Yankee Town, Southern City

Yankee Town, Southern City

Race and Class Relations in Civil War Lynchburg

Steven Elliott Tripp

NEW YORK UNIVERSITY PRESS
New York and London

The American Social Experience

SERIES

James Kirby Martin

GENERAL EDITOR

*Paula S. Fass, Steven H. Mintz, Carl Prince,
James W. Reed & Peter N. Stearns*

EDITORS

NEW YORK UNIVERSITY PRESS
New York and London

© 1997 by New York University

Library of Congress Cataloging-in-Publication Data
Tripp, Steven Elliott, 1956-
Yankee town, southern city : race and class relations in Civil War
Lynchburg / Steven Elliott Tripp.
p.   cm.—(The American social experience series ; 36)
Includes bibliographical references and index.
Contents: Yankee town, southern city—Religion, rum, and race—
The many battles of Lynchburg—These troublesomes times—To crown
our hearty endeavors—The mauling science—Epilogue :
Lynchburg's centennial and beyond.
ISBN 0-8147-8205-1 (alk. pap)
1. Lynchburg (Va.)—Race relations.   2. Social classes—Virginia–
–Lynchburg—History—19th century.   3. Virginia—History—Civil War,
1861-1865.   I. Title.   II. Series.
F234.L9T75   1996
305.8'009755671—dc20   96-35602
                                        CIP

New York University Press books are printed on acid-free paper,
and their binding materials are chosen for strength and durability.

Manufactured in the United States of America

10 9 8 7 6 5 4 3 2 1

For Elise, Nathan, and Hannah

Contents

Illustrations

Acknowledgments

I t is with a mix of relief and pleasure that I finally have an opportunity to thank those who have helped me see this project through to its completion. I am grateful to the staffs at the National Archives in Washington, D.C., the Alderman Library at the University of Virginia, the Perkins Library at Duke University, the Southern Historical Collection at the University of North Carolina at Chapel Hill, the Virginia Historical Society in Richmond, and the Virginia State Archives in Richmond.

Many people in Lynchburg helped make my frequent visits productive. Without exception, churches, private libraries, and private organizations allowed me to examine their records in full and to use what I thought relevant. Most of my research was conducted at Jones Memorial Library, the Lynchburg city clerk's office, and the Lynchburg Museum. Each offered me a place to work and all the attention that I needed. I am especially grateful to Patt Hobbs and Adam Scher of the Lynchburg Museum System and Sarah Hickson and Ed Gibson of Jones Library.

As a graduate student at Carnegie Mellon University in Pittsburgh, Pennsylvania, I was fortunate to work with an excellent dissertation committee. Peter Stearns and John Modell each offered penetrating criticisms and sound advice that have helped me sharpen my conceptual understanding of race and class. Although I can't claim to be in their league, I am a better historian for having worked under them. My greatest professional debt is to Joe William Trotter. Over the years, he has been all that a mentor should be—patient, dedicated, enthusiastic, and forthright. I am very thankful that I had the opportunity to work under him.

A number of people at Grand Valley State University in Allendale, Michigan, have made completing this project a pleasant experience. Two generous grants from the university helped me see this project to completion. I am especially grateful to the university's library staff, especially Laurel Balkema and Milly Holtvluwer in interlibrary loan. They helped me locate a number of obscure sources and saved me countless hours in doing so. Equally important, they never yelled at me when I failed to return books and microfilm on time. I am also grateful to my colleagues in the history department—a wonderful and stimulating group of people who have made my life in academia extremely pleasant and meaningful. Thanks too to New York University Press, especially Colin Jones, director, Despina Papazogla Gimbel, managing editor, and Karin Kuczynski and Adam Becker, editorial assistants. Each has been extremely helpful and extremely patient as I readied this for publication.

Finally, a word of thanks to my family. In particular, I thank my parents, Marv and Jeanette Tripp, for teaching me to love learning, for encouraging me to do my best, for paying for my college education, and for not protesting when I told them I wanted to be a history major. I also thank my brother Tom and my sister Cindy for being so supportive over the years. I am especially indebted to my children, Nathan Elliott Tripp and Hannah Magdaline Gould Tripp, for interrupting my work on a regular basis. By doing so, they have given me great joy. And a special word of thanks to my wife, Elise Hansen Tripp. Quite literally, our marriage has been bounded by this project: we were married two weeks before I entered Carnegie Mellon's Ph.D. program, I completed the dissertation one week after our fifth anniversary, and I completed the book manuscript three weeks after our tenth anniversary. Through it all, Elise has been a wellspring of support. Although this work can hardly repay her for all that she has done for me, it is fitting that I dedicate it to her.

Introduction

This is a study of how the people of one Southern community—Lynchburg, Virginia—experienced four distinct but overlapping events: Secession, Civil War, black emancipation, and Reconstruction. It was a volatile period in the town's history. The combined effects of these events influenced all areas of life, none more so than race and class relations. Although relations between black and white, rich and poor, had long been contentious, the tumultuousness of the era gave lower-class blacks and whites greater incentive to redefine their place in the town's social order. The relative successes and failures of their efforts are largely what this study is about.

I am hardly the first to explore this topic. During the past decade, the question of how war and Reconstruction affected race and class relations has attracted a diverse but talented group of historians. Cumulatively, their work has already impacted on our understanding of Southern history. First, they have extended the enduring debate of continuity versus change in Southern history to include race, class, and gender relations. Second, through meticulous local studies, they have uncovered significant regional variations in an area that we once mistakenly termed the "solid" South.

About the only thing that these historians have not done is to come to some consensus on what has become the central question of nineteenth-century Southern history: How did the war and Reconstruction affect social relations in the South? Some suggest that the impact was negligible. They argue that the South's traditional elites—namely, planters—successfully fought off Yankee and lower-class insurgents to retain much of their prewar power and stature. Because of their success, the "New" South looked very much like the "Old" South.[1] Others contend that the era was one of profound change. They argue that the "crucible of war"—a favorite term of this group—and Reconstruction largely destroyed the planter regime. Within the resulting power vacuum, a number of groups competed for power, creating a new and more contentious era of race and class relations.[2]

For the most part, I find myself in agreement with those who have argued discontinuity over continuity, conflict over consensus—but not by much. In Lynchburg, the agents of change were so many and so diverse that it took years for all segments of society to adjust to the new order. As the various groups tried to negotiate their status within an often volatile social structure, race and class relations became increasingly unsettled. By the end of Reconstruction, the transformation was still incomplete and the lines of conflict still not fully developed. As a result, the period ended with no clear winners and losers.

Moreover, change often occurred in a decidedly conservative context. By this I mean that individuals invariably tried to retain what they had, even as events propelled them in new and often unanticipated directions. This was especially true on the white side of Lynchburg's social structure. After all, most white residents embraced Secession and war to preserve a way of life, not to transform the existing social structure. For this reason, they looked to the past—or more properly, to their understanding of the past—to guide them through the crises of the 1860s and the early 1870s. Even as the crush of events accelerated the process of change, many individuals continued to be attracted to the past for the security it offered. In a word, it was a restive age for all who lived through it.

Although this is a study of all levels of Lynchburg society, I have tried to be especially attentive to the words and actions of Lynchburg's lower classes, especially lower-class whites—a group that has yet to receive its full share of scholarly attention. By looking at life in the grogshop, at the military encampment, and on the street corner and the shop floor, I have tried to suggest how ordinary people influenced the contours of race and class relations in one Southern town. In making my presentation, I break ranks with those historians who have argued that upper-class whites muted class antagonisms in the South by persuading lower-class whites to join them in a quest for white racial solidarity.[3] Ultimately, I argue that, after the war, social, political, and economic concerns compelled lower-class whites to defy elites' prescription for race relations. By acting on their own, lower-class whites expressed their frustrations with elite rule and contributed to the instability of postwar society. Although class conflict was not a central feature of mid-nineteenth-century Southern history, class antagonisms, often only vaguely articulated as such, did influence the reshaping of Southern social relations.

The study is organized chronologically and thematically. The study begins with an economic and demographic overview of prewar Lynchburg. Chapter 1 highlights some of the basic features of Lynchburg society, including the town's involvement in a market economy, the steep gradations of the social hierarchy, the diversity of the town's laboring population, and white residents' commitment to slavery, personalism, and paternalism. The second chapter provides a closer examination of Lynchburg's white and black laborers. Through an extensive study of religion, propriety, and leisure, the chapter suggests the general contours of lower-class life. The chapter highlights places of interclass and interracial interaction to suggest the normative patterns of behavior, especially vigilance and the ethic of honor, that informed prewar social relations.

The third chapter explores how war affected race and class relations at home and in Lynchburg's military regiments. Specifically, the chapter argues that Lynchburg's social organization was remarkably durable for much of the period. Although class and racial conflicts eventually came to the fore, they did so late in the war and then only in a haphazard fashion. By war's end, it was not clear if the town's antebellum civic leaders would have to surrender all or even part of their power.

The remaining chapters describe the new social environment that defeat, black emancipation, and federal occupation created. After an economic and demographic overview of postwar Lynchburg in chapter 4, the study returns to an analysis of the role of religion as a source of conflict and consensus, as evinced by elite-led moral reform efforts and the town's "Great Revival of 1871." Here in chapter 5, the study takes to task those historians who argue that racial solidarity furthered class solidarity. Finally, the study returns to an analysis of interracial violence and vigilance. In chapter 6, I argue that community-endorsed mob violence against blacks became increasingly rare as laboring whites refused to participate in elite-sponsored rituals. At the same time, however, overall violence against blacks actually increased as laboring whites resorted to individual acts of aggression to "protect" themselves, their jobs, and their neighborhoods against presumed black interlopers. Black residents often responded in kind. In contrast to most interpretations of postwar Southern violence, I argue that blacks often displayed a collective resolve to avenge abuse that frustrated civic leaders' attempts to control their behavior.

Lynchburg recommends itself for study for a variety of reasons. The most pragmatic is that the town has retained a wealth of private and public records. Many of these records pertain especially to lower-class groups—specifically, church minutes and membership lists, manuscript census materials, criminal court records, and army muster rolls. Using these records, I have been able to reconstruct lower-class life in a wide variety of settings, ranging from the grog shop to the prayer meeting.

More thematically, Lynchburg's demography makes it a convenient place to examine the interaction of diverse social groups. On the eve of the Civil War, the town was about 39 percent slave, 5 percent free black, 46 percent native white, and 10 percent foreign-born white.[4] In contrast to much of the rural South, the town's close quarters compelled these groups to interact daily in a wide variety of settings. As a result, Lynchburg is an ideal place to observe how various groups negotiated the normative standards of race and class relations.

Finally, Lynchburg offers a unique opportunity to analyze the impact of industrialization on Southern race and class relations. Prior to the war, Lynchburg was one of the leading centers for the manufacture of plug tobacco, with a level of entrepreneurial activity that rivaled the textiles towns of New England. Thus, this study invites comparisons with similar developments in Northern industrial cities.

In selecting an urban area, I am well aware that I lay myself open to the charge that I have chosen an atypical community as a forum for study. Indeed, no less an authority than C. Vann Woodward has argued that city and countryside were so distinct in the South that comparisons between the two are hazardous at best. According to Woodward, the face-to-face social arrangements of the countryside allowed rural whites to use direct, or "vertical," forms of race control. In contrast, cities added a "horizontal" system of segregation, characterized by an "impersonal complex of interlocking economic, political, legal, social, and ideological components to maintain white dominance."[5]

Although Woodward's thesis helps explain one of the most salient differences between urban and rural racial systems, the similarities between town and country may be equally significant. For instance, it still holds that most racial encounters in cities—especially cities as small as Lynchburg—were probably of the informal vertical variety. Moreover, poorer urbanites, who had limited access to formal institutions, probably relied almost exclusively on face-to-face encounters to determine the contours of race relations.

We should also question the wisdom of some Southern historians' search for the "typical" Southern community. Recent analyses of the nineteenth-century South suggest that it was a diverse region, marked by a large number of subregions with distinctive subcultures. Historians' quest for the typical Southern community has meant that they have depreciated the significance of the city in Southern society. Southern cities did not evolve in a vacuum. The South's cities, no less than the great plantations, were products of Southern politics, economy, and society. As this study demonstrates, white urban residents of the South had much in common with their rural counterparts—most notably, a commitment to slavery and white racial superiority.[6]

Finally, many of the events that changed the nineteenth-century South first occurred in the city. During and after the war, as black and white war refugees left the countryside, cities and towns became one of the first places where the two races confronted each other as social and political equals. Later, as Old South changed to New South, these towns played an increasingly important role in the region's social and economic reorganization, if only because they stood at the juncture of the rural South and the international market economy.[7]

Studying Southern cities will not unlock all the secrets of Southern history, but it can provide a new vista for interpretation.

CHAPTER ONE

Yankee Town, Southern City

On the eve of the Civil War, Lynchburg, Virginia, enjoyed a national reputation as a progressive, enterprising city. Founded in the mid-eighteenth century by Charles Lynch as a trading depot on the southern bank of the James River, the town quickly gained prominence as a regional tobacco market. One hundred miles upstream from Richmond, local tobacco farmers found Lynchburg a convenient place to ship their tobacco, store it, and have it inspected by state agents before selling it at auction to eastern merchants. By 1840, Lynchburg tobacco accounted for nearly one-quarter (23.4 percent) of all tobacco inspected in Virginia. As early as 1830, English traveler Anne Royall visited the town because of its reputation as a "place of considerable business." In 1851, a correspondent for the *Richmond Enquirer* stated that "there is not a town in Virginia more interesting than Lynchburg." Its citizens were "alive to internal improvements" and evidenced "industry, emulation, and business success." The editor of the nearby *Bedford Sentinel* was equally impressed, noting in 1858 that Lynchburg had become southwest Virginia's "seat of learning, art, trade, and manufacture." In time, the editor predicted, Lynchburg's "industry, energy, and enterprise" would make the city "second to none" in the state. Future Reconstruction governor Francis H. Pierpoint's tribute was less hyperbolic but even more pleasing to the town's business leaders. In an 1858 visit to Lynchburg,

Pierpoint told the editor of the *Lynchburg Virginian*, Charles Button, that Lynchburg had "more the appearance of a Yankee town than any other in Virginia."[1]

In many respects, Pierpoint's observation was apt. On the surface, antebellum Lynchburg looked very much like the emerging commercial and industrial centers of the North. When Pierpoint visited, Lynchburg had established a national reputation as a leading producer of one the era's most popular manufactured commodities—"plug," or chewing, tobacco. By all accounts, manufactured tobacco was the basis of the town's economy. Lynchburg's first factories appeared around the turn of the century; however, plug tobacco did not become a major commodity until the second quarter of the nineteenth century. By then, urbanization and industrialization had created a market for the product—the many laborers who chewed to relieve the tedium of their jobs and to exhibit their manhood. Yet it took considerable enterprise and economic acumen for the town to attain and secure its share of the market. Although Lynchburg's hinterland boasted some of the best tobacco farms in the nation, the town was too isolated from the eastern seaboard to take full advantage of its resources. During the second quarter of the nineteenth century, however, the city made a concerted effort to compete with eastern trading centers. In 1840, the James River and Kanawha Valley Canal was completed, providing Lynchburg an easier and faster route to Richmond and the Atlantic seaboard. The canal dramatically improved the town's economic fortunes. In 1830, Anne Royall counted fifteen tobacco factories in the town. In 1843, the *Lynchburg Republican* boasted that there were thirty factories and by 1850, the manufacturing census listed thirty-five factories in the city. These represented a capital investment of $600,300, a manufactured product valued at $1,183,000, and a labor force of 1,127. By 1860, there were forty-five factories in the city limits, representing an investment of $1,136,190, a product value of $1,907,882, and a total workforce of 1,054. In that year, Lynchburg factories accounted for 17 percent of the state's revenue of manufactured tobacco sales.[2]

Although other cities manufactured more chewing tobacco than Lynchburg, no other city pursued the trade with such a singular interest. According to a recent study of the antebellum Virginia tobacco industry, Lynchburg produced more tobacco in proportion to its size than any other city in Virginia and North Carolina, the principal tobacco-growing states. Only one-sixth the size of Richmond and one-third the size of

Petersburg, Lynchburg nonetheless produced tobacco valued at one-third that of Richmond and three-fourths that of Petersburg.[3]

Even more than of quantity, however, Lynchburg's tobacco manufacturers boasted of the quality of their product. Despite competition from Richmond, Petersburg, and Danville, Lynchburgers claimed that their product was the best in the country and unabashedly asked that their rivals refer to the town as the "Tobacco City." In July 1856, the editor of the *Lynchburg Virginian* tried to end all debate on the subject by triumphantly announcing that "it is a fact now settled beyond a doubt that Lynchburg is the best market for the sale of manufactured tobacco in the world."[4]

Although such claims were typical of nineteenth-century urban boosters, they probably had some basis in fact. Alexander Patten, a correspondent for the *New York Mercury* who traveled the South extensively in the late antebellum period, stated that "those who indulge in the finer kinds of manufactured tobacco know that it comes rather from Lynchburg, than Richmond." Although "away off" from the eastern seaboard, Patten noted, "Lynchburg has a renown that is universal." Even the town's rivals reluctantly agreed. After visiting a Lynchburg tobacco auction, a correspondent for the *Petersburg Express* admitted that Lynchburg attracted the "finest tobacco in the world."[5]

Tobacco gave the town fortune as well as fame. Due largely to the profits generated from the tobacco trade, Lynchburg's per capita valuation in 1859 was $1,262.31, making the town the second wealthiest city in the country. The tobacco manufacturers—or tobacconists, as they called themselves—led the way to Lynchburg's prosperity. According to the census of 1860, the town's sixty-three tobacconists accounted for about 29 percent of the town's personal wealth, 25 percent of the town's real estate wealth, and 27 percent of the town's total wealth. The wealthiest tobacconists accumulated impressive fortunes. Five possessed over $100,000 in total wealth. By far the wealthiest of these was Jesse Hare. In 1860, he owned real estate valued at $110,000 and a personal estate, including thirty-five slaves, valued at $800,000. Others were not far behind. Thirty-two of the town's sixty-eight tobacconists were among the town's wealthiest decile.[6]

Tobacco gave Lynchburg wealth and fame, but it did not give the town economic security. Tobacco manufacturing was subject to the same volatile fluctuations as other antebellum commercial enterprises. Despite the fortunes of a few, most tobacconists found the trade to be exceedingly unstable. Thus, Lynchburg experienced a rapid turnover in tobacco firms. In 1850, forty-one men owned tobacco factories. Of these, only sixteen (39 percent) remained in the business ten years later—even though the total number of tobacconists grew to sixty-one.[7]

Several factors contributed to the instability of the trade. Nature was obviously one culprit. To receive a good price for their product, Lynchburg tobacconists preferred the finest grades of tobacco. When fine-grade tobacco was in low supply, tobacconists could either end the manufacturing season early or make an inferior—and thus, less financially rewarding—product. Yet to grow fine-grade tobacco required near-perfect weather, fertile soil, and constant cultivation.[8]

Even more than from nature, however, tobacconists suffered from the structure of the trade itself. Less-affluent tobacconists often complained that the product marketing system worked against them. Virginia tobacconists relied on Northern factors to buy their product, who then shipped it north to distribute for sale. Unfortunately for the tobacconists, these factors usually bought the tobacco on credit and paid off only after they sold the product. As a result, most tobacconists relied on bank loans to continue their business operations. In times of economic stability the system worked well, since banks were quick to extend liberal credit to most tobacconists. In times of economic dislocation, however, many tobacconists suffered. During the panic of 1857, most Northern factors defaulted on their payments. In the midst of the crisis, one Lynchburg tobacconist predicted that while those of "large means" would be able to recover even if conditions did not improve in a year or two, "the man of small means" would soon be "hopelessly ruined."[9]

Fierce competition also made tobacco manufacturing a volatile enterprise. Much of the competition was local: Lynchburg tobacconists competed with one another to buy the best tobacco, concoct the best flavors, and obtain the most favorable agreements with factors. At the same time, however, Lynchburg tobacconists began to feel pressure from other quarters. Despite the town's national reputation as the tobacco capital, Lynchburg tobacconists found themselves in an annual struggle to attract growers with the best produce to their warehouses. Although Lynchburg always competed with seaboard cities for the tobacco trade, the competition reached a new level of intensity when railroads from Richmond, Petersburg, Alexandria, and Baltimore began to reach the interior of the state during the late 1850s. With the arrival of the railroad in the Piedmont, Lynchburg found that it no longer possessed the advantage of geography. As a result, Lynchburg's status as a tobacco market began to slip. In 1856, the same Petersburg correspondent who reluctantly praised Lynchburg tobacconists for their commitment to excellence also observed that Lynchburg no longer attracted the number of tobacco farmers it once had. He was an astute observer. From 1853 to 1858, the number of hogsheads inspected and sold at Lynchburg declined each year, so that by 1858, Lynchburg sold only 70 percent of its 1853 total. During the same period, Lynchburg's percentage of state sales declined by half, from 20.2 percent to 10 percent. Ultimately, this increased competition among local tobacconists, who now found themselves paying exorbitant prices for whatever good weed they could find. As their costs rose, their margins of profits declined.[10]

Civic leaders responded to the burgeoning urban rivalry with the economic foresight that they believed set them apart from other Southern towns. During the 1850s, town fathers embarked on an ambitious program of internal improvements that they hoped would solidify the town's place in the regional tobacco market, as well as enable the town to diversify its economic base. The result was a decade of almost frantic railroad construction, funded largely by local taxes and private subscriptions. By 1860, Lynchburg was the crossroads for three railroads. Lynchburg's first line, the Virginia and Tennessee Railroad, built in 1850, enabled the town to surmount its eastern barrier, the Blue Ridge Mountains, to reach the fertile farmlands and rich mineral deposits of southwest Virginia and eastern Tennessee. The second line, the Southside Railroad, completed in 1856, linked the city to Petersburg, thus giving the tobacconists greater access to the eastern seaboard. The town's final antebellum project, the Orange and Alexandria Railroad, promised even greater changes by connecting Lynchburg to northern Virginia and, ultimately, the urban North.[11]

Civic boosters anticipated a new era of economic prosperity from their investments. Charles Button, editor of the *Lynchburg Virginian*, predicted that Lynchburg would one day surpass Richmond in tobacco production by monopolizing the inland trade. Even more boldly, he suggested that the town might one day rival Wheeling for its iron foundries and Alexandria for its flour mills. Other business leaders were equally hopeful that the railroads would usher in an even greater era of economic prosperity born from expansion and diversification. According to the Board of Directors of the Virginia and Tennessee Railroad Company, the town's emerging status as a rail center would make it an ideal location to manufacture and ship the rich salt, copper, iron, coal, and gypsum deposits of southwest Virginia. To promote the town's interests within the state and beyond, civic boosters established a Board of Trade, a Mechanical Society, and an Agricultural Society.[12]

Although civic boosters never realized much of what they set out to do, by the end of the decade they did witness a new age of economic prosperity. Beginning in 1858, with the competition of the Orange and Alexandria Railroad, Lynchburg's tobacco industry slowly rebounded. In 1860, the town exported 9,301 hogsheads of tobacco, roughly the same amount it exported during the flush times in the beginning of the decade. At the same time, the town regained some of its share of the state trade moving, from a decade-low 10 percent in 1858 to 12 percent in 1860.[13]

Other industries also profited from railroad construction. Although tobacco remained the dominant industry, Lynchburg's status as an important crossroads to points east, west, and north attracted a number of new industries and encouraged a few older ones to expand their operations. On the eve of the Secession crisis, Lynchburg and vicinity were home to six foundries, including one that provided the passenger and freight cars for the Virginia and Tennessee Railroad; eleven grist mills; four coachmakers; two coppersmiths; and one fertilizer manufacturer. Although most of these businesses were relatively small, there were a few exceptions. John Bailey's coachmaking establishment, housed in a cavernous, abandoned tobacco factory, employed fifty workers. Two of Lynchburg's foundries were also relatively large establishments. Francis Deane, former proprietor of the Tredegear Iron Works in Richmond, operated an iron foundry that manufactured passenger and freight cars for the Virginia and Tennessee Railroad. In 1860, he employed twenty-five workers, and his product value was $52,800. A. G. Dabney's Phoenix Foundry was only slightly smaller. In 1860, the foundry employed thirty-five workers and produced $40,000 worth of iron fixtures for the town's tobacco factories.[14]

Button, for one, was impressed. In 1860, he observed that, because the number of new businesses had grown appreciably in the last few years, "now every suitable locality for business is occupied."[15] The scale and pace of economic activity allowed Lynchburg to reassert that it rivaled the North in business expertise and ingenuity. Visitors helped spread the word. In late 1859, David Forbes, newly arrived from the countryside, wrote his mother that he believed his economic prospects were excellent:

"I believe I will like Lynchburg," he told her. "This is a hardworking community and a very rich one."[16] A correspondent for the *Bristol News* agreed. During an 1858 visit, he observed that Lynchburg was once again "a prosperous and expanding city" with an extensive and diverse economic base. As future governor Pierpoint did, the writer alluded to the North as a way to explain Lynchburg's economic dynamism: "Whatever truth there may be in the charge of our cute Yankee friends on the upper side of Mason & Dixon's line that the Old Dominion is a century behind the age," the correspondent suggested, "it would puzzle them to find any evidences of the fact in Lynchburg with its canal and railroads continually pouring into it the merchandise of the East and the produce of the West, to be exchanged and distributed throughout the country by energetic businesses."[17]

Despite the capitalistic enterprise of its business leaders, Lynchburg was not a "Yankee town" for one reason—slavery. Compared to most other Southern cities, slaves comprised a large segment of the town's population: in 1860, nearly 40 percent of Lynchburg's population were slaves. Moreover, a large cross-section of white Lynchburg was personally involved in slavery; perhaps as many as 40 percent of all white household heads rented or owned at least one slave. Yet slavery's importance to Lynchburg transcended mere ratios of slave ownership. Economically, socially, and politically, slavery made Lynchburg a Southern city.[18]

Most obviously, slaves created Lynchburg's renowned wealth by their forced labor in the tobacco factories. The world of the tobacco factories was a world of black slavery. The factories employed over a thousand workers, virtually all of whom were black and most of whom were slaves. Probably close to half of Lynchburg's slaves worked in the tobacco factories.[19]

Tobacconists' reliance on slave labor suggests that the tobacconists were fundamentally products of Southern culture and not strict economic animals. Although tobacconists were able to adapt slavery to their factories, the system that emerged was labor-intensive and costly. In many respects, tobacco factory slaves were quasi-free laborers. Over half of the town's factory slaves were hired by the year. Many of these negotiated their own contracts and were allowed to keep a share of their owner's rent. In addition, most tobacconists offered their slaves cash incentives of $3 to $5 a week for "overwork." According to a recent study of Virginia's antebellum tobacco industry, this incentive system may have made slave

Marketplace and Ninth Avenue leading to Court House. (Jones Memorial Library; hereafter JML)

labor less profitable than free labor. Although the total cost to hire, board, clothe, and supervise slaves, estimated between $225 and $275 a year, was less than wage estimates indicate for free labor, cash incentives, averaging at least $120 a year, "increased labor costs significantly enough to eat away much of the profit margin."[20]

Lynchburg as seen from the Court House. (Lynchburg Museum System; hereafter LMS)

Given the high cost of slave labor, the tobacconists' decision to rely predominantly on slaves rather than on free laborers was probably as much social and demographic as economic. Throughout Virginia, white laborers and tobacconists classified tobacco factory labor as "nigger work." The designation probably hurt both groups. On the one hand, the most talented black factory workers, with weekly incentives as high as ten dollars a week, probably made more than the town's poorest white laborers. On the other hand, tobacconists competed for workers in a region hampered by a severe labor shortage due to the southwest movement of the internal slave trade and the town's small free black population. Thus, during the 1850s, local slave hiring rates for prime factory hands increased 35 percent, making Lynchburg the most expensive place to hire slaves in the state. Even so, Lynchburg tobacconists did not try to broaden the pool of available laborers by attracting whites into the factories. Even after a few Richmond tobacconists reported that they had successfully introduced rural white female workers into their factories, Lynchburg's tobacconists remained true to slave labor. Perhaps the economic nature of the trade dissuaded most from experimenting with the labor supply. In the usually profitable but sometimes volatile world of tobacco manufacturing, owners may have believed it made more sense to rely on the proven skill and camaraderie of black workers than to introduce a new and possibly reluctant population into the factories.[21]

No doubt, social convention also played a part. More than likely, Lynchburg tobacconists simply felt more comfortable managing slave labor than free. Most Lynchburg tobacconists were, after all, Southerners. Many were born in the surrounding countryside, where plantation slavery still dominated the economic pace of life. Through family visits, seasonal vacations to Virginia's famous springs and resorts, and weekend retreats to their family estates, Lynchburg tobacconists continued to have an intimate connection with Virginia's traditional rural culture. Perhaps for this reason, they eschewed the more descriptive occupational title "tobacco manufacturer" for the more pastoral and gentlemanly "tobacconist."[22]

Even the work routines at their factories were more in keeping with the rural South than with the urban North. Like their rural counterparts, Lynchburg's tobacco factory owners had to accommodate themselves to the demands of their workers. Although most tobacconists hired white overseers to supervise their factories, slaves and free black laborers largely determined the production process by their skill and collaborative work culture. Factory hands completed the process in three steps—stemming, flavoring, and pressing. Each of these stages required only rudimentary tools and few machines, enabling the workers themselves to determine the pace of work and the quality of the product.[23]

When tobacco entered the factory, adolescent and female workers steamed each leaf until it was pliable, then "stemmed" it by removing the midrib. Next, "dippers" soaked the tobacco in huge vats filled with a black syrup that usually consisted of sugar, licorice, caraway, cloves, nutmeg, cinnamon, and other spices. Workers, often sweating profusely as they stood over the hot vats, stirred constantly to prevent scorching or burning. When the tobacco was adequately flavored, they placed it in the open air of the factory roofs. To improve the bouquet, laborers then sprinkled the leaf with more spices, rum, and sweet oil. Next, male and female "lumpmakers," seated at benches in large rooms similar to Northern sweatshops, molded handfuls of the leaves into rectangular plugs. Once inspected and approved by an overseer or manager, the lumps were sent to the pressroom. In the pressroom, another set of workers fitted the plugs into "shapes"—rectangular molds subdivided into compartments. These were put in a screw press, which a "screwman" operated with a long lever. The screwman repeated the process until the plug aligned perfectly with the edges of the pan, groaning with each pull or push of the huge lever. When the lumps were adequately pressed, workers placed them in boxes and the boxes on ironbound billets. Again, the screwman placed all his strength on the lever to fasten and brand the box top. The plugs were then ready for shipment to Northern distributors.[24]

Just like plantation slaves, black factory hands constructed elaborate mechanisms to control both the work and the workplace. In the pressroom and lump room, senior workers used rhythmic chants and whistles to control the pace of work. According to Patten, the *New York Mercury* correspondent, factory laborers whistled from dawn to dusk. After work, Patten noted, black laborers reassembled on street corners, "whistling away the night." Like the work that inspired the music, each tune was a complex harmony that required several participants. At night, one group would start to whistle. Soon another group would pass, "whistling their loudest and best." This, in turn, Patten observed, "incites the first to displays of their fullest capacity; and thus the concert goes on."[25]

At times, factory slaves' quest for workplace control reached extremes. In one instance, Button of the *Virginian* reported that a slave employed at the factory of David Burton had abruptly announced that "he intended going into a trance." According to Button, the slave predicted that he would stay in that state for three days, "at the expiration of which time he expected a divine revelation and commission . . . as missionary to the world." At the appointed hour, the slave "picked the softest board for a couch" and fell into a deep sleep. Not one to report without comment, Button encouraged Burton to assert his authority, suggesting that a "sound thrashing" might "produce marvelous results." The more experienced Burton abstained, claiming that it was wiser to keep the peace by "humoring the darkie's eccentricity." Whatever the worker's intentions, the incident reflects the control tobacco factory workers had over the work environment.[26]

Slaves worked not only in Lynchburg factories but also in Lynchburg homes as domestic servants. In 1860, there were about eight hundred house servants, nurses, cooks, and domestics in Lynchburg, virtually all of whom were female slaves.[27] Here, too, social conventions and economic forces helped create the concentration. While male slaves demanded top dollar in Lynchburg because of the tobacco factories, female slaves attracted far less interest. Although many female slaves worked in the tobacco factories as stemmers, supply far outstripped demand. As a result, a large cross section of white Lynchburg residents found that they could buy or hire female slaves on relatively good terms. In addition, most whites identified domestic service as "slave work." As a result, few even considered employing whites or free blacks in domestic service.[28]

Not that employers had much of a choice. During the late antebellum period, most free female job seekers stayed clear of domestic service. Southern white women avoided domestic service for a number of reasons. Not only did domestic service carry a racial stigma, but it carried the stigma of servility as well. Moreover, most white women, especially young, single white women, had access to more lucrative and "respectable" jobs, such as seamstress work. Of the 230 white women gainfully employed in Lynchburg, only 12 worked as house servants; 5 of these were Irish, a group that tended to dominate domestic labor in the urban North. In contrast, 182 worked as seamstresses, mantuamakers, milliners, tailors, and the like. For their part, free black women also tried to avoid domestic labor. No doubt, they also wanted to avoid the stigma of slavery and the loss of personal autonomy. In addition, most black women were single parents. As such, they found that the demands of domestic labor interfered with their family obligations. Instead, they preferred jobs with set hours, such as tobacco work, or jobs that they could perform at home, such as washing or sewing. Yet, because they did not have the range of choices that white women had, free black women were about twice as likely to work as servants as were free white women.[29]

Whether they employed slaves in the factory, in the home, or in some other line of business, whites expected slavery to follow the rural ideal of master paternalism and slave deference. Although white Lynchburgers recognized that the anonymity of urban life increased blacks' ability to avoid the watchful eye of whites, most masters nonetheless tried to retain personal control over their slaves. Masters of house servants had the greatest success in following the paternalist model, because the social intimacy of the Southern household enabled them to develop closer relationships with their slaves. For this reason, race relations in the slave-holding Lynchburg household looked very much like those in its rural counterpart.

From the masters' perspective, house servants were members of their families—their perpetual children, who were in constant need of discipline. To fulfill their paternal responsibility, the masters diligently supervised their slaves' behavior. Some found this an exhausting responsibility. Jacob Mitchell, the doleful minister of the Second Presbyterian Church, confided in his diary that he was completely vexed by one of his servant girls, who was "behaving very badly." Plaintively, he prayed, "Lord teach me how to control her." After the war, Elizabeth Langhorne Payne, a member of one of the town's wealthiest families, remembered her father's servants with both fondness and frustration. Although she recalled that they behaved "unusually well" much of the time, they were always "indisposed to work." As a result, she spent much of her day hounding them to be more industrious and responsible.[30]

As the slaves' moral guardians, Lynchburg masters were concerned with how their servants behaved off the job as well as on. Masters believed that urban slavery provided house slaves too many temptations to stray from the fold and too many opportunities to develop alternative value systems that undermined their masters' quest for hegemony. Thus, many masters tried to govern their slaves' personal lives whenever possible. Charles Blackford, a prominent Lynchburg lawyer, refused to let his servants go into the city on their days off for fear that they might make their way to Buzzard's Roost, a section of town infamous for its doggeries, gambling halls, and whorehouses. Blackford had good reason to be concerned. According to observers, servants liked to mingle with the rest of the town's slave community in rumholes and grogshops. Masters feared that when their servants frequented these locales, they would be corrupted by low whites, free blacks, and unruly tobacco factory hands.[31]

Masters, in return for their self-sacrifice, protection, and benevolence, expected slaves to be obedient and loyal. After slavery, many masters maintained that the best of their former slaves had conformed perfectly to the ideal. Some time after Reconstruction, an anonymous biographer recalled that her favorite servant, Queen, was an integral part of her family. In fact, she maintained, while Queen's exterior was rough and dark, "inwardly" she was "all white and fine." According to the writer, Queen understood that personal service was a "sacred trust" and thus stayed with her mistress after the war. Ruth Hairston Early, another postwar writer, eulogized the many black mammies she had known growing up in Lynchburg. According to Early, these women possessed such "childlike dispositions" that they were utterly devoted to their young charges.[32]

Although few masters would admit to it, the bonds of dependence worked both ways. While many servants relied on their masters for food, shelter, and protection, masters needed slaves to help them fulfill their roles as patriarchs and matriarchs. With considerable pride, Charles Blackford recounted to Northern friends his family's Christmas tradition of dispensing gifts to their many slaves. "By sunrise" Christmas morning, Blackford noted, all his slaves—both those who worked in his household and those he hired out—"would be dressed, washed, combed, and knocking for admittance at our chamber door to 'catch' me as they call it." According to Blackford, his servants' eagerness to receive presents from his hand proved that white Southerners knew what was best for their chattel. "Where would the happy little ones have now been if their ancestors had not been rescued from barbarism?" Blackford challenged his Northern friends. "What would be their condition if they were now freed in the Infidel State of Massachusetts?"[33]

Whites found it far more difficult to establish the bonds of paternalism in the tobacco factories. Master-slave relations in the tobacco factories often bordered on the impersonal. Whether hired or owned by their employer, most slaves lived free of their masters' supervision in garrets near the factories and along Lynchburg's narrow alleys and ravines. Here they tried to establish an autonomous life for themselves. Indeed, through overtime earnings they procured much of their own food, clothing, and even lodging.[34]

Although some masters welcomed the opportunity to escape the more annoying responsibilities of paternalism, most looked upon the growing indications of black independence with considerable misgiving, if not with gnawing anxiety. Even though they could still extract good labor from their slaves through cash incentives, direct supervision, and physical punishment, most masters did not want obedient workers; they wanted obedient children. Like their rural counterparts, tobacconists legitimized slavery by arguing that blacks needed their perpetual care. Without their assistance, they predicted, blacks would confront a horrible fate. Famed storyteller and essayist George Bagby, a Lynchburg native, curtly remarked that "niggers are not niggers unless they are slaves." According to Bagby, free blacks would not work without white supervision. When left on their own, they were no better than "a hand without muscle" or "a tender without any locomotive." In short, "a nigger without a master" is "latent power off the track." William Blackford, lawyer Charles Blackford's older brother, agreed. A prominent engineer who dabbled in the tobacco trade, William contended in his postwar autobiography that slavery had been only a boon to blacks. "Never before were labor and capital brought together under circumstances more advantageous to the development of the laborer," Blackford maintained. "Nor was there ever a greater blessing bestowed on the negro race."[35]

The problem for most masters was how to establish control over their slaves in the atomizing environment of the city. Unable to use traditional means to establish paternalistic control, the tobacconists and other urban slaveholders tried to accommodate themselves to urban realities. In doing so, they hoped to find new ways to establish the bonds of paternalism. Slaveholders tried to increase their power over their slaves by using a variety of urban institutions—including churches, charitable organizations, and law enforcement agencies—to attend to their slaves when they could not.

Most often, masters tried to encourage devotion from their slaves through organized and public acts of benevolence. During the 1850s, Lynchburg slaveholders supported several black Sunday school programs and the construction of a black church, Court Street Baptist. Although Lynchburg blacks requested these institutions to gain even greater autonomy, the actual result was a compromise. Blacks gained separate services, but whites retained considerable influence by controlling finances, providing benevolence during hard times, and serving as the principal ministers and educators. Ultimately, whites used the programs to legitimize their paternalistic guardianship over their slaves. Writing in the *Lynchburg Virginian* in 1859, one white evangelical justified black religious instruction by noting that blacks were no better than "unlearned children" who required special religious instruction; otherwise, they would become slaves to their passions. Without proper religious education, the writer predicted, blacks would quickly fall to "the temptations of ease or idleness, to drinking or riot, to filching for their supply or their pleasure and extravagance, or to any present gratification."[36]

Although whites viewed their efforts as selfless acts of benevolence, they recognized that not all slaves would respond positively to their efforts to invoke the bonds of paternalism. When slaves resisted their overtures, slaveholders invariably turned to local law enforcement agencies to help them discipline their property. Even then, however, masters continued to assert that they should have the last word over their property. Thus, the local police department was essentially a creature of Lynchburg slaveholders and operated to enhance their power and prestige. When arrested, slaves were usually sent to the mayor, William Branch, for summary judgment. For petty crimes, slaveholders granted Branch considerable discretionary power. Although Branch regularly ordered slaves to be whipped for such petty crimes as drunkenness and breaking curfew, most masters considered this such a routine form of punishment that they rarely complained. Indeed, some masters probably encouraged Branch to conduct the punishment so that they could retain more benign reputations.[37]

More serious slave crimes required greater sensitivity. Although Lynchburg courts generally recognized the master's right to his property, public concerns about safety also had to be considered. As a result, masters often let the courts pass judgment before deciding how to act.

In 1858, three slaves—Carey, William, and Morriss—were arrested for setting fire to William Miller's tobacco factory. The crime created considerable anxiety in Lynchburg, setting off wild rumors of slave insurrectionary plots. Each of the slaves came before Branch, who immediately sent them on for trial. Two of the slaves, William and Morriss, belonged to Miller. With Miller's full cooperation, the two were quickly tried and sentenced to be executed. However, the owner of the third slave, William Speed, a prominent lawyer and politician, however, demurred. Even though the court's investigation concluded that Carey was an accomplice, Speed insisted on the slave's innocence, claiming that his slave Carey "had no connection, directly or indirectly, with the burning of the factory." As a result, he refused to turn his slave over to the authorities. In response, the circuit court decided not to press the indictment. Unwilling to challenge a master's sovereignty outright, the court asked Speed through a letter in the local press to sell Carey, claiming that it was for the public good that the slave not be "permitted to remain and go at large in the city." The court's action placed Speed in an uncomfortable position. As a member of city council, Speed dared not undermine the legitimacy of the courts and the racial solidarity of the community. As a slaveholder, however, he did not want to lose his property without compensation. And as a benevolent master, he may have felt a responsibility to protect his slave from injustice. In a public response to the court, also printed in the local press, Speed tried to please all sides, at least nominally. Deeming it his "duty to say" something "in vindication" of his slave, Speed asserted Carey's innocence one last time. At the same time, however, he reluctantly promised to fulfill his "obligation to society." Despite the "loss" and "pain" he and his slave would experience, he promised to remove Carey from town as "soon as I can conveniently do so." With these measured words, Speed gave notice that although he would comply with the wishes of the community in this instance, he reserved ultimate authority over his slaves.[38]

Lynchburg slaves responded to their masters' paternalist overtures in a variety of ways. A few, no doubt, had reason to be grateful to their masters. As slaves, they recognized that it was better to serve under a kind master, no matter how condescending and insensitive, than under a cruel one. In retrospect, many expressed appreciation for those masters who took special interest in their welfare. After emancipation, an ex-slave named Territ told Jacob Yoder, a Freedmen's Bureau agent, that he planned to continue working for his ex-master because he had been one of the rare enlightened slave owners. He not only treated his slaves kindly but even encouraged them to learn to read. Postwar civil rights advocate Orra Langhorne, while traveling on a train to Lynchburg, met an elderly black woman who was returning to visit the home and grave of her former mistress. The elderly woman fondly recalled that her mistress had shown "excessive indulgence" toward all her slaves. She told Langhorne that her former owner had been "very much attached to her slaves," so much so that she "could not be induced to sell any of them" or force them to work beyond what was necessary to keep up the household. As the mistress grew old, she freed her slaves one by one, sending her favorite ones north so that they would not be kidnapped into slavery after she died. In her will, she made cash provisions for all of her former slaves.[39]

Most servants, however, were not so fortunate as to receive such indulgences. Instead, long hours of servile labor, racial barbs, the constant presence of white supervision, and the enduring threat of arbitrary punishment were all features of life in the white household for most servants.[40] Occasionally, slaves protested by refusing to do work, stealing small items as payment for work rendered, or talking back. In some rare instances, servants were more daring. During the war, William Luck informed a friend that he had been forced to whip his "negro boy Penn" for the first time. Evidently, Penn viewed the punishment as excessive and "left for parts unknown." Luck believed he would never see the slave again.[41]

Most slaves, however, were unwilling to take such chances. Forced into the role of servant, they had little choice but to play their part, even as they tried to stretch the bonds of paternalism. Charles Blackford's slaves seem to have been especially adept at this. By showing up at Blackford's door every Christmas morning, they helped Blackford retain a conception of himself as an indulgent master. At the same time, however, they used the occasion to compel Blackford to compensate them in some small way for the year's service.[42]

Tobacco factory slaves had reason to appreciate their status—especially in comparison to slaves in the surrounding countryside. The peculiarities of the factory system enabled factory slaves to enjoy some of the liberties of free society that most slaves never knew. To begin with, slaves were often given the opportunity to earn extra money by working overtime. Under the "task" system, each slave was assigned a specific job. When the job was completed, the slave was then paid for any additional work he did. Usually the slaves made only a few extra dollars per week, but during the busiest seasons they could earn as much as ten dollars per week. As a result, tobacconists testified that they rarely had difficulty motivating their slaves to work. Moreover, except for those owned by the tobacconists themselves, slaves were often responsible for their own hire. During the last week of every year, experienced hands bargained their own contract. Because tobacconists depended on workers with experience, hiring rates could run as high as two hundred dollars a year for an adult male, one hundred dollars for an adult female, and fifty dollars for a youth.[43]

The advantages of the factory system for black laborers were such that many slave owners who rented slaves to the tobacconists complained that their slaves became spoiled for any other kind of work.[44] Factory slaves' apparent high standard of living impressed even the most doubtful visitors. During the war, Charles Ostrander, a wounded Northern soldier hospitalized in Lynchburg, marveled that while he never "believed it possible," Lynchburg slaves "seem to be the best dressed and happiest people here." Less hyperbolic, a Boston Presbyterian minister visiting on the eve of the war confided to a local clergyman that despite his abolitionist leanings to the contrary, Lynchburg slaves "did not at all have the appearance of a down trodden race."[45]

Even so, factory laborers endured a hard life. Although they were compensated better than most slaves, the work was grueling, the hours were long, and they still had to labor under the customary conditions of Southern servitude. Tobacconists, despite their claims that slaves and free blacks responded to financial incentives, continued to rely on physical abuse to maintain labor discipline. For this reason, overseers, armed with whip and pistol, were a ubiquitous sight in most factories. In addition, hired slaves, by far the largest segment of the workforce, faced the annual insecurity of being uprooted from work and home.[46]

In rare instances, factory slaves lashed out against the system and the individuals that held them in bondage. According to reports published in the local press, black laborers tended to be far more contentious of authority than whites. During sample periods in 1858 and 1860, Button's *Lynchburg Virginian* reported six cases of black violence against employers, but only one case of white employee-employer violence. Although Button may have exaggerated the seriousness of some of these incidents to encourage employers to be diligent in their supervision of their black employees, the black workers' behavior is still extraordinary compared to the apparent passivity of white workers. Factory laborers who openly resisted, however, did so at considerable risk. When a Richmond overseer shot and killed a recalcitrant black laborer, the editor of the *Virginian* endorsed the overseer's behavior, noting that "nothing short of the use of the deadly weapon will produce subordination in our factories."[47]

In truth, most factory laborers rarely had to rely on violence to seek redress at the factories. Working in gangs, black factory laborers retained considerable discretionary power on the shop floor. As a result, they could use means other than violence to protest cruel treatment and gain some semblance of justice. Extant evidence suggests that slaves and free blacks were far more likely to steal from their employers than whites. Although Button reported few cases of white theft from employers, as much as 40 percent of all reported black thefts were against employers. Evidently, much of this crime was used to fuel what historians have termed the "gray market." By appropriating goods from their masters and selling these items to other blacks, poor whites, and white grocers, slaves and free blacks raised cash to pay for both necessities and leisure activities. More often than not, Lynchburg slaves stole what they manufactured with their own hands as a salient protest against their exploitation. Although such behavior reinforced whites' opinion that—as Button termed it—blacks' "moral culture is, at best, defective," for those blacks who stole, the economic and psychic gains outweighed the disadvantages.[48]

Nevertheless, few Lynchburg blacks openly rebelled against the system of slavery. Constrained by their own powerlessness, most simply tried to make the best of their circumstances by creating—as best they could—an autonomous world. Through their churches, their families, their leisure activities, and their work, they attempted to bring order and dignity to their lives.

Perhaps the most telling indication of how slavery affected Lynchburg society is how it shaped relations between slaveholders and nonslaveholders. When slaveholders protected slaves from Lynchburg's municipal authority, supported black churches, or allowed a favored servant to use the dining room for a wedding feast, they risked alienating their poorer white neighbors, who no doubt resented the special relationship that slaveholders sometimes developed with their slaves. Fearing that disaffected lower-class whites might threaten the security of slavery, Southern slaveholders tried to bolster their allegiance by convincing them that despite the slaveholders' overtures to some slaves, theirs was an exclusive community, by and for whites. Specifically, apologists for slavery argued that slavery guaranteed prosperity, social mobility, and independence for all hardworking Southern whites.[49]

By the late 1850s, slaveholders had nearly mastered the rhetoric of the pro-slavery argument. Yet they could hardly rest easy. The declining proportion of slaveholders, the growing concentration of wealth, and the deterioration of the soil made the pro-slavery argument increasingly problematic.[50] Southern cities like Lynchburg posed a unique set of problems for pro-slavery apologists. Not only were the extremes of wealth more evident in the cities, but many white urban laborers were themselves dispossessed farmers who had already lost their cherished independence and autonomy. Often in desperation, they moved to the cities to live and labor in conditions that, by their view, were much too similar to slavery. Thus, urban slaveholders, no less than their rural counterparts, had to go beyond mere rhetoric to give nonslaveholding whites a stake in the community and in slavery. In Lynchburg, slaveholders used many of the same methods as their rural counterparts as they tried to accomplish this

Tobacco factory scenes. (*Harper's Monthly,* 1879; LMS)

task. Through grand gestures of paternalism, Lynchburg slaveholders tried to show their less wealthy neighbors that slavery offered tangible rewards for them.[51]

To begin, many Lynchburg slaveholders followed Southern custom by trying to remain intimately involved in the lives of their less wealthy white neighbors. Living near them was one way to do this. Entrepreneurs who employed skilled and semiskilled laborers in their shops were especially insistent on this point. In contrast to employers in the industrializing North, many Lynchburg employers tried to retain the patriarchal relations of the preindustrial store and workshop. Growing up in the 1850s, John Meem Payne recalled that most artisan shopkeepers resided at or near their places of business. Evidently, they encouraged their workers to do the same. According to the 1859 Lynchburg city directory, one-fourth of all skilled workers lived either at their employer's home or at his shop. Most others lived in the same neighborhood.[52]

Even those who did not employ white laborers often chose to live among them. Although the 1850s witnessed an increase in the physical separation of the classes, the process was hardly complete by the end of the decade. Traditional residence patterns continued to dominate. In his block-by-block description of Lynchburg, Payne recalled only two wealthy residential enclaves during the 1850s. Otherwise, most city blocks were a mix of artisan shops, large brick and small wood homes, tobacco factories, and merchants' storefronts. Many of the most prominent citizens of Lynchburg lived on the most densely populated streets in town, near the central business district. This group included Mayor William Branch; attorney G. Woodville Latham; the town's wealthiest tobacconist, Jesse Hare; and six of the town's twelve city council members. These individuals lived in the center of town at least in part because they believed it was incumbent on them as civic leaders to remain a conspicuous part of the town's daily life. They were not alone. Forty-four percent of the town's tobacconists, 60 percent of the town's professionals, and 63 percent of the town's proprietors lived in or within two blocks of the central business district, where most of the town's laborers lived.[53]

Not that proximity created social harmony. Some wealthy residents tired of what they perceived to be the vulgar habits and mannerisms of their poorer neighbors. Living and working on Main Street, in the heart of the city, Charles Button of the *Lynchburg Virginian* had ample opportunity to observe his poorer neighbors. He did not like what he saw. More than once, he used sarcasm in his city column to create the separation between himself and the poor that geography would not allow. In one of his more caustic social commentaries, Button lampooned the "prevailing mode of fashion" of his female neighbors as they went about their daily routines. Button observed that "the reigning style for four o'clock in the morning toilets, is bare feet, toes very red, handkerchief around the head," hair "uncombed in style, *a la scullion*," and a gorgeous "three-penny calico dress *a la natural*," confined at the waist with a "superb girdle, made of a string." Before heading off to work, they added one additional adornment—"a broom and slop-bucket." Changing for an evening's rest, their costumes included "stockings, down at the heels . . . a great deal of terra firma under the finger nails," and, in obvious reference to the Irish, "hair stuck loosely over the head—the emigrant ship style—for greater facility in flavoring soups and gravies." For their part, many poor residents resented their wealthy neighbors for their large homes, fine carriages, and fancy clothes, not to mention their insufferable acts of condescension.[54]

Even so, other forces were also at work. By sharing the same streets, sidewalks, and stores, rich and poor whites also learned to coexist on reasonably peaceful terms. Moreover, because they lived only a few blocks away from the poorest sections of town, civic leaders found it exceedingly difficult to disavow their traditional obligations to assist the poor in times of extreme want. Wealthy women such as Lucy Otey, wife of the president of city council, and Sabra Ramsey, wife of a Presbyterian minister, often commented on the travails of their less wealthy neighbors and made it a point to visit their poor neighbors during times of economic dislocation.[55]

Many of Lynchburg's wealthier citizens also employed credit networks to strengthen the ligaments of community with their less wealthy neighbors. Historians have long recognized that credit was indispensable in the rural South because of the agricultural cycle and the lack of currency. What is less appreciated is that currency problems also plagued tobacco towns like Lynchburg, because of the tobacconists' dependence on Northern factors and Virginia's antiquated banking system.[56] As a result, most white Lynchburgers relied on credit from time to time. Many lower-class whites benefited from the informal networks that emerged. Because they possessed fewer financial resources, lower-class whites often required more time to pay their debts. Thus, entrepreneurs' offers of credit helped soften the sometimes harsh realities of Lynchburg's commercial economy. In addition, as historian Rhys Isaac has observed, debt and credit reinforced the personalism of Southern social relations by reducing "the impersonal now-and-done quality inherent in cash transactions, sustaining in its place a network of continuing, face-to-face personal relationships."[57]

A number of diverse Lynchburg businessmen and professionals extended credit to their customers, some more extensively than others. Samuel Garland, Jr., and Charles Slaughter, two of Lynchburg's wealthiest and most prominent antebellum lawyers, gave most of their less wealthy clients liberal terms to pay their legal fees. In their 1857–1861 account books, the law partners meticulously recorded all their business transactions, noting the date of service and the date of repayment. For their most complex and time-consuming cases, they charged fees that ran into the hundreds of dollars, making it necessary for clients to pay them back in installments over a number of months or even years. Yet even those who were charged comparatively modest fees of five to ten dollars were given liberal terms of repayment. In the four years before the war, the lawyers represented forty-four white widows and skilled and unskilled laborers. Of these, only nine paid their fees within a month of services rendered. The rest were much less prompt: three paid their bills within the year, three more paid their bills within two years, five took from two to three years, and two took more than three years. When Slaughter closed the firm's books in 1863, after his partner's death, twenty of their former clients had failed to make any payments and two had made only partial payment.[58]

The large number of delinquent payments may have been in part due to the quality of clients lawyers sometimes attract, but it also reflects how two prominent Lynchburg residents chose to do business. Indeed, Slaughter and Garland proved almost as lenient in their nonlegal business dealings. Besides their joint practice, the two owned several houses and apartments in Lynchburg that they rented to widows and laborers. According to their financial records, they rarely pressured their tenants to pay their rents with regularity. During one ten-month period early in the Civil War, eight individuals rented dwellings from the two lawyers. None paid rent every month, and only two, both white men who lived in the most expensive rentals, paid uniform sums when they did pay. The rest paid what they could, when they could. Some planned ahead. Maria Graham, a widow, paid six months' rent at the beginning of the year. Others could not plan ahead and had to rely on the generosity and patience of their landlords. In successive months, Betsy Rambee paid $1.00, $2.65, $2.00, $2.00, $2.00, no payment, $5.00, no payment, $2.00, and no payment. During the same period, Mrs. Monarty paid $4.50, $3.00, $2.00, no payment, $5.00, $5.00, no payment, $5.00, and no payment.[59]

Merchants were often less willing to accept credit. At the vanguard of the emerging market economy, merchants tended to be less appreciative of the social value of casual credit and debt networks. Nevertheless, special circumstances and the pull of tradition often compelled merchants to offer credit, despite their disinclination to do so. George Washington Clement was one merchant who preferred to do business on a cash basis. Even so, his account book reveals that nearly once a day he extended credit to his customers. On rare occasions, he even bartered with his customers to help them reduce their debts. In the middle of the panic of 1857, for example, Clement noted in his ledger that he had accepted six pairs of shoes from John Wells "in payment of his store account." Clement gave other evidence of his concern and generosity for his customers. About once a week he loaned a customer money, usually to help the customer pay off a debt owed someone else.[60]

Besides offers of credit, many wealthy Lynchburgers found different ways to assist poorer whites financially. Some went out of their way to patronize local artisans and laborers. Button was especially enthusiastic of this practice. In his local column, he advertised the superior skill of Lynchburg craftsmen and commended his readers to buy local. Other civic boosters went a step farther. In 1857, civic boosters organized the Lynchburg Agricultural and Mechanical Society. At its annual fair, the organization staged competitions to encourage Lynchburg home industries, offering cash prizes for the best agricultural implements, wagons, tinware, stoves, tobacco molds, furniture, and other local products. By the end of the decade, promoting free labor had become a favorite cause for many local boosters, perhaps because it dovetailed with another pet cause of Southern capitalists—creating an independent Southern economy. By underlining the crucial role that laboring whites played in the South's economy, Lynchburg's capitalists hoped to show artisans and mechanics that their conception of the ideal South was a truly integrated community of artisans, capitalists, farmers, and slaves—each complementing the other to create a dynamic and self-sufficient regional economy.[61]

Many artisans and shopkeepers not only accepted this logic but learned to exploit it to full advantage to sell their products. During the 1856 presidential election, J.H.C. Winston, a local Lynchburg cabinetmaker, advertised that "an opportunity is now offered FIRE EATERS, of every grade and stripe, of manifesting their devotion to Southern institutions, by sustaining Southern manufactures, instead of buying the WORTHLESS NORTHERN TRASH which floods our Southern cities." A few months after John Brown's raid, John Bailey, the town's largest carriagemaker, made a similar plea to Southern nationalists. Under the mock headline "Abolitionists Killed in Lynchburg," Bailey suggested that "the way to kill the Northern fanatics is to buy your Carriages, Buggies, and Wagons at Bailey's." In this way, patrons would not send their "money North to enrich and enable the Abolitionists to make Sharpe rifles and Spears to send to our Negroes to kill us with." Patronage, especially when aligned with certain political issues, was a powerful force of social unity in the late antebellum South.[62]

Not every laborer was in a position to profit from wealthy patrons. Without permanent jobs, day laborers lived an especially precarious existence. In 1860, roughly two-thirds of all white unskilled laborers reported that they had neither real nor personal property. Many artisans were not much better off; nearly one-half of all white nonproprietor artisans also reported no property. Lynchburg could be extremely inhospitable for such people. Because one industry dominated Lynchburg's economy, the town was vulnerable to sudden economic collapses. And when the economy faltered, as it did in 1856, 1857, and after Lincoln's election in 1860, those without property were particularly vulnerable because they lacked the resources to live without a steady income.[63]

Rather than develop permanent institutions to assist the town's poorest citizens, however, civic leaders preferred to rely on spontaneous and personal gifts of benevolence. Button, for one, believed this approach was more in keeping with the paternalist ethos. In one of his periodic pleas that wealthier citizens assist the poor, he complimented his readers for their good works. He observed that, although "we have few charitable associations organized as such," the town had acquired a reputation as an "eminently benevolent one," largely because so many "delighted in doing good" and were always "open to proper appeals." Following the dictates of paternalism, Button encouraged citizens to make their gifts as personal as possible, noting that "a kind word sometimes exercises a magic influence."[64]

Elites believed their generous acts of charity precluded the necessity of a systematic program of public assistance. The municipal government's primary contribution to the relief of the poor was to allocate funds to the "overseer of the poor," an elected official whose primary tasks were to distribute wood during the winter and to care for the town's twenty or so vagrants, who were housed in the dilapidated poorhouse.[65]

Most private benevolent organizations were equally limited in scope. To ensure that they would have plenty of opportunity publicly and personally to show their benevolence and moral stewardship, elites kept all existing institutions small and dependent on constant infusions of private donations. Even church poor funds were often paltry. Although Jacob Mitchell, minister of Lynchburg's Second Presbyterian Church, dispensed aid to the poor daily, he often had to solicit wealthy individuals before making his rounds. Through such practices as these, elites made sure that poorer residents knew whom to thank for whatever assistance they received.[66]

The town's largest permanent charitable organization was the Dorcas Society, a Methodist women's organization that included many of the town's wealthiest matrons. The Dorcas Society provided year-round assistance and operated a Sunday school program for impoverished white women and children. In pursuing these ambitious activities, however, the Dorcas women also tried to make benevolence as personal as possible. Like every other voluntary organization, the Dorcas Society depended solely on individual donations to survive. As a result, the extent of its assistance varied from month to month and sometimes proved inadequate to the task. Moreover, in times of severe economic crisis, the Dorcas women allowed their organization to be usurped—compliantly, it seems—by male civic leaders, who may have wanted to show that they, not women, were the true benefactors of the town.[67]

Even in times of great need, public relief remained tied to personalism and paternalism. In the middle of the Secession crisis, for instance, the treasurer of the Dorcas Society reported that the organization had run out of funds. At the same time, however, gentlemen of property and standing busily orchestrated several grand gestures on behalf of the poor. Not surprising, most of their plans enabled them publicly to exhibit their wealth, power, and generosity. In the face of widespread economic dislocation, town fathers urged their peers to help mitigate the suffering of the poor by lowering housing rents and slave-hiring rates. Others publicly encouraged their friends to curtail their extravagant lifestyles and provide for the poor instead.[68]

As the economic crisis worsened, however, wealthy citizens recognized that symbolic acts of self-sacrifice did not relieve the sufferings of the poor. In response, a group of Lynchburg's wealthiest male citizens—an assembly that included four tobacconists, six merchants, two lawyers, and a physician—formed a society to raise money for the poor. Observing that "there never was in our city so much suffering," the society laid out an ambitious relief program. First, the committee organized a number of fund-raising ventures, including public lectures and tableaux at Dudley Hall. These lavish events were especially designed to give Lynchburg's wealthiest citizens a public forum in which to demonstrate their benevolence. As the crisis continued, members of the relief society expanded their efforts. As they did, however, they continued to adhere to the ethic of paternalism. The organization divided into two subcommittees to care for the city's two wards. Members of each subcommittee were then instructed to walk from door to door to solicit donations. Once sufficient funds had been collected, members of the relief society would visit each needy family.[69]

Through these gestures, Lynchburg relief organizations not only restricted how the poor received assistance but also determined who deserved assistance. Yet Lynchburg's relief organizations rarely excluded individuals because of their moral character per se. Button, for instance, suggested to his readers that as long as the poor individual was a member of the community, he deserved assistance. Sympathetically, he reminded his readers that "there are always some who find it exceedingly difficult to obtain even the necessaries of life" in a "town the size of Lynchburg." Although some are "idle, dissolute, and depraved . . . we should not be too rigid in any case," Button continued, but "manifest a proper sense of gratitude by doing what we can . . . no matter what their antecedents." For this reason, Button suggested, the poor of the community actually helped society by reminding elites of their charitable responsibilities.[70]

Yet if the morality of recipients was not of uppermost importance to charitable organizations, ethnicity and race were. Perhaps as a way to elevate native laboring whites, elites discriminated against those who were closest to native white laborers in status—free blacks and the Irish. Although these were the two poorest groups in town, charitable organizations systematically excluded them from benevolence. The Dorcas women were especially determined to show that charity was only for native whites. The Society assisted only individuals who attended its Sabbath school. This strategy effectively excluded free blacks and "foreign paupers": free blacks, because they were not allowed to attend the school; the Irish, because most would not attend a Protestant institution. In ways such as this, elites defined the boundaries of the Lynchburg community.[71]

A final way in which civic leaders attempted to integrate less wealthy whites into the community was through politics. Here civic leaders operated on more volatile ground. In many antebellum communities, politics operated as a source of class, ethnic, and religious division, not as a source of unity. This potential existed in Lynchburg as well. Late antebellum state and national elections in Virginia were characterized by intense partisan campaigns, as Democrats and Whigs contended for the popular vote in a series of close elections. At least in theory, this political competition offered lower-class residents an opportunity to bring their views to the fore. Especially after 1851, when electoral reforms expanded the franchise to include all adult white males, both parties had to remain sensitive to the feelings of the electorate to be successful. Whether party leaders wanted to or not, their activities helped democratize politics.[72]

In Lynchburg, political leaders were not immune to the democratizing tendencies of two-party politics. During the late 1850s, leaders from both parties made regular overtures to mechanics and laboring men. For Whigs, the stronger of the two parties in Lynchburg, the decision to do so must have been an uncomfortable one. Skeptical, if not downright fearful, of the new political realities that democracy created, Lynchburg Whigs had long chastised Democrats for courting the masses rather than standing on principle. According to the editor of the *Lynchburg Virginian*, the Whig Party organ, local Democratic leaders were demagogues who appealed to the lowest instincts of the voters through vicious and vulgar language that excited the populace without encouraging them to reason.

The *Lynchburg Virginian* was equally critical of the party's rank and file. After the local Democratic Party achieved a resounding victory in the national election of 1852, the editor bitterly condemned their adversaries as "disorderly and "mob-like . . . composed . . . of all shapes, sizes, and colors." According to the editor, the tumult was merely the inevitable result of the party's obsession for the principles of freedom and equality. Conservative Whigs even blamed the sectional crisis on the dissolute effects of too much democracy. Writing in the *Virginian*, "Virginius" concluded that the fundamental difference between North and South was that the North affirmed "the absolute political equality of all," while the South was "founded upon the coincident distinctions of *class and race.*" According to Virginius, democracy corrupted Northerners, ultimately enabling radical abolitionists to ascend to power in the North. In an editorial response, Button praised "Virginius," noting that "nobody will admit more readily than we that Democracy is aggressive and that the principle of 'equality' . . . is dangerous to society." He offered one corrective, however. Button cautioned that the thirst for equality "exists even in Virginia." Indeed, Button concluded, "we are suffering now one of the evils deplored by 'Virginius,' to wit, 'universal suffrage.' "[73]

Despite their fears about democratic politics, Whigs had little choice but to try to attract popular support if they wished to remain the dominant party in Lynchburg. During the 1850s, many local Whig politicians began to claim that they, not the Democrats, were the true friends of labor. Internal improvements and economic expansion, they claimed, created jobs for the city's mechanics and laboring men. During the secession debates, Whigs attempted to claim the voice of urban labor outright by suggesting that agrarian-based Democrats would lead the South into a war in which urban laborers would be forced to do most of the fighting.[74]

Local Democratic leaders were far more comfortable appealing to the lower classes. As the party of Andrew Jackson, local Democrats could call on a number of political issues that lower-class whites throughout the South had long found attractive: a time-tested commitment to equal rights for all white men; a pledge to keep government small, inexpensive, and respectful of individual liberty; faith in popular democracy; an abiding distrust of economic change; and an outright intolerance of free blacks.[75]

Although the Democratic Party organ, the *Lynchburg Republican*, survives only in fragmentary form, extant evidence suggests that local Democratic leaders used these issues to full effect but molded them to fit the unique circumstances of Lynchburg politics. Buoyed by the decline of the Whig Party at the national level and the growing popularity of states' rights, local Democrats believed they could break the Whigs' hold on Lynchburg if they could appeal to the town's commercial-oriented artisans. To prove to Lynchburg voters that they were not against economic expansion, local Democrats adopted some of the Whigs' favorite campaign issues. By the end of the decade, Democratic candidates routinely announced that they, too, supported internal improvements, as long as these did not fasten too great a burden on "the shoulders of our already oppressed citizens." In the 1857 and 1859 state elections, Democratic legislative candidates went even farther, noting that they enthusiastically supported Lynchburg's most ambitious project, the construction of the recently completed Virginia and Tennessee Railroad, a work that one Democratic circular described as "the salvation of the city" because it created jobs for "thousands of mechanics." Apparently, the economic interests of Lynchburg Whigs and Democrats were not as different as they were at the national level.[76]

This was not the only point of convergence. Leaders from both parties were careful not to let too much democracy enter Lynchburg politics. Even as party leaders fashioned campaign issues to attract popular support, they also tried to consolidate their power. Through a variety of measures, party leaders tried to dissuade popular insurgents. This was especially true in municipal elections. Through a variety of means, party leaders made a concerted effort to keep partisanship—and the rancor it sometimes produced—out of local elections. Whigs, although they might have dominated the local government, preferred to share power with Democrats rather than introduce partisan politics to local elections. Thus, the editors of the *Lynchburg Virginian* usually endorsed a number of Democrats for local office, without mention of their political orientation, but otherwise avoided discussing municipal candidates.

In Lynchburg, the careful bipartisan management of municipal elections meant that stature, almost as much as party affiliation, determined whether one gained local office. Whether Whig or Democrat, municipal political leaders were always men of wealth and reputation whose families had long been active in Lynchburg politics and commerce. In 1860, Lynchburg's twelve city council members included four tobacconists, four merchants, two lawyers, the manager of the Virginia and Tennessee Railroad, and a banker. Each owned at least four slaves, and half had estates valued at more than fifty thousand dollars. Ten were among the wealthiest 5 percent of Lynchburg residents; the other two had close relatives who were, and they were themselves among the wealthiest decile. Ten of the twelve were incumbents; the other two replaced retired council members. Each won by an overwhelming majority.[77]

When insurgents did appear in municipal elections, elites united to quash their campaign. Just a few weeks before the 1859 municipal election, Fleming Coleman, a carpenter, announced that he intended to run for police master. Neither party endorsed Coleman. Indeed, the Whigs went out of their way to ridicule his candidacy. Button referred to Coleman, a native Virginian, as "Flemini J. Colemonie" and mocked his fitness for office by riddling his press announcement with misspelled words, ungrammatical sentences, and lower-class slang. Disheartened, if not distraught, by the reception his candidacy received, Coleman promptly withdrew from the race.[78]

Even in state and national elections, where political campaigns were far more volatile and partisan, party leaders took steps to control popular participation so that lower-class insurgents could not challenge the existing social and political hierarchy. Party leaders—most of whom were individuals of wealth and standing within the community, not professional politicians—controlled the process from nomination to election. In many respects, the entire process was a ritual of deference. A few months before an election, party officers selected a candidate. In a printed letter to the party organ, they announced their selection and appealed to the individual to accept. Invariably, they also mentioned the candidate's moral integrity, republican selflessness, and respected stature within the community. In most cases, the candidate readily accepted the invitation, but only after noting his personal lack of ambition for power.

By the time the general population became active participants in the political process, party leaders had already scripted their role. Just before the election, party leaders organized political rallies and directed local vigilance committees to get out the vote. They also supervised the polls on election day. As a result, citizens had little opportunity to act on their own initiative. Even at the polls, citizens confronted the power of local elites. Each citizen gave his vote aloud, in the presence of the candidates or their neighborhood lieutenants. In these ways, Lynchburg politics retained many of the customs of traditional Virginia political culture. Even though Lynchburg society may have lacked some of the day-to-day, face-to-face contact that made this ritual such a powerful bulwark of deference in rural Virginia, the ideal remained. Through the very public and personal act of voting, Lynchburg citizens were required to show their gratitude for past favors and to confer honor and esteem on public figures. Indeed, the enduring political power of Lynchburg's elites suggests that voters continued to be compelled—at least in part—by considerations of personal obligation and duty.[79]

Although Lynchburg's elites enjoyed considerable success in their efforts to retain the support of lower-class whites, by the late 1850s, the message they were sending their less wealthy neighbors had become rather muddled. For one thing, a few prominent citizens harbored rather ambivalent feelings toward laboring whites. Former mayor and editor of the *Lynchburg Virginian* Elijah Fletcher noted that local railroad contractors preferred slave laborers to free white laborers because they deemed the former "equally efficient, more moral and much easier managed" than the local pool of white road workers. As a result, Fletcher observed, "none . . . will employ White Labor if they can procure black." Evidently, Fletcher agreed with their assessment. At the age of sixty-two, he set out to construct a new wing for his mansion, hiring white men to do it "for almost the first time" in his life. He regretted the decision. In the midst of the construction project, he complained to his brother that it was not going well. Determining that they were lazy and dishonest, he concluded that he could "not well leave them" alone. As a result, he cancelled his annual summer trip to visit family in Vermont so that he could oversee the construction project.[80]

More often, elites found themselves torn between two very distinct ethics. Though deeply committed to traditional Southern customs and habits, even the most stalwart were not immune to the emerging values of commercial capitalism. Indeed, as entrepreneurs and professionals in a commercial city, they were the leaders of the economic transformation of their region. As such, they found themselves slowly, albeit imperfectly, adopting values and patterns of behavior that were often antithetical to their most cherished beliefs. In the large cities of the North, their counterparts often proved to be less interested in maintaining the traditional ties of the organic community. Instead, the North's new middle class extolled new values of individualism, dignity, self-discipline, and privacy. Equally important, they often promoted their class interests by dissociating themselves from the rest of society—an act that threatened to destroy the corporate nature of early American society.[81]

Lynchburg's antebellum entrepreneurs and professionals did not make such a complete transformation. Most were too much the products of the rural South to make a clean break from traditional patterns of community. Nevertheless, the process had begun. In words and deeds, Lynchburg elites occasionally acted in ways that undermined a strict adherence to the ethic of paternalism. For one thing, some elites had begun to absent themselves from daily interaction with lower-class whites. To promote their distinct interests and differentiate themselves from the mass of whites, they became increasingly exclusive in their social relationships. A few built private Italian villas, the architectural rage of the day, on the tops of Lynchburg's highest hills. With enclosed gardens, spacious grounds, and secluded entrances, the homes placed a premium on privacy. Indeed, one of these neighborhoods, Diamond Hill, was surrounded by deep ravines and could be accessed from the city only by narrow footbridges. More common, civic leaders organized exclusive societies, such as the Young Men's Christian Association and the Board of Trade, or transformed old ones, such as the Masons, to distinguish themselves from the rest of society and to create stronger ties with those who shared their business interests.[82]

John William Murrell House, circa 1860. Murrell, a tobacco and sugar merchant, built his Italian villa on Garland Hill, a remote area that became one of Lynchburg's first exclusive neighborhoods. (JML)

As civil leaders separated themselves from the town's poorest whites, they began to withdraw many of the services they had once offered the poor. Merchants, for one, became less willing to offer credit to their customers. With increased regularity, entrepreneurs through newspaper advertisements began to press their customers to settle their accounts promptly. As one clothier ruefully put it, he "had not yet learned to do business (with wholesalers) without money." When Virginia banks suspended payment during the panic of 1857, several merchants decided this was a fitting time to change the way they did business. Although most had little choice but to extend credit during the panic, a few withdrew from the practice completely when the crisis ended. John Adams and Thomas Anderson, who operated a rather modest establishment, were among the first to discourage credit customers. In March 1858, they advertised their business as a "CASH GROCERY STORE," stating that they were "determined to do business on, and strictly adhere to, the CASH SYSTEM."[83] Other entrepreneurs announced that they planned to be far more discriminating when they granted credit in the future.

Beginning in early 1858, a growing number of merchants began to publish the general terms under which they would offer credit to customers. Unfortunately, grocers' and merchants' newly developed fiscal conservatism probably left many artisans and most unskilled laborers in the cold. When Nathan Kabler, a dry-goods merchant, died during the war, 140 people owed him money. Of the 89 who could be identified by either the 1859 city directory or the 1860 manuscript census, 19 were skilled laborers who owned their own businesses, 10 were skilled laborers who worked for someone else, and 2 were unskilled. Evidently, Kabler did not think it his responsibility to extend assistance to all whites—only those he did not view as serious credit risks.[84]

Market considerations eroded the influence of paternalism in other ways as well. As entrepreneurs like carriagemaker John Bailey and foundry owners like A. G. Dabney and Francis Deane became more dependent on regional and national markets, their businesses became more vulnerable to seasonal fluctuations in trade. Particularly in the winter months, these employers often had to let many of their workers go. This, in turn, created a more transient working population, which severely undermined the type of community Lynchburg elites hoped to fashion. Yet even many laboring whites who were not transients were often not recognized as members of the community. When B. L. Blackford and D. P. Payne, booksellers, created a business directory in 1859, they included most of the town's artisan-shopkeepers but only 75 of the town's 369 white nonproprietor artisans and only 2 of the town's 371 white unskilled laborers.[85]

Some members of the upper class became so enamored with their new business values that they tried to apply them to some of the town's social problems. A few began to suggest that public institutions should replace private charity. Writing in the *Virginian* in 1859 under the Dickensian nom de plume "Utility," one civic leader suggested it was time to build a municipal workhouse so that the poor could learn the value of work and self-discipline.[86]

Given the uncertainties and inconsistencies of the age, some individuals seemed to embody both cultures at once. In many respects, Colonel

Augustine Leftwich, one of Lynchburg's most established tobacconists, was the embodiment of Southern gentility. According to travel writer Anne Royall, Leftwich was a "stout noble figure and a very gentlemanlike man," with manners that were "polished and familiar." On sunny days, he strolled to his factory, dressed completely in white, accompanied by one of his slaves, who held a large umbrella over Leftwich's head. But Leftwich was more than just a Virginia cavalier; he was also an astute businessman who spied on his competitors to maintain an edge.[87]

Similarly, Samuel Garland, Jr., and Charles Slaughter, for all their efforts to attend personally to the needs of their less wealthy neighbors and clients, acted in ways that sometimes must have alienated the poor. Both lived on the most remote hill of the city, Daniel's Hill. Their neighbors were virtually all kith and kin, creating a tight social network of Lynchburg's most prominent citizens. In the last years before the war, the social gatherings of this small social circle became increasingly extravagant. As the economic crisis that accompanied the Secession winter worsened, their parties exposed class differences like no other event in Lynchburg's immediate past. Despite widespread unemployment and admonishments by some civic leaders to curtail their lavish displays of wealth, one intimate of Garland recalled that "the winter of 1860 and 1861 was . . . one of unprecedented gaiety." Led by Mr. and Mrs. Samuel Garland, Jr., "the leaders of our society," this exclusive social circle attended "party after party in rapid succession" in search of "relief from the oppression of [our] forebodings." At one of this group's more outlandish affairs, a theme party of an Irish wake, guests dressed in costumes "representing different characters among the lower classes of that race."[88]

It is difficult to determine how laboring whites responded to civic leaders' imperfect efforts to retain their loyalty through paternalism. No doubt, many white laborers needed little encouragement to support slavery. The vast majority of Lynchburg's laboring whites were native-born Southerners and viewed slavery as a fundamental aspect of their society. Indeed, Lynchburg society offered whites little opportunity to develop an alternative perception of race because of the homogeneous nature of the community. Although the town was originally settled by Quakers, most had moved away by the 1850s, victims of the Upper South's growing intolerance for abolitionism. Most of those who remained in Lynchburg through the 1850s had long since made their peace with slavery. As a result, the Quaker Meeting House in the suburbs of town slowly fell into disrepair.[89]

The few who questioned the morality of slavery were extremely circumspect in doing so. As a boy growing up in Lynchburg, John Douglas recalled only one instance in which his father, Joel Douglas, a machinist from Philadelphia who opposed slavery, criticized the institution. One day, while walking through town, father and son came upon a white man whipping his female slave. Though John noticed that his father was disturbed by the incident, they passed by in silence. Finally, when he was sure no one else could hear, John's father muttered to him that "some day this will be wiped out in blood." Most of the time, the elder Douglas was so circumspect that he kept his true feelings from his son. As a result, John confessed he paid little attention to the morality of slavery when he was a boy. Instead, he remembered only that Lynchburg slavery "was milder in comparison with states farther South." Even the market house's slave auction block "made no impression on me at the time."[90]

John Douglas was not alone in his casual acceptance of slavery. In contrast to laborers and artisans in other Southern towns and cities, Lynchburg's laboring whites demonstrated little resentment toward slavery. In large part, this was because only a handful of slaves competed outright with whites for jobs. Because male slaves were so attractive to tobacconists, owners had little economic incentive to teach them other skills or hire them out as laborers. Although it is impossible to determine the exact number of skilled slave laborers, an estimate can be hazarded by assuming that an adult male slave's occupation was related to the occupation of the artisan who rented or owned him. By this method, the number of skilled slaves was probably not much greater than forty. Most of these were dispersed throughout the skilled trades and thus did not pose a threat to any single class of artisans.[91]

Rather than oppose slavery, white artisans apparently accepted the status quo. Those who could afford to do so, mainly shopkeepers and master craftsmen, rented and owned slaves of their own. Indeed, a larger proportion of shopkeepers than of professionals and entrepreneurs owned or rented slaves: 73 percent of all male proprietors held at least one slave, compared to 58 percent of professionals and entrepreneurs. In contrast, only one-fifth of nonproprietor artisans held slaves. Here, too, the decision may have been more economic than moral. Of the wealthiest decile of nonproprietor artisans, 56 percent held slaves.[92]

Shopkeepers' decision to own and rent slaves did not necessarily mean that they repudiated their free-labor ideology. Nor did they necessarily turn their backs on white laborers when they employed slaves. Although some shopkeepers may have used slaves in their shops, the majority probably did not. Instead, most preferred female house slaves, probably because they were cheaper. In all, 62 percent of the shopkeepers' slaves between the prime working ages of fifteen and sixty were female. Moreover, of the thirty-two shopkeepers who used slaves, twenty-nine had at least one female; of this group, eighteen used only females. In contrast, only fourteen held one or more male slaves, and only three held only males. In short, shopkeepers demonstrated no aversion to slavery per se. Like most native and adopted Southerners, they accepted slavery as part of the status quo.[93]

The relatively large number of slaveholding artisans in Lynchburg was due in part to the availability of female slaves. But it was also the result of the provincialism of the town's population. In contrast to other Southern cities, where European and Northern-born immigrants often comprised a majority of the artisan class, Lynchburg failed to attract either group in great numbers.[94] Isolated from the eastern seaboard by its rugged geography and unattractive to many artisans because of its large slave population and the dominance of the tobacco industry, Lynchburg's artisan class remained predominantly Southern. In 1860, 73 percent of the town's free artisans were born in Virginia, while another 4 percent came from other Southern states; in contrast, only 15 percent were Europeans, and 7 percent were Northerners.[95]

Lynchburg's provincialism may also have encouraged the town's few non-Southern artisans to accept slavery. Without a large non-Southern enclave to draw support from, Northern and foreign-born artisans may have felt compelled to behave in concert with their Southern counterparts; as a result, they demonstrated little of the intense antislavery sentiment seen in other Southern communities.[96] Instead, non-Southern shopkeepers and skilled workers were just as likely as Southerners to hold slaves.[97]

Many artisans and laborers who did not own slaves also believed that they had good reason to support the institution of slavery. For one thing, all white Southerners, including nonslaveholders, understood their status in relationship to black slavery. As historian J. Mills Thornton III has observed, Southern whites believed that slavery protected their independence and liberty by ensuring that few of their kind would "ever have to depend directly upon other white men for their sustenance." Evidently, even Lynchburg's poorest whites accepted this basic tenet of Southern republicanism. Although they were dependent on white benevolence, as well as on impersonal market conditions, they believed they needed only look at the condition of Lynchburg's slaves to recognize the superior status that their race gave them. Laboring whites understood that although they could lose a great deal in the volatile economic world of the nineteenth century, they could never lose their whiteness. As a result, they would never feel completely dependent.[98]

If most nonslaveholders had distinctive reasons to support slavery, paternalism helped solidify their support of the status quo in at least two ways. First, paternalism gave all laboring whites, not just those who owned slaves, an economic stake in slavery's survival. Patronage, in particular, revealed to many laboring whites, especially those with coveted skills, that there was a great deal of money to be made by serving the needs of Lynchburg's upper classes. Consider, for instance, those artisans involved in the building trades. During the 1850s, some of Lynchburg's wealthiest citizens engaged in a virtual mania of home construction, building mansions to exhibit their wealth and status. In what became an obvious effort to outdo one another, elites relied on the skill of local artisans to make their homes increasingly luxurious. While a few, most notably Elijah Fletcher, expressed a preference for slave laborers, most preferred skilled white artisans to execute the detailed work that they demanded. For this reason, a large number of Lynchburg's artisans benefited from Lynchburg's housing boom. By 1859, Lynchburg boasted three building contractors; seven master carpenters; six cabinet shops; one marble works; two brickyards; four painting and glazing outfits; four stove, tinware, and roof manufacturers; one sash, blind, and door-molding establishment; and one iron foundry that specialized in ornate fences and balconies. Together, these establishments employed 147 skilled white craftsmen.[99]

Many other types of artisans also catered to elite tastes. Lynchburg's 1859 city directory and the 1860 manufacturing census list four confectioners, four dressmakers, six milliners, three tailors, six shoemakers, three cigarmakers, five carriage manufacturers, two gunsmiths, and seven jewelers. Even those with no single marketable skill benefited from elite patronage. Samuel Garland, Jr., regularly augmented his workforce of slave laborers by hiring a variety of white day laborers to take care of his home, gardens, and rental property.[100]

Second, paternalism made it easier for less wealthy whites to accept the current social hierarchy. As much as they may have resented elites for their wealth and power, paternalism gave artisans access to an elite world that they otherwise would probably not have known. Even as they expressed disgust for the haughtiness of upper-class culture, most recognized the advantages of securing the favor of their elite neighbors. As the less wealthy artisans well knew, such alliances not only brought more work but helped them to enhance their reputations as craftsmen and as citizens.

On occasion, paternalism could create mutual feelings of respect and devotion between leaders and those below them. When George W. Glass, a manager for the Virginia and Tennessee Railroad, retired, his workmen were so grateful for past kindnesses that they staged an elaborate banquet to thank him publicly for his "gentlemanly conduct" toward them, noting, among other things, that they considered Glass a "number one" gentleman who had earned their respect "to the fullest extent." As part of their public tribute, mechanics and apprentices gave Glass gifts of appreciation.[101]

In most cases, however, relations between leaders and the led did not match this romanticized ideal of mutual devotion. No matter how intimate civic leader and citizen became, paternal relations were still based on power and inequality. Even prosperous shopkeepers and artisans sometimes found that they had to swallow hard in their dealings with elite patrons. Consider, for instance, the relationship between William Massie, a local tobacconist who lived on a plantation a few miles from Lynchburg, and Henry Didlake, a carriagemaker. Sometime during the spring of 1853, Massie commissioned Didlake to build a carriage he had designed. Shortly after Massie received the completed carriage, the luggage-rack bar broke—evidently because it was too small for its intended use. Furious, Massie sent an emissary, J. M. Cobb, to Didlake to repair the bar. Cobb made it clear to Didlake that Massie was disappointed in his work and expected satisfaction. He instructed the hapless artisan "for Gods sake [to] put up the carriage right," because Massie was "not only a good judge of work, but . . . very particular to have things done [his] own way." Didlake complied. In a letter that accompanied the repaired carriage, Didlake assured Massie that he "had attended in person to setting up the carriage and examined most closely, just as closely as I could do." And while he gently suggested that Massie's carriage design was difficult to follow, he assured Massie nonetheless that "you are the best and only judge in this matter." Plaintively, he suggested that Massie let "Mrs. Massie take a ride in the carriage," predicting that she would find it to be "the most pleasant riding and running carriage she ever rode in."[102]

Didlake was not the only skilled artisan to experience Massie's disfavor. During the war, Massie again used Cobb as an emissary, to chastise an unnamed loommaker for the poor quality of his work. Like Didlake, the loommaker apologized, telling Cobb that because "he is anxious that the loom should please," he would visit and repair it at a cost of $1.50 a day, or half his normal daily rate.[103]

Although Massie may have been an unusually difficult patron, the measured responses of Didlake and the loommaker suggest that both were accustomed to such episodes and knew how to appease their benefactors. They were probably not alone. By their willingness to play their prescribed role in affairs of deference, Lynchburg shopkeepers and artisans retained their clients and reaffirmed the social hierarchy—even if it occasionally cost them their dignity.

Poorer whites probably found elite paternalism even more difficult to accept. Most viewed even the kindest gesture as symptomatic of their marginality and a reminder of their relative powerlessness. Because poorer whites had fewer marketable skills, were more transient, and behaved in ways that elites found repugnant, elites' overtures to them were less frequent, less substantive, and often exacted at an even greater loss of honor. Receiving benevolence must have been an especially unpleasant experience for most poorer whites. Not only did they have to admit publicly their inability to live independently, they often had to listen to the moralizings of their benefactors before receiving assistance. Early in the 1850s, the Dorcas Society suggested that "the touching instances of woman's sorrow" were largely the product of man's "idleness and intemperance." According to their report, men of the poorest class were "miserably destitute—entailing ignorance, poverty, and crime upon their offspring." Indeed, they were so "destitute of principle" that to provide aid for them "would seem to be an abuse of public confidence." Women were only slightly less at fault. While noting many instances of "women's suffering," the Society rebuked others, noting that some were so miserable that their children would be "bettered by absolute Orphanage." Individuals could be just as condescending. Mary Blackford, the matriarch of one of the town's most respected families, kept a charity box on hand to assist her poorer neighbors but otherwise treated them with disdain. According to her grandson and biographer, L. Minor Blackford, Mrs. Blackford made it clear to all who knew her that she never "wanted to do anything for them as a group except to deny them the privilege of buying alcohol."[104]

No doubt, lower-class whites resented such depictions of themselves. Yet if they resented their status and the roles they were expected to perform, they generally suffered in silence. The extant evidence reveals only a few, isolated instances of poorer whites openly expressing their frustrations. In June 1859, a writer to the *Virginian* caustically asked Button "why it is that the Aristocracy are never required to serve as Jurors" while mechanics were always chosen, even though such service required them to "leave their businesses and lose two dollars to make one."[105]

For the most part, however, artisans and laborers kept such thoughts to themselves. Yet even as they acquiesced to elite claims of their right to rule, laboring whites searched for ways to assert their own identities and to express their own vision of the good life. Ironically, slavery offered them some opportunity to do so. Because of slavery, Lynchburg had no need for a large police force to watch and control its laboring population. After all, most Lynchburg laborers were slaves, and by power of tradition, all whites were called to supervise slaves' behavior. As a result, laboring whites were free to go their own way much of the time and to develop relationships with upper-class whites only when necessity compelled them to do so. As products of a culture that virtually idealized personal autonomy, this was no small advantage.[106]

Moreover, Lynchburg's laboring whites had access to a competing social and political vision to that espoused by most of the town's civic leaders. As many historians have observed, antebellum Southern slavery gave rise to two contradictory, and sometimes competing, social and political ideologies—deference and egalitarian republicanism. While most elites were uneasy with the political and social democratization of the late antebellum period, artisans and laborers embraced the changes and worked to broaden and defend their rights and freedoms whenever it was practicable to do so.[107]

Unfortunately, economic dependence and political powerlessness prevented Lynchburg's white laboring men from openly challenging elite dominance. As a result, most tried to evince their egalitarian ideals through other means. On the one hand, laborers and artisans developed a distinct leisure culture that minimized—and often excluded—upper-class involvement. On the other hand, laborers and artisans occasionally reached beyond their own emerging class to forge new relationships with elites that were not impeded by traditions of deference and paternalism. The ways in which they did this are the topic of the next chapter.

Religion, Rum, and Race:
Lower-Class Life in Antebellum Lynchburg

On Sunday, January 6, 1861, sixteen-year-old Jannett Cleland, the only daughter of the town's gas fitter, presented herself for membership at Lynchburg's First Presbyterian Church. Although Cleland had grown up in the church, she confided in her diary that the day had been "the most important . . . of my life." To Jannett, the ceremony had been a dramatic event. Along with several other probationers, she was asked to make a public confession of her faith to demonstrate her fitness for church membership. Although the ritual momentarily isolated her before the congregation, the ceremony affirmed her as a new member of the church community. Immediately after her testimony, the minister and the church elders received her into membership with "their right hand as a token of fellowship." Later that day, she participated in her first communion.[1]

Jannett believed her decision to join the church expressed a profound change in her life. In simple words, she tried to express the essential meaning of her act: "How do I describe this day? . . . I have this day decided before the world that I would live for Christ." By this she meant that she had abandoned a secular life to practice her faith within the context of a church community—a community that promised to encourage her, educate her, and discipline her if she broke her pledge.[2]

Jannett knew from experience that remaining true to her pledge would be a difficult task. A few months earlier, First Presbyterian had disciplined her father, James Cleland, for "indulging too frequently in the use of ardent spirits." Because of his transgressions, James was first visited by a committee of elders and then brought before session to repent. By then, James had sobered from his spree and was in remorse. According to the clerk of session's report of the event, James "expressed . . . deep sorrow at the wound he had inflicted on the church and his Christian standing." Admitting that he "had been overcome at an evil hour," he "promised with the help of God that he would abstain in the future." After a stern lecture from the pastor, James was readmitted to church membership.[3] Unfortunately, James did not keep his promise of sobriety. Although church elders did not discipline him again, he gradually drifted from their supervision to frequent the bars of the Buzzard, the town's vice district, much to the sorrow of his daughter, who remained an active member of First Presbyterian.[4]

The Clelands' experiences were probably not characteristic of all laboring families, black and white, in the antebellum South. Not all daughters piously joined evangelical churches when they came of age, and those who did may not have taken membership as seriously as Jannett. Similarly, not all male laborers were drunkards who spent their leisure hours prowling cramped doggeries—bars that often featured gambling and prostitution. Nevertheless, the Clelands' experiences suggest the perimeters of lower-class life in the urban South. Although church and grogshop endorsed different values and attracted different segments of the lower classes, they were two essential institutions of urban life. As such, they were products of the same culture and society and served similar functions. Each appealed to poorer whites' and blacks' desire to be free from elite domination and control. In both spheres of life, laboring whites and blacks tried to create order, stability, and a sense of self-worth in a community that often seemed to demean and marginalize them.

Most white Lynchburg churchgoers were staunch evangelicals—the spiritual descendants of a style of Protestantism that emerged from the revivals that swept through the South during the early nineteenth century. In some respects, Southern evangelicalism was an intensely individualistic religion. Southern evangelicals believed that each person stood alone before God for both judgment and salvation. In this relationship, they believed that they were utterly helpless. Isolated from other believers, they could confess their sins, but they could not change by their own initiative; instead, they must wait upon God's grace for forgiveness. In their day-to-day experiences, however, evangelicals also recognized the need for mutual support. Once penitents had experienced conversion, they were welcomed into a new community that promised to nurture and protect them from the temptations of the outside world. In turn, the new members were expected to take an active role in the life of the church. The key concept for evangelicals was "participation." Evangelicals believed that even the most devout believers needed to be immersed in a church community in order to maintain the discipline necessary for personal holiness. Moreover, full participation in a church provided converts an opportunity to draw upon the prayers, experiences, and emotional support of other members.[5]

Evangelicals' insistence that all were dependent on God for salvation made them—at least, in theory—extremely egalitarian. In their quest for moral purity, evangelicals claimed that the only true measure of a person's worth was his or her relationship to God. Consequently, they rejected all distinctions based on wealth and social status. For this reason, the South's lower classes were most attracted to the Baptist, Methodist, and, to a lesser extent, Presbyterian denominations. In the first decades of the nineteenth century, evangelicalism often appeared as a religion of protest. "Plain folk" found in evangelicalism a way to express their resentment at being excluded from what they believed to be an archaic social structure of the aristocracy. According to historian Donald Mathews, early evangelicals tried to "replace class distinctions based on wealth and status" with "nonclass distinctions based on ideological and moral purity."[6] Although some evangelicals lost their insurgent edge as they became more prosperous, studies of specific Southern communities suggest that many evangelical churches, particularly in the rural South, continued to attract those groups on the margins of Southern society—namely, lower-class whites, blacks, and women. This has led one historian to conclude that many churches "contained more equality than did any other public place" in the South.[7]

The practices and membership patterns of Lynchburg's evangelical churches do not completely support this assertion. By 1860, most of Lynchburg's white evangelical churches were a hybrid of historical Southern evangelicalism and the more rigid social organization of urban life. In many respects, Lynchburg's evangelicals espoused the same religious principles that attracted lower-class groups throughout the South. Like other evangelicals, Lynchburg residents often expressed contempt for worldly ambition. When future United States senator John Warwick Daniel was asked by his sister if she should join a church, he observed that his advice was hardly necessary since she had already "renounced the fading glories of this world and claimed that better part which does not perish." Instead of offering advice, Daniel prayed that God "shield you from the temptations and exposures with which your pathway will be fraught."[8]

Occasionally, evangelicals drew moral lessons from the lives of wealthy Lynchburg residents whose financial successes seemed to come at the expense of personal salvation. Jacob Duche Mitchell, pastor of the Second Presbyterian Church, kept a running account of the spiritual failures of the town's business elites in his diary. When the town's wealthiest citizen, Jesse Hare, died, Mitchell expressed pity that "the poor man" had "made over $2,000,000 but had been cast into eternity with a faith unfit to meet his God." In another instance, Mitchell recorded the death of R. G. Bell, a "flourishing merchant" and "for many years a member of the Church." Sadly, "he had been cut from the Church for intemperance" and fittingly, Mitchell believed, "died without a cent."[9]

Lynchburg's Protestant churches also retained many of the customs that evangelicals used to foster fellowship across class, racial, and gender lines. As with early evangelical churches, physical contact was often an important part of Lynchburg's Protestant worship services. Evangelicals believed that such contact helped cement the bonds of community by demonstrating the love of Christians for one another.[10] Thus, in some Lynchburg churches, repentant sinners and new converts were asked to come forward for the "laying on of the hands." When new members joined a church, church elders offered the right hand of fellowship. In some churches, this ceremony was followed by a "love feast" or, as with Jannett Cleland, communion.[11]

Church members also used discipline to reaffirm the egalitarian bonds of the church community. Although disciplinary hearings occurred irregularly at most churches, they remained an important way for some church communities to control deviance and maintain communal harmony.[12] Regardless of denomination, these hearings followed a pattern that consistently supported these goals.

In most instances, proceedings began when one or more members accused a fellow member of committing a specific offense against the church community. In late 1858, William Miller and J. A. Hamner of First Baptist accused fellow member Virginia Spence, the wife of a bank cashier, of dancing at a party. On January 10, 1859, the male members of the church appointed Hamner and Miller to visit Spence, present their case before her, and solicit her response. For her part, Spence took a conciliatory stance. While she declared that "she did not regard dancing as sinful," she also stated that "she did not think that she would engage in it again as it was contrary to the rules of the church and she did not wish to be thrown out." Evidently, Spence's candor surprised the two elders. At a subsequent meeting, the church decided that because "the report of the official committee was not entirely satisfactory," the church would delay action until their regular meeting in two weeks. They informed Spence of their action. This time, Spence responded by letter. Although she maintained that she saw "no harm in dancing," she repeated her promise to abstain in the future. Citing 1 Corinthians, she stated that "if meat make my Brother to offend, I will eat no more meat." Evidently, the biblical reference was enough to persuade all of Spence's sincerity. The church resolved to "forgive" Spence and restore her membership, on the condition that she would view her letter as a "pledge that she will not again engage in dancing."[13]

Spence's experience is suggestive of mid-nineteenth-century evangelical church polity in a number of ways. First, the proceedings were generally democratic, in that a number of people shared power. Because the entire church considered the matter, Spence's two accusers could not easily act independently of the church; if they did, they, too, would risk disciplinary action. Instead, Spence's fate became a matter for the entire church body to decide. Members even allowed the accused a voice in the proceedings. Although the church's constitution prohibited women from voting and holding church office, church elders allowed Spence to have her say. Ultimately, she not only defended her actions but negotiated a settlement by invoking a higher authority, the Bible.

Second, church polity ensured that the proceedings would be relatively fair. Although having the accusations aired before the entire congregation may have embarrassed Spence, the public forum also protected her from gossip and innuendo by bringing the matter into the open. Furthermore, the church allowed Spence to face her accusers and respond to their charges, not once but twice. Then, too, it probably helped Spence that the congregation was in no rush to settle the matter. The waiting period between meetings may have allowed tensions to ease and protected Spence from an ill-considered response by the church.

Finally, members apparently instigated the disciplinary hearing to strengthen the church community, not simply to drive out deviants. As a result, the church offered Spence considerable opportunity to recant. When Spence refused to do so but reaffirmed her commitment to the church and to God, the church accepted a negotiated peace and—perhaps to win a moral victory—"forgave" her, even though she had not formally repented.[14]

In those instances when the accused did not reaffirm the church community, church members did not always act so charitably. Several months after Spence made peace with the congregation, the congregation heard charges against another member, Brother P. Bowyer, for dancing at a public hall and for irregular church attendance. Rather than address the charges, Bowyer lied and alibied. First, he claimed that he had not danced, even though witnesses saw him on the dance floor. In addition, he excused himself from regular attendance at church, claiming that his poor health made it impossible for him to go out at night. Unconvinced, church members summarily excommunicated Bowyer.[15]

Yet if Lynchburg's white Protestant churches retained the form and rhetoric of historical evangelicalism, the membership patterns at most Lynchburg churches diverged in several important ways. For one, Lynchburg churches generally failed to attract a large cross section of the community. Most white laborers and their families did not attend church regularly. Fewer than one in three joined a Lynchburg church.[16] Of course, some laborers were more attracted to religion than others. Skilled laborers and their families tended to be far more regular churchgoers than the more transient and economically unstable unskilled laborers: 68 percent of laboring-class churchgoers came from the families of skilled workers. In addition, female laborers and the wives of laborers tended to be more attracted to religion than male laborers. Roughly two-thirds of all of Lynchburg's laboring-class church members were female. In this, Lynchburg's laboring class closely matched local and regional patterns.[17]

Despite the participation of working-class women, however, laborers and their families still comprised only a small percentage of Lynchburg evangelicals. In most of Lynchburg's Protestant churches, laborers were a distinct minority of the congregation. At First Presbyterian, one in four church members was from a laborer's family; at Second Presbyterian, Court Street Methodist, and St. Paul's Episcopal, the ratio was closer to one in five.[18] Equally significant, when laborers attended these churches, they often played circumscribed roles. Despite the egalitarian rhetoric of evangelicalism, laborers rarely received positions of authority in

Lynchburg churches. Instead, ecclesiastical power usually went to those who already wielded power outside the church. At St. Paul's, six vestrymen were tobacconists and six were professionals. The leaders of Court Street Methodist, Protestant Methodist, and the two Presbyterian churches came from much the same group; all were tobacconists, professionals, or merchants. In 1860, three of the town's twelve city council members were either church elders or trustees, while another three were close relatives of church elders. Charles Button, who probably influenced public opinion in Lynchburg more than anyone, was also a church elder.[19]

In many respects, evangelical churches sent the town's lower classes a mixed message. On the one hand, they preached an egalitarian message that God was no respecter of a person's worldly stature. On the other hand, they accepted lower-class participation only within a limited sphere of activities. This is dramatically revealed in Jacob Mitchell's visitation diary. Throughout his tenure at Second Presbyterian Church, Mitchell kept a daily record of his activities. He did this—at least, in part—as a matter of duty: Presbyterian churches required their ministers to keep daily logs of visitations and preaching engagements so that the ministers remained accountable to their congregations. Mitchell documented his pastoral duties more or less regularly from 1857 to 1861, at which time his participation in the Confederate war effort made daily entries impossible. Before the war, however, he often wrote more than the church required. Most of the time he used the small book as a diary to chronicle his spiritual sojourn with what he believed to be an indifferent congregation. As a result, his records contain much useful information on church polity.

In his daily entries, Mitchell could be as benevolent as he was self-righteous. Although he seemed to take special interest in the moral failures of Lynchburg's more prominent citizens, he was extremely compassionate toward the poor and unfortunate. To these, Mitchell saw himself a source of spiritual strength, moral guidance, and charity. Throughout the year he visited white and black, the sick and the dying, the widowed and the lonely. During the winter months, he provided food, clothing, and fuel to virtually anyone who asked. He visited those facing difficult circumstances almost daily until the particular crisis passed.

In the fall of 1857, one of Mitchell's members, John Crawford, was arrested for gambling. Evidently, his gambling debts were so high that his family was near poverty. Undeterred by Crawford's moral failings, Mitchell made frequent visits to his home to care for the family. When Crawford's gambling cohorts tried to collect from him while he waited in jail for his trial, Mitchell contacted a lawyer to help speed Crawford's release so that he would be able to work off his debts. Although Mitchell often condemned wealthy residents for their immorality, he refused to censure Crawford. Instead, he noted only that he "hoped he will reform."[20]

Despite these benevolent gestures, Mitchell usually remained personally aloof from his poorer neighbors. A systematic analysis of his pastoral visits for August 1857 and January 1861 reveals that he tended to visit only two classes of people—the prosperous and the very poor. And most of the time, he visited the prosperous. From August 1 to August 18, 1857, Mitchell made forty-three visits to local residents. Of the nineteen individuals he visited who can be identified through 1860 federal census, fifteen were professionals, two were unskilled whites, and two were blacks (one slave and one free). Mitchell's January 1861 visitations followed a similar pattern. In that month he visited forty-seven Lynchburg residents, twenty-nine of whom can be identified. Twenty-two of his visits were to professionals or their families, two were to skilled laborers, two were to impoverished whites, and three were to slaves.

Mitchell's visitation records also suggest that he preferred to spend his time with some groups more than others. His most frequent visits were to professionals, men he probably considered to be his peers. Judging from his diary, two of his closest friends were D. B. Payne, one of the town's wealthiest merchants, and Charles Mosby, a prominent lawyer. He often dined with these gentlemen, which suggests that his visits were as much social as pastoral. In contrast, Mitchell visited poorer residents only when they needed charity or spiritual counsel; otherwise, he seems to have left them alone.[21]

Some worship services also reminded poorer members of their humble status. Through pew rents, wealthy members purchased the best pews in the sanctuary and thus separated themselves from their less wealthy brothers and sisters. Although many nineteenth-century evangelicals questioned the use of pew rents, others did not. At least two of Lynchburg's seven Protestant churches, St. Paul's Episcopal and Court Street Methodist, used them as a way to raise revenue for church expansion. To defray costs, these churches sold their pews to church families. Members were then expected to pay an annual "rent" of about 10 percent of their pew's appraised value. In 1858 Court Street Methodist appraised its first floor pews from $100 to $355, with pews in the front and center priced higher than pews in the rear corners. Pews in the second-floor gallery were designated "free pews" for those who could not afford the high rents. The resulting seating arrangement was a microcosm of Lynchburg's social order. Although the congregation of Court Street Methodist included fourteen laboring families, nearly all pew holders were merchants and tobacconists. Of the thirty-three rented pews for which the owner could be identified in the 1860 manuscript census, merchants, tobacconists, and professionals owned twenty-eight. In contrast, artisans owned only three. All of the artisans tended to be men of substance: one was a hatter and co-owner of a clothing store; the other two were master craftsmen, each of whom had accumulated more than $11,000 in property. Most of Court Street Methodist's laboring members were not so fortunate. Along with a few small grocers and clerks, laborers were practically relegated to the periphery of the church sanctuary. On the eve of the Civil War, church seating had begun to reflect the city's social structure.[22]

Only two of Lynchburg's Protestant churches had much success in reaching the town's poorer citizens. Throughout the period, First Baptist and Centenary Methodist continued to attract sizable numbers of laborers to their worship services. First Baptist's congregation included three skilled proprietors, twenty-three skilled laborers, and twenty unskilled laborers, who together accounted for 43 percent of the congregation. Even more impressive, over half of Centenary Methodist's members were skilled and unskilled laborers.[23]

These churches were exceptional in their efforts to reach poorer citizens, at least in part because they made a forthright effort to integrate all their members—or at least, all their male members—into the church polity. For instance, First Baptist opted for an extremely democratic form of church government. Although the church constitution allowed for only a few church officers with nominal power, most major decisions were made by common consent of all male members. In addition, the congregation tried to make its decisions unanimous. As a result, the majority had to bargain with the minority before the church could act. On May 29, 1859, the congregation elected Brother C. Tyree as the new pastor by a vote of seventeen to fifteen. A week later, the church moderator reported that "he had cause to believe that considerable dissatisfaction existed with the Brethren" about the selection of Tyree. As a result, they took another vote. This time, H. W. Dodge defeated Tyree by a vote of twenty-two to fourteen. Although a clear majority, the vote did not reflect an overwhelming consensus. As a result, they voted again. This time, Dodge won by a vote of twenty-nine to four. Evidently, this was close enough to the desired unanimity: after the vote, the congregation dispatched the moderator to ask Dodge to fill the pastorship.[24]

Centenary Methodist did not match the democratic yearnings of First Baptist, but it, too, provided its lower-class members with leadership roles. In contrast to Lynchburg's wealthier churches, the lay leaders of Centenary Methodist represented a large spectrum of the town's social structure. In 1858, the Board of Stewards included two grocers and one skilled artisan, Henry Jones, a clockmaker. In addition, the church appointed two artisans in the building trades to act as lay preachers— perhaps to evangelize to others of their class.[25]

These two churches may have differed from the wealthier churches in other ways as well. Impressionistic evidence suggests that First Baptist and Centenary Methodist adhered to the traditions of their evangelical heritage more faithfully than did Lynchburg's other Protestant churches. For instance, First Baptist members, in contrast to all other evangelicals in Lynchburg, reaffirmed the equality of all believers by addressing one another as "brother" and "sister." Furthermore, the two churches guarded the bonds of community more zealously than did other churches. Although all churches supervised the moral behavior of their members, First Baptist and Centenary Methodist appear to have been unique in their willingness to discipline those who simply stopped attending church. From 1857 to 1861, First Baptist disciplined seven members, excommunicating three of these—all for failing to attend church regularly. Centenary Methodist chose a less public way to discipline backsliders. Each member was assigned to a Sunday school class; the leader of the class— usually a church officer—monitored moral behavior. At the end of the year, his observations became part of the church record. In 1859, Centenary's Sunday school records show that the church removed seven members and six probationers from the membership rolls for irregular attendance.

Unfortunately, the extant evidence does not explain why less wealthy whites preferred churches that demanded more commitment. However, it is tempting to speculate that they viewed their churches' rigid attendance demands not as an attempt to control their behavior but as an affirmation of their importance to the church. In contrast to those churches that placed lower-class members on the periphery of the church polity, First Baptist and Centenary Methodist emphasized that all members were important to the community and to God.

Centenary Methodist's commitment to these egalitarian traditions of historical evangelicalism may have cost it dearly. In 1851, forty-six of the church's members seceded to form a new church, Court Street Methodist. Their numbers included most of the original congregation's wealthiest members. Of the thirty-nine founders identified through either the city directory or the manuscript census, twelve were from the families of tobacconists and twenty-two were from the families of professionals. In contrast, only four were from families of artisans or laborers.[26] Although church records do not explain why these particular members split from Centenary Methodist, secondary accounts suggest that the different spiritual objectives of rich and poor may have played a determining role. According to some sources, those who left wanted an organ in the church—an adornment that evidently appalled those evangelicals who remained uncomfortable with such worldly refinements in a house of worship. Here, as in most Southern communities, lower-class evangelicals adhered to a much stricter moral code than did their wealthier counterparts.[27]

Location may also have been a factor. Centenary Methodist was near the heart of the town's business district, just a few blocks up from Buzzard's Roost. The founders of Court Street Methodist built their church only a few blocks away. But because of the steep hills, Court Street Methodist had the appearance of being removed from the bustle of the center of town. Moreover, the new church bordered Federal Hill—a neighborhood that was becoming the near-exclusive domain of Lynchburg's wealthier citizens. Quite possibly, wealthy evangelicals built Court Street Methodist as part of their emerging desire to separate themselves spatially from the poverty and congestion of the town's center. Whatever the reasons for the division, the subsequent histories of the two churches suggest that they disseminated very different messages. While Court Street Methodist became increasingly estranged from its evangelical heritage, Centenary Methodist, like First Baptist, remained a democratic refuge for many laboring whites.[28]

Yet if Centenary Methodist and First Baptist treated laboring whites differently than did Lynchburg's other evangelical churches, neither church fomented class animosity. Although a slight majority of Lynchburg's churchgoing white laborers attended these two churches, neither was the exclusive domain of laboring whites. Instead, both churches also attracted sizable numbers of professionals and proprietors and their families. At Centenary Methodist, one in five members came from the family of a proprietor or a professional; at First Baptist, the number was nearly one in three. As a result, laboring whites who attended these churches came in regular contact with wealthy citizens. Yet they did so on very different terms from those prevailing in the secular world. While wealthy residents expected poorer residents to treat them with deference and respect outside the church, the traditions of Centenary Methodist and First Baptist encouraged wealthy whites to treat their less wealthy brothers and sisters as moral and spiritual equals. For their part, many laborers and their families may have recognized that limited upper-class participation in their churches worked to their advantage. As was true of many urban laborers throughout the United States, Lynchburg laborers often joined churches to demonstrate their adherence to the new urban values of self-discipline, self-control, and temperance. Through intimate contact with the upper classes, laborers enhanced their reputations as respectable members of Lynchburg society. Moreover, in a volatile world, some laborers may have used church membership to bolster their self-worth through moral exclusiveness. In church, they not only showed that they lived by the same values as were held by some of the town's most successful businessmen but also distanced themselves from those of their own class who refused to conform to these new values.[29]

This interclass civility within churches was often matched by civility between churches. Despite their theological differences, members of the various churches refused to be divisive. Instead, all sides made a concerted effort to set aside their differences for the sake of Christian unity. Members often visited one another's churches to worship with families and friends. During regional denominational meetings, ministers routinely allowed rival denominations to use their pulpits and their church buildings. Even Court Street Methodist and Centenary Methodist remained relatively cordial. After the schism, both congregations made overtures to end the divisiveness. After Court Street was completed, members allowed Centenary Methodist to use the basement for their black Sunday school program. On occasion, the ministers of the two churches exchanged pulpits.[30]

Of Lynchburg's Protestant churches, only St. Paul's Episcopal Church remained somewhat aloof from the town's evangelical community. Some of the town's most prominent individuals attended the church, including the mayor and half the city council. Apparently, many of the church's members were too accustomed to the deferential style of Lynchburg politics and society to feel comfortable mixing with the more egalitarian denominations. According to Mary Barbara Grant Moorman, a lifelong member of Centenary Methodist, St. Paul's minister, William Kinkle, was "a very high churchman" who was inflexible in his conservatism. When the Methodist Conference met in Lynchburg, Kinkle "would close his church and go out of town to preach" rather than "offer his pulpit to another clergyman not of his faith."[31]

Several factors explain the general lack of conflict within the town's evangelical community. First, although evangelicals took their theological differences seriously, they recognized that the similarities among them were also important. On the one hand, they understood that the religious community they joined referred to both a specific congregation and the body of all believers. On the other hand, all evangelicals believed they shared a common adversary—the forces of sin in the world. As James B. Ramsey, minister at First Presbyterian Church, reminded his congregation, "The church is in an enemy's country, ever surrounded by foes." In this environment, Ramsey warned, it must be "upon the hearts of all her members" to "counteract the insidious advances of the world." Particularly during religious revivals, evangelicals were reminded that they must remain united in their sacred mission to redeem their society. Although each church conducted its own protracted meetings, religious enthusiasm sometimes spread throughout the town as ministers and laypeople attended one another's meetings. Indeed, many evangelicals made a point to attend all protracted meetings in order to demonstrate their commitment to their spiritual brothers and sisters, regardless of denominational affiliation or social status. Even Episcopalians sometimes joined in this religious enthusiasm. After a Methodist revival in 1853, the president of city council, a staunch Episcopalian, hosted a dinner to thank the participating itinerants for their good work.[32]

Second, it also helped that the more egalitarian congregations did not go too far in their commitment to egalitarian principles. Although Centenary Methodist and First Baptist provided greater opportunities for nonelite white males to influence church policies, they generally did not extend these opportunities to blacks and women. As a result, the two churches, no less than Court Street Methodist and St. Paul's Episcopal, bolstered the racial and gender status quo.

Blacks were especially marginalized in white churches. Although all Protestant churches accepted blacks as members, they did not encourage them to join their regular congregations. Instead, churches tried to serve the spiritual needs of blacks by establishing separate Sunday school programs and worship services. The few blacks who attended white church services occupied a precarious status within the church. Although listed as "brothers" and "sisters" in some of the church membership rolls, they were accorded a decidedly inferior status within the church hierarchy. Not only were they not allowed to vote and hold office, but, during church services, they were relegated to negro pews in the back of the sanctuary.[33]

Only First Baptist tested the racial status quo—and it did so only briefly and perhaps unintentionally. When members realized what they had done, they immediately took steps to return to the customary standard. The incident evolved around First Baptist's relationship to its black missionary church, African Baptist. The episode began innocently enough, from a bit of white philanthropy. On January 12, 1852, Calvin Ford, a tobacconist, acting on a request by African Baptist, proposed that First Baptist "free herself from any participation as a church in the ecclesiastical management of the affair of the African Baptist Church." Ford's resolution was not an act of complete emancipation for the black church. Amendments to the resolution gave First Baptist the right to abrogate the agreement if a majority of members changed their minds. In conformity with municipal law, First Baptist retained the right to approve the next minister of the black church. Nevertheless, Ford's resolution would give the black church considerable latitude: members would now be allowed to receive and discipline their own members, establish their own programs, and influence the selection of the next minister. Although the resolution did not endorse blacks' spiritual equality, the gist of the document was that blacks could manage most of their spiritual affairs, with only intermittent assistance from whites.[34]

The resolution passed without formal opposition. Most white Baptists seemed eager to agree to the black church's demand for increased autonomy, in part because they trusted the sincerity of their black brothers and sisters and in part because they hoped such an act would further the Baptist cause among the town's black population. As one proponent argued, the move would make the African Baptist Church more popular and thus "do much toward pulling down the strong hold of the wicked" within the black community.[35]

Within a few months, however, several members of First Baptist expressed misgivings about the church's decision to loosen its relationship with African Baptist. Under the pretext that the agreement violated municipal law, Brother Allison recommended that First Baptist reclaim control of African Baptist. Despite Ford's protest that the agreement was legal, and without any apparent prompting from civil authorities, First Baptist voided the agreement and appointed a Committee of Five to supervise African Baptist again.

For their part, the black Baptists wanted nothing to do with the new arrangement, stubbornly insisting that the white church honor the first resolution. Evidently, the collective resolve of African Baptist offended the Committee of Five. In its report to First Baptist, the Committee of Five stated that the black congregation's conduct toward the committee was "in the highest degree offensive and reprehensible . . . and we think amounting to rebellion against the highest ecclesiastical authority known to the said African Church." In reaction, members of First Baptist set aside their egalitarian ideals. To reclaim their authority over African Baptist, they excommunicated all members of the church, recalled the church's pastor, and withdrew financial support.[36] For the next seven months, relations hit an impasse. Indeed, feelings remained so hostile that at one point First Baptist considered a proposal to abandon African Baptist and its mission to the town's black population—a move that might have destroyed the black church, since it was extremely dependent on the white church's financial assistance.

Finally, in July 1853, First Baptist succeeded in breaking the will of the black church. On July 11, members of African Baptist asked for forgiveness and promised "to make satisfactory concessions for the wrongs done the white church." Evidently, one of their concessions was to abandon their former aspirations of autonomy. When blacks were restored to membership a few days later, it was as members of First Baptist, not of African Baptist. Whites would allow them to continue to attend African Baptist, but only with the clear understanding that they were under the sovereign authority of First Baptist. The parent church excommunicated those black members who could not accept the new terms.[37]

Only a few members of First Baptist dissented. To show his support for the black congregation, J. C. Clopton accepted their invitation to become pastor of their church. Others, most notably Calvin Ford, continued to support the African church in its quest for greater autonomy. In response, First Baptist treated these members even more harshly than it had treated the recalcitrant members of African Baptist. Perhaps to show their intolerance for those of their own race who undermined the twin principle of white man's rule and white racial solidarity, members voted to excommunicate Clopton and pressured others, including Ford, to leave. Even after the church resolved its differences with African Baptist, church leaders remained intransigent toward those of their own race. Although church members reinstated Clopton after he publicly apologized for his behavior, they refused to reinstate Ford and two of his allies. Evidently, the congregation could forgive those who experienced moral lapses, but it could not tolerate those who violated the racial customs of the community. From that point on, the white members of First Baptist conformed to the prevailing standards of race relations.[38]

On the surface, women's status within Lynchburg churches was not quite as clear-cut as the status of blacks. Because women comprised an overwhelming majority of Lynchburg churchgoers, they could wield considerable influence over church affairs. Churches depended on women to handle many of the day-to-day responsibilities of the church. White Lynchburg women taught in Sabbath school programs for blacks and white children, organized relief efforts, and assisted with worship music. In addition, women, especially wealthy widows, performed important financial services for their congregations. This may have been especially true of Centenary Methodist and First Baptist, because their members tended to be poorer. In 1859, Centenary Methodist's female members organized a fair to defray costs for a new church building. At First Baptist, male members rarely made financial decisions without first conferring with the church's female members, an implicit admission of the power of women's purse strings.[39]

Through their membership, women developed networks and associations that allowed them both to socialize with one another and to exert a moral influence over the community at large. Centenary Methodist's Dorcas Society, a national philanthropic organization, provides a case in point. Although nominally Methodist, women throughout Lynchburg's evangelical community joined the organization. By the end of the antebellum era, the Dorcas Society was probably the most popular women's organization in the town. Various committees, each composed exclusively of women, organized fund-raising efforts and implemented programs to aid to the poor.[40]

Nevertheless, Lynchburg's Protestant churches never formally recognized women's power and often supervised their behavior to maintain patriarchy. Like all Southern Protestant churches, Lynchburg churches barred women from leadership positions and denied them an official voice in church governance. Even First Baptist and Centenary Methodist treated women as extensions of their husbands and families. For married women, this meant that church records rarely listed their first names, even when their husbands were not members.[41]

Church-affiliated women's organizations also followed the conventions of Southern patriarchy. Like the churches, the Dorcas Society listed its members by the husband's full name. Even more telling, the Dorcas women often went out of their way to show proper deference to the men of Lynchburg. The organization always invited local ministers to attend its meetings and solicited their advice as a way to demonstrate its acquiescence to male leadership. In its annual reports, the organization occasionally pointed out that it owed much of its success to the generous donations of the town's patriarchs.[42]

The very fact that so many women joined Lynchburg's churches was itself a testament to the enduring influence of patriarchal values on women's behavior. Although spiritual concerns and the rare chance to socialize and influence community moral standards attracted many women to church organizations, societal pressure was also an important consideration. Like men, many women on the margins of polite Lynchburg society viewed church membership as a pathway to respectability. For women, however, one's moral reputation often meant the difference between social acceptance and social death. Respectable Southerners, male and female, were unequivocal in their understanding of how white women should behave. As historian Elizabeth Fox-Genovese succinctly notes, the ideal Southern lady was married, dependent, pious, and deferential. Thus, while society forgave men for their moral transgressions, the South's double standard gave women no such indulgences. Single and working women in particular were often the subject of considerable public scrutiny because of their presumed independence from male control. Religion offered these women at least some relief from public disapprobation. Church membership not only offered these women a badge of morality but placed them once more under the paternal care of male leaders.[43]

Even so, the cost of conformity could be very high. Consider, for instance, the fate of an anonymous diarist who moved to Lynchburg shortly after her husband of twenty years abandoned her and their adolescent son for another woman. Because she had neither family nor financial resources, the woman apprenticed her son to John Bailey, Lynchburg's largest coachmaker, and boarded with an old family acquaintance. Alone and with only her son to support her, she agonized each day about the fate of her marriage. If respectable Lynchburg residents pitied her, they rarely showed it. Instead, she was often the target of gossip for her presumed failure to keep a husband. Rather than face the overwhelming silence of her neighbors, she spent most of her days taking long walks in the surrounding countryside, praying that her husband would return to her. As it became increasingly clear that he had left her for good, she began to wish simply for release from Lynchburg society. At a particularly low point, she confided in her diary that "really I wish I had wings—so that I could fly far away from here for no peace of mind can I see." On another occasion, she stated simply that life was nothing to her but a "burden." Her church offered little comfort. Indeed, church attendance was an especially trying ordeal, because she believed all eyes were upon her when she attended. Nevertheless, she attended church faithfully, perhaps because she believed she had little choice. If she did not attend, she feared she would lose all semblance of respectability in the eyes of proper society. One Sunday, as she prepared to attend an evening prayer service, she confided in her diary that "it is a cross, but I must take it up." As it was, attending church allowed her to live on the periphery of polite society and to demonstrate her abiding commitment to the evangelical community. Evidently, not everyone found the same acceptance and spiritual peace that Jannett Cleland discovered when she joined First Presbyterian. Although Lynchburg churches offered residents some respite from the inequalities of Southern life, they did not offer them a complete escape.[44]

The anonymous woman's experiences with proper Lynchburg society suggest that most evangelicals tended to think in terms of moral absolutes, believing there was a clear, discernible line between the sacred and the profane. Thus, while they aspired to live by values of self-control, harmony, and moderation, they accused nonevangelicals of intemperance, self-indulgence, unwarranted aggressiveness, and disorder.

For their part, most nonevangelicals were also impressed by the differences between themselves and the religious community, but many would have disagreed that theirs was a valueless, pathological environment. Instead, most could rightly claim that they, too, wanted stability and order. Unfortunately, most of the evidence about lower-class secular behavior comes from the columns of Lynchburg's two prewar newspapers, the *Virginian* and the *Republican*. As a result, information is often anecdotal and flavored by each paper's desire to amuse, shock, and moralize. Nevertheless, these sources and others provide numerous indications that lower-class residents tried to create a stable environment for themselves.

Most obviously, Lynchburg's lower classes sometimes took the initiative to protect their neighborhoods from family members, neighbors, and fellow workers who threatened their peace and safety. In many instances, the individuals acted in self-defense or in defense of others. In December 1859, Peter Sullivan, an Irish gardener, asked the night watch to arrest his live-in son-in-law, John Lynch, because the latter was a habitual drunk who often became violent when intoxicated.[45] Some neighbors were especially aggressive in their efforts to protect women from abusive men. According to Virginia Daniel, her neighbor Mark White developed the habit of coming to her home late at night, "abusing and insulting her grossly." One night, she finally summoned the courage to "order him away and never to put his foot in her door again." He complied, but only to return a few nights later. Daniel again told him to leave. This time, he struck her. When Daniel cried for help, neighbors rushed in and threw White out. Neighbors also interceded on behalf of Lucy Bowles, to arrest her abusive husband. Late one Saturday night, Mr. Bowles returned home after a long drinking binge. With an ax in one hand and a bottle in the other, he told his wife that he intended to kill her. Fortunately, Lucy was able to outmaneuver her drunken husband and escaped through a bedroom window. The following Monday, neighbors accompanied Lucy to the mayor's office to testify against Mr. Bowles. Thanks to her neighbors' corroborating testimony, the mayor ordered Bowles either to pay a large fine to keep the peace or to leave town. Bowles chose to leave town.[46]

On occasion, less wealthy residents also banded together to rid their neighborhoods of undesirable grogshops and houses of ill fame. In one instance, neighbors of Bill Sprouts asked the municipal authorities to close his house of prostitution because it "disturbed the peace of the entire neighborhood." The watch readily complied by arresting and caging the notorious Sprouts.[47]

Yet if Lynchburg's lower classes steadfastly tried to maintain the peace, they ascribed to a very different code of propriety from the one endorsed by most churchgoing citizens. The experience of Dacre Kinnier, an Irishman who owned a small grocery, with his church, First Presbyterian, suggests how some lower-class whites diverged from evangelicals. In 1853, Kinnier and his family, recently removed from Ireland, joined First Presbyterian. In 1857, church elders excommunicated Kinnier for keeping a "disorderly house." Although the elders did not detail their indictment against Kinnier, years later Kinnier's son John recalled that his father ran afoul of the congregation on two counts—he sold liquor and he served liquor to blacks. John, then clerk of session at First Presbyterian, defended his father's actions by observing that Dacre had acted according to his cultural heritage. According to John, Dacre hoped to replicate groceries of his native Ireland, creating a comfortable setting where men could drink and socialize on market day. Indeed, John claimed that Dacre believed he was performing a community service by providing a neighborhood meeting place.[48]

John also believed that Dacre's violation of the South's racial mores was attributable to his father's foreign heritage. John noted that his father served blacks because he was ignorant of the South's system of racial stratification. Believing slavery to be "very strange" but impressed by America's democratic traditions, Dacre encouraged persons of all classes and races to frequent his establishment. Unfortunately, the elders of First Presbyterian were less than tolerant of Kinnier's imperfect adjustment to Southern culture. Because Dacre refused to acknowledge that he had done anything wrong, the church condemned him as disloyal, to the church and to the South. When Dacre refused to relent, they excommunicated him. Embittered from his first brush with Southern evangelicalism, Dacre Kinnier never joined another church.

Apart from his Irish heritage, Dacre Kinnier was not exceptional. Many Lynchburg residents, especially those of the lower classes, rejected evangelicals' understanding of propriety as alien to their own cultural heritage and somewhat impractical. Most of Lynchburg's laborers lived in shanties along the narrow alleys and deep ravines that intersected the city's major streets. Although elites occasionally tried to reach out to them through benevolence and other gestures of paternalism, for the most part the poor lived an isolated existence in an environment that was often tumultuous, sometimes violently so. As they saw it, evangelical values of self-control and self-regulation were more often than not liabilities, not virtues. As a result, they clung to an older system of ethical behavior—the ethic of honor.[49]

Like many Southerners, Lynchburg's lower classes ascribed to the belief that a man's worth came from how others viewed him. To retain status, one had to be able to back his words with deeds and to rebuke aggressively any challenge to his reputation. For this reason, Lynchburg's lower classes—again, like most Southerners—felt compelled to defend themselves from even the slightest insult.[50]

Unfortunately, historians have provided little information on the nature of lower-class honor. Yet if Lynchburg is representative of the South, lower-class honor differed from upper-class honor in several respects. Lower-class whites, in particular, may have been more likely than upper-class groups to use violence as a way to gain or defend their honor.[51]

Because they had fewer opportunities to attain status, they may have felt the pangs of insult much more keenly. As a result, Lynchburg's poorer whites often let old feuds fester—sometimes for years—before one side or the other took action. In seeking vengeance, they did not always rush to the fray.

Perhaps in an attempt to demonstrate their manliness to friends or simply to draw public attention to the contest, one or both of the assailants often announced their desire for revenge well before they intended to take action. In 1860, William Hendricks, a cartman, killed Thomas Johnson, a canal boatman, during a dispute at a Buzzard home. A jury convicted Hendricks of murder and sentenced him to hang. During the trial, witnesses testified that a "cool and sober" Hendricks "had repeatedly threatened to kill Thomas Johnson within the last two months" over some "old grudge." He finally found his chance at a social gathering attended by many of their mutual friends. Without warning, Hendricks began to abuse Johnson verbally. When Johnson responded to Hendricks in kind, Hendricks pulled out a knife and stabbed Johnson in the neck. In another instance, two Irish laborers, Dan Callen and Dennis Sullivan, spent months, according to Button's published account of the trial, "discussing the merits of each other in terms not very courteous" in "both public and private places." One night, they finally came to blows. When a night watchman attempted to break up the fight, observers stopped his interference, so that "one man should not be bate mor'n t'other." Apparently, Southern laborers believed that the sweetest form of revenge came when the individual carried out the deed in public and in the presence of his peers.[52]

At times, an individual's desire for vengeance became an all-consuming passion. For years, Jack Woodall had plotted the murder of Hezekiah Ford, because Ford's testimony had earlier sent Woodall to jail. When the two met by chance at a cockfight outside town, Woodall struck Ford on the head with a stone, then stabbed him several times. Unfortunately for Woodall, Ford turned out to be a brilliant adversary. When he gave his testimony in court, Ford swore he would send Woodall "to a place where the dogs wouldn't find him." The courts made good on Ford's threat by sentencing Woodall to the state penitentiary. During his final plea, a desperate Woodall tried to convince the judge that this had been Ford's intent all along—to provoke him to violence so that he would be sent to jail. In another instance, Theodore Bennett attacked Powhatan Parrish from behind and nearly choked him to death. Once caught, Bennett justified his action by claiming that "some years since he had been severely thrashed by Parrish in Richmond." This "being the first favorable opportunity . . . for resenting that affront, he concluded to take advantage of it."[53]

Not all demonstrations of personal honor were premeditated acts of vengeance. When insulted, lower-class white men believed it essential to demonstrate their manhood through the ferocity of their response. Adversaries sometimes clashed over the smallest of slights. In one instance, Edward Moore, an Irish shoemaker, attacked another Irish laborer, John McLoughlin, twice in one night, after McLoughlin called Moore a "hypocrite" because he did not know his Scriptures. In another incident recorded by Button, George Stump "offered a most gross indignity to the revered and venerated grandparents" of Calvin Shenault. A short time later, Shenault met Stump walking with his mother. Undeterred by the presence of a woman, Shenault attacked them, kicking and punching them both as they fell to the ground. When Stump retaliated by complaining to the mayor, Shenault provided a very different version of the incident. He testified that the Stumps were the aggressors and had even succeeded in knocking him to ground, sitting on top of him, and pummeling him with blows to the face and body. Unconvinced, the mayor bound Shenault over to the grand jury.[54]

Such incidents suggest the distinctive ways in which lower-class whites defended their honor. First, in contrast to the ritualized patterns of upper-class defenses of honor, lower-class defenses of honor provided the participants greater opportunity to express rage through spontaneous acts of aggression. Moore did not get his fill the first time, so he attacked McLoughlin again. To get satisfaction, Shenault attacked not only his adversary but his adversary's mother as well.

This suggests a second dimension of lower-class honor: women were often active participants in the fray. As a result, lower-class defenses of honor often became family affairs.[55] Although women rarely initiated affairs of honor, they were often aggressors. In one such case, the wife of Patrick Spillers urged him to fight their neighbor John Mulligan after the latter had insulted her during an argument. At his wife's insistence, Spillers grabbed an ax and came at Mulligan. Luckily, Mulligan escaped. In another incident, Catherine Reid, the wife of a coachmaker, suspected Mary Snyder of seducing her husband. Fearful that the affair might bring scandal to the family and that Snyder meant to replace her in her husband's affections, Catherine Reid began to stalk Snyder, waiting for an opportunity to get revenge. When she finally caught Snyder in her hus-band's place of business, Mrs. Reid attacked. According to Snyder's court testimony, Catherine Reid blackened both of Snyder's eyes and whipped her "until she could scarcely stand up." Finally, passers-by heard Snyder's muffled cries of "murderer" and rescued her.[56]

In time, Snyder also sought vengeance. Shortly after the episode with Catherine Reid, William Stone, an elderly clerk, told virtually anyone who would listen that Snyder was a lewd woman, "guilty of whoredom, fornication, and incontinence." Snyder tried to defend herself. Fearing that she would lose her "good name, fame, and credit among her neigh-bors and other good and worthy citizens," she brought suit against Stone. The use of the civil courts in defense of honor was nothing new.[57] But for a woman to sue a man hardly conformed to nineteenth-century gender conventions. In this instance, Snyder proved no match for the powers of patriarchy. Although most witnesses supported Snyder's contention that Stone intended to slander her, the jury concluded that "the words were not spoken by the defendant with malice." Evidently, lower-class honor, like evangelical religion, provided women some opportunity to act on their own but not enough to challenge male authority directly.[58]

Third, the state often played a crucial role in determining the fate of affairs of honor. When lower-class incidents escalated beyond the princi-pals, legal authorities often stepped in to reinstate order. Yet in many cases, the law was neither a passive nor a neutral party. Quite often, one side or the other used the law as a last resort to get satisfaction. Evidently, some exploited the police and courts to perfection. As noted earlier, Hezekiah Ford used the courts to make good on his threat to Jack Woodall that "he would have him back in the Penitentiary before long."[59]

Women, in particular, relied on the courts to satisfy vendettas without resorting to violence. This was probably Mary Snyder's intent when she brought suit against Stone. In another instance, Mary Callen asked the mayor to arrest her neighbors Mr. and Mrs. King, because, according to Callen, they had threatened to kill her. The Kings protested, arguing that the opposite was closer to the truth: Mrs. Callen took advantage of Mrs. King's petite frame to abuse and ill-treat her. In this case, the mayor sided with Callen, but not before each side tried valiantly to defame the other.[60]

Unless one side or the other appealed to local law enforcement officers for assistance, civic leaders usually allowed lower-class combatants to settle their own disputes. When two Irish laborers came before the mayor for fighting, Button encouraged the mayor to let the two continue their dispute, because it was not worth the city's expense to interfere in a case that did not affect its better class of residents.[61] As long as only whites were involved, the mayor and the watch usually did just that. Even though lower-class white affairs of honor were generally volatile and violent, municipal authorities were reluctant to intervene. In a sample of 448 mayor's court cases reported in the *Lynchburg Virginian* from 1858 through 1860, Button recorded only ten instances in which the mayor tried whites for fighting.[62] Of these, Mayor William Branch deemed one individual dangerous enough to send to the state court for trial, sentenced another to a short stay in the town jail to "cool off," and released the rest without substantial punishment. Among those he released were the residents of a boardinghouse who beat up a fellow occupant, Patrick Ryan, after he disturbed their sleep with drunken singing. Because of the wounds he sustained, Ryan made complaint to the mayor. Although he "presented a most pitiful sight" with his many cuts and bruises, the mayor took no action. Believing that "the thing was done in the best possible humor," Branch "professed entire satisfaction with all that had occurred."[63]

When lower-class whites were accused of more serious crimes of violence, they often received light punishments. In 1858 and 1860, the grand jury and the mayor sent only fourteen cases of assault to the state courts. In the six cases in which the accused's occupation could be determined, four of those accused were white laborers.[64] Three of these were dismissed without trial; the other, a shoemaker accused of beating a clerk, was fined thirty-five dollars and released. Even when the accused endangered his victim's life, the courts did not necessarily punish the individual to the full extent of the law. In the sample years, seven white laborers were indicted for malicious stabbing. Of these, two were dismissed before trial for lack of evidence, two were fined less than thirty dollars, and three received jail terms of one to three years. In all the cases of violence, only one received the maximum punishment: William Hendricks was hanged for the murder of Tom Johnson.[65]

Civic leaders' acceptance of most forms of lower-class white violence was matched by their tolerance of other forms of lower-class white impropriety. As long as lower-class whites confined their drinking, gambling, and whoring to their own neighborhoods and did not involve blacks, elites generally tolerated their behavior. Consider Mayor Branch's reaction to William Lloyd, a white laborer picked up by the night watch for public drunkenness. After spending the night in jail to sleep off his inebriation, Lloyd went before the mayor. Branch released him, reasoning that Lloyd "had in nowise interfered with the rights and privileges of his neighbors" and thus "he was the soul who suffered most from his indiscretion." Such leniency was fairly common. Even though newspaper reports suggested that public drunkenness was primarily a lower-class phenomenon, and contemporaries blamed much of the town's white lower-class violence on liquor, Branch rarely used his court to try to reform those lower-class whites arrested for drunkenness. Nor did he try to abate public consumption by making examples of those who came before him in court. Most white offenders—even repeat offenders—escaped with only a lecture or a night or two in jail to "sober up."[66] To Branch, most drunken whites were a nuisance, not a threat to social order. Only the Irish were treated differently. To rid the town of this group, Branch more often than not expelled them.[67]

Even when drunkenness led to violence, civic leaders remained unconcerned, as long as the incident did not seriously disrupt the lives of the innocent. Apparently, most believed that the liberties and temptations of urban life inevitably led to a certain amount of public disorder. Despite the endless stream of cases of rowdyism that filled the mayor's court docket, Button, for one, believed the town to be a "comparatively quiet" community. On one particularly "calm" day, Button described lower-class life in Lynchburg:

> There were several fights in the more disreputable parts of the city, in all of which old General Barleycorn took a prominent part—but these ebullitions were not sufficient to raise the mercury of fifteen thousand people. And so in spite of . . . the agency of Mr. John Barleycorn our world wags on and the city is . . . quiet.[68]

Civil authorities treated other moral offenses by whites just as lightly as they regarded public drunkenness. Like other Southern communities, Lynchburg accepted prostitution as a necessary evil, the consequence of man's passionate nature. For this reason, Lynchburg officials rarely prosecuted bawdy-house owners, and officials arrested prostitutes only when they wandered into respectable parts of town.[69] As a result, the trade flourished in Lynchburg. By 1860, there was one prostitute for every thirty-three free men, a ratio comparable to other Southern cities and much higher than New York's one to every fifty-seven or New Haven's one to seventy-six.[70]

Gambling was only slightly less tolerated. In 1858, the grand jury of the hustings court handed down twenty-three indictments against nineteen individuals for either keno or faro gambling. Of these cases, the prosecution won only thirteen, fining each of the accused individuals thirty dollars. In 1860, the grand juries of the hustings court and the circuit court handed down fifty-five gambling indictments against forty-one individuals. Eventually, the courts dropped all of these cases for lack of evidence.[71]

Civic leaders' indifference allowed lower-class whites that much more opportunity to enjoy their leisure hours any way they saw fit. In the years before the war, Lynchburg's lower classes even established a section of town, Buzzard's Roost, that specifically catered to their leisure pleasures.[72] Located along the river basin on the southern edge of town, the Buzzard became a favorite place for all who liked whorehouses, doggeries, and gambling dens. Its reputation was so notorious that a Frederick, Maryland newspaper correspondent asked to visit the "far famed locale" on his tour of the city. Evidently, the neighborhood did not disappoint. He reported that the Buzzard was "a wretched looking place . . . ten-fold worse than the meanest place to be found" in any other city he had seen. During the 1930s, Wyatt Tucker Hill, interviewed by the Federal Writers' Project, remembered the Buzzard with equal fascination. According to Hill, "the roughest element of the town, or I might even say the world, hung out there."[73]

Wealthy Lynchburg's tolerance of lower-class white impropriety emerged from a number of sources. Some civic leaders were only too willing to allow Buzzard life to continue unmolested, because sensational stories of unseemly poorer whites not only confirmed their worst class prejudices but legitimized their own claims as moral guardians of the community. Middle-class shopkeepers, merchants, and petty professionals, in particular, were eager to find ways to distinguish themselves from those below them. Accentuating how the lower classes failed to conform to modern standards of propriety was one way to do this. Not surprising, Button's colorful commentaries on white lower-class crime assisted the middle classes in their objective. When Button reported criminal behavior, he invariably accentuated the racial, ethnic, and class attributes of the accused offender and intimated that each segment of the lower classes possessed moral defects peculiar to itself. In Button's colorful arsenal of appellations, black offenders were "loafers," "unruly," and "degraded"; the

James River and Kanawha Canal #1. (*Harper's Monthly*, 1857)

James River and Kanawha Canal #2. (*Harper's Monthly*, 1857; LMS)

Left and above are two illustrations of Buzzard's Roost, the notorious vice district at the basin of the city.

Irish were "reckless," "violent," and "hedonistic"; and native whites were morally "abandoned," "worthless," and a "discredit to the race."[74]

In their own way, Southern evangelicals also contributed to the town's toleration of the Buzzard. Although their moral absolutism made them uncompromising in their condemnation of sin, as Southerners, they had few illusions about the perfectibility of humankind. Instead, they believed that because sin was endemic to society, even the most pious person was prone to its temptations. This pessimism made Lynchburg evangelicals extremely skeptical of the efficacy of social reform. At best, they could try to save souls, but they could not save society. Thus, Lynchburg's respectable citizens made few efforts to pressure the city government to enact blue laws for moral uplift.[75]

Nor did civic leaders necessarily view drunkenness as an impediment to economic productivity and commercial expansion. When Button learned that one of his printers, Isaac Higginbotham, had been arrested in a "state of glorious exhilaration on Christmas day, caused by imbibing freely of his favorite beverage," he ridiculed Higginbotham in the press but disclosed that he would take no further disciplinary action. Even after the night watch arrested Higginbotham two more times during the next three months, Button refused to fire the printer. Although Button admitted that Higginbotham too often "indulged in a line of conduct . . . beneath the dignity of . . . a gentleman of his profession," he explained to his readers that Higginbotham was simply a victim of his own personable nature, "which not infrequently eventuates in trouble to himself and mortification to his friends." According to Button, this made Higginbotham pitiable and a legitimate object for public humiliation, but not someone deserving of job discipline.[76]

Of course, some did more than just tolerate lower-class whites' indiscretions; some were truly intrigued by Buzzard life. Although developing standards of propriety discouraged most members of respectable Lynchburg society from frequenting whorehouses, gambling dens, bawdy theaters, and groggeries, many still thirsted to know how the other half lived. Button, through his regular coverage of the mayor's court, generally satisfied their curiosity. Indeed, the public's desire for details was so great that on those rare days when no cases came before the mayor, Button playfully chided Branch for not providing his readers with some provocative tale of sin and degradation. After a particularly uneventful week, Button claimed that he even paid the mayor a visit to "impress upon His Honor the necessity of his furnishing us something in the way of an item," lest the daily column remain boring.[77]

Lynchburg's black community rarely enjoyed such indulgences. Instead, civic leaders responded aggressively to all cases of black impropriety. While Lynchburg's law enforcement agencies often seemed to encourage lower-class whites to settle their differences, these agencies rarely provided blacks the same opportunity. In one incident, Thomas Cousins, a black laborer, assaulted an old friend, Gundey Juelius, because he believed Juelius had made improper advances toward his wife. When Mrs. Cousins told her husband of his friend's behavior, Button noted, the husband revenged "the iniquity in the most summary manner." Night watchmen found Cousins and Juelius scuffling on the street and promptly threw them both in jail. In court the next day, the mayor refused to recognize Cousins's defense of his wife's honor as a legitimate form of behavior. Instead, the mayor gave Cousins the maximum sentence he could give a black man, thirty-nine lashes. In another instance, John Deane, a slave, met an old nemesis, Allen Langhorne, also a slave, at a Buzzard gambling den. The two played faro, but as they did, each began to insult the other. After a short while, Deane had heard enough and assaulted Langhorne. Again, the night watch arrested both men. Again, Branch gave the apparent aggressor—in this case, Deane—the maximum sentence of thirty-nine lashes. These cases were typical. Branch prosecuted black combatants vigorously. Of the thirty-six blacks arrested for violent behavior in 1858 and 1860, as reported in the newspapers, only three were released without punishment; the rest either received jail time or were whipped.[78]

Blacks received harsher treatment by Lynchburg authorities in other ways as well. Unlike lower-class whites, blacks found that Lynchburg's law enforcement agencies rarely tolerated their off-hour behavior, no matter how circumspectly they tried to behave. Because most lived in cramped and dilapidated garrets and shacks, men and women spent most of their leisure hours congregating on street corners, in alleys, and in Buzzard groggeries. Here they socialized with one another, usually in small, same-sex groups. According to urban historian Roger Lane, blacks were often "aggressively competitive" with one another in these encounters. Chance meetings provided an opportunity for individuals to assert their boldness through "semiritualistic insults," in which they ridiculed an adversary's sexuality, intelligence, lineage, and courage. To blacks, evening and Sunday meetings were an essential part of their daily lives—a time to let off steam, meet people, sustain their pride, and assert their voracity. Unfortunately, whites failed to appreciate the intricacies of urban black culture. Most viewed black street culture as a minor annoyance, an indication of the inherent difficulty of trying to establish social order in a city that was almost 50 percent black. During times of political or social turmoil, however, whites viewed black street culture far more sinisterly. Especially after John Brown's raid, whites became fearful of black collective behavior and thus increasingly intolerant of blacks' leisure activities.[79]

White authorities were especially critical of the Buzzard's influence on slaves and free blacks. Throughout the period, civic leaders accused Buzzard grogshop owners of pandering to enslaved and free blacks at the expense of social order. To dissuade blacks from frequenting these locales, Mayor Branch vigorously prosecuted all blacks who were arrested for rowdy behavior, public drunkenness, and breaking curfew. Although the *Virginian* listed only a fraction of the cases of this type that went before the mayor, nearly all individuals in the cases reported received some form of punishment. In contrast to the tolerance shown disorderly whites, even recidivist whites, Branch treated most blacks with considerable severity. Of those cases of public drunkenness reported, thirty of thirty-eight slaves and free blacks were whipped. In cases of curfew violations, forty-five of eighty were whipped, and another six were fined. The number of lashes varied from as few as ten to the maximum of thirty-nine.[80]

Besides punishing drunken blacks, civic leaders tried to stop the black liquor trade at its source. As usual, Button championed the cause. Initially, Button attacked the liquor trade because he believed that it encouraged slaves to steal from their masters. According to Button, grogshop owners "in every corner of the city" will "furnish liquor to any negro that can purloin property enough from his master to pay for it." After John Brown's raid, however, Button and others raised new concerns about the effects of grogshops on Lynchburg's black population. In a letter to the *Virginian*, "V.F.J.R." argued that these doggeries were favorite meeting places for slaves and free blacks and, as a result, were potentially dangerous to the public peace. While V.F.J.R. did not accuse any slaves of incendiarism, he painted a picture of doggery life intended to disturb concerned white residents. On one Sunday morning, he claimed to have witnessed as many as twelve blacks assembled outside the door of a Buzzard dramshop, drinking and gambling. Yet although they were all "drunk and talking very loud," the authorities failed to respond. The writer concluded that if "such disreputable conduct among the slaves is allowed in broad daylight, and that on Sabbath morning, what are we to expect after night closes—worse of course."[81]

On one level, whites' anxieties are difficult to comprehend, especially considering the town's toleration of lower-class white violence and impropriety. After all, blacks didn't do anything that whites didn't do. Moreover, the two groups shared a similar orientation toward life. Like lower-class whites, blacks believed that theirs was a hostile, competitive, and violent world. Thus, like whites, blacks admired aggressiveness and rage as necessary virtues for survival. For this reason, black violence was often related to the defense of honor. According to Button's newspaper accounts, both the Cousins-Juelius and the Deane-Langhorne quarrels were essentially contests of honors.[82]

Perhaps even more important, black violence, like individual acts of lower-class white violence, tended to be fairly insular. Apart from the few cases in which black workers assaulted their employers (discussed in chapter 1; also see table 2:8 in the appendixes), blacks tried to avoid conflicts with whites. As they well knew, even the smallest incident could incite the wrath of the entire white community. To protect themselves from abuse, blacks closely monitored their own behavior. Unlike whites, blacks often intervened when they witnessed those of their own race fighting, so that they could prevent the authorities from arriving. When possible, blacks simply tried to stay away from whites. Perhaps this explains why tobacco factories—a place lower-class whites would never enter—became popular meeting grounds for black residents. These cavernous structures served as churches, funeral parlors, and—usually without the owner's knowledge—gambling dens.

Of course, there were times when blacks could not avoid interacting with whites. With few economic resources, blacks were especially dependent on the white-owned groceries and grogshops in and around the Buzzard. Although civic leaders suspected that grog shop society openly flouted all social conventions, the truth was that blacks and whites rarely socialized at the same locales. Newspaper accounts make clear that most of the whites found in "black" doggeries were either the owners or their employees. Although these whites relied on black customers to make a living, there is little evidence that they developed any sort of social intimacy with their patrons. Instead, black-white relations in the grog shop generally mirrored the inequalities of the dominant society. Since these locales were among the few places blacks could buy liquor, congregate, gamble, and fence their stolen items, blacks had to conform to the owners' expectations of race relations if they wanted to be served. In short, Buzzard grogshops may have provided blacks a respite from slavery, but they did not provide them a respite from being subordinate to whites. Even in the Buzzard, blacks found it more difficult than lower-class whites to distance themselves from the hierarchical structure of Lynchburg society.

Even so, whites remained suspicious of any form of black initiative. The resilience of the liquor trade, in particular, convinced many whites that they were becoming impotent in all matters related to race. Developments outside Lynchburg added to whites' fear: the demise of the Whigs as a viable national party, John Brown's raid at Harper's Ferry, and the growing success of the Republican Party suggested to white Lynchburgers that they were fast losing control of their destiny. Throughout the presidential election of 1860, local politicians consistently played on a common fear—that current political trends threatened the very basis of white dominance. Black behavior at the Buzzard confirmed whites' worst fears of what might happen to all society if they lost complete control of their slaves. Thus, policing the Buzzard became a kind of litmus test for white society, an opportunity to prove their ultimate authority. To regain command of the racial environment, civic leaders began to propose a wide variety of new strategies.

White citizens became especially frustrated by the behavior of the white entrepreneurs who sold liquor to slaves. Indeed, most of the first initiatives concerned stopping this group from selling to blacks. Button, for one, believed that existing agencies could stop the liquor trade if they simply enforced existing laws prohibiting the sale of liquor to slaves. A short while later, however, he reluctantly admitted that the police were virtually helpless, because "these gambling and drinking parties have their spies out at all times, and before our officers can reach them, the birds have flown." To combat the perfidy of these entrepreneurs, Button suggested a radical approach: allow blacks to testify against grogshop owners. Although Button admitted such a law violated Southern whites' view of racial propriety, he countered that "any man who is mean enough to sell whiskey to a negro" deserved the public humiliation of being arraigned on the testimony of one.[83]

Few were willing to take this radical step; for while all agreed that liquor salesmen were a nuisance and dangerously opportunistic, most believed that the real problem was not the few whites who broke the law by selling to slaves but the large number of blacks who paid them to do so. If local magistrates were truly concerned about white behavior at the Buzzard, they probably would have taken steps to close the district. But they never publicly contemplated this strategy, nor did they make a point of arresting whites who frequented the Buzzard. Evidently, civic leaders trusted the loyalty of lower-class whites enough not to interfere in their leisure-time activities, even though these leisure activities sometimes placed them in contact with blacks. Instead, most believed it was more important to control the town's black population than the few "mean" whites who violated the South's code of racial propriety.

Thus, the mayor, city council, and police focused their energies on controlling the behavior of blacks. And they relied on increasingly radical measures in their efforts. One day, after V.F.J.R. complained about Buzzard groggeries, Branch instructed the police to make regular Sunday sweeps and "arrest every negro in the Buzzard (except those resident in that locality) who may be found on that street . . . without regard to what they may be doing when found." When this failed to stop the vice, Lynchburg's municipal officers decided to go one step farther. During the

1860 election and thereafter, Branch called on the town's newly organized militia companies to assume responsibility for controlling black society. Although the companies were originally established to defend the town from slave insurrectionists and Northern incendiaries in the wake of John Brown's raid, Branch summoned the militia for even the smallest of slave infractions. As their responsibilities increased, so did the number of organizations. By the beginning of 1860, white residents had established a cavalry, two rifle units, and nine neighborhood vigilante organizations to patrol the town at night.[84]

Vigilantism was nothing new to Lynchburg. At various times in the town's brief history, white residents had believed they had good reason to fear incendiaries. When this happened, residents organized patrols to catch presumed conspirators and to stop others from joining forces. White Lynchburgers were hardly unique in this behavior. Abusing alleged black and white incendiaries became something of a ritual in the Old South—an opportunity for slaveholders and nonslaveholders alike to demonstrate their mutual dedication to maintaining the racial status quo.[85]

Yet even if Lynchburg's reaction to black lawlessness was somewhat predictable, the use of militia units to police slaves still revealed a great deal about the racial and class climate of the town on the eve of the war. For one thing, the organizational response in 1860 was far more ambitious than earlier efforts. Unlike previous vigilante operations, participants in 1860 did not view their organizations as temporary, organized to stop a specific incendiary movement. Instead, recent national events coupled with the intractable behavior of local blacks at the Buzzard convinced civic leaders that the problem of slave control had reached crisis proportions and required the establishment of formal military organizations to handle the situation. Thus, individuals who joined these units were expected to demonstrate an even greater commitment to the racial status quo than those who had joined previous vigilante organizations. At least in the beginning, lower-class whites embraced this commitment. Although evidence is fragmentary, extant records suggest that sizable numbers of laborers, petty grocers, clerks, and the like joined these units.[86]

Lower-class whites' motives for volunteering varied from individual to individual. Some, no doubt, simply wanted a legally sanctioned excuse to carry a gun, wear a uniform, enjoy the company of other men, and bully blacks. Some viewed military organizations as an opportunity to enhance their reputations through community service. Others genuinely believed it was incumbent upon them to protect and secure their community. Still others were probably reluctant participants, individuals who felt coerced by community pressure to demonstrate their loyalty to slavery.

Regardless of motive, whites of all classes responded to the perceived crisis with similar fervor. The presidential election campaign of 1860 was an especially tense time in Lynchburg. Already on edge after Harper's Ferry, militia units remained on constant alert. As the election neared, citizens began to perceive even the most innocuous behavior as dangerous. A few weeks before the election, the mayor called out two militia units to capture "two drunk negroes" for breaking curfew. The units arrested the black men, then beat them until they were unconscious. Once the black men were incapacitated, the militia released them.[87]

Unfortunately, such episodes provided only a momentary relief from anxiety. By the eve of the election, new rumors had spread of an impending slave insurrection. On the night before the election, Sabra Ramsey told her husband, the minister at First Presbyterian Church, that every man in town was "armed in fear of an invasion." Sabra, however, was more fearful of the enemy within. Born and raised in the North, she found it difficult to understand the brutality that often accompanied slavery. As the streets became more tumultuous, she expected to hear news that the militia had found an unwitting victim. "I did not fear . . . an insurrection," she confided to her husband, "but I did fear overt acts of violence from such an excited state of feeling." Indeed, with so many armed young men wandering the streets, she braced herself for the worst: "I expected there would be street shooting and midnight murder of some poor blacks accused and convicted of what they had never dreamed of." Fortunately, she believed, "the prayers of God's own dear people" prevailed, and "evil passions" abated without the needless loss of life.[88]

Even so, blacks could not rest easy. Perhaps even more than the militia members themselves, blacks understood that the militia provided lower-class whites an opportunity to do what they could not do during more peaceful times—abuse blacks without fear of loss of status or incrimination for destruction of property. In short, the restraint lower-class whites customarily displayed toward blacks began to abate amid the prewar ferment. No doubt, fear induced much of the violence. Although historians generally conclude that there was little real threat of slave rebellion during the Secession winter, contemporaries were not so sure. According to John Douglas, son of a mechanic, patrolling was a grueling and terrifying ordeal. Shortly after the battle at Fort Sumter, Douglas, then just thirteen years old, joined a vigilance committee to protect the town from Northern and slave incendiaries. Every evening, for several weeks, he and the other members of his squad met at the home of the commanding officer. After fortifying themselves on "real coffee," they went to their assigned beats. On most nights, Douglas patrolled the lonely roads on the outskirts of town, near the college. Alone and vulnerable, Douglas anxiously waited for the first break of morning light so that he could return to the safety of his home. "I confess," he later recalled, "that I was often compelled to pull my cap down tight on my head to keep my hair from lifting it off." Indeed, Douglas was so scared that he was not sure how he would have acted if a crisis had arisen.[89]

Given the disagreeable nature of militia service, it is surprising that so many eagerly accepted the roles assigned to them in their military units. Although white laborers often displayed seemingly antithetical desires to separate from elites and, at the same time, to develop more egalitarian relations with them, in the militia they reverted to traditional standards of behavior. In virtually every unit, laborers elected the town's leading citizens to the most prestigious roles, usually by unanimous vote. This deference was partly out of expediency. In many units, elites not only treated soldiers after drills but also paid for their uniforms and armaments. Thus, less wealthy residents were only giving elites their due by electing them to military command.

At the same time, however, deference to elites reflected the community's level of anxiety. Faced with the twin crises of Republican insurgence and possible slave insurrection, white residents anxiously looked to traditional leaders to guide them. True, laboring whites had long demonstrated a willingness to let elites lead by electing them to political office. Yet in many respects, the deference exhibited in the militia was far more meaningful than anything that ordinary citizens had shown before. For one thing, it was more immediate and personal, because the militia placed nonelites and elites in daily contact with one another in a relationship that was inherently hierarchical. Moreover, by deferring to elites now, poorer whites put their own lives at risk to protect the lives of others. As Douglas patrolled the streets, his commanding officer—described by Douglas as "one of the most prominent men of the town"—stayed home.[90]

The behavior of lower-class whites did not denote a complete victory for the forces of tradition and hierarchy. Participation in the militia was only one aspect of their lives. In other ways—most notably, religion and leisure activities—laborers continued to strive for greater autonomy and equality. During the Secession crisis, laborers continued to attend different churches and frequent the Buzzard. Nevertheless, laborers' participation in the militia and their willingness to accept the counsel of traditional leaders in the midst of the crisis suggest that recent portrayals of the prewar South's fragile social structure do not hold for Lynchburg.[91] Instead, class relations remained dynamic. Rich and poor Lynchburg residents did not solve the tension between hierarchy and equality, integration and autonomy. Instead, they learned to let these countervailing forces operate in an unsteady equilibrium. In some ways, they had to do this, for in the years before the war, neither rich nor poor whites provided a clear indication of what they wanted. The rich may have extolled the virtues of hierarchy and the organic society, but their behavior sometimes belied their stated desires. At the same time, lower-class whites were equally inconsistent, acting at times to support deference and at other times to undermine it.

Perhaps the only issue in which rich and poor whites demonstrated any coherence at all was in their commitment to slavery. As a result, they frustrated blacks, the group that provided the most consistent message of what they wanted in their unceasing effort to gain freedom. In virtually every avenue of life, blacks struggled to gain autonomy and freedom. And at nearly every turn, whites frustrated their efforts. Whether whites could continue to do so during the dual epics of war and emancipation remained to be seen.

The Many Battles of Lynchburg

Lynchburg Goes to War

The events of the Secession winter of 1860–1861 convinced Lynchburg's men of property and standing that they ruled a society united by bonds of deference, paternalism, white superiority, and economic ascendancy. Five years later, they would not be so confident. Military mobilization, poverty, and death created animosities that elites were unable to control, much less resolve, as they had once done. True, not all the intracommunity conflicts directly challenged the foundations of the South's old order. Laboring whites and blacks often complained about issues that in hindsight seem insignificant or unique to the war itself. Nevertheless, by constantly testing the traditional structures of power, lower-class whites and blacks helped create a new social environment that would significantly affect the direction of postwar race and class relations. Indeed, the most fundamental features of race and class relations in postwar Lynchburg—most notably, laboring whites' alienation from civic leaders' political designs, the development of black collective activism and separatism, and the increase in violence as an essential feature of racial interaction—can all be traced to the war.

Yet if the war helped foster change, the changes themselves often took place within a decidedly conservative context. Because Lynchburg's antebellum civic leaders retained much of their wealth and stature throughout the war, less powerful groups found it difficult to challenge them in overt ways. Most tried only to stretch the traditional bonds of paternalism. Ultimately, poorer whites and blacks learned that war created new opportunities for them to test elite control, but it did not offer them the opportunity to break entirely from the past. Moreover, whatever lower-class whites and blacks achieved during the war came at a high price—four years of poverty, desolation, and death.

Lynchburg's civic leaders approached the Secession crisis with considerable anxiety. Through the long Secession winter, most remained steadfast Unionists. As businessmen, they feared the growing hostilities would disrupt their lucrative tobacco trade in both the North and the South. As political conservatives, they blamed Northern and Southern extremists for bringing the crisis to a head, arguing that ideological fanaticism violated one of the fundamental principles of republican politics—that good order rested on the self-sacrifice and cooperation of all citizens. The town's few ardent Secessionists were no less apprehensive. Although Secessionists tended to be somewhat more virulent in debate, they shared Unionists' concern that constant agitation and malicious debate might do irreparable harm to the community by fragmenting the ruling class.[1]

As the crisis unfolded, the two sides saw their worst fears realized. From the presidential election campaign in the fall of 1860 to the firing on Fort Sumter in April 1861, the issue of secession dominated public discourse. As political rallies became more frequent, the rhetoric of the opposing sides became increasingly virulent. Unionists routinely insinuated that states' rights Democrats were demagogues who had long conspired to destroy the Union to advance their own political careers. For their part, Democrats condemned Unionists as timid at best and abolitionist sympathizers at worst. Even so, leaders from both parties tried to control the nature and extent of partisan name-calling. Particularly after Abraham Lincoln's election, Whig and Democrat party organs encouraged their readers to remain tolerant of one another's beliefs and publicly praised the intelligence and virtue of their adversaries, even as they attacked their views. When the Virginia state legislature called for a special election to select representatives to a state convention to consider secession in late 1860, Charles Button, editor of the Unionist *Lynchburg Virginian*, was especially magnanimous. In an overture of goodwill, Button published the speeches of all the candidates and carefully tempered his criticisms of the Secessionist candidates, James Goggin and Thomas Kirkpatrick. While noting that both men were skillful lawyers and good citizens, he suggested that they lacked the composure and statesmanship the desperate times required of political leaders. Secessionists also searched for ways to build consensus. For the special election, Democratic leaders opted to split their ticket, endorsing a longtime Whig, John Speed, and a moderate states' rights Democrat, Charles Slaughter.[2]

As debate continued, elites looked for new ways to convince the public and reassure themselves that beyond the nettlesome issue of secession they could act in concert for the good of the community. In January 1861, just a few weeks before the convention election, "ministers and leading members of the various churches of the city," including both Secessionists and Unionists, met to sign a pledge promising to act with moderation and Christian forbearance during the crisis. At about the same time, local leaders formed a relief society to assist the poor hurt by the harsh winter and the decline of trade during the Secession crisis. In early April, all city officials were reelected in a lackluster election that was nearly void of any public discussion of secession. But perhaps the most poignant demonstration of elite unity occurred every evening at the Fair Grounds, where the town's numerous militia companies drilled for home defense. The highest-ranking officers came from the town's most prominent families and included both Unionists and Secessionists.[3]

Nevertheless, the issue of secession refused to go away. Although Lynchburg voted for Unionist candidates in the presidential election of 1860 and the state convention of February 1861 by ratios of two to one, observers noted that Lynchburg's Secessionists were becoming increasingly outspoken in their criticisms of the North. At the same time, Unionists began to quarrel among themselves as some began to place conditions on their continued loyalty to the Union. Charles Blackford, a young lawyer in town, was among this group. Although Charles was president of the Lynchburg Young Men's Union Club, he admitted to an uncle that his loyalty to the Union had waned. In a January letter, Charles initially noted that although he believed Virginia's "peculiar position . . . requires her to remain in the Union." However, a few paragraphs later he confessed that his "ante-election Union sentiments" were "oozing away and the fires of my National patriotism expiring." He blamed Northern voters for his waning enthusiasm for union. Because they had elected Lincoln "by majorities greater than ever given any man since Washington," they "indicated a complete endorsation of his obnoxious views . . .

and a declaration on their part to make war upon us and our institutions." For this reason, Blackford "was inclined to think that prompt secession is the only remedy," for it would quickly bring Northerners "to realize the condition of affairs at the South." When Mary Blackford, Charles's mother, learned of her son's slow conversion to secessionism, she confessed to her brother, John Minor of Charlottesville, that she preferred to die rather than see her sons fight against the flag she had "labored to train" them to "love and die for."[4]

Others debated the issues more publicly than did the Blackfords. As the town became more fragmented, public debate became increasingly rancorous. In response, Button reprinted the words of an editor from another town, who advised his readers to "avoid excitements and collisions," so that they might "harmonize as far as possible without sacrificing principle." Button added that if every man would respect the opinions of his neighbors, "then might we with more reason hope for a peaceful end of our national troubles."[5]

Ultimately, civic leaders attained political consensus, but not in the way that most had hoped. On April 12, 1861, Confederate batteries attacked Fort Sumter. The day after the fort fell to the Confederacy, Lincoln called on all loyal states, including Virginia, to help raise an army to defend the Union. The two events galvanized public opinion for secession. Years after the war, W. H. Morgan recalled that although he had been a Unionist "when Lincoln determined to make war on the South . . . it did not take me two seconds to cast my lot with Virginia." Robert E. Withers made much the same claim. After Manassas, he told a wounded Yankee officer that before Fort Sumter he "had been an outspoken opponent of secession." Once Lincoln called for "Virginia's quota of troops to coerce the seceded states," however, Withers also joined the Confederate cause. Evidently, his was a complete conversion: when his daughter was born in late April, Withers named her Virginia Secessia. Even Dr. John Terrell, a pacifist Quaker and devout Unionist, converted to the cause "once the first shot was fired." Terrell even contemplated joining the local cavalry unit, before a fellow physician convinced him that he would serve the cause better if he used his talents in the medical corps.[6]

In the crush of events, few contemplated how much their ideals had changed in just a few days. On the first anniversary of the state convention election, William Blackford, Charles's father, paused to read his diary entries from the previous year. After doing so, Blackford confided in his diary that he scarcely believed it was possible to undergo "so radical a change of sentiment" in so short a time. "It makes me question the identity of mind," he confessed. "I then had strong hopes that the Union might be preserved."[7]

Fort Sumter unified white Lynchburg like few other events in the town's history. Robert Glass, of the Democratic *Lynchburg Republican*, suggested that the crisis had introduced an "Era of Good Feeling," ending all differences of opinion about the best way to protect Southern rights. Now, Glass asserted, "every man is ... willing to march shoulder to shoulder, breast to breast," down the "path of Glory and if need be death." Button agreed with his political adversary, noting that "the occurrences of the past few days have developed a oneness of sentiment and feeling among our citizens, a feeling of undying opposition and resistance to the further encroachment of Black Republicanism." Glass and Button were essentially correct in their assessment of the political climate. On May 23, 1861, the state's secession ordinance was submitted to Lynchburg voters. The ordinance was approved unanimously by the town's 1,486 voters. Early military enlistments also confirmed the press's observations. In the months following the outbreak of war, citizens' enthusiasm for military service reached its peak. From April through December, some 401 Lynchburg residents volunteered for military service in ten local companies; the next year they were joined by another 68 from two more locally raised companies. Citizens from all social classes played prominent roles in the establishment of these units.[8]

Not only were white Lynchburgers unified; they also rallied around their traditional leaders as they confronted the crisis. During the first months of the war, voters demonstrated a preference to be led by those already in power. Although artisans and laborers comprised more than half of all military enlistments, they helped elect the town's traditional political and social elites to officer positions—usually by unanimous or near-unanimous votes.[9]

Meanwhile, opposition to secession virtually disappeared. Although a few remained pro-Union, their numbers were small and their voice was relatively weak. On the same day that Lynchburg citizens unanimously supported secession, a few individuals met at one of the town's Methodist churches to pray for Union. This proved to be the last time that Unionists met publicly. After this, those who continued to doubt the efficacy and the morality of the Confederate cause learned either to accept the public will or to harbor their objections in silence. No doubt, some felt their silence coerced. Although there is no evidence that Lynchburg Unionists were physically abused, they may have been intimidated by the town's treatment of "suspicious" outsiders. In the days after Secession, Button and Glass counseled readers to be on the lookout for spies. Subsequent events seemed to justify their advice. In late May, Mayor William Branch ordered the arrest of George Gross, a Northern laborer, because Gross allegedly told friends he was a Republican and opposed the further expansion of slavery. Although Gross assured Branch that he would not fight in a war against slavery, Branch remained suspicious and remanded Gross to jail. After a month, Branch asked the governor to handle the case. The governor asked Gross to take an oath of allegiance to the Confederacy. Gross complied and was released. Two months later, however, Branch arrested Gross again—this time for aiding the federal army at the Battle of Manassas.[10]

Sobered by such intolerance, Unionists learned to keep their views to themselves. Throughout the war, William Blackford's wife, Mary, a steadfast Unionist and opponent of slavery, refused to discuss her views with anyone but her brother. Though she confessed to him that she felt "sometimes as if I had no country," she buried her convictions in her maternal role, determining to help her five sons survive their military enlistments by doing whatever she could for the local war effort. Though frequently ill, she was a regular contributor to the Soldiers' Aid Society. Still, she never completely converted to the Confederate cause; instead, she prayed for the restoration of the Union, and she continued to write down her observations on the evils of slavery in her notebook, *Notes Illustrative of the Wrongs of Slavery*. Joseph Douglas, a machinist, also kept his views to himself. An opponent of slavery and the Confederacy, Douglas stayed in Lynchburg through much of the war, silently biding his time. Late in the war, he moved his family to Philadelphia, where they would finally be free of the sin of slavery. These, however, were the exceptions. Most citizens embraced the war with such enthusiasm that they probably never paused to consider the consequences of their decision to do so.[11]

Lynchburg at War

Encouraged by public expressions of political unity, Lynchburg residents turned their attention to the soldiers. From the first, Lynchburg citizens viewed Lynchburg soldiers as an extension of themselves, the embodiment of their own unselfish dedication to the cause. When the first companies left the Lynchburg railroad depot on April 23, 1861, ceremony organizers made sure that the soldiers knew exactly whom they were fighting for. Before departing, the three regiments paraded through town for the last time. As they marched, young women threw them trinkets and flowers as remembrances, while hundreds—perhaps even thousands—of other citizens looked on. At the corner of Main and Bridge Streets, in the heart of the central business district, they listened to an invocation by the Reverend Jacob Duche Mitchell, one of the town's most ardent Secessionists. With his usual blunt fervor, Mitchell reminded the men that the way in which they acquitted themselves in battle would reflect on the community they represented. When the soldiers departed on the Southside Railroad, they carried with them further reminders that theirs was a battle in defense of kith and kin—flags sewn by women of the town, some depicting such local scenes as the Blue Ridge Mountains.[1] Company flags were not simply emblems of the community but symbolic admonitions to the soldiers that theirs was a fight for hearth and home. By "defending the flag," a popular phrase in Civil War parlance, soldiers were defending those who made the flag—the women and families they left behind.[2]

Even after soldiers settled into the military life, civilians and soldiers continued to strengthen the link between camp and home. Most obviously, soldiers kept in touch with family and friends through private letters and newspaper correspondences. In addition, large numbers of Lynchburg residents took advantage of their proximity to the front lines to visit the campsites. Family members, public officials, ministers, and diverse private citizens made frequent visits, offering moral support, wagon loads of supplies, and news from home. Through their extensive and regular interaction with soldiers, Lynchburg residents not only learned of camp-life experiences and military heroics but retained a claim of moral stewardship over their soldiers.[3]

Initial reports back home were not comforting. Citizens and soldiers had hoped the unity, self-sacrifice, and moral integrity that seemed to have characterized the days following Fort Sumter would carry over into the war. Especially in the early days and months of the war, Lynchburg regiments seemed on the brink of disintegration, as soldiers and officers complained loudly and often about their military experiences—and even more loudly about one another.

For many soldiers, the problems began immediately after they settled into their first encampments. The physical surroundings were an affront to soldiers who believed they were about to embark on a noble and heroic cause. From the outset, soldiers had to make due on inadequate rations, meager supplies, and living conditions that seemed almost inhuman. John Henry, a printer who enlisted as a private in the Home Guard, spent his first nights of army life in a "rat-possessed shanty" just outside Richmond. As his troop awaited their first marching orders, they found that their host city was ill prepared to care for them. Sarcastically, Henry described his first meal with his outfit:

> In due time, it was announced that supper was ready. With appetites whetted by a long fast, we marched into the dining room, whilst visions of biscuit and butter, coffee *a la francaise*, steak, mutton chops, ham and eggs, muffins, waffles, etc., etc., danced through our brains (they never got lower in our system). But, alas, how are earthly hopes doomed to disappointment! ... The only object that met our anxious gaze ... was a barrel containing some putrid and decomposed matter, said to be beef! Here was a feast for the gods! Rotten beef and live maggots. There was one advantage connected with it, to wit: When a portion of the beef was put in the mouth, the maggots would crawl down our throats with it, thus relieving us of the trouble of chewing and swallowing.[4]

Others found camp life equally inhospitable. Edmond Moorman, a sergeant in the Beauregard Rifles, spent most of his first months in Norfolk, quartered in a building that he described as "one of the filthiest places I ever saw." According to Moorman, the house had been used as a yellow fever hospital some years earlier and had since been abandoned. Nevertheless, the "awful stench" remained, "leaving a very unfavorable impression on our company."[5]

Soldiers found that their supplies were as wanting as their quarters. In June 1861, Charles Blackford, now a lieutenant in the Wise Troops of the Second Virginia Cavalry, observed that his men had "already lost all modesty of begging." Pitying their poverty, Blackford refused to discipline them. Yet even if he had, it might not have made much difference; throughout the war, begging and foraging—or perhaps, more accurately, theft—were part of the Southern soldier's daily routine.[6]

The coming of the first winter posed new problems. Although many soldiers left Lynchburg supplied with homemade quilts and coats, most abandoned these items as they marched to their summer encampments. As winter approached, many Lynchburg soldiers panicked at the thought of keeping warm with only an army-issue blanket and tent to protect them from the elements. Those with some means, mainly officers, encouraged wives, mothers, and sisters to send new provisions. Ever resourceful, Blackford sent his wife a design for a stove and asked her to find someone in town to make it and deliver it to him. Stationed near Manassas, Robert Garlick Hill Kean, a sergeant for the Home Guard, told his wife in October that he could "not conceive . . . what I shall do about keeping warm this winter. I am bitterly cold every morning by day break, even now when weather is just becoming frosty. When the thermometer is at zero I shall perish outright." Kean eventually solved the problem by gaining an administrative position with the Confederate government in Richmond. Most soldiers did not have such options, and suffered for it.[7]

In time, bad food, crude quarters, and crowded conditions created severe health problems. At the end of the second month of service, an anonymous soldier, writing in the *Lynchburg Virginian,* observed that many in his regiment, the Home Guard, had already been debilitated by sickness, especially dysentery. Even officers, who were able to import many of the amenities of home life to the battle front, were not immune. After eighteen months in the service, thanks perhaps to his custom-made stove and regular foodstuffs from home, Blackford recounted with considerable pride that he had been absent with illness only thirteen weeks, 16 percent of the time. As the war continued, problems of disease lessened slightly; nevertheless, by the end of the war, 36 percent of all fatalities within Lynchburg companies were attributed to disease.[8]

Soldiers were also frustrated by the sheer tedium of camp life. Because confrontations with the enemy were few during the first year of the war, soldiers were forced to stay in their camps for days on end, waiting for the moment of battle, when they would finally get a chance to display their courage. As they bided their time, soldiers often felt as if they were going to waste. Just three months after mustering into service, a soldier complained that "we are waiting!—waiting patiently as we can for whatever the fortunes of war may have in reserve for us. . . . Days have passed—weeks have passed, and months have passed and yet we are in undisturbed occupation of the vacated premises." For some, the tedium of camp life was torture. In letter after letter, Charles Blackford told his wife, Susan, that he was becoming increasingly depressed. Anxious about battle and wanting to return to his family, he found himself "spending hour after hour in the spirit of a martyr." Ever fearful of what might happen, Blackford told his wife that he would rather be an enlisted man, figuring that they at least had the daily routines of picket duty and defense preparations to keep them occupied and out of trouble.[9]

The common soldier felt otherwise. Most believed there was little that was enviable about their status. During his regiment's stay near Norfolk in 1861, Moorman remembered that they had nothing to do to break up the "monotonous strain of camp-life" but drill twice a day, giving them the dubious distinction of becoming "very expert . . . in a very short time." Soldiers detested picket duty even more. Alone or in small groups, soldiers were commanded to stand watch for up to twelve hours at a time. Unable to make even a crude shelter, for fear any disruption of the landscape might make the enemy suspicious, pickets were often left unprotected from the elements. John Henry believed picket duty to be the most "harassing to the soldier" of all the "duties of the camp." On one "unpleasant and disagreeable" night, Henry recalled, he was ordered to stand in the rain until daybreak in "water and mud a foot deep." He confessed that it was all he could do to remember that he "was a Virginian, fighting for his . . . fireside." Picket duty could be as dangerous as it was uncomfortable. Alone in the black of night, soldiers were vulnerable to attack from both Yankee and Confederate scouting parties. In the Second Virginia Cavalry, officers were so afraid pickets might mistakenly shoot one of their own that they prohibited them from using their weapons for anything but self-defense. Although officers hoped the edict would spare lives, it had just the opposite effect, because it left Confederate soldiers virtually defenseless against Yankee attacks. For this reason, Charles Blackford condemned picket duty as a "barbarous custom."[10]

As bad as the privations of camp life were, soldiers were even more disturbed by the behavior of many of their officers. Before the war, lower-class citizens had rarely had to test the bonds of deference and paternalism. From the perspective of lower-class whites, customary patterns of social relations had worked well enough, because elites generally came through when their benevolence was needed but otherwise had the good sense to leave the lower classes alone. Now, as soldiers, lower-class whites realized that the behaviors and decisions of their leaders had a much greater impact on their lives than previously. If only for the sake of survival, soldiers carefully observed and evaluated how their officers conducted themselves. Especially in the early goings, they did not always like what they saw.[11]

More often than not, soldiers found that their officers fell short of what they expected of military leaders. Soldiers were especially critical of officers who used their authority to abuse their men, physically and psychologically. One morning, Henry and a few of his cohorts reported late for the company drill. The commanding officer, Captain George

Latham, a prominent lawyer from Lynchburg, decided to make an example of them by putting them in the guardhouse. Henry was indignant, complaining that he had been sick with an "irritation of the bowels and dysentery," caused by eating bad meat. He denounced the sentence as unfair and unwarranted, since he had proved his loyalty by "meeting the enemy everywhere he had shown himself." The whole episode was, in his words, "humiliating" and a reminder of the "hardships a man has to undergo when he volunteers to fight for his country." In rare instances, soldiers took a more direct approach against abusive officers. Charles Blackford told his wife that one of his soldiers nearly beat up a fellow officer. According to Blackford, the officer provoked the soldier by verbally abusing him and his mates. In response, the soldier told the officer "that if he did not take what he had said and beg his pardon for cursing him he would give him a thrashing on the spot." The officer promptly apologized. Blackford, who professed to be an enlisted man's officer, praised the soldier for his resolve.[12]

Soldiers also complained that their officers rudely ignored the sufferings of their men even as they enjoyed the privileges of rank. In January 1863, "a citizen," writing as a "friend of the soldiers of the 11th regiment," complained that many soldiers went without overcoats, tents, and blankets because "none of the officers who are here on furlough will take the trouble to procure the items from the commandant." About the same time, Samuel Oakey, a tailor from Lynchburg serving in the Home Guard, warned his family that he would not be able to give them much support because his commanding officer, Kirkwood Otey, had not seen fit to pay him for some time. Nor did Oakey think he was "likely to get it soon." By late 1864, Button reported that a soldier had confessed to him that he and his fellows had not been paid for eight months. Like most of his class, the soldier blamed the officer for the mistake.[13]

Soldiers were also critical of officers who, to enhance their military reputations and military career needlessly endangered soldiers' lives. Precisely because they believed they sacrificed so much, soldiers had little patience for any who abused and exploited their courage and patriotism. Invariably, soldiers complained that while they were willing to fight for the cause, they were not willing to risk their lives simply to indulge the whims and poorly conceived plans of untested officers.

John Henry was as willing as most to engage the enemy in battle. After his first experience in combat, a small skirmish at Manassas, he proudly recorded in his journal that he and his regiment had conducted themselves as seasoned veterans. Upon hearing the call to arms, "the men exhibited no signs of excitement, but coolly and calmly took their arms" and fell in with the regiment, faithfully following their officers' every command. Within a few months, however, Henry bitterly complained that his officers risked his life too readily with ill-conceived strategies. He was especially mortified by his officers' behavior at Blackburn's Ford, the first military engagement of the war. First, his commanding officer ordered the regiment to wear colored arm bands, so that they could distinguish themselves from the enemy—a sure sign that the impending battle had not been well orchestrated. Still later, the same officer commanded Henry's unit to act as advance scouts in an open area infested with Yankees. Much to Henry's relief, the plan was not executed. "And it was well for our company, at least, that it never was," Henry observed, for they would have been "overpowered at once." Although such second-guessing was most prevalent early in the war, some soldiers retained a healthy suspicion of the motives of their officers. At the Battle of Drewry's Bluff in May 1864, General Archibald Gracie ordered the Eleventh Virginia Infantry to replace a regiment that had run away from the fight. Before being compelled to go, some soldiers protested that it was a foolhardy mission, because no other regiment had been able to hold the ground.[14]

At bottom, many soldiers suspected that some of their officers had significant character flaws that undermined their ability to be effective military leaders. During the first year of the war, soldiers came to suspect that many of their officers were unfit for command. And indeed, some were—though not necessarily the ones whom soldiers suspected. Before he proved himself in battle, many suspected that Sam Garland, commander of the elite Home Guard, would not cut it as an officer, because he seemed to be too much the scholar. Privately and publicly, they voiced a preference for Captain Maurice Langhorne to lead them. After a few battles, however, soldiers realized they had been wrong about both men. While Garland proved his valor under fire, Langhorne proved to be indecisive and vain. In time, soldiers began to assert that they did not want to serve under Langhorne. Eventually, their protests forced Langhorne to retire from the field. Other homegrown officers faced a similar fate. At Manassas, Captain James Blankenship of the Lynchburg Rifles, a Virginia Military Institute graduate and the former military instructor at Lynchburg College, behaved so poorly that he lost the confidence of his men—most of whom had been his former students. He, too, was forced

General Samuel Garland, Jr., circa 1862. Garland was a prominent Lynchburg lawyer and politician who also won distinction in battle. He was mortally wounded while rallying his men to charge at South Mountain during the Antietam campaign. (LMS)

to resign. Colonel Christopher Winfree, a Lynchburg tobacconist, was the focus of rumors of cowardice after Bull Run. Although he tried to defend himself in the press, he left the military before the end of the first year.[15]

In addition, many soldiers questioned the morality of their officers. They knew that while waiting for battle, many of their officers engaged in what Charles Blackford disdainfully called "drinking and whoring." Soldiers, many of whom came from evangelical churches, which condemned such licentious behavior, quickly sent word home that some of their officers endangered the purity of the cause and were thus unfit for military duty. Even those soldiers who were no more pure than their officers criticized their superiors' behavior as dangerous and irresponsible, given their leadership roles. More than once, soldiers complained that the iniquitous behavior of an officer had lost a battle or undermined and corrupted the morale of those under him.[16]

Occasionally, isolated complaints turned into angry denunciations against all officers. In November 1863, soldiers recuperating at Lynchburg hospitals were ordered to board trains to Salem, Virginia, to help that town protect itself from a rumored federal invasion. The train ride took more than twelve hours, during which time the soldiers—many of them still quite ill—were forced to ride in open boxcars, exposed to the cold night air, without benefit of fire to keep them warm. Enraged, "a convalescent" exposed the inhumanity of the episode in a letter to the *Lynchburg Virginian*, saving his harshest criticisms for the officers who ordered them out:

> Even though it may seem puerile, we must hold up to public rebuke the disrespectful and unfeeling conduct of some of the barred officials who accompanied us—their disregard of the complaints of the sick; the abusive, nay, scurrilous epithets applied to men whose social position, moral and intellectual worth would compare most favorably with that of these pampered youths for whom parental influence or some propitious gale of fortune, and not personal merit, secured positions of responsibility. They could see nothing worthy of admiration in the self sacrificing patriotism of men whose best energies have been devoted to our glorious cause.... Their tattered, worn out garments, their shoeless feet, and emaciated features excited not the generous sympathy and respectful consideration to which they were so richly entitled.[17]

Soldiers rarely confined their complaints about officers to the camp. To hasten reform and get a bit of revenge, soldiers learned to broadcast their complaints and accusations to anyone who would listen. Civic leaders were an especially receptive audience. Eager to retain the support of their volunteers, and concerned about the moral purity of the cause, elites often broke class ranks to champion the soldiers. Button was an especially effective and loyal advocate for the soldiers. Perhaps to soothe his conscience for not fighting, or perhaps to exhibit his commitment to paternalism, Button quickly established himself as the soldiers' advocate. In his local column, Button usually took the soldiers' side in camp disputes and regularly chastised military leaders for not taking better care of their hapless enlisted men. When soldiers complained that many of their officers were drunks, Button, a leader in the local Sons of Temperance, lectured the guilty officers, informing them that their insobriety endangered their men and reflected poorly on the "model army" the community had tried to create. In another instance, Button took several unnamed local officers to task for treating their enlisted men as "hireling soldiers" and for acting as "martinets." Since it served his purposes, the conservative Button even gave voice to the soldiers' republican ideals, asking the accused officers, "What right has a man who but a few short months ago was a plain civilian . . . to be so puffed up with a little temporary distinction and command as to sport with the sensibilities of men who are his equals if not superiors in everything but office? . . . The poor soldiers endure hardships and privations enough." If this rebuke was not sufficient, Button gently reminded the guilty officers that "all these unwarranted rigors will operate most seriously to the detriment of the service when it shall be necessary to call for more troops to replenish the ranks."[18]

The dual onslaught from citizens and soldiers placed military officers from Lynchburg in a precarious position. On the one hand, many officers resented the constant scrutiny and character assassinations from people who they believed were largely below their stature. On the other hand, most had entered the military to enhance their reputations and to validate their stature in the community back home. As a result, they felt they desperately needed the approval of their men. With little experience or training in the art of military leadership, most officers tried to retain both stature and popularity by relying on the familiar ethic of paternalism. Although most officers expected to earn their men's respect through demonstrations of military leadership and acts of courage, soldiers quickly learned to press the advantage by demanding that officers provide more tangible rewards for their allegiance. Faced with the prospect of losing face among their peers, in camp and at home, many officers complied and, in doing so, stretched the limits of their paternalistic ethos to accommodate their soldiers. Charles Blackford's experience as an officer suggests just how far some were willing to go.[19]

Like many of Lynchburg's well-connected young men, Blackford entered the military as an officer, the first lieutenant of a locally raised cavalry unit. With no formal military training, Charles learned the art of command by observing his superiors. In letter after letter to his wife, Charles explored the reasons that some officers failed and others—namely, himself—succeeded. In his chronicles, he created an informal manual on the art of military leadership for the Confederate Civil War officer.

Surprisingly, Charles seemed to learn the most by observing the least popular officers. Charles was especially critical of his own commanding officer, Captain John Langhorne, Lynchburg's most prosperous miller and scion of one of Lynchburg's wealthiest tobacco manufacturing families. Very early on, Charles assessed the measure of the man. In the late spring of 1861, he wrote his wife that "our captain is entirely incompetent . . . and he never can be made any better." Evidently, the enlisted men agreed with Blackford's assessment. Blackford predicted that because "they have no confidence" in Langhorne, most "will disgrace themselves" at the first sign of battle "by running and I will not blame them for it." A few weeks, later Charles repeated this observation, noting this time that "there are only 5 men in the camp who will not sign a petition to remove him and they are his relatives." Yet even they "feel no hesitation" to criticize him.[20]

Charles believed Langhorne's failure to win the respect of his men stemmed from two crucial shortcomings—Langhorne failed to take better care of them, and he was immoral. According to Charles, if Langhorne had been more considerate of his men, they might have forgiven him his lack of experience as a commander. Instead, Langhorne remained aloof from them. Like some others of his rank, Langhorne demonstrated "an utter disregard of the feelings of the officers and the welfare of the men," treating them more like "slaves" than like enlisted men. Symptomatic of Langhorne's failings, he often failed to order the necessary supplies, so that "more than once" his regiment had "been on the eve of starvation." Yet instead of admitting his mistakes, Langhorne "made up for his deficiencies as an officer by the violence of his profanity and the amount of whiskey he drinks." This made him appear even more incompetent. In one of his more wicked deeds, Langhorne arrested a hapless soldier for drunkenness, then proceeded to abuse and embarrass him in front of his regiment by tying his hands, gagging his mouth, "and actually making thrusts at him with a bayonet." To Charles and the rest of the company, Langhorne's behavior was not only unwarranted but was hypocritical, and, it endangered the South's cause. Like many engaged in the war, Lynchburg soldiers believed that God would use the war to bless the virtuous and punish the wicked. To ensure victory, the Civil War generation believed that civilians, soldiers, and officers must be morally vigilant. But Langhorne was a drunk. From Blackford's perspective, there was no room for such a man in the Confederate army.[21]

With considerable pride, Charles contrasted his popularity with that of Langhorne. According to Charles, the men under his charge loved him as much as they hated Langhorne. *"Without exception,"* he told his wife, his men had shown him "nothing but *kindness*" and devotion. When passing by his pickets one day, a soldier warned him to be careful lest "Lincoln's men would take me." In response, another replied, "If they take him, he will be retaken or the Wise Troop will die in the attempt." Obviously pleased, Charles noted that "there was an earnestness about the manner of saying it that satisfied me highly."[22]

Although the soldiers were probably genuine in their praise of Blackford, their obvious effort to make their affections public suggests that they had ulterior motives. By proclaiming their preference for one of Langhorne's subordinates, the enlisted men of the regiment may have been trying to shame Langhorne into resigning his commission. For this reason, they informed not only Blackford of their preference for him as a leader but anyone back in Lynchburg who would listen as well. According to Charles's wife, Susan, all her friends and acquaintances knew that Charles, not Langhorne, was the favorite among the troops. Indeed, it was such common knowledge in town that Charles Blackford would be the enlisted men's candidate for the next captain that the Langhorne family accused Charles of plotting Langhorne's demise.[23] Meanwhile, back in camp, Langhorne's soldiers became increasingly brazen in their efforts to defame Langhorne by exalting Blackford. One night, Charles returned to camp to find that the men had erected a sign proclaiming it "Camp Captain Blackford." Charles was moved but also distressed. He confided to Susan that he had "determined not to accept the captaincy" should it become available, believing that such a course would silence "those who are saying that I am at the bottom of the matter."[24]

Charles Blackford, circa 1880. (LMS)

A month later, however, Charles changed his mind. In August 1861, he accepted the captaincy after being elected by a unanimous vote. Yet in ascending to a higher office, Charles soon realized that it would be much more difficult to retain his popularity than it had been to gain it in the first place. Charles found that to stay in the good graces of his men, he had to attend to their needs constantly . After only a few months in his new office, he told his wife that a captain must be part "dry-nurse" to be successful. He was not exaggerating by much. To retain his popularity, he regularly shared a portion of his provisions with his men, kept a constant vigil over the sick and wounded, and instructed his wife to do the same with those who had been sent home. As the winter of 1862 approached, he purchased new blankets for all of the thirty or so soldiers under his direct supervision. When on leave, he spent much of his time visiting sick or wounded soldiers, procuring supplies at his own expense, and checking in on the families of his men. In addition, he occasionally suspended military discipline to win the favor of his troops. When his men complained that they were worked too hard, he pleaded with his commanding officer to lessen his demands. Understanding that his soldiers hated and feared picket duty, he tacitly allowed them to barter with their Yankee counterparts and to visit their camp, figuring that "it was better that this sort of thing should exist than that the pickets should be constantly firing at each other." When soldiers were AWOL—especially those who simply returned late from an approved leave—Charles often refused to arrest them himself, though he sometimes encouraged his commanding officer to do so. Finally, Charles recognized the limits of his own authority, professing a commitment to lead by example, knowing that his men would not follow him if he tried to intimidate them. For this reason, he was particularly solicitous of his noncommissioned officers, observing that because they knew they had his "love and confidence . . . we work together like a band of brothers."[25]

Initially, Charles thrived in his new position, openly boasting that he had won his company's loyalty through his intuitive leadership abilities. Yet within a few months, Charles began to take a much different view of command. Though his popularity never declined, he began to long for what he termed a "more independent position." After only four months as captain, he told his wife that he could no longer "stand the responsibility of command" because he lacked the physical makeup. "I am too sensitive and nervous," he confessed to his wife; "it wears me out body and soul." Specifically, he had grown tired of the daily ordeal of caring for his regiment. On the one hand, he was "subjected to all the whims and caprices of so many ranking officers in the regiment." On the other hand, he was forever preoccupied with "all the annoyances of a company dependent upon me for everything." To console himself, he fantasized that he could retire his rank and become a private, believing that it would be a "great relief to have all the responsibility resting on the commanding officer instead of myself." Instead, Charles enlisted the assistance of his father to gain an "independent" commission. After nearly twelve months of waiting, Charles got the escape he craved—an appointment on General James Longstreet's staff. No longer would he be burdened by the demands of office.[26]

Meanwhile, Langhorne continued to have problems. For two months, he stoically remained with his company. Although he considered resigning, he delayed doing so because he feared he would be even more humiliated if he returned home without a commission. Yet as a discredited officer, he was virtually useless to his regiment. He soon alienated his commanding officer, Major Richard Radford, who tried to court-martial him to induce him to resign. The scheme worked. In November 1861, just a few weeks after he was threatened with court-martial and four months after he lost his unit, Langhorne left the military and returned to Lynchburg. Two of Langhorne's relatives followed close behind. During the early stages of John Langhorne's troubles, Sergeant Marion Langhorne encountered difficulties with his men and decided to transfer to another position. Later, William Langhorne, also a sergeant in the company, tried to escape service in a more deceptive manner. Under the pretense of poor eyesight, he resigned his commission. Blackford, for one, could not hide his disgust. Labeling William's medical discharge a sham, he wondered how this Langhorne would face the shame of his fraud back home.[27]

Regardless of what awaited the Langhornes when they returned home, Lynchburg soldiers had accomplished what they intended. By their actions, they forced three officers to resign or leave and compelled another, Blackford, to comply with their demands, to the point that he nearly wore himself out. The Langhorne-Blackford episode is symptomatic of how the early years of the war encouraged changes in class relations. First, Lynchburg's soldiers learned something about their strategic role in Lynchburg's social and political hierarchy during a time of crisis. By casting off one leader for another, Lynchburg's soldiers did not simply take advantage of elites' dependence on them; they learned that the social hierarchy was now malleable. Second, they learned that they had greater ability to determine the content of their relationships with elites. Thus, when Langhorne attempted to act imperiously toward his men in order to display his status, the soldiers revolted, opting for a leader who was both more benevolent and more democratic in his leadership style.

Unfortunately for the soldiers, they soon found that they could go only so far in their efforts to lessen the hardships of war. No matter who was in command, they still had to live in unhealthy camps, fight the war with inadequate and inferior supplies, and receive poor compensation for their sacrifice. In time, soldiers learned that ultimate power usually rested at the top of the military hierarchy, not at the bottom. Often enough, soldiers gained indulgences from an immediate commander only to have them taken away by a higher-up.

In addition, many officers began to change their leadership strategies. As Charles Blackford learned through bitter experience, it was simply too difficult to be all things to all people. Over time, many officers determined that it was sometimes more important to win the respect of their superiors than it was to win the affection of their men. While marching toward the field of battle, Major Robert Withers of the Eighteenth Virginia Infantry noticed that three of his fellow officers were allowing fainthearted soldiers to leave their units so that they could avoid the anticipated battle. By the time the regiment arrived at the designated site, so many men had absented themselves that the commanding officer, General J.E.B. Stuart, had to abort the attack. Furious, Stuart had the three officers court-martialed. By his complaint, each was summarily dismissed from military service. A short time later, one of the three reenlisted and was promptly reelected to his old rank. By now, however, he was a changed man; Withers noted that he served the rest of the war without further incident.[28]

Slowly, officers worked to consolidate their power, concomitantly limiting the rights of soldiers. Regimental elections, initially tolerated by most officers as a way to gauge one's popularity, soon became anathema. Many officers grew tired of the constant electioneering that they were compelled to do to keep their companies. Others came to view regimental elections as an unwelcome intrusion of democracy in an institution that required order, regimentation, and hierarchy. William Blackford, Jr., Charles's older brother and an officer in Stuart's cavalry, complained that it was always the officers who "exerted themselves the most to establish discipline" who became unpopular with their men. Thus, Blackford noted, officers believed it was "better to keep with your men, whatever the consequences, if you don't want to be turned out some day." Eventually, this is what happened to William. Although he was one of Jeb Stuart's favorite officers, Blackford lost his regiment after a rival officer promised to give the unit indulgences that Blackford routinely denied them. Rather than lower himself to solicit votes, Blackford took a staff position with the Engineering Corps and, later, with Stuart. After 1862, the Confederate army gradually stopped conducting regimental elections largely because of the complaints by officers.[29]

Officers' quest to establish greater authority over their men received assistance from Confederate conscription laws. During the first year of the war, soldiers showed their displeasure with army life by simply leaving the military. Often this left many officers without companies or units to lead—an embarrassing fate for men accustomed to power. In early 1862, Robert Garlick Hill Kean noted that the first wave of volunteers had just about served the length of their enlistments. With so many about to leave the military, he wondered what some officers would do without men to lead. Kean predicted most would try to save face by "rushing to Richmond" for staff positions. In fact, officers worked hard to keep their men or to attract new ones. Many promised their soldiers long furloughs or special details for agreeing to stay with their old units. After conscription laws were passed in 1862, this changed. More and more soldiers found themselves in the military without the leverage of deciding the terms of their service.

In an indirect manner, conscription laws curtailed the power of enlisted men almost as much as they enhanced the power of officers. In early 1862, soldiers heard rumors that Confederate authorities were threatening to draft any soldier who did not reenlist with his unit when his tour of duty was up. Soldiers, most of whom had signed only one-year enlistments, were furious. In anger, James Old, a private in the Eleventh Virginia Artillery, threatened to desert, but he later thought better of it. Charles Phelps also complained that the new law created considerable consternation in his unit, the Beauregard Rifles. According to Phelps, most of the men hated their commanding officer, Marcellus Moorman, and wanted out. Yet they believed they had little choice but to reenlist under him.[30]

With these advantages, officers ushered in a new period of officer-soldier relations. After the first year of the war, officers began to pay greater attention to army discipline and less attention to gaining reelection. To demonstrate their new orientations, many officers physically withdrew from their troops and spent more time among their peers and superiors. In addition, many officers made it more difficult for soldiers to obtain leaves of absence and nonfighting details. Perhaps most important, officers became much less forgiving of soldiers who disobeyed orders. Freed from the democratic excesses of the Confederacy's original military organization, some officers began to lead with a high-handed severity. During the final months of the war, William Blackford was reassigned to command a unit stationed in the entrenchments at Petersburg, Virginia. This time, he treated his men as he thought fit, without worrying about how they might respond. In charge of a regiment composed mostly of raw and reluctant conscripts, Blackford and his fellow officers commanded with a cold severity that they justified as necessary for the Confederacy's survival. According to Blackford, executions for desertion became a regular event in the trenches. Indeed, some officers buried the executed in the breastworks to remind soldiers of what might happen to them if they tried to escape. In one instance, an arrested soldier claimed he was no deserter but had just gone off to help himself to some buttermilk from a nearby farm. Although most of the officers believed the soldier's story, the colonel, deeming that "the discipline of the regiment required an example to be made of" him, had the man court-martialed, with the recommendation that he be shot.[31]

In many areas of the South, the new severity coupled with the old privations created considerable disaffection among soldiers and potential soldiers. In reaction, many poorer whites embarked on a war against the South itself. Economic hardship, oppressive state and local government officials, and unresponsive officers convinced many lower-class whites that the once-noble cause of the South had degenerated into "a rich man's war and a poor man's fight." In response, they began to resist military service. Some simply withdrew their support of the war. Others adopted more violent methods, most notably guerrilla warfare, bushwhacking, and social banditry. Regardless of method, the result was the same: by challenging the existing hierarchical system, poorer whites in many locales helped to destroy much of the Old South.[32]

During the last years of the war, Lynchburg soldiers became extremely divided in their view of the war. The most radical engaged in a clandestine war against the South. Late in the war, Confederate spies determined that the Heroes of America, a secret antiwar society that was vaguely Unionist in its stance, had made inroads into southwestern Virginia. Furthermore, they suspected that "Hero" operatives regularly traveled through Lynchburg. Although investigators found no evidence of the organization in Lynchburg, they believed that the organization existed in several nearby communities. In rare instances, disaffected soldiers took out their frustrations in random and less organized acts of collective violence and crime. In July 1864, a group of six deserters and a fugitive slave camped in the countryside of Lynchburg. For several weeks, they sustained themselves by raiding local residents. When a group of Lynchburg vigilantes discovered their camp, the two sides engaged in what Button described as a "regular battle," which the vigilantes eventually won.[33]

For the most part, disaffected Lynchburg soldiers acted individually, not collectively. Early on, some simply refused to reenlist. Unfortunately, Confederate recordkeepers did not always register the date of discharge; thus, it is difficult to determine just how many Lynchburg soldiers availed themselves of this choice.[34] Nevertheless, the overall exodus throughout the South was enough to encourage the Confederate government to enact conscription laws in 1862 and 1864. Within Lynchburg regiments, the steady depletion of the ranks caused considerable concern for those who remained. At the end of the first year of the war, William King, a high-ranking officer in a unit made up of many laboring men, the Lynchburg Artillery, expressed relief that a slim majority intended to reenlist—just enough to enable him to keep his commission. In October 1862, Charles Blackford told his wife that there were simply too many officers for the number of men in his regiment. By then, enlistment and recruitment had become such vexing problems that it was already standard practice for many commanding officers to spend a few months each year back in Lynchburg, trying to raise troops to fill their companies.[35]

As conscription laws effectively ended most soldiers' ability to retire from military service legally, some determined to do so illegally. Although Confederate records do not provide exact numbers, it seems clear that a sizable number of Lynchburg soldiers deserted during the war. Compared to some other regions of the South, however, the numbers from Lynchburg were relatively small. Although Confederate officers were not the best bookkeepers, the available evidence suggests that until the last months of the war, when defeat seemed certain, most soldiers remained with their units. Officers from Lynchburg's twelve local units recorded only twenty cases of desertion. In truth, the number may have been higher. According to the same source, another sixty-one, or 15 percent, disappeared from company rolls during the last year of the war. Although none of these was formally listed as a deserter, it is likely that many of them were.[36]

Soldiers abandoned the military for a variety of reasons. Contemporaries and some historians have explained desertion as an indication of the underlying Union sentiment among Southern laborers and poorer farmers. Although the argument is usually overstated, there is evidence that some of Lynchburg's deserters were less than loyal to the Southern cause.[37] William Henry Morgan recalled that one member of his regiment left because "he was a *nullius filus.*" Believing that "he had nothing to fight for" in the Confederacy, the soldier deserted to the Union army.[38]

Yet if some deserters intended to weaken the South's cause, the majority acted from other motives. Most were probably animated by the same concern that had once induced them to support Secession and the war—to defend family and neighborhood against a threatening foe. Especially as the economy worsened, as the number and scale of the South's defeats increased, and as the Yankees moved closer to Lynchburg, soldiers became less hopeful that their support could affect the outcome. Disillusioned more with the course of the war than with the cause, most held on until defeat seemed certain before returning home to protect their families and homes from possible invaders. In addition, many simply believed they had suffered long enough and were now entitled to go home. After all, most deserters were relatively poor. Of those who can be identified, two-thirds were laboring men and three-fourths held neither real nor personal estates.[39]

Writing from the Petersburg breastworks, William Allen, a farmer from the hinterland of Lynchburg, witnessed firsthand the disintegration of the Confederacy from desertion. Due to the grim living conditions of the breastworks—continuous fighting, constant brushes with death, confined and primitive quarters, and cruel officers—many soldiers simply burned out and decided to leave. According to Allen, most did so because they feared dying in the breastworks. By late March 1865, Allen's comrades understood that the Confederacy had no chance of winning. Those who deserted preferred to risk capture, court-martial, and a possible firing squad to waiting to be killed by mortar shells. For his part, Allen decided to remain, even though friends urged him to go with them. He stayed not because he still believed in the cause but because he feared being caught by his own side. Perhaps he should have decided otherwise. On March 26, 1865, Yankees opened fire on Allen's encampment. Allen was hit three times; he died instantly.[40]

Button, for one, understood that desertion was less an act of rebellion than an act of survival. In reaction to reports in late 1863 that the Confederate Congress had enacted a law that would impose the death penalty for desertion, Button suggested a more tolerant approach. While noting that the crime has always been regarded as "heinous," he cautioned that "we shall, if we look about us, see much to palliate it now." Button argued that many left the army simply to help their impoverished loved ones. He further suggested that if the Confederacy truly wanted to stop desertion, they should improve morale by raising soldiers' pay to a living wage. Whatever their reasons for leaving the military, Lynchburg's deserters contributed to what historian Paul Escott has termed the "quiet rebellion of the common people," which led to the eventual defeat of the Confederacy.[41]

Yet if soldier disillusionment eventually helped destroy the Confederacy, there were many who refused to waver in their allegiance during the war. Until the last months of the war, those who stayed to fight were adamant in their support of the cause. Even as they complained about hardships, countervailing forces often encouraged Lynchburg soldiers to remain loyal to their units, to their officers, and, ultimately, to the Confederacy. Although often frustrated by their experiences in the war and highly critical of many of their civic and military leaders, most Lynchburg soldiers did not reach the level of alienation and class animosity seen elsewhere. As their public petitions and private letters suggest, Lynchburg soldiers doggedly persevered in their allegiance to the Confederacy, even as they attacked some of their leaders. When angry, they plaintively reminded elites of their customary responsibilities to honor and protect those who sacrificed for them.

In hindsight, contemporaries realized that the large number of desertions contributed to the defeat of the Confederacy. At the time, however, the significance of the desertions was not always clear. Indeed, enough soldiers remained that some in the military were convinced Robert E. Lee's surrender was premature. William Blackford recalled years later that although desertions were "steadily weakening us," only "those in authority" were aware of how serious and widespread the problem was. "We in the army," Blackford noted, "had not the least idea of it." As far as Blackford could tell, those who stayed on were still willing to fight. Until the end, Blackford claimed he and his men looked "forward to beating the enemy . . . as a matter of course and we would have been bitterly opposed to any compromise."[42]

Given the dangers that soldiers in the Confederacy faced and the public's reluctance to stigmatize those who deserted, it is somewhat surprising that more did not leave, and did not leave sooner. Yet the crucible of war, even as it exposed class animosities, did not always embitter soldiers to their cause. Just as often, soldiers became more devoted to the fight and more dedicated to their brothers in arms. Consider how James Old, a landless farmer who lived just outside Lynchburg, responded to military service. Although Old joined his neighborhood regiment shortly after Fort Sumter, he soon regretted his decision. A month after being mustered into the Southern Guards, he instructed his brother John not to join up. Instead, he confessed that "if I was out of this I never wood join another." In subsequent letters, he explained to family members why his initial enthusiasm had waned. Although his letters were infrequent, the message was consistent. During his ten months of service, he often complained about the dangers of picket duty, the gruesome nature of the warfare, the capricious and arbitrary power of his commanding officers, and the lack of adequate food, clothing, and supplies. When he learned that the Confederate army might draft him when his enlistment was up, he declared that he had had enough. "I have not forgot how to walk," he informed his mother; "I will desert if they go that way." He further claimed that most of his comrades felt the same. If the Confederacy tried to draft them all, he predicted, "most of the army will fight against the south" or "go home."[43]

Instead of walking, however, Old stayed in the army. Over the next few months, he changed from a reluctant soldier to a dedicated supporter of the Confederate cause. A month after he informed his family that he might desert, the transformation began. When informed that his brother and a neighbor had been drafted, he admitted that he felt "sorry" for their families, but he advised them to look beyond personal hardships. "This war is going to bee a desperat one and A short one I think, and wee will Need all the men that we can get," he told his brother. Far from feeling like the victim of Confederate decision makers, Old took on a new identity—as a defender of kith and kin. If the Yankees won, Old asked, "what will become of ous and our homes and families they will bee Taken from ous." For Old, there was now only one alternative: "we aught to do all that wee can and fight them untill the last drop of blood has gorn."[44]

Old was not the only soldier whose dedication to the war increased over time. As the war continued, many soldiers found new reasons to fight—reasons that sometimes surmounted their fear that, as "poor whites," they were being abused as a class. Thomas Kelley, a mechanic, came from a neighborhood just outside Lynchburg, with its fair share of dissidents. His cousin Samuel Sublett lived in the same neighborhood and complained loud and often that this was a "rich man's war and a poor man's fight." Kelley himself was reluctant to fight for the cause; like many laborers, he waited until the threat of conscription before joining up. Yet once he had, his views of the war changed dramatically. As a common soldier in Lee's Army of Northern Virginia, Kelley experienced firsthand Ulysses S. Grant's war of attrition. Even as the fortunes of the Confederacy deteriorated, Kelley, much like Old, rallied to the cause. During the summer of 1864, Kelley excitedly reassured Samuel's wife, Martha, that no matter how strong the Yankees were, the South would prevail, "as long as there is as many brave Boys to defend it as there are here now especially while General Lee is here to lead us." As a sign of confidence, Kelley predicted that the end was near: "you will Soon hear of old Yankee Grants Army being completely whiped and again driven a cross the Potomac. then old Abe will be thrown out as soon as his time expires . . . and a peace candidate will be elected. . . . this will give us independance."[45]

Even in defeat, many soldiers remained committed to the cause, although not necessarily to the fight. During his travels through the South immediately after the war, John Dennett struck up a conversation with a soldier from Lynchburg. According to Dennett, the soldier was ready to surrender in April 1865, because he had lost the desire "to shoot at anybody or be shot at by anybody anymore." He further claimed that if they had another war, "they would have to burn the woods and sift the ashes before they'd find him in it." "The South was sick of fighting and the North was too strong," he freely admitted, so "yes, he was willing to acknowledge himself beaten for good and all." Nevertheless, he remained unrepentant and unreconstructed. He told Dennett that if there were a foreign war, most Confederates would "join Maximilian" rather than fight for the United States. As for him, he wanted to escape "Yankeedom" by going to Brazil but couldn't afford to, because he had only six dollars in his pocket.[46]

Lynchburg soldiers' dedication to the cause can be traced to a number of factors. In Kelley's case, it probably helped that at the time he wrote his parents, his regiment was doing fairly well, having just defeated Grant at Cold Harbor in one of the bloodiest battles of the war. Kelley bragged that "so far we have whiped the Yanks in every engagement and you never Saw Such a Slaughter in all your life as that of the Yankees."[47] Even so,

Kelley often pondered defeat. Like most of his compatriots, he had few illusions about what it would mean. After a few years of fighting, Lynchburg soldiers had seen firsthand what they believed to be Yankee depredations. This, perhaps more than anything else, convinced Kelley that the South must persevere. In describing Yankee atrocities to his family, Kelley admitted that "it is so bad I am ashamed to write it to my own people ... if you are a good hand at guessing you will no doubt know what I mean." Yet having disclosed this much, Kelley could not resist some vague descriptions: "I could tell you of deprivations committed on Young Ladies in this part by the Yankees both black and white that would bring tears out of your eyes ... they are certainly worse than broots ever was I am told that they practis Such every where they go more or less. Such people should not prosper."[48]

Whether Kelley's observations about Yankee barbarities were true or not, a number of soldiers also believed the worst of the Yankee invaders. Lewis Blackford, another of Charles's brothers who served in the Confederate army, wrote his father of the "horrible barbarities of the Federals." According to Lewis, the Yankees treated all Southerners like slaves. Unwilling to employ a commissary, "they live off the citizens: killing their cattle and poultry, insulting the women, hunting down the men like wild beasts." John Henry, who complained loudly and often about abusive officers, stayed in the war in part because he believed Yankees meant to subjugate the South. Calling his enemies "murderers, assassins, and robbers," Henry charged that the "accursed scoundrels" carried "large quantities of handcuffs ... doubtless intended to be put upon their victims."[49]

If the stories were not enough, late in the war Lynchburg soldiers and citizens experienced firsthand what might happen to their community if they did not persevere. On June 18, 1864, the federal army attacked the city. Although Confederate forces drove off the Yankees later that day, the short-lived battle confirmed white Lynchburg's worst fears of what Yankee victory would mean. As the federals retreated, they looted and burned several homes in the surrounding countryside, terrorizing the white citizens and liberating the slaves. As Button summarized, "They sacked houses and destroyed furniture, not sparing even the poorest people. In short, their object seemed to be to destroy all they could."[50]

Knowledge of such abuses convinced Southern soldiers that theirs was the righteous cause. Early on, John Henry admitted that although the North possessed superior numbers, "upon our side [are] the prayers of a nation, young in years, but strong in a righteous cause, and dependent to

Heaven for the success of our army." By his thinking, Confederate soldiers were the "Sons of the Virginians of '76." Some time later, Kelley made a similar argument. Late in the war, he assured his family that even though the Yankees had shown they would stop at nothing to destroy the South, Southern virtue would eventually prevail, for "Christ says he that holdeth out faithful to the End Shall be Saved."[51]

Yet those who endured the war until the end were not just dedicated to the destruction of the enemy; they were also dedicated to one another. Those who stayed to fight developed a singular allegiance to the men in their regiments. In assuring his family that victory was near, Kelley made special mention of the heroism of his unit, the "brave boys" who had faithfully defended the South. Others agreed. Indeed, those who stayed often felt personally betrayed by those who decided to leave. During the autumn of 1864, Kelley reported that in his company of Lynchburg and Campbell County soldiers, almost one-half were presently absent, leaving a heavy burden for those who stayed behind: "the remainder of us have as much duty as we can perform, one picket every third night and on duty in the trenches between picket tours." Walter Henderson's company faced similar difficulties. In late 1864, he cautioned his wife that the perfidy of some endangered the lives of the faithful. "The men who dodge . . . are sent home on furloughs," he observed, while "those that have done their duty are required to be sacrificed."[52]

For many Lynchburg soldiers, allegiance to their unit often meant allegiance to their officers. Although soldiers were quick to condemn incompetent officers, they were devoted to those who proved their worth. As historian Reid Mitchell has observed, Confederate veterans' idolization of their generals began during the war, when, as soldiers, they developed unswerving loyalties to those officers who led without pretense and who willingly suffered along with their men. Even as they tried to drum out incompetents and to stretch the boundaries of paternalism to gain the advantage, soldiers never completely abandoned the customs of deference. John Henry, for one, demonstrated complete loyalty to those who proved themselves in word and deed. When General Pierre Gustave Toutant Beauregard, the hero of Fort Sumter, assumed command of all the forces stationed at Manassas, Henry claimed that the men almost instinctively fell under his control, because they sensed "the utmost confidence in his ability and military capacity." Henry was equally devoted to the first commander of his regiment, the "beloved" Major Carter H. Harrison. When Harrison died at Bull Run, Henry lamented that it "sent a gloom over the entire regiment." No doubt, military life encouraged soldiers to look to traditional leaders first. Stated baldly, the military's hierarchical power structure, its regimentation of life, and its physical separation from civilian society offered soldiers limited access to alternative value systems. As a result, military life often encouraged soldiers to be conservative in orientation.[53]

To many soldiers, faithful officers, as the leaders of the cause, came to personify the persevering spirit of all the troops. Thus, Kelley told his family that as long as "General Lee is here to lead us," victory was certain. Others also looked to their officers for courage and fortitude. While General James Longstreet convalesced in Lynchburg after being wounded at Seven Pines, soldiers stationed in Lynchburg pestered the nurses for news about his health. When word came that he would recover, they cheered.[54]

Ultimately, such devotion translated into action. During General George E. Pickett's charge at Gettysburg, soldiers in the Eleventh Virginia Infantry followed a succession of officers as, one by one, they fell by the wayside. Only one other Confederate regiment lost more men at Gettysburg. At Drewry's Bluff, William Morgan and his men obediently followed Colonel R. F. Maury toward the enemy, even though the force of enemy fire felt like "a heavy storm of wind and rain" that forced them to lean forward, as if moving through it "required great physical exertion." When the battle was over, Morgan credited the commanding officer, General Archibald Gracie, with enjoining them to go forward despite their protests that the mission was suicidal. Even in the chaotic last days of battle, soldiers retained an allegiance to certain officers. In April 1865, as rumors swirled through town that the Yankees were about to invade Lynchburg, many detailed and wounded soldiers decided to return to Lee's army. According to one of the town's military doctors, their desperation to be with Lee was a singularly "melancholy occurrence," but "it was the place they seemed to think of all others, as they had been accustomed to think the safest."[55]

For many soldiers and officers, shared experiences often created shared ideals. Most officers detested Yankees every bit as much as their soldiers did. Forty years after the war, Morgan still claimed that Yankees took delight in abusing citizens, the wounded, and prisoners of war. By his view, "the average Yankee has a very poor conception of what is right and honorable" and could not understand those who did. Charles Blackford was so convinced of Northerners' moral failings that he believed Yankees

Christopher Silas Booth was a student at Lynchburg College when Virginia seceded. He immediately joined the illustrious Home Guard. The photo captures his youthful resolve and enthusiasm for war. (Privately owned by Louis Booth, Lynchburg, Virginia; used by permission)

deserved any punishment that came their way. In a letter to his infant daughter Nannie, Blackford described a "most remarkable thing" while touring the carnage of a recent battle—the sight of a dead Yankee and his faithful dog, starving at his feet. For a brief moment, Blackford allowed himself to pity the man and his family, telling his daughter, "Perhaps far away in the north his little children still hope for their father and picture . . . the pleasures with which they will welcome him home and how they will come and play with that faithful dog—War is a sad thing!" In the next moment, however, Blackford regained his composure and instructed his daughter not to sympathize with the dead Yankee. "The wretch had . . . come down here to murder you and Mama and all of us and burn our houses," Blackford reminded her. "I am glad he was killed and as long as they stay here we must be glad when any of them die—the more of them the better." Charles's brother William hated the enemy so much that he encouraged his men to plunder their camps and homes whenever it was expedient to do so. After Lee's surrender, Thomas Munford, a brigadier general and a Lynchburg native, urged his men to continue the fight, reminding them that the Yankees still meant to make them slaves, despite their overtures of peace and reconciliation. If the South were to submit now, Munford warned, the Yankees would "rivet the chains they have been making such gigantic efforts to forge" and would "surely make us wear [them] forever." [56]

Soldiers and officers often agreed on who their internal enemies were as well. Though soldiers and officers remained contentious throughout the war, they found common cause in their desire to rid the military of incompetents. Consider, for instance, the fate of Jack Alexander, a lieutenant in the Second Virginia Cavalry and one of Charles Blackford's closest friends. A wealthy farmer and tobacconist, Alexander went to war for the fame and adoration but wanted nothing to do with "the rules of military life." Instead, he chose to rely on "his wit and good fellowship" to lead his men. His convivial style worked during the early days of the war. Indeed, after only a month of service, soldiers of the Second Virginia Cavalry elected him second lieutenant. In a short while, however, his fellow officers began to question his military soundness. On one occasion, he was sent to Leesburg, Virginia, for some special duty. "Finding it a very charming place to be stationed," Charles Blackford reported to his wife, "he determined to stay there." When Alexander's immediate commander, Colonel Richard Radford, ordered him to come back, he refused. Finally, General Beauregard commanded Alexander to return with his regiment. Not wishing to have his men leave Leesburg, Alexander returned alone. Perhaps to remind Beauregard that he, too, was a man of some stature, he came to his appointment dressed in an "elegant suit of black velvet, with ruffled shirt and fancy-topped boots in a handsome carriage drawn by two handsome black stallions." According to Blackford, he looked more like "the Prince of Wales . . . on a visit" than a military officer. Although his soldiers and some of his peers were amused, Beauregard was furious. He refused to see Alexander and ordered him to return within forty-eight hours with his men or face a court-martial. Alexander complied, but it was probably too late to salvage his military career. By now, most professional officers wanted nothing to do with him. A year after the Leesburg incident, he tried to advance in rank, but Jeb Stuart intervened, showing the War Department papers that he hoped would be "a perpetual bar to his promotion." In time, soldiers became disenchanted with Alexander as well. Although they appreciated his gregarious nature, most understood that because of his poor judgment, he was not the sort of officer they wanted to follow into battle. In early 1863, Alexander's company asked his superiors to relieve him of command.[57]

Soldiers and officers also came together to condemn those who refused to make greater sacrifices for the cause. Officers especially endeared themselves to their men when they joined with them in a public rebuke of soldiers and civilians who did not do their share in the field. Late in the war, Charles Blackford served with a regiment detailed to defend Richmond. As they passed a regiment that had so far stayed clear of battle, they mocked the unit for their clean clothes, neat homes, and small gardens, shouting, "You stay there boys, and make onions for us. We'll do the fighting for you and won't let you get hurt."[58]

Soldiers and officers often extended their criticisms to include wealthy civilians who tried to use their stature to escape the hardships and dangers of war. Soldiers were the first to raise doubts about the priorities of wealthy noncombatants. Even in the early months of the war, many of Lynchburg's soldiers believed that the war would eventually become a poor man's fight, because the wealthy would rely on kith and kin to escape military duty. Samuel Sublett, for one, believed this from the start. According to Sublett, examining doctors were especially suspect, because they were all "quite partial to wards the rich" while "a poor man did not stand any chance." Sublett claimed that doctors "would not let them off on no circumstances," because "the poor people hav got the fighting to do" while "the rich can take their pleasure."[59]

As the war continued, soldiers' criticisms of wealthy civilians became more vociferous. Increasingly, soldiers accused prominent civilians of profiting from the troops' sufferings. Soldiers were especially critical of merchants and "speculators," individuals who hoarded scarce items to sell at inflated prices. Some demanded that these "gougers" and "extortionists" be made to atone for their disloyalty by paying a special tax on the profits they made during the war. Others suggested that the Confederate Congress institute price-fixing. In a letter to the *Virginian*, "a soldier" argued that unless Congress regulated prices, soldiers and their families would be made "slaves" to the rich "in every sense of the term." Citing a letter written toward the same purpose and published in a Richmond paper, the soldier further argued that these unpatriotic merchants were no better than "Yankees," traitors to the Confederate cause, conspiring to "starve the soldiers' families and laboring class in the Confederate States."[60]

Officers came to share their soldiers' hatred of civilians who profited without sacrifice. George Munford, an officer in the Second Virginia Cavalry, blamed extortionists and hoarders for destroying his unit. With prices so high on fuel, clothing, and horses, most of his men could not afford the necessary two mounts to stay in the cavalry. As a result, Munford bitterly observed, less than half his regiment was fit for service.[61]

Officers and soldiers shared other concerns. Both worried about the welfare of their families. Although most officers had greater financial resources than did their soldiers, many were strapped for cash during the war. Because of inflation and hoarding, many wives of military officers were forced to make sacrifices. By the middle of the war, Susan Blackford took in boarders to improve family finances. Later, the Blackfords sold their home, most of their furnishings, and a few of their slaves. With her husband's blessing, Susan boycotted many of their old merchant friends because they engaged in what the Blackfords considered to be war profiteering.[62]

Late in the war, as the Confederacy's fate became clear, many soldiers and officers came to believe that civilians were largely to blame for the South's reversal of fortune. Although soldiers rarely made specific accusations against civilians, their letters reveal a gnawing fear and growing resentment that they had been abandoned by those whose support they most needed. To N. E. Lucas, civilians became another obstacle to overcome, not a source of moral and material support. In a letter to one of his neighbors, Lucas stated that although he often experienced the "blues," he would never stop fighting, because "it will be ten times as hard for us who have whipped them so often to knuckle to them at last." Even though many civilians had abandoned them by "failing to support the army with food and clothing," Lucas promised that he and his brothers in arms would not surrender. Instead, they would "merely make themselves into daring reckless bands of guerrillas whose last hope it will be to sell their lives at a dear cost." Launcelot Blackford agreed. The youngest Blackford and the only one not to receive a commission, Launcelot knew firsthand what a soldier's life was like. When his sister Mary Isabella announced her plans to marry a young soldier, "Lanty" told her to "be sure to let Churchill's *regiment* appear on the card," because he "would not have it appear" that his sister "married any body but a soldier, particularly now." By his view, "men that ain't soldiers may be very well in their way," but he preferred "not to have any such in the family." Late in the war, an anonymous soldier, writing in the *Lynchburg Virginian*, was even more candid. The writer claimed that soldiers in his regiment "now, as of yore, have faith in the cause, and . . . have become greatly awakened to their condition" and the need for a complete victory against the hated Yankees. At the same time, however, the writer doubted that civilians were animated by the same spirit. If they were, the soldier contended, then "General Lee (God bless him) would, in three weeks, be reinforced by no less than 20,000 men." It was time, the writer continued, "for weak kneed public men" to put aside all doubts and all fears and "elevate themselves" to the "greatest task of the occasion." Unfortunately for the soldiers, few citizens came forward during the last months to accept the challenge.[63]

Officers joined soldiers in blaming civilians for undermining the Confederacy. Late in the war, Charles Blackford became especially critical of the Lynchburg press, claiming that local editors seemed to "take infinite delight in publishing everything to increase the depression and chill the enthusiasm of the army." While admitting that "our sky is dark," Charles argued that "the worst feature is that our people seem to be letting down" and appeared to have "gone into a fainting fit." After the war, Robert Withers bluntly suggested that the South lost the war because too many of the South's original Secessionists refused to fight. "It is not to be wondered at, that, as the war progressed and its privations, hardships, and dangers constantly increased," Withers observed, those who originally opposed Secession would eventually "become more and more dissatisfied" after seeing the bad example set by those who had wanted the war in the first place.[64]

In so many ways, Lynchburg soldiers' military experiences contributed to the fragmentation of society back home. Those who left the army before the end of the war demonstrated that they were alienated by both the substance and the style of Lynchburg social relations. Not only did they believe that the cause was not worth the hardships and the risks, but they left the military disenchanted with the town's traditional leaders, whom they saw as weak, arrogant, and petty.

Those who stayed in the army had a more ambivalent reaction to the war. On the one hand, prolonged military service encouraged many soldiers to remain loyal to traditional leaders and to see themselves as the true defenders of the community. On the other hand, many soldiers and officers began to identify more closely with the profession-based community of the military than with the geography-based community of Lynchburg. As they did, they became critical of some of their friends and neighbors back home. By the end of the war, many openly condemned civilians for refusing to make greater sacrifices, while a few hinted that the stay-at-homes were largely responsible for the army's defeat. It remained to be seen how the faithful would get along with civilians when these soldiers and officers returned from the war.

The War in Lynchburg

The war proved to be a far different experience for civilians from that for soldiers. Civilians often had a less personal stake in the war, experienced the war in a more heterogeneous community, and had a greater range of personal freedoms than did enlisted men. Although most Lynchburg residents remained loyal to the Confederacy and dedicated to the traditions and customs of their society, the war created disputes that civic leaders and civilians were hard pressed to resolve during the war itself. As a result, the process of social fragmentation took a far more profound course in town than it did in the military.

The first months of the war offered little indication of the chaos and disorder that was to come. Publicly and privately, civilians congratulated themselves for doing their part for the war effort. Indeed, initial enthusiasm for the war was so high that Charles Button's chief concern was that the town might have sacrificed too much for the cause. Because Lynchburg had provided a disproportionate share of men, provisions, and money to the Confederacy, Button feared the town might exhaust its resources or be unable to defend itself against a Yankee invasion.[1]

To publicize the town's united commitment to the war, the daily newspapers regularly announced the charitable and patriotic efforts of its citizens. The Ladies' Relief Society, organized in May 1861, provided uniforms for poorer regiments, offered refreshments to soldiers as they traveled through town, and organized donations for Lynchburg soldiers and their families. By January 1862, the Society reported that it had provided 1,789 coats, 2,195 pairs of pants, 1,454 shirts, 493 pairs of drawers, 523 pairs of gaiters, 1,175 cartridge boxes, sixty-six beds, ten overcoats, "several hundred" haversacks, canteens, "whole sums of uniforms and hats trimmed and altered, and a large amount of work taken in from day to day for soldiers passing through our city." In the fall of 1861, a handful of women from the Ladies' Society dramatically expanded their field of service by establishing the Ladies' Relief Hospital for wounded soldiers. Although it was the smallest hospital in town, it became one of the largest volunteer-staffed hospitals in the Confederacy. Assuming the role of matrons, Lynchburg's most prominent women supervised a legion of hired nurses, whose salaries they paid through charitable subscriptions. Legitimizing their activities as the natural outgrowth of their maternal instincts, the Ladies provided amenities to sick and wounded soldiers. While other hospitals rarely had the time or the inclination to care for soldiers' individual needs, the women of the Ladies' Relief Hospital brought flowers to their patients, chatted with them, read to them, wrote letters for them, served them buttermilk and delicacies from their own tables, and provided whatever moral support they could.[2]

Men also demonstrated their support for the Confederacy through public and private acts of patriotism and self-sacrifice. Besides contributions to the Soldiers' Aid Society and the Ladies' Relief Hospital, men occasionally raised other types of financial donations. After Fredericksburg, Virginia, was leveled by a battle in late 1862, William Blackford, Sr., raised four thousand dollars for the town's refugees. In addition, Blackford and others made frequent trips to camps with gifts of food and supplies. One resident, John Tilden, a tinner, made caring for Lynchburg soldiers his personal avocation. Until late in the war, Tilden made regular supply trips to Lynchburg soldiers, usually to deliver gifts from private individuals and the Ladies' Relief Society. For his good deeds, local residents unanimously elected Tilden city sergeant in 1864. William Kinkle, the town's Episcopal minister, was almost as zealous as Tilden in his ministrations to the poor. Although many residents remembered Kinkle as haughty and elitist, he became far more empathic during the war.

According to one of Kinkle's parishioners, the minister virtually "stripped himself to aid the suffering" families of poor soldiers. Even the Lynchburg Tobacco Manufacturing Association got into the act by regularly providing Lynchburg soldiers with their much-beloved "chew."[3]

After a short time, however, residents learned that the simple act of volunteering to help the cause sometimes created disputes and conflicts. At least some male residents resented the efforts of the Ladies' Relief Hospital. Dr. William Otway Owen, a Lynchburg resident and chief surgeon of all Lynchburg's Confederate military hospitals, tried numerous times to close the Ladies' Hospital. He once told his superiors that "women and flies" were the two most undesirable hospital pests. Other doctors agreed. During the Battle of the Wilderness in May 1864, Lynchburg became the primary repository for wounded soldiers. In a short time, the town's hospitals were overwhelmed. To alleviate the wounded soldiers' suffering, women tried to enter the three military hospitals, to give them food and bandages. Most surgeons objected to the intrusion and tried to force the women to leave. Only after they realized

Lynchburg soldiers celebrate as they leave to fight the enemy in western Virginia in the summer of 1861. (*Harper's Monthly*, 1861; LMS)

that they could not hope to take care of all the casualties did the surgeons reluctantly allow the women to stay.[4]

Doctors were not the only ones who objected to women's conspicuous involvement in the war effort. Button was an early and vocal critic. In April 1862, he ridiculed the leaders of the various women's organizations, claiming that most only wanted notoriety and an officer's status. Some women also believed that certain tasks were inappropriate for their sex. Addressing the public through the *Virginian*, "a lady" chastised women for trying to raise funds for an ironclad ship. By her view, women should stick to projects closer to their prescribed roles, namely, "the care of our sick and wounded soldiers . . . working to make their clothes, and best of all . . . administering in various ways, to their spiritual good." Raising funds to build a battleship, she asserted, was a duty better suited to men and "not one belonging to us, as women, to perform." Concluding her remarks, she pleaded that women "not leave the place our Creator seems to have assigned us" or advocate "'women's rights' as Northern women mistakenly have done."[5]

As civilians reacted to women's expanded role in civic affairs, other conflicts also emerged. Those who made up the rank and file of voluntary organizations occasionally complained about the arrogance of the town's civic leaders. Susan Blackford, although she had married into a prominent Lynchburg family, often felt rebuffed by the leaders of the Soldiers' Aid Society and the Ladies' Hospital. In addition, she occasionally noted that some citizens failed to do all that their wealth and stature allowed them to do for the war effort. In letters to her husband, she complained that many of those who were supposed to lead the war effort at home were far too condescending, distant, and egotistical to be of much use.[6]

Meanwhile, Protestant and Catholic leaders sometimes clashed as well. Like many white Lynchburg residents, Jacob Mitchell, minister at Second Presbyterian Church, treated Catholics as a group apart and did all he could to exclude them from the Lynchburg community. He regularly derided Catholics' contribution to the war effort. Although the Sisters of Mercy, a Catholic order, were the only trained female nurses in town and the only ones brave enough to serve in the smallpox ward, Mitchell belittled their efforts as self-serving and claimed that the "sisters of mercy of protestant hospitals" were equally helpful but did not make "such loud professions of self-denial." Père Louis-Hippolyte Gache, the town's only Catholic chaplain, often fought back in kind. Gache became a bitter rival of Mitchell and took great pleasure in foiling Mitchell's efforts to proselytize to the soldiers in town.[7]

None of these disputes evolved into a major conflict. Most people aired their complaints as gossip, as unguarded entries in private diaries or letters, or as statements in the public press which were quickly assailed by other members of the community. None of the disputes hindered Lynchburg's attempts to help the war effort. Nevertheless, the early conflicts suggest that appearance of unity and self-sacrifice that residents tried to create for themselves was problematic from the beginning. Individuals disagreed on their place in the community, the roles their leaders assumed, and, ultimately, who rightfully belonged to the community. As the war attracted new groups into Lynchburg and unleashed more tumultuous forces, town residents would find it exceedingly difficult to retain the unity and order that they had celebrated in the prewar years and even more in the early months of the war.

Ironically, the first group to become a serious threat to the safety and well-being of the community was the group whose duty it was to protect the town: the hundreds—sometimes thousands—of soldiers stationed around Lynchburg. Whether they were in town to recuperate, work in the hospitals, rest on their way to the front, enjoy their leave, or escape detection from the Confederate army, they quickly transformed Lynchburg from a center of manufacturing and trade to what William Blackford, Sr., aptly called a "garrison town." Many of those who came brought with them a very different code of morality that ultimately led to conflicts, especially with members of the propertied classes.[8] Just as many soldiers came to believe that civilians did not appreciate their efforts, many Lynchburg civilians, especially the town's civic leaders, came to believe that the soldiers in their midst were ungrateful, immoral, and perhaps even barbaric. From the beginning, soldiers looked to Lynchburg as a place to relax and unwind. Inevitably, they attracted a growing number of entrepreneurs—including barkeeps, prostitutes, gamblers, and dancehall matrons—to cater to their quest for pleasure. Thus, by the end of the first year of the war, Lynchburg's red-light district had spread beyond the Buzzard to the heart of the central business district on Main Street.[9]

Most Lynchburg citizens had not anticipated such developments. Civic leaders had hoped that the war would encourage soldiers to practice a morality consistent with the righteousness of the Confederacy's cause. As a result, many civilians became truly scandalized by soldiers' desire for baser pleasures. Within a very short time, town residents learned that it was much easier to celebrate the virtues of their soldiers in the field than of those who loitered on their streets and in their groceries and shops.

Just a month after the first soldiers camped outside the city at the Fair Grounds, the city council passed a liquor curfew, forcing all restaurants and barrooms to close by 10:00 P.M. As with most of its prewar efforts to stop the vice traffic, however, council learned that it was nearly impossible to enforce the laws it passed. By December, Button complained that most grogshop owners were ignoring the curfew. Undeterred by the city codes, soldiers stationed in Lynchburg wandered the streets at night in a "partial state of abandonment . . . plied with mean liquor . . . and unmanageable to our police."[10]

Faced with nightly drunken melees, town officials adopted more extreme measures to control the whiskey trade. In January 1862, council doubled the night watch to twenty, hoping that a larger patrol might enforce the curfew better. When this failed, civic leaders gradually adopted measures to ban the sale of liquor all together. One month later, after a drunken row at a cockfight resulted in the death of a soldier, Mayor Branch closed all grogshops. Although Branch had no legal power to do this, no one disputed his move; indeed, some criticized him for not having acted with greater resolve. Two months later, the hustings court, after considerable urging from city council and local newspapers, sustained the mayor's edict and announced that it would not grant any liquor licenses for the next year. Within a few weeks, however, civic leaders admitted that they had failed to eradicate the trade. Some liquor dealers moved across the bridge to Amherst County, while others simply concealed their livelihood by opening their alley doors to do business.[11]

Almost immediately, concerns about how to impose order divided the town. Although most civilians came to accept the efficacy of applying a more stringent code of conduct to the soldiers, many were not at all sure it was the town's responsibility to do so. Mayor Branch was among this group. Before the war, Branch had used the mayor's court to enforce a distinctly Southern brand of justice. Because he believed it was impossible either to reform or completely to control those under his jurisdiction, he used his considerable discretionary power to allow most whites to enjoy their vices, as long as they recognized elites' right to rule and did not threaten property. Branch preferred to rule by the same code during the war. In early 1862, he claimed that as long as "no stores are being broken open and robbed" and "no private houses entered by thieves," tougher measures were not necessary.[12]

Others disagreed. A week before the 1862 municipal election, "a tax payer" condemned Branch in the public press and nominated James

Saunders, a prominent lawyer and alderman, as a mayoral candidate. Button, long a friend and supporter of Branch, gave Saunders his tacit endorsement as well. Without explicitly endorsing Saunders, Button suggested that it might be time for a change. "Revolutions," Button warned, often "promote violence and bloodshed," making human life cheap and property "doubly insecure." To ensure that their community did not go this way, Button encouraged the "good people of Lynchburg" to elect those who are "vitally interested in having an efficient municipal government." Otherwise, "rum-sellers, rum drinkers, and rowdies" who supported the current administration would again have their way.[13]

In the end, the reformers were not able to defeat Branch, but they did deprive him of his customary near-unanimous election. For the first time in Lynchburg's memory, popular politics had unabashedly entered a municipal election. No doubt, this development concerned many civilians, and it may explain why, during the next few months, the two sides tried to reach some sort of rapprochement. On the one side, the new council enacted tougher liquor licensing laws and increased the size of the night watch from ten to thirteen. On the other side, those who had been most critical of the vice trade began to change their assessment of the problem. Initially, residents had viewed soldiers as victims of unscrupulous grog dealers who tempted them to go astray. As the drunken rows continued, however, some residents concluded that the only true victims were the townspeople themselves. In May 1862, Button, presuming to speak for the civil authorities, warned soldiers that because they had abused the town's hospitality toward them for so long, council would be more aggressive in the future. Unfortunately, town leaders were in no position to enforce such vague threats. The night watch was both too small and too inefficient for the present problem. Rather meekly, Button suggested that military officials should take better care to discipline law-breaking soldiers. Over the next several months, civil authorities echoed Button's plea, urging military officials to take care of their own. Finally, in August 1862, the military responded by establishing a provost guard in the city to police soldiers.[14]

Ultimately, the guard proved to be as ineffectual as the civilian police. In May 1863, after John Barleycorn incited yet another row between soldiers, Robert Glass of the *Lynchburg Republican* implored military authorities to take action, suggesting that "some sort of military discipline ought to be maintained by the officers of the regiments," so that the men were "kept in order and not permitted to cut and splurge about the streets." In hindsight, the establishment of a provost guard had only one positive result: it gave citizens a common enemy. Civilians now condemned the Confederate army, instead of their own leaders, for the town's continuing lawlessness and crime. Thus, the following year, Branch and the city council were again reelected without significant opposition.[15]

Meanwhile, civilians became increasingly estranged from the soldiers in their midst. The longer the soldiers stayed, the more civilians complained. After volunteering in one of the city's military hospitals for a few months, Lucy Rodes told her cousin that she had nearly lost patience with the soldiers whom she tended. According to Rodes, most did not need the attention: "You know," she told her cousin, "every factory and every other house . . . is filled to overflowing with this class of fellows all *playing sick.*" Rodes complained that many of these soldiers thought nothing of going door to door and begging for food. In one instance, two soldiers, "the toughest looking characters you ever saw," entered Rodes's house, demanding that she play her piano while they rested on her porch. Deathly afraid of the intruders, she complied until her fingers were too numb to continue. William Blackford, Sr., agreed that many soldiers demanded too much of the civilians. After his son Launcelot praised his parents for opening their home to wounded soldiers, William responded that he was glad they did not have any soldiers at present. "There has been a great deal of old soldiering," William told Launcelot, "and the kindness of families has been grossly abused by men lingering when they were fully able to rejoin their corps."[16]

Others observed far worse abuses by soldiers. Writing in June 1864, just days after a Yankee regiment tried to raid the town, "a sufferer" protested that there were simply too many soldiers in town. With nothing better to do, the writer complained, they spent their days begging for food or, worse, "seeking opportunities to rob premises and injure property." The situation was especially bad near Camp Davis on the eastern edge of town. According to Button, the military commander neglected to post a guard at the camp. As a result, "soldiers roved about without restraint," committing "depredations on the surrounding civilians with impunity, even laughing at those whom they despoil." Finally, in August 1864, after constant complaints from civilians, the commanding officer of the camp posted a guard and threatened the death penalty for any soldier caught "plundering or pillaging."[17]

Women felt especially vulnerable. To overcome the anxiety of living in a large house by herself, Susan Blackford took in boarders and made her most faithful house servant, Gabe, sleep in the first-floor hallway. When economic concerns forced her to move out of the house, Charles encouraged her to stay with his parents, where she would be "under the guardianship of her natural protectors." Still, Charles and Susan remained concerned about Susan's safety. Sadly, Charles concluded, the "war has so demoralized the people" that he feared Susan would probably not be safe anywhere.[18]

From the soldiers' perspective, many of the town's criticisms of their behavior seemed wholly unwarranted. Those who were so inclined viewed drink as a right, if not a necessity, given their patriotic sacrifices to the cause and their miserable circumstances. Soldiers detailed to Dr. John Terrell's smallpox ward threatened to "mutiny" if Terrell, a temperance man, followed through on his vow to cut off their whiskey supply. They were so adamant that Terrell not only relented but eventually agreed to pay them in liquor. In August 1864, after city council attempted to close the doggeries, John Lucas, a private with a Georgia battalion stationed in Lynchburg, protested through the public press. Irritated that civilians were becoming too meddlesome, he argued that "soldiers ought to be left alone and have a drink when they feel like it." According to Lucas, council's act smacked of hypocrisy. If the town aimed to close the soldiers' low doggeries, he argued, they should do the same with the "large hotels, where a man gets poisoned in the most approved style."[19]

Even more than as a place of refuge, doggeries played a strategic role in soldiers' efforts to make ends meet on an inadequate wage. When John Henry's unit first arrived in Richmond, the only establishment that opened its doors to them was a doggery. All other places either refused to serve soldiers or were too expensive. Much to Susan Blackford's chagrin, her brother-in-law Lewis Blackford often visited gambling halls and saloons, because he could not afford to eat at nicer restaurants. After Susan lectured him on the evils of gambling, Lewis replied that he could pay as much as three dollars for a meal at a respectable hotel and "get nothing to eat." By contrast, when he went to a saloon he could get a "fine dinner" by betting that much on a card game.[20]

Soldiers were less forthright in explanations of theft, though obviously, need was a motivating factor. In addition, many who learned to pillage and scavenge at their camps and in the countryside may simply have continued the practice when they arrived in town. Whatever the cause, many soldiers adopted an almost nonchalant attitude toward thievery. In his autobiography, written years after the war, William Andrew Fletcher recalled that his regiment stopped in Lynchburg just long enough to change trains as they made their way to the front in northern Virginia. While there, they noticed a hogshead of sugar on the railway platform and an apple orchard nearby. Using their wits, they mixed the two to make stewed apples to eat while they waited. Fletcher did not regard the act as theft. By his view, the apples and the sugar were the soldiers' due— a small treat for the sacrifices they made as defenders of the cause. Apparently, other soldiers held to a similar ethic. In 1863, military officials posted a guard at the Lynchburg-Amherst Bridge to keep soldiers from raiding the farms on the other side of the James River.[21]

As civilians became more discontented with their presumed protectors, they searched for ways to bring soldiers back into the fold. Elites were especially hopeful that religion might serve this purpose. After all, many soldiers and civilians approached the war as a kind of religious crusade; as such, they viewed the outcome of every battle as divinely ordained. For this reason, the war years were marked by periods of intense religious enthusiasm, as soldiers and civilians tried to make the Confederacy worthy of God's grace and protection. In the military camps, this enthusiasm culminated in the winter of 1863–1864, as a revival swept through the Confederate armies, converting large numbers of soldiers and officers.[22]

In Lynchburg, religious enthusiasm never peaked as it did in the military camps. Nevertheless, civic leaders remained acutely interested in the Confederacy's spiritual health. During the war, each of Lynchburg's five largest evangelical churches experienced at least one revival. These events attracted large numbers of civilians and soldiers alike. In addition, periodic fast days, ordered by President Jefferson Davis and enforced by civil authorities, reminded Lynchburg residents of the religious basis of the war.

Civic leaders hoped that religion would give Lynchburg's civilians and soldiers, whether at camp or in town, a common identity and a common purpose. As Robert Glass of the *Lynchburg Republican* reminded his readers, those who could not fight were expected to pray for those who did. After all, Glass reasoned, "the soldier's duty leaves him but little time to aught else but fight." Therefore, it was every civilian's duty "to pray and beseech God" for the soldiers, so that their cause might yet be blessed. Many did not need Glass's encouragement. Especially after the first Confederate defeats in the spring and summer of 1862, God-fearing soldiers persistently asked those at home to pray for them. Conversely, those at home admonished soldiers to be ever diligent in their religious affairs. Robert Brown told his son Sandy that "while I would urge you to perform your duty as a soldier and a true Southerner, I must not omit to exhort you to remember your duty to your creator. In my opinion he who is the best christian will always be the best soldier."[23]

Devout Lynchburg residents displayed their religious convictions to soldiers in more concrete ways as well. As soldiers moved in and out of Lynchburg during the first weeks of the war, churches opened their doors to the troops and provided them with Bibles and religious tracts. Later, churches helped establish a reading room for sick and wounded soldiers. Especially in the early years of the war, local religious leaders played an active and conspicuous role in army camp life. Jacob Mitchell, who just a few months before the war contemplated leaving Lynchburg because he doubted whether the town needed his pastoral services, found new purpose in life as an army chaplain. For the next several months, Mitchell spent his time tending to soldiers in Lynchburg hospitals and at military encampments. By the end of the war, Mitchell was one of eight chaplains whom the town supported to tend to the spiritual needs of soldiers stationed in Lynchburg.[24]

Nevertheless, religion served as an imperfect source of social cohesion between soldiers and civilians. Although some soldiers participated in the town's religious activities, others resented civilians' missionary efforts, claiming that citizens simply could not understand the troops' spiritual and physical needs because they had not made the sorts of sacrifices they had. As the violence and destruction of war continued, many soldiers became indifferent to religion. According to historian Gerald Linderman, a nagging skepticism replaced the religious enthusiasm that swept through the military camps in the winter of 1863–1864, as soldiers came to terms with the brutality of the war and the capriciousness of life. In addition, more immediate concerns slowly replaced the time soldiers once had set aside for religion. Rather cynically, Samuel Oakey told family members that a minister near his camp preached twice a day to soldiers, but "the boys are very slow about going to the altar" because there "are too many vegetables here for them to steal." For many soldiers, the day-to-day struggle for survival took precedence over spiritual concerns. In peace, they might have shared the civilians' view that activities such as drinking and stealing were repugnant to Christian living, but in war, the soldiers acquired a more tolerant attitude.[25]

Civilians were often shocked by what they perceived to be the soldiers' lack of morality. When Lucy Rodes found out that, despite a series of military setbacks, her cousin Sandy Brown had refused to attend church, she reminded him that there was a connection between soldiers' spiritual state and the fate of the Confederacy. Using the first person plural, perhaps to soften the sting of her reproach, she gently reminded Sandy that "we must put our trust in him." Although she expressed confidence that "God is on our side and He will achieve our independence," Lucy concluded that the recent setbacks could only be attributed to the South's sinfulness. "Ours is a wicked nation," she told Sandy. "For our great sinfulness . . . [we] deserve to be given up to our merciless adversaries." Yet "if we repent and do better than formerly, and look more to God we *will undoubtedly* receive his favour." Despite the rebuke, Sandy remained indifferent.[26]

As soldiers began to view civilians' religion as a source of judgment rather than support, they became less receptive to the charitable overtures of Lynchburg's religious community. With delight, Père Louis-Hippolyte Gache, a Catholic priest and a bitter enemy of chauvinist evangelical Protestants, observed that the town's ministers faced considerable resistance in their attempts to minister to the Confederate army. Gache, who worked as a chaplain and nurse in one of Lynchburg's military hospitals, was especially pleased that Mitchell, an ardent revivalist and Protestant evangelical, failed to make more of an impact on the soldiers under his care. Commissioned as a chaplain early in the war, Mitchell had hoped to organize regular meetings in each of the town's three military hospitals. When Mitchell announced that he intended to hold prayer meetings at the hospital on College Hill, the chief surgeon of the division told him that army regulations forbade preaching in the wards. When Mitchell moved his meeting to the hospital yard, only a handful bothered to attend; and these quickly deserted him after just a few minutes of preaching, when a young Irish Catholic orderly—a "wily rogue from Erin's green shores," according to Gache—unceremoniously rang the dinner bell. "Before the clock had struck five," Gache reported, "all of the congregation was at the table and the preacher was left alone, his arms stretched out and his mouth gaping, still standing on the grassy mound." A week later, Mitchell tried again, at another Lynchburg hospital. Once again, an Irish Catholic—this time a nun in charge of the nursing staff—thwarted his efforts. With the implicit support of many of the convalescing soldiers, the nun refused to allow Mitchell to preach in the hospital ward. Frustrated and angry that native soldiers had chosen to follow two despised Irish Catholics, Mitchell again despaired over his inability to revive sinners. A few days later, he resigned his commission from the Confederacy and, according to Gache, never entered a Lynchburg hospital again. Though somewhat extreme, Mitchell's experiences provide a telling indication of just how military life altered soldiers' view of civilians. From the soldiers' perspective, the Catholics had proved themselves worthy of the troops' respect through yeoman service on the battlefields and in the hospitals, while Mitchell had only discredited himself by moralizing about their wretched spiritual state.[27]

In a short while, Lynchburg residents realized that they would have more problems to contend with than just the immorality of their soldiers. The declining state of the economy became especially worrisome to many residents. Lynchburgers entered the war sharing Southern entrepreneurs' hope that separation from the North would stimulate home manufacturing to create a golden age of commercial enterprise and expansion. During the early years of the war, businessmen waited anxiously for old businesses to expand and new ones to emerge. When wagonmaker John Bailey and foundry owner Francis Deane received contracts from the Confederate government, Button and others hoped these would provide the impetus for Lynchburg to diversify its economy, so that it might finally become a major industrial center. Despite a few lucrative government contracts, however, the golden age never came. Although the war stimulated both private and public industrial enterprises throughout the South, particularly in iron and textile manufacturing, relatively few profited from these successes. For most Southerners, the war was a time of intense economic suffering. The reasons that so many suffered during this period of unprecedented economic growth have been well documented. Insufficient domestic food supplies, an incomplete and deteriorating transportation network, the disruption of trade, and hyperinflation caused distress throughout the South, but especially in urban centers like Lynchburg.[28]

Rather than analyze the complex causes of their misery, however, Lynchburg residents looked for scapegoats. Residents became especially suspicious of merchants. Like most urbanites of their era, white Lynchburgers ascribed to a Victorian business ethic. They believed that the ideal businessman was one who was honorable in his business practices and who engaged in work that contributed to the well-being of the community. In the midst of shortages and rising prices, however, most agreed it was doubtful that the town's entrepreneurs were living up this code. Most nonmerchants thought not. Unable to fathom the vast impersonal forces that influenced market conditions, they blamed escalating prices on the greed of local and regional entrepreneurs.[29]

The first group of capitalists to be scrutinized were the salt dealers. In November 1861, local merchants claimed that they were running out of salt and would have to raise prices. Skeptical residents immediately accused merchants of hoarding. In an attempt to pressure merchants to bring the price down, civic leaders organized an indignation meeting and devised plans to buy salt directly from the saltworks in southwestern Virginia. The results were mixed. Although residents failed to impose a just price on salt, they did force merchants to locate more salt so that, for a short while, the price went down.[30]

The following year, as prices on items began to rise to four to ten times their prewar levels, residents spread their wrath to nearly all entrepreneurs. By that time, Jacob Mitchell had come to refer to all merchants as "extortioners." That many were members of his church did not lessen his contempt. When shopping, he often tried to browbeat them into lowering their prices. In his diary, he lamented that unless God "interposes, the extortioners will ruin our cause." Button agreed. Calling extortion "the prevailing vice in the Southern Confederacy," he wondered how long the Southern people would "bear the heavy exactions . . . that war makes."[31]

As the economic crisis worsened, many residents began to employ the very practices that they condemned. As they did, the line between legitimate and illegitimate economic behavior became increasingly hard to distinguish. Speculating became an especially popular sideline for virtually all citizens of property. To retain some semblance of their prewar standard of living, wealthier individuals bought up large quantities of Southern staples—tobacco, salt, and sugar being the most popular—then sold them when prices rose. In doing so, they ran the risk of themselves being accused of hoarding.

Many found it easy to rationalize this form of behavior. Button, for instance, claimed that the Confederate government's system of random and often excessive impressment made hoarding almost necessary. Others hoarded and speculated because they believed it the only way to survive. In July 1863, Charles Blackford, fearing that inflation and shortages would only get worse, instructed his wife to buy provisions for eighteen months, so that they would be able to ride out the worst of it. Charles could afford to do so; throughout the war he speculated in tobacco and, at the time, still had enough on hand to help his family live a fairly comfortable life.[32]

Speculating and hoarding became so widespread that many suspended judgment on the practice. Walter Henderson, an officer in the Confederate army, filled many of his letters to his wife with instructions on which items to sell and which items to buy. That he might have indirectly contributed to the suffering of his men did not enter into his thinking. In November 1861, Susan Blackford criticized John Meem, a drygoods merchant in town, because he bought a bolt of negro cloth, waited a few months, then sold it at three times its value. Resolutely, she told Charles that she would "never darken his door again," because she did not think "he ought to be countenanced" for hoarding. A few years later, however, Susan complimented several of her husbands' friends for their ability to make large profits by selling their surplus firewood and cloth. In time, even citizens of modest means adopted the practice to stretch their limited incomes. John Lipscomb Johnson, a hospital chaplain and the minister of the African Baptist Church, speculated simply to make ends meet. In the latter part of 1864, when Confederate money was nearly worthless, Johnson bought three barrels of brown sugar, a commodity that he shrewdly noted "everybody wanted" and that was "getting higher everyday." For the next several months Johnson sold and bartered the sugar by the cup to make ends meet.[33]

Over time, speculation helped sustain the wealth of Lynchburg's entrepreneurs. In 1863, the Confederate government ordered all tobacco factories to close, so that tobacco farmers would switch to food crops and tobacco factory laborers could be used for the war effort. Without a source of revenue, Lynchburg residents began to hoard and speculate on the tobacco they had on hand. Some made a killing. William Blackford, Sr., did so well in the trade that he climbed out of debt for the first time in years. During the last year of the war, and for some time thereafter, elites used plugs and hogsheads of tobacco as money. By the end of the war, Charles Button noted that it was not uncommon to see wealthy residents ambling down the main streets of town with their pockets full of tobacco plugs to trade or sell. Since the War Department did not consider tobacco to be a "necessity of life," it did not condemn the trade. Nevertheless, because tobacco was an item that poorer residents could not hope to acquire, it no doubt symbolized the growing disparity between rich and poor. Moreover, by refusing to show their confidence in Confederate money, speculators contributed to inflation and indirectly forced poorer residents to barter what little they had.[34]

While the town's wealthiest civilians were sometimes tested by the economic problems of the Confederacy, those of limited resources were often broken by them. Laborers—with few financial reserves—suffered the most. Although some, especially craftsmen who owned their own shops, were able to remain solvent by making contracts with the Confederate government, most were not so lucky. In March 1862, Samuel Sublett stated that the rise in prices made it difficult to plan for the future. "The price of everything to eat and to ware is very heigh and keeps rising every day," he told a friend. As a result of inflation, he could not "say what the prices are thay are one price one day and the next day they are higher." Glass of the *Republican* agreed that hyperinflation made it nearly impossible for the poor to survive without assistance. In October 1862, with butter selling at one dollar a pound and bacon at almost that much, he noted that it was "impossible for anyone on $5.00 to buy food at the market." Shortages only added to the problem. In March 1864, Glass noted that there were less than one hundred pounds of beef, one and a half bushels of potatoes, and three bushels of turnips for sale at the market house. "Rather a lean bill of fare for 15,000 people," Glass concluded.[35]

Inflation quickly led to widespread suffering among the poor. During the first winter, Susan Blackford predicted that many merchants would "literally drink the life blood of the poor families who are left here." Women, many of them without husbands and sons to help earn money, were especially bad off. "It is dreadful to think upon," Jannett Cleland, daughter of the town's gas fitter, observed: "so many widows working hard for a few dollars to keep life in her and her children, distracted by harder times and the loss of friends." Unless relief came "in some form," Cleland continued, no one knew "what they will do this winter." A year later, Susan Blackford raised the same concern. "Unless we have peace," she told Charles, "I fear many of our poor people will starve."[36]

With fewer resources than the town's wealthier residents, laboring men and women did whatever they could to survive. John Douglas recalled that at the beginning of the war, his father, a machinist, did his best to prepare for the anticipated hardships by "laying in quite a bit of flour and bacon." Because they were unable to hoard as much as wealthier civilians, however, they soon found their supply exhausted. To survive amid food shortages and inflation, Douglas, then still a youth, was forced to "help fill the family larder" by selling newspapers to soldiers in the local military hospitals. Meanwhile, his father, though still employed, relied increasingly on government rations and charity to make ends meet. Eventually, poverty mixed with doubts about the efficacy of the cause compelled the family to move to Philadelphia to live with relatives. Necessity drove women to even more desperate measures. Late in the war, Button told the story of Sarah J. New, "a widow lady," who lived with her children in a condemned brick building. When the building collapsed, New lost what little she had, including an old sewing machine she used to support herself.[37]

Some less wealthy residents tried collective efforts to protest and improve their circumstances. In December 1861, a month after the first salt indignation meeting, "labouring and mechanical men of the city" planned a second meeting to "devise some means by which they could obtain salt for their families." Perhaps because they had been frustrated by the first meeting, and because they believed that the upper classes, especially merchants, created the shortage by hoarding and speculating, organizers of the meeting made a special point to invite only laboring men. Although no record exists of what transpired at the meeting, the exclusiveness of the meeting must have troubled civic leaders, who had always prided themselves on their ability to care for the poor.[38]

As the war continued, protests against high prices and food shortages became increasingly common. In April 1862, "One of the People," writing in the *Lynchburg Virginian*, suggested that the hustings court institute price-fixing "to curb extortioners." Unless something was done, he warned, "the people would take the subject of redress into their own hands."[39] Poor civilians became especially uneasy a year later, when the army's new food conscription laws threatened to deprive towns like Lynchburg of essential commodities. During the crisis, Father Gache informed his superiors that he had heard rumors that the poor of the town intended to replicate the recent food riots of Petersburg and Richmond. In those cities, poor residents, mostly women, staged massive demonstrations, accusing the Confederate government of starving the poor of the city by conscripting an inordinate amount of the state's food supply to the military. Apparently, Button also heard the rumors. A few days after Gache wrote his report, Button observed that "there seems to be a wide-spread apprehension, almost a panic that we are in danger of starvation." Button tried his best to allay the public's fears with a twofold argument. One the one hand, he categorically denied that the town was in danger of starvation. Indeed, he argued, Georgia alone had corn enough to feed the Confederate army. On the other hand, he joined the citizenry in their condemnation of the Confederacy's impressment policy, claiming that the present system fed the army at the expense of the cities. Giving voice to the complaints of the poor so that they would not resort to more radical means, Button encouraged Congress to reform its policies.[40]

Although the town remained calm, the rumors reflected the upper class's understanding that the poor were becoming increasingly restive in their poverty. In a few instances, the poor did take matters into their own hands. With some relish, Robert Glass told his readers about a poor youth who valiantly tried to protect his cart—his only source of income—from impressment officers. When the officers approached the young man about the cart, he quickly disassembled it, hiding a small wheel cap as he did, so that the cart would not work. When the officers tried to search the boy for the cap, he announced, that "I dar you to search me, you no right to put your hand in my pocket, no how." When one of the officers commanded him to be quiet, he shot back, "I ain't goin' to do it, my mouth is my own." Finally, when threatened with arrest, the young man handed over the cap but still claimed that he would be "dad skinned" if he would drive the cart for them.[41]

In the winter of 1863, draymen and wagon drivers, in an unprecedented action, rebuked city council's efforts to fix their rates at prices that were "entirely disproportionate to . . . the times and consequently unremunerative." Without waiting for a reply from council, the drivers raised their rates, with the threat that unless a "liberal public sustains us . . . we shall be compelled to withdraw our teams from the streets." Evidently, the threat worked; one month later, the draymen published a second notice, raising their rates for a second time by as much as 33 percent a load.[42]

Not all laboring men were so successful in their demands. A year after the wagon hucksters' protest, white machinists employed in the shops of the Virginia and Tennessee Railroad made an equally forceful stand by striking for a 50 percent increase in their daily wage, from $11.00 to $16.50. In reaction, the company tried to intimidate the men. Because all were detailed men, the company asked the provost to send the men back to their regular outfits. The provost did more than comply: he arrested the strikers and sent them to the guardhouse.[43]

Perhaps the best indication of laborers' restiveness is that crimes against property rose dramatically in the last years of the war. Unfortunately, it is difficult to determine the full scope of the problem by quantifying police records, because the town's night watch was hopelessly undermanned during the war. Nevertheless, contemporaries were convinced that thefts and robberies were on the increase. As early as July 1862, Button claimed that the situation was "intolerable" and chastised both military and civil authorities for failing to patrol the streets with better care. In January 1863, residents of the city, including "the most quiet and respectable citizens," organized a vigilance committee to hunt down a notorious thief. When the mob caught him, Glass of the *Republican* reported that they demonstrated a "strong disposition" to "apply the code of Judge Lynch to him." Although cooler heads prevailed, Glass hoped the incident "shall serve warning to the garroters and burglars among us. The patience of our people has been worn thread bare by the repeated acts of villainy committed by these rascals." Button also supported the use of extralegal methods to curb crime. After a series of burglaries and robberies in the spring of 1864, he encouraged residents to "form themselves into patrol parties . . . well-armed . . . [to] keep a vigilant watch for . . . desperadoes." A week later, the hustings court acted on Button's suggestion and organized four patrols to police the city. By the court's order, each would be manned by private citizens, operating much like the town's militia. Evidently, the new patrol system intimidated very few thieves. Just a month later, Button noted that the town still resembled a "carnival of theft." At the end of the year, he again called for an increase in the size of the peace-keeping forces.[44]

Civic leaders generally blamed most of the thefts on outsiders—so-called ruffians and rovers. Authorities suspected that these individuals first arrived in Lynchburg as deserters or to escape conscription. Unable to find work and reluctant to ask for public assistance for fear of detection, they relied on the town's black market to earn their keep. In one of the better-documented cases, a gang of thieves, headed by a Maryland man named Brown, stole over two hundred watches from a local jeweler. Brown then sold all of them to the owner of one of Lynchburg's most notorious "dens of vice and iniquity." When the police raided the place, they found stolen items from several other thefts as well.[45]

Yet if many of the boldest crimes were committed by outsiders, some native Lynchburgers also relied on theft as a means to survive during the economic crisis. At least three of Brown's five accomplices were laboring men from Lynchburg. Even so-called respectable civilians sometimes succumbed to crime. In 1864, First Presbyterian Church excommunicated two unnamed members for fencing tobacco stolen by slaves.[46]

Most of the time, poorer residents were not so audacious in what they stole. Like the many soldiers in town who stole to supplement their meager rations, laboring whites usually relegated their thievery to items that they could use for their own purposes, such as clothes, food, and money. In February 1865, Button noted that petty thievery had become so widespread that the grogshops now served as marketplaces for the buying and selling of stolen goods. Unfortunately, without better documentation of wartime crime, it is impossible to determine precisely how many—or how often—Lynchburg residents turned to thievery to survive. Whatever their number, that some were willing to go beyond the law to survive suggests how desperately poor many in town had become.[47]

It is also difficult to determine if crimes against property reflected poorer whites' opposition to the war. During the last months of the war, such seems to have been the case. As public order eroded, individuals turned their wrath toward those people and institutions that they considered to be the source of their suffering—namely, war profiteers and military stores. For most of the war, however, crimes against property were far more random. True, most targeted the rich, but never exclusively. In desperate times, everyone was a potential victim, including soldiers, small shopkeepers, travelers, and slaves. Moreover, if thieves hoped to make a statement about the war, they found that municipal and military police curtailed their ability to do so. By patrolling the central business district, the police forced thieves to relegate their activities to the suburbs, where they engaged in more petty forms of thievery—robbing smokehouses, gardens, barns, and homes.[48] This is not to say that thieves made no statement by their activities. By engaging in crimes against property, some lower-class whites may have demonstrated their growing dissatisfaction with constituted authority, a general weariness of the deprivations of war, and a desire to regain some measure of their customary economic independence by appropriating what they needed for themselves.

Yet if strikes and crimes against property suggest that poorer residents were beginning to break from the traditions of paternalism and deference, it is easy to exaggerate the extent and significance of such activities through most of the war. The pettiness and randomness of much of the crime suggest that the perpetrators did not see their effort as an organized attack against property. Then, too, even as some poorer residents tried to take matters into their own hands, others became more dependent on wealthy benefactors.

For their part, elites tried to encourage the poor to look to traditional means of public assistance. Faced with widespread suffering and growing restiveness, Lynchburg's civic leaders expanded their definitions of charity and public assistance. No matter that the state began to extend public assistance as well; civic leaders quickly learned that state aid would not be sufficient and rushed to fill the vacuum. In doing so, they made sure that personalism would not be a casualty of the war.[49] Before the war, the overseer of the poor's annual budget rarely exceeded one thousand dollars. In the winter of 1862 alone, council allocated five thousand dollars for the purchase of wood fuel for the poor. In addition, state and local governments experimented with price-fixing. By the last year of the war, needy families could buy cornmeal, rice, and salt, well below market value, at a special store for the deserving poor. Private charitable organizations also increased their activities during the war. Through most of the war, civic leaders raised special funds to buy wood fuel, clothing, and food for the poor. Meanwhile, churches continued to provide whatever they could. First Presbyterian doubled its poor fund during the second year of the war and doubled it again the following year.[50]

Along with these gestures, wealthier residents also looked for other ways to assist the poor. From the beginning of the war, the Soldiers' Aid Society paid the wives and daughters of poorer soldiers to make uniforms for Lynchburg regiments. Similarly, the matrons of the Ladies' Relief Hospital, feeling that it was beneath them to cook, clean, and nurse the soldiers, hired poorer women to take on these duties. Many residents, especially women, also acted independently of organizations to provide charitable assistance. Lucy Otey, founder of the Ladies' Relief Hospital, and Narcissa Owen, the wife of the president of the Virginia and Tennessee Railroad, regularly visited poor families with provisions. After Mary Blackford's husband died in early 1864, she spent virtually all of her leisure time visiting poor residents and sick soldiers, to fill the void in her life. Button, perhaps to make sure that charity would retain a personal component, encouraged poor residents to apply for aid at his office, so that he could find appropriate benefactors to assist them.[51]

Quite often, poorer residents actively encouraged civic leaders to increase their charitable efforts. Although they might have hoped to gain greater independence and autonomy during the war, economic necessity often forced them back to elites. When they returned to the upper classes for help, the poor continued to employ the language of deference. The creation of the special charity store provides a case in point. During the summer of 1863, after two years of complaining about escalating food prices, "the mechanical and laboring men of Lynchburg" called another meeting, this time to establish a store for the needy of the city, where they could buy the "necessaries of life" at cost. On this occasion, however, they invited a number of prominent citizens, including the president of the city council, to persuade municipal leaders to help fund the store. Duly impressed, the president assured the crowd that council would endorse the plan at its meeting the next day. True to his word, council allocated twenty-five thousand dollars and established a Committee of Supply to organize the store. Once the store was organized, civic leaders maintained complete control of its operation. Council, not trusting the spending habits of the poor, refused to give direct cash donations. Instead, they allocated money to the storekeeper and let him buy whatever he believed his customers needed.[52]

Although requesting and accepting assistance must have been humiliating for individuals who grew up in a culture that celebrated independence as an essential attribute of whiteness, most had little choice but to rely on the paternal care of Lynchburg's civic leaders and to do so without complaint. Few could challenge elites directly. A few strikes and an increase in crimes of property notwithstanding, Lynchburg's civic leaders remained remarkably resilient throughout the war. Because most were able to retain their financial resources through the war, Lynchburg's civic leaders remained a force to be reckoned with. The striking railroad mechanics learned this the hard way. When they realized that they would lose not only the strike but maybe even their jobs, they reverted to the language of deference. The day after the managers threatened them with conscription, the mechanics called on the president of the railroad, Robert Owen, and told him that all they wanted was enough to "support themselves and their families." Touched, perhaps, as much by their change in tone as by their obvious need, Owen granted their request. Through one of his administrators, he told them that he "would pay them as much as the employees of any other railroad in the state" and that he would "see that detailed farmers would sell them provisions at government prices."[53]

Poor women, by far the largest group of recipients of public and private benevolence, were especially vulnerable in their dealings with Lynchburg's philanthropists. Although the families of soldiers received provisions from the state, these proved to be inadequate. As a result, women were often compelled to ask local benefactors for assistance. Yet to receive aid, they usually had to prove their good character and devotion to the Confederate cause. Both the Soldiers' Aid Society and the Ladies' Hospital hired only women whose husbands or sons served faithfully in the war. Similarly, Button advertised the needs only of poor families who had family members who were casualties of the war or who were presently in the military.

As the war continued, the question of who deserved assistance became irrelevant, as sources of charity began to evaporate. By the end of the third year of the war, many leading citizens reluctantly curtailed their charitable giving. In early 1864, Susan Blackford stopped giving financial assistance to the poor. Even with a house full of boarders, she found that she could not make ends meet. As a result, she sold nearly all her family's possessions, put the house up for rent, and moved in with Charles's parents. In doing so, she became something of an object of charity herself. Others also had to make adjustments. In late 1864, George Ramsey, son of Presbyterian minister James Ramsey, noted that it was no longer just the poor who suffered but many who had once been "regarded as wealthy." Faced with food and fuel shortages, George noted that many residents were moving to the surrounding countryside, where food was more plentiful.[54]

Small wonder that Button and other civic leaders had difficulty raising support for public benevolence during the last months of the war. Despite constant reminders that many in town were suffering, financial contributions could not keep pace with need. When a "good citizen" volunteered to help raise fifty thousand dollars to help the poor during the last winter of the war, few rallied to the cause. Instead, for the first time in years, Lynchburg civilians made no sustained, organized effort to help the poor with fuel, clothing, and food. Evidently, elites were no longer capable of taking care of their own. How the poor survived that winter is not known.[55]

Meanwhile, attempts to stop suffering at its source largely failed. Price-fixing worked well for a time, but not during the hyperinflation of the last year of the war. Moreover, the poor found few supporters among the town's propertied classes for wholesale structural change. Most feared that any further governmental control over the economy would lead to a corresponding decrease in local autonomy. Fundamentally, citizens of wealth and stature believed that the problem was not so much structural as moral. Button argued that the only real remedy to the South's economic ills would come through greater self-sacrifice and discipline by those who possessed wealth and power. For this reason, he encouraged civilians to "desist from every effort to increase the power of the Government." Perhaps the most radical reform he suggested was to encourage city council to liberalize the local peddling ordinances, so that the town's refugees and poor civilians, not just hucksters "whose only motive may be gain," could sell items at the town market. Unfortunately, Button did not specify what the poor would sell or who would have money to buy their items.[56]

While most laboring whites found that their fortunes and their place in Lynchburg society declined during the war, Lynchburg's blacks had more mixed experiences. Many used the chaos of war to test the limits of white authority. The most adventurous used the proximity of federal troops, the disruption of civil authority, and the absence of large numbers of white males to make their escape. Although it is impossible to determine how many Lynchburg slaves ran away at this time, the number was large enough to concern most slave owners. As early as June 1862, Button complained that the federal army regularly "enticed" blacks from their "comfortable homes" to work in crowded Northern cities. When six slaves owned by the James and Kanawha Canal ran away a month later, Button remarked that "the stampede" continued unabated.[57]

In truth, Button probably exaggerated the number of runaways during the early part of the war, perhaps to encourage whites to be more vigilant. In all likelihood, far more left after the spring of 1863, when federal troops retained a constant presence in the Shenandoah Valley and the Blue Ridge Mountains. Moreover, when slaves did leave, their numbers probably resembled a steady trickle, not a stampede. During the last month of the summer of 1863, the *Lynchburg Virginian* published nine runaway notices for six men and three women. Of these, all but one were believed to have left the area. A year later, when federal troops attacked Lynchburg, witnesses noted that the army "carried off" several slaves as they retreated over the Blue Ridge Mountains.[58] To ensure that more did not run away, some masters commonly told their slaves that the Yankees would kill any blacks they found. The ploy seldom worked. Ex-slave Edward Lynch told a Freedmen's Bureau worker that when his master instructed him to "hide himself in the woods" during the Battle of Lynchburg, he retorted that "it would be more suitable for . . . Master . . . to hide himself."[59]

The enslaved did not always wait for the federal army to escape; nor did they stay with federal troops once they had left. Many runaways, perhaps for the sake of kith and kin, remained close to home. In the countryside, they formed small groups of maroons, scavenging and looting by night to survive. In June 1863, Glass complained that the "whole country is filled with absconding negroes." Like most whites, Glass refused to believe that Lynchburg slaves left on their own volition. Instead, he believed that most had been "enticed away from the service they owe their masters by Yankee deserters." He feared that these "cowards" encouraged slaves to seek revenge on their former owners and predicted that many more owners "would be murdered" and their property "made the prey of fire and other modes of destruction." For the rest of the war, whites remained fearful of black marauders. Consonant with the growing sense of social chaos, white concerns occasionally bordered on hysteria. According to a female resident living on the outskirts of town, runaway blacks regularly burgled families of their food supplies, often in broad daylight.[60]

Nevertheless, most Lynchburg slaves remained subjugated until the end of the war. For these blacks, war evoked a great range of experiences, in which occupation often played a determining role. Those employed as servants generally survived the war better than most. For one thing, many servants retained a closer relationship with their masters than did other slaves. As a result, they could rely on paternalistic overtures of their masters to save them from many of the hardships of war that befell other slaves and many whites. Unless they were sold by an economizing master, servants could expect to live in the relative security of knowing that they would have food, clothes, and shelter. During the first years of the war, some masters indulged their slaves in grandiose overtures of kindness. When William Blackford's cook, Elvira, married a servant of James Langhorne in late 1862, the two masters rented the lecture room at Court Street Methodist for the ceremony. Afterward, the Blackfords allowed the wedding party to use their dining room for the wedding supper. Facetiously, Blackford recorded that "the company was 'select'" and well behaved.[61]

As financial constraints made it difficult for masters to provide such indulgences, favored servants could still count on other forms of assistance. Many servants asked their masters to help them avoid conscription, so that they could escape the exhausting and often hazardous labor associated with army life. When Charles and Susan Blackford's slave William was impressed by the Confederate army to build ramparts in Richmond, the servant begged Susan to have the order rescinded, claiming that the work would kill him. Unwilling to risk the life of a valuable servant, Susan made Charles's father intervene on the slave's behalf. Other masters were also concerned about the well-being of their favored, and often most expensive, slaves. So many slaveholders complained that conscript officers had taken prized servants that Button protested on their behalf. In one of his many diatribes against the encroaching power of the Confederate government, Button argued that because the city had given more to the Confederacy than any other town in Virginia, its most prominent citizens should not be expected to forfeit their favored servants. Later, he endorsed a proposal that would suspend the manufacture of tobacco, so that factory slaves could perform the military labor deemed too torturous for house servants.[62]

For many house slaves, the war itself served to mitigate some of the worst abuses of slavery. Perhaps at no other time were whites forced to admit their dependence on their servants—and this acknowledgment often won servants new freedoms. With her husband away, Susan Blackford relied on an old family slave, Gabe, to fill many of Charles's roles. Thus, when Charles expressed concern that Susan would be alone in the house, Susan assured him that he need not worry, since she would have Gabe stay in the drawing room to protect her. Later, after thieves broke into their home, Charles told Susan that he was glad Gabe was a good watchman but wished that it was legal for him to fire a gun, so that "he could shoot some of the rascals." Years after the war, Susan eulogized Gabe as a "model of fidelity," claiming that "his devotion and sympathy" made him "worthy of all praise." Indeed, because he "guarded the premises and my wants as would a father or a brother," she regarded him as "more of a friend and a protector than a slave." Susan rewarded Gabe's devotion in a number of ways. During her frequent trips to visit Charles, she often left Gabe in charge of the house and the other slaves, with only minimal supervision from Charles's family. At various times, she even allowed Gabe to travel alone to Richmond. Toward the end of the war, when she could no longer afford to keep him as her servant, she hired him out to work at a wire factory, in hopes that this war-related job would protect him from conscription.[63]

Lynchburg house slaves did not simply wait on the benevolence of their masters to weaken the bonds of slavery. As the war progressed, some exploited the disruption of social relations to stretch the boundaries of paternalism to its limits. Susan's relations with some of her other servants provide a case in point. Very early on, Susan discovered that not all her slaves would be as obedient as her trusted Gabe. Before the war, Charles had been the chief disciplinarian in the Blackford household. Although Susan carefully defined each slave's jobs, Charles, not Susan, corrected and punished slaves if they failed in their duties. In addition, Charles decided which slaves to hire out and which to keep at home. As a result, Susan had little experience managing the half-dozen slaves left to her charge during the war.[64]

From the first, some slaves—especially men—took advantage of her. Scarcely six months after Charles left, one of his favorite house servants, Jack, ran away after Susan's brother threatened to whip him for some misdeed. When Jack was finally caught in Lovington, twenty miles north of Lynchburg, Susan confessed to Charles that she did not know what to do with him. For the next few weeks, she tried to persuade Charles to sell him or hire him out. At first, Charles was sympathetic. But when he learned that Susan intended to send Jack to the saltworks, Charles abruptly changed his mind, arguing that the distant locale would make it too easy for Yankees to "take" him. Instead, Charles suggested that Susan attempt a rapprochement. He instructed her not to "treat Jack too harshly," since "it will only make him worse." After all, Charles reasoned, "there are two sides to every quarter and perhaps he does not think himself as bad as you and your Brother do." Moreover, Charles continued, "he has been punished considerably now" and did not deserve anymore.

Although Charles's instructions eased tensions for a bit, Susan's relationship with Jack slowly degenerated again. Sometime in 1863, Jack ran off. For a while he followed federal troops through Virginia. Then, in October 1863, he became ill. Too sick to travel with the military, he made his way back to Charles's sister Nannie, where he rightly surmised he would "receive all sympathy and all attention." Despite Jack's many misdeeds, Charles remained magnanimous, suggesting that it was "just like a negro to return to his master when sick and neglected by those who *freed* him."[65]

Some of the Blackfords' other slaves proved equally adept at taking advantage of Susan and Charles's separation to make life easier for themselves. William, for one, relied on his persuasive powers to negotiate better conditions. In late 1862, he persuaded Susan to protect him from conscription. Although Susan was only too happy to protect a favored slave from the dangers of military life, the truth was that she did not need his services during the war and wanted to rid herself of the cost of his upkeep. Rather than waste William's services, Susan determined to hire him out to the local express agent. Unfortunately, William demurred. Suggesting that Charles would not want a favorite slave to take a job that required him to work on Sundays, William again asked Susan for special consideration. Reluctantly, Susan agreed to look for something that would suit him. Finally, Susan found William a job that would please both him and her husband—in the already overstaffed and financially strapped Blackford household, as Susan's dining-room servant.[66]

Susan understood that the servants were taking advantage of her. Yet without more assistance from Charles, she felt unequal to the task of bringing them under control. The best she could do was encourage Charles to discipline them during his infrequent visits home. This Charles was not always willing to do. When Charles refused to discipline a cook for failing to make biscuits the day before he arrived home, Susan remained indifferent to him during his entire stay, telling him only after he left that she thought he was altogether too lenient with the servants and too cruel to her.[67]

Occasionally, Susan got what she wanted. Maria, one of the Blackfords' three female servants, was even more determined than Jack in her efforts to take advantage of Susan. From the time Charles left, Maria posed special problems for Susan. As another of Charles's old family servants, she had little respect for Susan and showed it by routinely ignoring her orders. At one point, Susan complained to Charles that she hoped to sell Maria, for no other reason than to free herself "of the bondage I have been under since she has been here." The final confrontation came after Maria refused to work while Susan was bedridden with a bad cold. Susan threatened Maria, but Maria ignored her. Instead, Maria coolly informed Susan that she had no right to discipline her, moreover, Maria demanded to talk to Charles about her ill treatment. This time, Charles was unable to ignore such a blatant challenge to his wife's authority. He instructed Susan to sell Maria. Within a few months the servant was gone.[68]

Although the range of behaviors that the Blackfords' slaves displayed may have been exceptional for one household, their unremitting efforts— often successful—to use the war to secure increased freedoms from their masters were not. Although most slaves generally used methods that inevitably reinforced slaveholders' beliefs in the virtues of paternalism, the servants' failure to be more forthright in their quest for independence during the war did not reflect their lack of desire to gain freedom but rather their understanding that the methods of accommodation still worked best. As Maria's case suggests, slaves who went too far risked dire consequences. Indeed, so many masters tried to unload recalcitrant slaves during the last months of the war that slave dealer J. G. Hargrove advertised that he could no longer guarantee the good character of his slaves. Instead, he urged buyers to "try the virtue of the rod" to "make them do their duty." In Lynchburg, war made the conditions of slavery more malleable, but slave discipline did not break down completely.[69]

Lynchburg's other large group of black workers, tobacco factory laborers, found the war to be a mixed blessing at best. For the first year and a half of the war, most of the town's fifteen hundred slave and free black tobacco laborers continued to work in their old occupations. At the end of 1863, however, the state law prohibiting the manufacture of tobacco threw most tobacco factory laborers out of work.[70] From the laborers' perspective, the law was a disaster. Not only did it rob them of one of the most profitable and prestigious occupations available to their race, but it threatened to destroy one of their best sources of racial autonomy—the tobacco factory.

Conscripts found that their new jobs provided them few of the advantages of the tobacco factories. Most were absorbed into Lynchburg's many hospitals, by far the largest employer of blacks during the war. As many as four hundred were conscripted as washers, cooks, and nurses—occupations that placed them in constant contact with white supervisors, coworkers, and patients. Blacks who were conscripted into the town's government shops—mostly to construct and repair wagons—may have found their new circumstances slightly more palatable. Although they, too, were forced to work under the close supervision of white artisans, a shortage of skilled slave laborers in Lynchburg may have encouraged some supervisors to train their conscripts in the needed trades. Thus, by the end of the war, there were as many as 145 slave blacksmiths and metal strikers in Lynchburg, far more than in the prewar years.[71]

The least fortunate conscripts did not get to stay in Lynchburg. Many—although it is impossible to determine how many—were immediately sent to larger cities such as Richmond and Petersburg for the duration of the war. Still others were sent to neighboring towns for short-term assignments, sometimes at a moment's notice, to build fortifications, to repair railroad lines, and temporarily to increase armament production. As a result of such practices, Lynchburg's black factory laborers learned that their already fragile community would be made even more tenuous because of conscription.

Despite the best efforts of the Confederacy, many black factory laborers escaped military conscription. Even though military personnel frequently complained that they needed black laborers to relieve white soldiers of the most servile labor, many black laborers were able to avoid conscription through the timely assistance of their masters or, failing that, through deception. In doing so, many in this group sentenced themselves to a life of extreme poverty. Masters, unwilling to support nonproductive laborers, simply gave their slaves year passes and told them to find work for themselves. Virtually cut off from further white assistance, they lived in a sort of quasi freedom that anticipated their postwar economic status. Some tried to outbid white laborers for the few remaining jobs in town. Others scavenged, peddling their surplus items at the marketplace. Most charitable institutions offered little assistance. Two exceptions were African Baptist Church and Court Street Methodist's black Sunday school program. Both attracted large numbers throughout the war.[72]

Whites only slowly realized that blacks' growing autonomy, no matter how precarious its foundation, might impede whites' ability to control them. At first, many whites were content to make fun of blacks' efforts to assert themselves. After Easter festivities in 1863, Glass casually observed that the town had been full of "grinning darkeys arrayed in fine clothing and their best looks." Glass was especially taken by the large number of black entrepreneurs who catered the event, selling "old clothes, black eyed peas, dressed chickens, and fever and ague pies." Far from rebuking blacks for overrunning the city on the Sabbath, Glass delighted in the carnival atmosphere. Such a "time honored resort," Glass reasoned, "contributes to the happiness of our black peasantry."[73]

A few months later, Glass was less certain that such behavior was altogether innocent. When a respected citizen from a nearby plantation was brutally murdered by five of his slaves, Glass used the occasion to launch into an attack against Lynchburg's black community. In his view, local blacks had become "too free for their own good and that of the community." Behavior that he had once portrayed as innocuous Glass now presented as far more sinister. He claimed to be especially appalled that owners allowed their slaves to "drive hacks and promenade the streets dressed in fine silks or other costly vestments." Glass suggested that such slaves needed to be reminded of their lowly status. Toward that end, Glass encouraged owners to punish their slaves whenever they displayed such impudence.[74]

As the cause of the Confederacy deteriorated, whites became increasingly suspicious of any efforts by blacks to loosen the bonds of servitude and dependence. White residents were especially distrustful of blacks' entrepreneurial activities. Although whites probably exaggerated the size of blacks' wartime businesses, they feared that their expansion was but the first step in the development of an independent black business community. As such, it was but another indication of blacks' growing independence from white control. In January 1864, "A Sufferer" contrasted his poverty with what he perceived to be the general prosperity of Lynchburg's black population. Bitterly, the writer asked why *"the negro . . . carries the most change in his pocket and flaunts in the finest clothing to be seen on our streets?"* In fact, he believed he knew the answer: blacks were thieves. According to the writer, unemployed blacks routinely stole from whites, and what they did not keep for their personal use they sold at the market house. He complained that the business was so widespread that blacks had come to monopolize the market house, forcing honest white hucksters—many of whom were unemployed laborers—either to leave town or to find a new line of work.[75]

Within the next few weeks, others endorsed the "sufferer's" complaints. A second letter writer, "Comus," suggested that city officials prohibit slaves from using the marketplace, so that whites could reclaim it for themselves. Button went even further. Asserting that most blacks had become "a nuisance and a pest to us" because they had been "reduced to such extremities as to compel them to steal," he suggested that they be conscripted as military laborers. Conveniently, this would make them the military's problem, not the civil government's.[76]

Occasionally, whites exhibited a more violent side in their antiblack sentiments. As rowdyism increased in Lynchburg, blacks became a favorite target. Before the war, random violence against blacks was relatively rare—in part because whites recognized slaves as valuable property, and in part because the two races generally tried to avoid each other. When whites had attacked blacks, they generally did so as part of well-orchestrated mob actions, usually led by civic leaders, against one or two black recidivists. During the war, these prohibitions continued to play an important role in governing race relations, but they no longer carried quite the same force. As Lynchburg became home for a large population of rootless and impoverished white males, it was perhaps inevitable that they directed some of their aggressions against blacks. For this reason, much of the wartime white violence against blacks was random, suggesting that the perpetrators' intent was not necessarily to teach a certain class of blacks a lesson but to terrorize the entire black community.

And terrorize they did. Just a few months after the war began, Button chastised soldiers stationed in Lynchburg for carelessly aiming their guns at blacks in an attempt to scare them. According to Button, "a number" of blacks had already been "accidentally" shot because the soldiers had mistakenly believed their guns to be empty. At other times, violence against blacks was intentional. In one incident, conscript officers shot Thomas Wray, a tobacco factory slave, from behind as he fled their dragnet.[77] As civil authority in the town eroded, blacks learned that they had more to fear than just undisciplined soldiers. Like many whites, they fell prey to rowdies and ruffians. Unlike whites, they could not use legal and extralegal means to avenge and protect themselves. Nor could they rely on benevolent whites to come to their assistance. Although the local press noted widespread random violence against blacks, whites gave less attention to stopping such crimes than they did to other forms of criminal behavior.

As a result, Lynchburg blacks were left to their own devices. Blacks responded to these new threats in a variety of ways, most of which only fed whites' anxieties. On the one hand, many blacks adapted by retreating into their own community, thus anticipating what historian Joel Williamson has termed the "disengagement of black culture from the white way."[78] Although the suspension of the tobacco factories destroyed a cornerstone of their community, blacks continued to use the buildings to establish autonomous social and religious institutions. By the end of the war, most blacks had left Lynchburg's white congregations for either the African Baptist Church or more clandestine churches that met in the abandoned tobacco factories. At about the same time, blacks also established their own amusement halls, so that they could enjoy the company of their own race after hours.[79]

On the other hand, some blacks—particularly those who had been more or less abandoned by their masters after the tobacco factories closed—became more aggressive toward whites. Although whites may have exaggerated black hucksters' involvement in theft to discredit them, there is little doubt that slave and free blacks, like soldiers, deserters, and white laborers, became increasingly involved in crimes of property to survive. As early as May 1863, six months before the factories closed,

Glass noted that the "amount of [black] petty thievery being carried on in the city is unprecedented." Property holders contended that blacks were as brazen as whites in their efforts to steal and intimidate. The same letter writer who complained that Confederate soldiers terrorized her neighborhood asserted that blacks were equally unruly. She recalled one incident in which a black mob "called" upon a white woman, "demanding . . . lodging and something to eat." When the woman refused them, they threatened her but were forced to flee when neighbors heard the woman's call for help.[80]

Such incidents were exceedingly rare. No doubt, white perceptions of black behavior owed as much to wartime hysteria and fears of impending black emancipation as to any acts of black terrorism. More often, blacks found revenge in less conspicuous, though equally effective, ways. Evidently, many blacks were especially adept at taking advantage of soldiers as they traveled through Lynchburg. According to Button, Lynchburg blacks regularly tried to sell soldiers pies made out of dog meat, figuring that the soldiers would be too hungry to detect the ruse.[81]

Yet even in the midst of war's mounting chaos, there were limits to how far blacks could go. If they were too overt in their acts of insubordination, they risked disciplinary action, if not revenge, by the entire white community. Wounded Confederate soldiers were especially sensitive to the treatment they received from black hospital conscripts. Weak and vulnerable, most Confederate soldiers—as proud white Southerners— probably did not feel entirely comfortable with the idea of being left unprotected in the hands of black hospital conscripts. As a result, they were extremely sensitive to even the smallest slights by black orderlies. On their way to the hospital, for instance, soldiers often complained that black ambulance drivers handled them too roughly. In reaction, they asked the city's medical department to dispatch whites to the depot "to control the negroes." Soldiers made similar complaints about black nurses in the hospitals. In one instance, a slighted soldier decided to get revenge. Daniel Sullivan, a Confederate soldier, claimed that one of his nurses, Joshua Burns, was so cruel to him that he vowed to settle the score when his wounds healed. Almost three years after the war, Sullivan found Burns back in Lynchburg. True to his word, Sullivan followed Burns home and beat him up.[82]

Fearful of white reprisals and hopeful of a more peaceful solution to the problem of slavery, most blacks did not act in an openly hostile manner toward whites. This may explain why Button and other civic leaders confidently asserted throughout the war that the South could enlist any number of blacks to fight against the North. Indeed, when the war ended, the town's provost marshal was in the process of organizing a black regiment.[83] Nevertheless, the scattered occurrences of black restiveness were significant, if only because they anticipated postwar race relations in Lynchburg. Where blacks had once been victims of racial violence, during the war, a few became perpetrators themselves. Like many of the town's poorest and less powerful whites, these blacks used the disruption of civil authority as an opportunity to assert and protect themselves. In doing so, they also contributed to the process of social erosion.

Assailed from below by soldiers, poorer whites, slaves, and free blacks, Lynchburg's men of property and standing soon began to quarrel among themselves as well. After passing through uneventful municipal, state, and Confederate elections in 1863, some predicted the end of party wrangling and divisiveness. The municipal election campaigns of 1864, however, suggested that such hopes were illusory. Early on, Button noted that there was an exceptionally large field of candidates. "A voter," writing in the *Lynchburg Virginian* stated that the cause was obvious: many men wanted to escape military service by gaining political exemption. To stop this practice, he suggested that citizens vote only for those individuals who were already exempt from military service because of age or disability. In addition, he suggested that voters give special consideration to those who had shown consistent devotion to the war despite their inability to serve in the military. He was especially gratified to see that John B. Tilden, who faithfully took supplies to soldiers in the field, was running unopposed for city sergeant. According to the writer, Tilden's unanimous election would send him a much deserved message of gratitude. "A constant reader" seconded "a voter's" support of Tilden, noting that the unanimous election of Tilden, dubbed the "soldier's friend," would also be a sign of the town's united support for the war.[84]

Unfortunately, citizens agreed on little besides Tilden's election. Although Mayor Branch was reelected without significant opposition, the election of council representatives was hotly contested. During the campaign, "many voters" announced that they intended to defy "a voter's" plea and would endorse "gentlemen" of stature, irrespective of whether they were "subject to duty in the field." By their view, it was better to have "men long known and well tried" in the crisis than men who were simply unfit for military service. Button endorsed their conservatism, claiming that those who wanted to make military eligibility an issue were nothing more than "put-everybody-in-the-army men (except themselves)." Most residents thought differently. Of the three members of city council who were military-eligible, two were voted out. Since both the winners and losers were men of property and standing, the election results probably had little to do with class per se. Instead, the election revolved around the nagging question of what constituted legitimate community service and true patriotism. Those who had served in the military or who had family members who did resented those who had received exemptions, even if the later had demonstrated their patriotism in other ways. Informed by letters from loved ones in the field, these voters knew that detailing and exempting eligible citizens only increased the dangers and the adversities for those who stayed to fight.[85]

Women may have helped sensitize male voters to this issue. Writing in support of John Tilden's candidacy, "Matron" endorsed Tilden as the "Ladies' Candidate," because he had won over "every mother and daughter of Lynchburg" by his commitment to "mitigate the sufferings of our sons and brothers in the army." Although "Matron" refused to comment on the more divisive council race and indeed apologized for "trespassing" on "the affairs that pertain exclusively to our worthy lords," her support of the public-spirited Tilden was perhaps a polite message that women expected more self-sacrifice of their political leaders. Privately, women were sometimes less polite. When Stonewall Jackson's body passed through Lynchburg, the town organized a funeral procession. Among the pallbearers was Colonel Maurice Langhorne, who had been forced to retire from the field early in the war. Susan Blackford was furious. Informing Charles of the incident, she stated that Langhorne "was of course making a tremendous ado about nothing and so were all the substitute men." She reported that she and her brother were both "indignant that Mayor Branch should let men be pall bearers who had substitutes in the army."[86]

At times, individuals framed the issue of military service and self-sacrifice in vague, though discernible, class terms. In February 1865, members of the town's Second Class Militia, the town's only defense unit, petitioned the state government to have all the militia officers removed from office. Most of the members of the unit were of the middling sort— artisans, clerks, and small grocers—all too old or infirm to be in the regular army. In their petition, the militia claimed that the officers of the unit used their status "as a barrier" to "keep them from the field." Indeed, the petitioners argued, the officers cared more about their reputations than they did about the welfare of the unit. As a result, they showed up only when "there is some excitement . . . flitting around performing some mythical duties" as a way to impress the public of their patriotism. Otherwise, the officers ignored the militia's efforts to improve the town's home defense. The soldiers claimed that while they "were eager to contribute whatever service they can to the defense and security of the state," the behavior of their officers had "caused so much dissatisfaction as to render the Battalion . . . utterly inefficient and useless."[87]

As the condition of the Confederacy continued to deteriorate, especially after the military reverses of the 1863 summer campaigns, the issue for many civilians became not how to serve but whether to serve at all. Perhaps depressed by the bleak outlook, a growing number of civilians demonstrated that they were no longer willing to make the same commitment to the cause that they were in the beginning of the war. The local defense unit, originally organized with considerable enthusiasm, had trouble attracting volunteers and proved reluctant to serve outside the town. When the nearby town of Salem asked for the Lynchburg militia to assist it, most members refused to turn out. As a result, Lynchburg's provost marshal had no choice but to send a company of convalescing soldiers to assist the town. Eventually, the Home Guard dissolved, and the Second Class Militia took its place as the town's only defense unit. Their contribution to the cause was mixed at best. In June 1864, military officials reported that the militia behaved gallantly in defense of the town when attacked by Union raiders. Later in the year, the unit again won accolades for helping defend the much-prized saltworks in southwestern Virginia. Yet unless Lynchburg had a direct stake in the military activity, residents proved reluctant to serve. Major Francis Nicholls, commander of the Lynchburg post, regularly complained that the soldiers under his charge were of "indifferent material" and unwilling to leave town, even when they were desperately needed. Since many of the officers were of military age, Nicholls suspected that they had joined the militia to avoid service in the regular army, a strategy of dubious legality. By the end of the war, when the Confederacy could no longer enforce its conscription laws, the local militia gave up nearly all pretense of patriotism. In February 1865, the acting commissary told Lee that interest in the militia was so low that there were now fewer than one hundred men willing to serve, "and they were unarmed."[88]

Others were equally reluctant to help the cause. As the South's fortunes waned, more and more tried to escape military service altogether. As early as June 1863, Button chastised eligible citizens for failing to enlist. To shame those who refused to volunteer, Button threatened to publish an honor roll and a blacklist, so that all would know who contributed to the war and who did not. Despite the threat, the problem of recruitment became worse with each succeeding month.[89]

Many civilians developed a far different view of patriotism from Button's. Evidently, many came to view conscription as the act of a powerful and arbitrary central government. As such, it was the very antithesis of what most white Southerners believed the Confederacy was supposed to be like. To defend themselves from such tyranny, civilians sometimes went to extreme ends to avoid fighting. Lower-class groups complained the loudest, recognizing that conscript laws placed most of the war's burden on them. Unlike their wealthy counterparts, poorer civilians could not escape service by hiring substitutes or claiming exemption because they owned more than twenty slaves.[90]

James Cleland may have been among those who viewed conscription as a form of class persecution. As the town's only gas fitter, Cleland had originally been excused because the city depended on him to maintain the municipal gasworks. As the Confederate army became increasingly desperate for men, however, conscript officers began to rescind most exemptions. In October 1864, the provost marshal gave Cleland notice that he would have to serve. Cleland wanted no part in the war. An alcoholic, he went on a drinking spree in a desperate attempt to persuade conscript officers that he was physically and morally unfit for the military. His plan failed. While still drunk, conscript officers enrolled him and shipped him to Richmond, where he was mustered into service. While there, he may have run across another Lynchburg resident, William Waller, who fled to Richmond at about the same time in hopes that conscript officers would have more trouble finding him in a larger city. Others may have tried even more outlandish ploys. According to Robert Withers, men in nearby Danville dressed as women, hid in secret closets and pits, and fled to the hills to live off the land.[91]

Meanwhile, a larger cross section of the community stopped supporting the war. By the winter of 1864–1865, even the most sincere efforts to help the cause failed for lack of community support. Although many residents claimed that they wanted to continue the fight, few had the means or enthusiasm to do so. Both the Soldiers' Aid Society and the Ladies' Relief Hospital stopped publishing the names of donators, probably because their numbers were so low. Even special events to aid soldiers did not garner sufficient public assistance. On New Year's Day in 1865, a group of civilians announced that they planned to give a holiday meal to soldiers camped near Lynchburg. Despite extravagant promises of a sumptuous dinner, the affair did not come off as planned. So few donated food and money that organizers were not able to serve everyone. The lucky few who did receive a meal got only a small portion—a bit of bread and two ounces of half-done pork. Although the incident was a disaster, Button, for one, refused to admit it. When a soldier complained to him about his meager helping, Button brushed his criticism aside, brusquely reminding the soldier that he and his cohorts "had better bear the disappointment gracefully, as they have to bear a great many others." Though still unapologetic, he told his readers that it would have been "much better that the dinner had not been attempted at all." [92]

Meanwhile, a growing number of residents began to hint that their persons and their property would probably be more secure if the South surrendered and rejoined the old Union. Although Button publicly chastised their lack of resolve, privately he must have been somewhat sympathetic to their concerns. By February, robbery had become a daily occurrence. Homes, stores, and banks were targets. Button claimed that he himself had been robbed repeatedly, at a loss of thousands of dollars. Perhaps without even realizing it, Button began to send his readers a mixed message. Although he consistently stated that the South must continue the fight at all costs, in less guarded moments he, too, admitted that he had tired of the war and wished it would end soon. [93]

To buoy public confidence, leading civilians orchestrated a mass meeting that they hoped would rekindle the public's commitment to the cause. Suggested in early February, the meeting did not come off until 2 March. This time, Button was more upbeat, terming the "war meeting" a great success. John Speed and J. O. Goggin, two of the town's most ardent Confederates, made speeches to what Button believed was the "largest meeting . . . ever seen in Lynchburg." After the speeches, participants unanimously approved a resolution stating that since the government of the United States meant to destroy the South, they would continue the fight, dedicating themselves and all that they had "anew to the cause in which we struggle." In a bit of rhetorical reverie, the signers claimed that they would "shirk from no duty, fear no sacrifices, shun no dangers, complain of no hardships, know no weariness, nor show no mercy, and that with God as our Helper, we will conquer." [94]

In the end, however, the meeting made little impact. Although public morale may have improved for a time, the meeting did nothing to increase supplies or enlistments for the Confederate army. Nor did the meeting alter white Lynchburgers' penchant for looking after their own needs first. When the Confederate government decided to impress the town's only undertaker, George Diuguid, residents denounced the decision, claiming that his services were desperately needed in Lynchburg. Yet the Confederate government had little choice but to draft Diuguid. There was almost no one else available. Similarly, when the Confederate government decided to enroll blacks for military service, so few slave owners volunteered their slaves for military duty that when the war ended a month later, the regiment had only a few members. Finally, when rumors of a Yankee invasion circulated in late March 1865, the military commander of the town was forced to organize a company of youths, some of whom were as young as twelve years old, because no one else—including many of the town's militia officers—would volunteer.[95]

And so, the South moved inextricably toward defeat. With Grant in pursuit, Lee abandoned Petersburg on April 1 and headed west in search of a way around the Union forces. On April 8, the Confederacy's high command instructed the Lynchburg provost, General Raleigh Colston, to make a firm defense of the town, in case Lee intended to make a stand there. Lee never made it that far. On April 9, he surrendered at Appomattox Court House, less than twenty miles from Lynchburg.[96]

Unsure of what to do, Colston's small regiment of young boys, old men, and convalescing soldiers disintegrated. Some tried to join regiments still in the field; others fled the city, fearing the Yankees were close at hand. As they left, renegade Confederate soldiers, many of them from Lee's army, made their way to Lynchburg to reorganize. According to one observer, the scene was chaotic. With no one to lead them, they wandered the streets aimlessly, "not knowing what to do, nor where to go." When General L. L. Lomax arrived later in the day with a small regiment to help prepare the town for battle, he was greeted by the mayor and council. They begged him to surrender the town to the first Yankee squad he could find. Lomax refused and did his best to quiet the citizenry. Meanwhile, more and more fugitives from Lee's army entered the town.[97]

Amid the confusion, residents tried to come to terms with Lee's surrender. Mary Early, daughter of a local minister, admitted that "my brain refuses to grasp the idea of this great calamity," even though "it is written on my brain in letters of fire." H. C. Sommerville, an army physician stationed in Lynchburg, was similarly distressed and incredulous. "What fearful news—who could believe it? I for one could not," he confided in his diary. "The thing seemed so . . . unreasonable that Lee's army should have to yield." Some soldiers also refused to accept that the end was near. Upon hearing the news of surrender, convalescing soldiers at Lynchburg's various hospitals determined to find Lee so that they could reorganize. According to Sommerville, the scene was a "sad and melancholy sight," for "among the number were many maimed and crippled. . . . These were to scatter, roam, and wander without protection or leader under whom they could seek shelter or safety."[98]

In the resulting chaos, civil authorities lost control of the town. Fearful of riot and plundering, wary civic leaders closed their businesses and suspended all city services. Perhaps they hoped that the Confederate military would take control, but Lomax's regiment could offer little help. According to a staff officer, William Lyne Wilson, the regiment was simply a "rabble of fugitive soldiers," most of whom were "famished with hunger and frightened" and thus in poor condition to police the town. Instead, they added to the chaos. When distraught civilians started throwing Confederate money and cotton bonds into the canal, soldiers fished them out in hopes that they might be worth something. Once they tired of this, they began to search for more corporeal treasures. After days of living on "parched corn and what meat they could pick up along the march," the soldiers were ready to let loose their frustrations. They started by looting the Confederate supply stores, while officers, according to Wilson, made "scarcely no attempt . . . to control the men." At about the same time, Sommerville recorded that "irresistible raids were made on the commissary and other buildings" by "the rabble." When they exhausted the military stores soldiers and citizens went after private property, stealing "clothing, tobacco, and shoes" from the canal boats and riverside warehouses. At long last, poorer residents had the opportunity to reclaim what the war had taken from them.[99]

The next day, civic leaders decided that Yankee rule was better than chaos and disorder. Acting like "whipped curs," according to one observer, the mayor and council promptly dispatched a committee to find someone to accept their surrender. Meanwhile, a small Union scouting party entered the town. Once again, town fathers hoped that an outside force might do what they could not—restore order. Once again, they were disappointed. The ranking officer, General John W. Turner, turned over what remained of all military stores to destitute whites and blacks. He then unceremoniously paroled five thousand soldiers and left them to fend for themselves. According to Sommerville, the three groups— blacks, poorer whites, and ex-soldiers—flooded the city streets, "ready to make violence on anything." The Union soldiers made only half-hearted efforts to keep the peace before leaving on 16 April.[100]

When the Yankee soldiers left, citizens of property retreated to their homes for safety. On April 20, nearly two weeks after Lee's surrender, Jannett Cleland noted in her diary that she had still not ventured far beyond her front door. Earlier that day, she missed church because her mother did not want her to leave the house during "these troublesome times." According to Cleland, it looked "like a revolution has broken out everywhere."[101]

So it must have seemed to many Lynchburg residents. Blacks, feeling more confident than ever of their impending freedom, finally allowed themselves an opportunity to celebrate and to articulate what they hoped the war's end would mean. A few days after the town formally surrend- ered, the black community congregated at the Fair Grounds—the place where the town's militia units had once paraded—to celebrate. Watching from a distance, Sommerville noted that the meeting was orderly, though disconcerting nonetheless. Some gave speeches, Sommerville noted, "and sundry doctrines were inculcated of a *moral, social, and political tone*"—fair warning that blacks intended to define freedom and their place in postwar Lynchburg for themselves.[102]

The war was over—and so, it seemed, was the old order of Lynchburg. During the days and weeks between Lee's surrender and Yankee rule, there was little evidence of the community that had grown prosperous, stable, and harmonious on the traditions of deference, personalism, and paternalism. Amid the disorder, elites made little attempt to behave as the benevolent patriarchs of old. Even faithful slaves were sometimes turned away. As the Confederacy crumbled around them, the Blackfords' favorite slave, Gabe, now traveling with Charles, asked Charles what he should do, now that defeat seemed imminent. Nearly despondent, Charles told Gabe that since he was now free, he could "do as he pleased," but he suggested that Gabe "should try to get work with the Yankees when they came." After a tearful farewell, Charles left him. It was the last time they saw each other. According to Charles, Gabe died shortly thereafter.[103]

Overmatched by poorer whites, blacks, renegade Confederate soldiers, and Yankees, civic leaders did not even attempt to retain public order, let alone social harmony. Instead, they called on an outside force—indeed, their hated conquerors—to keep the peace. Sequestered in the relative safety of their homes, they were left to ponder if the events of the last few months signaled the end of their old way of life and, if so, what they could now do to regain mastery over the community.

CHAPTER FOUR

"These Troublesome Times": Rebuilding Lynchburg after the War

In late March 1865, Charles Blackford, then stationed at Richmond, asked for and received a thirty-day pass to visit his wife and children, now living in Charlottesville with family. Before Charles could reach them, however, Lee surrendered. Unsure of the Confederacy's future, Charles determined to stay in Charlottesville with his wife. They rented a one-room apartment at the University of Virginia and waited for the chaos in the countryside to subside, so that they could return to their home in Lynchburg. With only a few dollars, they lived mostly on gifts from family and friends.[1]

After two months, Charles determined it was safe for him to return to Lynchburg. Because train service was still irregular, he went alone and most of the way on foot, making the entire sixty-mile journey in one day. When he reached Lynchburg, sometime after sunset, he immediately began to call on neighbors, asking for loans. Fortunately, one of the persons he met was an old family friend, W. T. Booker. Booker, a tobacconist, had profited from the war by speculating in tobacco. When Charles asked Booker for a loan, Booker "ran his hand down his pocket" and nonchalantly handed Charles five twenty-dollar gold pieces. Friend that he was, Booker told Blackford to repay him "when he could." The next day, Charles reopened his old law office and waited "for any employment that might come." It would be a long wait. Although the war had been over for several weeks, Charles recalled that most businessmen and shop-keepers spent their days sitting along the sidewalks of Main Street "gossiping and smoking." The more ambitious "passed the decadence of another day of . . . enforced idleness" by playing chess, backgammon, and cards. As the sun drifted overhead, these "idlers followed with their tables, their chairs, their pipes, and their games."[2]

Charles did his best to stay busy. "Rusty in the law," he stayed close to his office "to study to catch up." Meanwhile, he noticed that much of the town had changed. Many of Lynchburg's oldest business establishments had closed for lack of funds and, Charles feared, would probably never reopen. Others had been taken over by "complete strangers," most of whom Charles suspected were Northerners. As a result, the town seemed foreign, so much so that Charles feared he would not be able to reestablish his practice. Depressed by his lack of prospects, he confided in a letter to Susan that "it is a sad thought for a man to think that he cannot support his family and this is my condition now." After only a week in Lynchburg, he confessed that he found himself "giving way to my feelings for the first time in years," unable to "keep back a bitter tear."[3]

Other longtime residents also feared that they would not be able to reestablish themselves in postwar Lynchburg. Former Confederate administrator Robert Garlick Hill Kean returned to town at about the same time as Charles Blackford. Although Kean was far more stoic and calculating than Blackford, he was equally discouraged. Kean noted that the economy was "perfectly stagnant" because of an absolute want of money, a general distrust of federal currency, and "the impoverishment of the whole community." Kean also fretted about how black emancipation would affect Lynchburg. Specifically, he questioned whether civil authorities would be able to cope with black emancipation. By his estimate, "one half of the negroes" would be "unable by age, sex, infirmity, or want of character to support and take care of themselves." Because their former masters were impoverished, the state would have to assume responsibility for their care. But, Kean noted, this would prove unworkable, because the state too was reluctant "to take up the burden of a vast pauper system." The "inevitable result," Kean predicted, would be "destitution and suffering on a vast scale," followed by "vice, crime . . . disease," and finally jail. Already, Kean noted, emancipation had created "great confusion" in Lynchburg because so many destitute blacks had entered the town looking for jobs and charity.[4]

In truth, prominent residents like Kean and Blackford had less to fear than most. Although their sufferings were real, they possessed resources that allowed them to survive the economic crisis without experiencing the worst of it. Most owned tobacco, specie, or some other commodity that allowed them to acquire the essentials. Charles Blackford, for all his fears about insolvency, retained an estate of twelve thousand dollars from before the war. In addition, he had several friends who lent him money whenever he asked. Others had skills and talents that allowed them to escape the economic crisis unscathed. Lewis Blackford, one of Charles's three younger brothers, received an offer from the U.S. Topographical Service for a position as an engineer, shortly after hostilities ended. Although Lewis had recently vowed that he would never be subject to Lincoln or his henchmen, a few weeks of poverty changed his thinking. After talking it over with his four brothers, he accepted the position and moved to New York.[5]

Most poorer residents lacked these options. The tobacco factories that had long been the engine of Lynchburg's economy had not operated in two years and would not reopen until the fall, because few farmers had planted tobacco during the previous summer. As a result, many of the artisans and shopkeepers who catered to the tobacconists found little demand for their work during the summer of 1865. Many of the town's twenty-five hundred newly freed slaves also had no means of support by the war's end. Although some former masters allowed favored servants to retain their positions, old and infirm slaves and the thousand or so former tobacco factory laborers had no choice but to fend for themselves. Meanwhile, all local rail lines were down. As a result, most merchants had few supplies. And what they did have was priced too high for poorer residents to purchase. With the economy shut down, most whites and blacks became increasingly dependent on government handouts of food and clothing, provided by the newly established Freedmen's Bureau.[6]

Even with federal assistance, however, poorer residents suffered, perhaps even more than they had during the last months of the war. John Richard Dennett, a Northern newspaper correspondent who toured the South immediately after the war, noted in July 1865 that trade was "dead" in Lynchburg because "the people have no money, nor is there the prospect of their soon getting any." According to Dennett, shops were only "scantily supplied," and then only "with poor goods." A month later, Dennett interviewed an ex-soldier who claimed that since he had come home from the war, the most money he had seen was six dollars. Dennett was unmoved. By his view, most whites had only themselves to blame for their poverty. Although the railroads desperately wanted their labor to repair the roads, many refused the work because they feared they would be put alongside blacks. Instead, they preferred to lounge "listlessly . . . in the streets and in the bar-rooms."[7]

More than likely, the inactivity of most lower-class whites had less to do with Southern indolence than with the dismal state of Lynchburg's economy immediately after the war. According to Button, unemployed labor was "abundant . . . and cheap." Some were reduced to desperate and sometimes dangerous measures to make ends meet. According to newspaper reports, many poor whites had taken up selling old bullet shells to the iron industry, a dangerous business because the shells often exploded for no apparent reason. Others supported themselves by selling fried pies and cider at the market house and the railroad depot.[8]

Lynchburg blacks suffered even more. Not only did they have to compete with whites for the few jobs open to blacks, they had to compete with a growing number of black refugees as well. Resident blacks were sometimes less than hospitable to the interlopers. In early 1867, Louis Stevenson, a local Freedmen's Bureau agent, reported that resident blacks wanted the Bureau to encourage rural black refugees to leave the city so that there would be less competition for jobs. Bureau agents were sympathetic. To alleviate the suffering, Lynchburg area agents plaintively wrote to agents in other counties that they could provide laborers if residents needed them. Few of the black refugees left. By October 1865, the Bureau regularly provided food and clothing to more than one thousand freedmen every week. Housing was another matter. Before the war, blacks found shelter in alley garrets, lofts, and small apartments near the tobacco factories. After the war, the large influx of black refugees into town forced many to sleep in abandoned factories, on the sidewalks, and in ramshackle shacks, made from crates, newspapers, and metal sheeting, at the Fair Grounds, along the main highways, and in a vacant lot near the Freedmen's Bureau office on Main Street. The last locale became such a labyrinth of huts that whites derisively dubbed it the "Fort Snacks Hotel," in reference to both the charity of the Freedmen's Bureau to blacks and the many black shacks on the grounds made from the empty provision crates. During the day, refugees and native blacks congregated on sidewalks in the central business district. Their numbers were so great that whites often complained that they made it difficult for whites to pass without stepping into the streets.[9]

Even as the poor continued to suffer from the effects of postwar economic dislocation, citizens of property and standing slowly became more optimistic in their estimation of the town. Wealthier residents were especially heartened by the conduct of the federal military officials who controlled the town. Although conservative residents would eventually resent "Yankee rule," most expressed satisfaction with the federal officials' willingness to work with the town's political and business leaders during the first months of Reconstruction. Almost immediately, federal military officials began to address one of the biggest problems—public order. Commander J. Irvin Gregg, the provost of the town, quickly won the favor of civic leaders by instituting laws that both protected private property and worked to revive Lynchburg's war-ravaged economy. Through a variety of measures, Gregg attempted to stop the vandalism that had terrorized the propertied community in the waning weeks of the war. To clear the streets of the classes presumed to be dangerous, Gregg established a strict curfew system that initially, at least, forced all residents to carry passes. In an even more ambitious move, Gregg attempted to stop rowdyism at its source by shutting down the ill-famed Buzzard. During his first week in Lynchburg, Gregg ordered his men to close every doggery and brothel and to confiscate and destroy all liquor in town. In addition, he rounded up the town's prostitutes and garrisoned them in an abandoned tobacco warehouse, which Gregg summarily converted into a workhouse.[10]

During the first months of Reconstruction, federal officials regularly solicited the assistance of civic leaders. In doing so, they proved to be as lenient in their treatment of former rebels as was their president, Andrew Johnson. After just a few weeks in Lynchburg, Gregg informed his superiors that "interviews with several prominent men . . . convince me that the people desire earnestly to renew their allegiance in good faith." A year later, when the first postwar municipal elections were held, federal officials were equally accommodating to the town's prewar civic leaders. Following the dictates of moderate governor Francis H. Pierpont's policies, federal officials allowed all white males to vote. The result was a conservative sweep. William Branch, the town's longtime mayor, was reelected by a near-unanimous vote, and the new city council included seven incumbents and three former Confederate military officers.[11]

In time, federal authorities came to rely on the civil courts as much as on the city council. In November 1865, when cases of petty larceny threatened to overwhelm the small staff at the local Freedmen's Bureau, Bureau agents asked their superiors in Richmond to allow the municipal courts to help police the freedmen. R. S. Lacey, head of the Lynchburg Bureau, reasoned that because the crime rate was so high, "it seems advisable to invite all authorities, civil and military, to aid in suppressing the matter." His superiors quickly approved Lacey's suggestion. By these measures, the federal army gained considerable popularity among those propertied residents who had long since become weary of wartime violence and excesses. When the federal army returned the policing of Lynchburg to local authorities in January 1866, city council formally thanked the military police "for the very efficient and satisfactory manner in which their duties have been performed." [12]

As civil and military officials restored order, Gregg and other federal officials worked to revive the town's war-ravaged economy—usually on terms that benefited the business community. Recognizing the town's dependence on the tobacco trade, Gregg asked his superiors to allow Lynchburg tobacco manufacturers to resume production. To make trade possible, Gregg organized work crews of destitute blacks and whites to rebuild the railroads and repair the roads. In early 1866, Whitelaw Reid, another Northern journalist who visited Lynchburg after the war, noted that although the railroad from Lynchburg to Richmond was "not yet in running order," all other lines into town operated with "unexpected regularity," even as they were being repaired. According to Reid, the railroads had already attracted a number of Northern capitalists who were "swarming" the town, "looking for investments." As a result, Reid reported, many citizens had regained their prewar confidence. One prominent citizen told Reid that thanks to the military's presence, the town was no longer "in a fix for starving." "Niggers might suffer . . . if they grew too saucy," the man cautioned, "but the people were all right." Reid's informant boasted that wealthy residents had preserved "half a million of specie" and were eager to use it to buy whatever tobacco farmers and speculators had stored away. [13]

Initially, citizens were less certain of Gregg's and other federal agents' racial policies. Yet here, too, federal government representatives eventually won white Lynchburgers over—at least for a time. Although Gregg and the local Freedmen's Bureau agents believed it was their duty to establish free labor in the South, they shared conservative whites' view that blacks were as yet too ignorant and unprepared for freedom to control their own labor. Moreover, because Bureau agents shared civic leaders' belief that priority should be given to maintaining public order and reviving Lynchburg's economy, they resisted blacks' efforts to gain control of their own labor. The Bureau's response to black refugees was especially severe. From the first, the Bureau told able-bodied refugees that it was in their best interest to return to their former masters. When this advice failed to stem the tide of impoverished blacks entering the town, military officials tried more stringent measures. In January 1866, the Bureau encouraged, if not forced, many unemployed blacks to sign labor contracts with local farmers, in order to get most of them out of town.[14]

Federal officials could be equally unrelenting in their treatment of longtime black residents. Gregg set the tone almost as soon as he came to town. In May 1865, he instructed his lieutenants to issue rations only to the "destitute ... and absolutely helpless," to "enforce contracts for labor," to tell all blacks that "no freedman will be allowed to live in idleness," and to treat all loafers as "vagabonds." When federal officials supervised the reopening of the tobacco factories, they approved work conditions that favored the tobacconists at the expense of the black factory laborers. Often these new arrangements seemed little different from slavery. Throughout the summer of 1865, Bureau agents advised Lynchburg's blacks that they should "be content to work ... for their victuals and clothes" until the economy improved. Later in the year, agents briefly experimented with an apprentice system, whereby destitute adolescent blacks were committed to the care of white employers until they reached maturity. Most received no more than fifteen to thirty dollars a year. Finally, in February 1866, agents revived the chain gang, forcing all black petty thieves, loiterers, and the like to become reacquainted with forced labor by cleaning the city streets.[15]

Perhaps the most persistent point of contention between federal agents and resident conservatives was black education. During the first year of Reconstruction in Lynchburg, the Freedmen's Bureau established schools, employing freedmen and Northern philanthropists to teach the ex-slaves. By March 1866, the Bureau had established nine schools in Lynchburg and its vicinity. With classes as large as one hundred or more, these schools taught as many as 819 men, women, and children. Most native whites hated the Bureau schools because, as one local agent observed, "education is blacks' only passport to distinction." Local whites harassed and threatened Bureau teachers constantly, so much so that Jacob Yoder, superintendent of the local freedmen's schools, refused to go out at night during his first year in Lynchburg. White residents treated black students even worse. Blacks who dared to seek an education were fired from their jobs, ridiculed, and even beaten for their presumed impudence. Even so, the Freedmen's Bureau attempted to find some point of rapprochement with local whites. When the city council announced in 1866 that it wanted to assume responsibility for black education, Bureau agents and teachers politely encouraged them to consider how they might do so in a way that would be both fair and advantageous for blacks.[16]

Federal agents were not always blacks' adversaries. There were some vestiges of slavery that they simply would not tolerate. When ex-slaves complained that their white employers physically or sexually abused them or forced them to act in a slavish manner, agents intervened. In addition, Bureau agents zealously guarded blacks' right to organize and attend schools, political clubs, and mutual aid societies. The Bureau also monitored civil courts and interceded when judge and jury refused to give blacks justice. Most important, Bureau agents, unlike most Southern whites, hoped that their current labor policies would be temporary, necessary evils that would be rescinded when passions had abated and blacks proved that they could care for themselves. Still, most federal officials retained many of the racial prejudices of their day and often acted accordingly. Jacob Yoder typified Northern whites' ambivalent racial views. Although Yoder was an outspoken proponent of black political rights, he confessed in his diary that he did not believe blacks were as intelligent as whites. After only a few months in the South, Yoder concluded that the average black person was a slow learner because he had a smaller cranial capacity than the average white person. Although he never wavered from his belief that blacks would eventually learn to care for themselves—a view that put him at variance with most native whites—he doubted whether most would amount to much. By his view, blacks demonstrated "a great want of energy" and had "not proved themselves very reliable."[17]

At least in the short run, then, local federal officials seemed to favor former slaveholders. Charles Button of the *Virginian*, for one, believed as much. In early 1866, after observing Bureau agents forcing black refugees to sign labor contracts on local farms for the coming year, he announced that the Bureau had proved to be the white South's ally in race relations. With considerable satisfaction, he noted that most blacks did not trust the Bureau. Robert Garlick Hill Kean was more guarded in his assessment of the town's federal officials. Although he remained a vocal critic of all things Yankee, in the privacy of his diary he, too, expressed satisfaction with the Bureau's labor policies.[18]

The speed and ease with which federal authorities helped restore some semblance of order to Lynchburg, without upending the old hierarchy,

Lynchburg skyline as seen from Amherst County, 1866. ("General Steedman's Tour," LMS)

encouraged many civic leaders to believe that the town would quickly return to its prewar eminence as a wealthy manufacturing center. Ever the booster, Button observed in August 1865 that Lynchburg was rapidly "becoming itself again," as "old merchants . . . have resumed their former pursuits" and "the city fathers have returned to their parental labors." Almost casually, Button suggested that "the debris of war" had nearly all been "brushed away." While admitting that the scarcity of money had made Lynchburg's leading industry, the tobacco trade, exceedingly "dull," he confidently predicted that in a very short time "there will be an increasing demand for our tobacco," which would usher in a new age of economic prosperity for the Tobacco City. Others were also eager to demonstrate their confidence in the town's economic revival. By the end of the year, local business leaders, including iron manufacturers, tobacconists, and merchants, established a subscription plan to build a new railroad to Danville, Virginia, seventy miles south of Lynchburg.[19]

For a time, it appeared that Button's prediction would come true. In February 1866, local Freedmen's Bureau agent R. S. Lacey reported to his superiors that the tobacco industry had revived to the point that he feared "from present appearances this section of the state will suffer from a lack of negroes." With "wages increasing almost daily," he anticipated a time in which "no one in the district will need to be supported by government or county charity."[20] Button was equally satisfied with Lynchburg's postwar economic progress. In May 1866, he noted that the sales at the daily tobacco auctions were so brisk that "it had something of the aspect of the olden time to see the weed coming in so plentifully." By the fall of that year, Button boasted that Lynchburg's tobacco trade had returned to its prewar levels. Without releasing trade figures to document his claim, he also declared that the Lynchburg tobacco business had survived the war better than the business had in the larger tobacco cities of Richmond, Petersburg, and Danville. As a result, the town now "stands ahead of all rivals in the tobacco trade." Still later, in December 1866, after several Lynchburg brands took awards at a New Orleans fair, Button bragged with renewed bluster that the reputation of Lynchburg tobacco was again "co-extensive with christendome."[21]

Yet if town fathers hoped that tobacco would create a revival of the prewar status quo, they quickly learned otherwise. Retaining formal political power in the community during Reconstruction proved especially problematic. As former rebels, civic leaders learned that they no longer controlled their political lives. Things began well enough. Unionist Republican governor Francis H. Pierpont proved to be an early, though unwitting, ally. Like President Andrew Johnson, Pierpont believed the best course of action was to reestablish civil order as quickly as possible. Also like Johnson, Pierpont preferred to rely on Unionists and prewar Whigs to build the Republican Party in the South but was willing to reach out to ex-Confederates, as long as they were contrite and willing to repudiate Secession. Since most of Lynchburg's civic leaders had been conditional Unionists before Fort Sumter, they had little trouble convincing state and federal authorities that they would work toward the peaceful restoration of civil government in Lynchburg.[22]

Conservatives' restoration of power proved to be short-lived. When moderate and radical congressional insurgents within the Republican Party wrested control of Reconstruction from Johnson in early 1867, they immediately stripped all former Confederates of political power, invoked martial law, laid out the steps by which civil government could be restored, and directed Southern states to give blacks political rights. In Lynchburg, the difficult task of implementing the intricacies of congressional Reconstruction was initially left to Colonel F. M. Cooley, commanding officer of the newly created Military Subdistrict of Lynchburg. Although Cooley was no radical—he preferred to build the party around moderate whites, not blacks—he dutifully denied Lynchburg's old leaders their traditional positions of political power and went about the task of building a Republican Party in Lynchburg. With the military's protection, a loose coalition of blacks, relocated Northerners, and Southern Unionists was able to outpoll Conservatives to retain control of the municipal government through the late 1860s.[23]

Lynchburg's Conservatives did not hide their contempt for the new political environment. The old elite condemned the opposition with a ferocity seldom seen in prewar political contests. In a steady stream of diatribes, they portrayed Republican rule as illegitimate and alien, controlled by selfish, unprincipled, and designing carpetbaggers who rose to power by purposefully misleading "ignorant and misguided" blacks and poor whites. According to Conservatives, the Republicans' purpose was obvious—to humiliate the Southern people as they stole from state coffers and raped the South of its resources. In the conservatives' view, there was only one way to stop the pillaging: true Southerners must unite in opposition and reelect traditional leaders to power. These "best men," as Button termed them, would be the very antithesis of the reigning carpetbaggers—public-spirited, temperate, revered by the community, patriarchal. Once in power, they would again look after the interests of the entire community.[24]

At every turn, however, Conservatives found obstacles in their quest to regain the power they believed was rightfully theirs. By their view, blacks were an especially troublesome group. Even before they gained formal political rights, Lynchburg blacks defied conservatives' expectations of how they should behave. Blacks and whites first clashed over the most fundamental of issues: What rights did freedmen possess as free laborers? Despite white Southerners' early optimism that emancipation would not radically change blacks' status and economic role, blacks consistently defied the efforts of their former masters and Freedmen's Bureau agents to control their labor. From the first, blacks demonstrated a desire for three things: a fair wage as compensation for their labor, greater workplace autonomy, and the freedom to leave an employer when they so desired.

House servants, often the most trusted of black workers, were among the first to challenge the old limits of white authority. Many simply left their ex-masters as soon as it was convenient. Former Confederate soldier Thomas Kelley observed that "although the people in this country" have as "many negroes as they ever had," domestic arrangements had been disrupted. According to Kelley, nearly all blacks in his neighborhood had "changed their homes," believing that "they do not show their freedom untill they leave their master and go to live with some new person." Kean made a similar observation, commenting in his diary that most blacks had a "passion for change" that was most often demonstrated by leaving their former masters.[25]

Although most masters were only too willing to see troublesome and unproductive servants leave, they deeply resented the departure of their most trusted servants. When William Blackford's prized servant Phoebe left one night without warning, William used the event to comment on blacks' inability to care for themselves. Writing to his mother, he complained that Phoebe had broken "the connection of a lifetime" and plunged "into 'freedom' with . . . blind infatuation" and the misguided notion "that it is a state of freedom from cares and troubles." Without the least trace of concern, he predicted that "she and her husband are in a fair state to starve to death as any people I know," because "he is idle and thriftless" and "she is lazy and delicate." To compensate for the loss of a trusted servant, the Blackfords hired a "little girl of twelve" who they believed would prove much better than Phoebe. After all, William rationalized, "Phoebe had become much spoiled" since freedom.[26]

In fact, blacks rarely left on a whim. Many left in search of better working conditions or greater autonomy or to reunite with family members who lived elsewhere. When Maurice Langhorne offered to pay his servants a part of his tobacco crop if they would stay on, they refused, telling him that they preferred to work for the railroads because the railroads paid wages. Others complained that their masters gave them no choice but to leave. According to one military official stationed in Lynchburg, many former masters were "disposed to get rid of the old and helpless," forcing them to fend for themselves on the streets of Lynchburg. Other masters, financially and psychologically broken by the war, released their servants, claiming that they were no longer able to care for them. Still others forced their former servants to leave by their cruelty of treatment and their refusal to accept servants as free laborers. John Averitt, a black political leader who had been a trusted personal servant before the war, told the House of Representatives' Select Committee on Reconstruction that many masters colluded against their former servants in the first months after the war by lowering wages and raising rents. According to Averitt, one former master told him that these actions were part of a plan "to prove to the Yankees that you are not as well off now as you were when you were with us." At first, Averitt counseled other blacks to try to stay on good terms with their former masters, telling them, "Your master's temper is up, but talk with him patiently and probably his temper will cool down." After a time, however, Averitt, like many of his peers, lost patience with accommodation and quit his job. Eventually, he became active in the Republican Party, where he gained a local reputation as an untiring critic of whites' economic exploitation of black laborers.[27]

As blacks and whites contested who would control black labor, small incidents sometimes flared into bitter disputes. Shortly after the war, Jenny asked her former master, Charles Blackford, if she could take her daughter, who was still employed by Blackford, to a party in a rough section of the city. Ever the patriarch, Blackford refused, claiming that he had a responsibility to supervise the daughter's behavior "so long as she is under my care." For good measure, he accused Jenny of trying to ruin her daughter by turning her into a prostitute. Blackford's response infuriated Jenny. Although she had shown proper deference to him, he had refused to honor her parental rights over her daughter. In response, Jenny took her daughter away from Blackford and refused to tell him where she was. Unable to fathom how a once faithful servant could challenge his well-intentioned paternalism, Blackford retreated to sweeping accusations. Agitated, he declared that "freedom and the Yankees have demoralized them all."[28]

Not all black servants could afford to act as hastily and decisively as Jenny and her daughter. Many servants remained with their former masters because of financial and family considerations. Indeed, according to Kean, many blacks who escaped slavery during the war returned to their former masters when the war ended because of what Kean termed their "cat-like attachments to places." Had Kean looked more closely, he might have noticed that blacks, no less than whites, developed kith-and-kin networks in Lynchburg that often obliged them to return. Moreover, because the entire region suffered from the postwar economic collapse, many believed that it was simply safer to stay where they could receive assistance from both the white and black communities that knew them. Then, too, necessity often prompted some distressed servants to try to revive whatever they could of their former masters' old paternalism. When Maurice Langhorne's ex-servants' jobs with the railroad ended, they returned to work for him under the same conditions that he had offered them the first time—a part of his crop. Long after the war had ended, some blacks were still able to exploit the old bonds of paternalism to gain assistance from their former owners. In one remarkable case, Dr. John Terrell's favorite servant, Uncle Davy, left immediately after the war, despite Terrell's request that he stay. Ten years later, Davy returned, exhausted by poverty. According to Terrell, he "begged me to take him back and give him a home for as long as he lived." Gratified that the bonds of the old paternalism still held, Terrell agreed. Once again, he anointed Davy with favored status. When Davy died, Terrell buried him in his family's plot.[29]

Servants who remained in Lynchburg responded to their emancipation in a variety of ways. In writing their memoirs, many ex-masters made a special point of eulogizing their faithful servants, leaving the impression that the bonds of affection between servant and master were so strong that they survived the death of slavery. No doubt, some servants continued to give faithful service, seemingly unaffected by emancipation and Reconstruction. "Mam' Peggy," Mary Blackford's personal servant, may have been one of these. Peggy cared for Mary Blackford until Mary died in 1896. By this time, both were past eighty. Although Peggy received a small wage after emancipation, she never spent it because, according to Mary's grandson, the Blackford clan gave her everything she needed. After Mary died, Mary's son Launcelot assumed responsibility for Peggy and even hired a personal nurse to look after her when she could no longer care for herself. When Peggy died in 1911, Launcelot buried her alongside her former owner.[30]

Many servants were more contentious. Shortly after the war, Charles Blackford complained that "the debauchery here among the servant girls exceeds anything that I have ever known." Another employer was only slightly less critical, complaining that while her slaves did their jobs, she suffered from their "depredations" because they needed her constant supervision and repeatedly tested her "ignorance of domestic matters."[31]

Within a few years after the war, most whites concluded that the days of the docile and devoted servant had ended. Almost immediately after the war, former masters became nostalgic for what they perceived to be a better day of black-white relations. In their reminiscences, they made the faithful slave an icon of that lost age. In 1867, Button described one chewing tobacco advertisement that played to this nostalgia:

> The name of this exquisite specimen of weed is the "Old Virginian Gentle-man" and it has on the outside a most suggestive print, viz: an old Virginian

gentleman sitting in the shade with his feet cocked up against a tree and a little nigger "toting" him a coal of fire to light with. When we looked at this representation of bygone times, we reflected that it conveyed a picture of a state of things of which we may hereafter read in history, or in the pages of a novel, but which we shall never see again.[32]

Although the advertisement invoked a world that never was, it is nonetheless true that the postwar period saw an increase in disputes between servants and employers. Freedmen's Bureau records suggest that many servants were no longer willing to accept abuses that they endured in slavery. As long as the Bureau operated in Lynchburg, blacks turned to it in search of justice. According to the Bureau's Register of Complaints, blacks commonly asked the Bureau to stop their employers from using physical punishment as a form of labor discipline, to force employers to pay wages for work rendered, and to retrieve their children from former employers.[33]

Even as blacks looked to the Bureau for assistance, they also acted on their own to define the meaning of free labor. By controlling the pace of work, refusing to perform certain duties, redefining gender roles on the job, and, when possible, resisting their masters' physical assaults and sexual advances, black laborers asserted that they, not their former masters, now controlled their labor. Whites were hardly sympathetic. In a long editorial titled "The Servant Question," J. G. Perry, local editor of the recently established *Lynchburg News*, argued that "the wretched condition of our domestic servants is due . . . to the pernicious influence of the political delusion that 'all men are created equal.'" While Perry was willing to allow that all men might be equal before the law, he observed that "the man of money or position" does not wish to "adopt the equality or Fifteenth amendment as part of his domestic . . . constitution." Instead, the employer rightly believed that "whatever he pays for or can control is his." According to Perry, servants needed to understand that "a distinction of classes and a division of the duties of life among mankind is necessary to the transaction of the daily business of life." At base, most whites believed that black servants had forgotten their place and were thus no longer as useful as they had been. When city council published a booklet to promote the town's economic resources, it candidly advised prospective immigrants to bring their own servants, "because they may otherwise have difficulty in getting such as will give them satisfaction" in Lynchburg.[34]

Nonservants, especially tobacco factory workers, had greater opportunities to demonstrate their resolve to upend the customs of slavery. Before emancipation, Lynchburg's black tobacco factory workers had developed considerable craft autonomy and a tradition of collective activism against white authority. During the decline and eventual defeat of the Confederacy, Lynchburg blacks used the factories as a place to demonstrate their solidarity. At least two black churches organized during the war at deserted factories. After the war, the factories remained a center of black community life. During the early years of Reconstruction, at a time when they could find no other place to meet, freedmen used factories as schools, funeral halls, and fraternal association meeting halls. Two of Lynchburg's most prominent black leaders had strong connections to the factories and used factory networks to establish their political careers. Squire Taliaferro, a leader in the local chapter of the Republican Party, worked in the tobacco factories before entering politics. When the Republican Party began to lose power during the late 1860s, Taliaferro returned to factory labor to support himself. Samuel Kelso, a former slave who became a Freedmen's Bureau schoolteacher and political organizer, came from a family of tobacco factory workers, lived with a brother who worked in the factories, and may have been a factory worker himself before the war.[35]

As the social and institutional networks that evolved from the tobacco factories solidified to form visible institutions, the factory workers gradually began to employ their collective strength.[36] In May 1867, workers took advantage of the revival of the tobacco business to strike for better wages. Although records of the strike are scanty, a few things are known. First, hands at every factory participated, suggesting that their labor organization enveloped the entire community. Second, the strike ended in a partial victory. By staging the strike in late spring when, as Button observed, "labor is most valuable," the factory hands forced their employers to negotiate. The manufacturers, fearful of what a work stoppage might do to the industry during the height of the manufacturing season, agreed to raise the pay of the most highly skilled workers, the twisters, from $2.25 to $2.50 per hundred pounds of tobacco during the busy summer months. The settlement was not a complete victory. The tobacconists gave the twisters no promises on wages after the summer. Moreover, they refused to give raises to the more numerous and less valued pickers and prizers; instead, they insisted that those wages would be negotiated by individual manufacturers.[37]

The strike worried white Lynchburg businessmen. Days after the strike, local newspaper editors published editorials condemning all forms of labor union activity. Button not only denounced the strike but lectured tobacco manufacturers that their "passive yielding" was an "impolitic step, not so much to the present as to the future." Most were more disturbed by the behavior of the black strikers. In a lengthy editorial written months after the strike, Perry of the *News* cautioned "our colored laborers" that future labor activity would carry harsh repercussions. According to Perry, employers would interpret such action as no less than a threat to the "safety and property of the white race." As a matter of "self-preservation," employers would be forced to replace blacks with European emigrants. Although the tobacconists' dependence on the skilled labor of the factory workers seems to belie the validity of Perry's threats, his bellicose posture indicates how fearful business leaders were of continued labor agitation. Tobacconists now realized that the collective resolve of the tobacco laborers had ushered in a new age of labor-capital relations. And indeed, the late 1860s was a period of constant black labor agitation, not only by tobacco factory workers but by canal and railroad workers as well.[38]

Over time, Lynchburg blacks became equally assertive in politics. When the Reconstruction Act of 1867 finally gave them the elected franchise, blacks used existing institutions—namely, the churches, Freedmen's Bureau schools, voluntary associations, and tobacco factories—to organize for both local and state elections. In their first political campaign, the 1867 state election of delegates to the constitutional convention, Lynchburg blacks helped the local Republican Party achieve a stunning victory. All three Lynchburg delegates were Republicans: former slave Sam Kelso and former Unionists Samuel D. Williamson and William Lydick.[39]

From the outset, blacks found that their assertiveness was not always welcome within the party. Indeed, their first sustained political challenge came not from Conservatives but from moderate Republicans who wanted to make the party more attractive to Southern whites by curtailing the power of blacks. With the assistance of Cooley and the Freedmen's Bureau, the moderates did just that. When the military commander of Virginia, General John Schofield, appointed city officers in 1868 and again in 1869, he followed the advice of local moderates and chose only whites, most of whom were longtime residents of Lynchburg and many of whom were prominent citizens before the war. As municipal and state elections were reinstituted, Moderates gained control over the party machine and effectively excluded blacks from most positions of influence. After Kelso's election as a delegate to the 1867 convention, no blacks were nominated by the party for political office at any level of government until 1871.[40]

Initially, blacks made few formal complaints about their unequal status within the party. Even Kelso acquiesced to the moderate platform during his first years of public service. As a delegate to the state constitutional convention, Kelso encouraged his fellow black members to accept segregated schools and to entrust Southern whites with the task of educating blacks. When Republican moderates in Washington questioned the convention's decision to disfranchise all Confederate municipal and military officers, Kelso asked the convention to reconsider the issue. Such concessions earned him grateful praise from state Conservatives. In January 1868, the editor of the *Richmond Enquirer* described Kelso as "one of the most respectable looking Negroes in the Convention," a man who "dresses well, and is certainly worth the respect as any negro that could have been appointed."[41]

As blacks gained political experience and became more cognizant of their differences with moderates, they became increasingly assertive within the local party. In August 1868, Robert Glass of the *Republican* observed that many freedmen had become disenchanted with the Republican Party because the executive committee had barred them from advancement within the party. A few months later, black Lynchburgers began openly to criticize some of the decisions of the local party officers. In March 1869, they pressured city council to fire the chief of police, a moderate appointee, for abusive treatment. Blacks' dissatisfaction with Republican moderates came to a head in late 1870. After the moderate-dominated city council reinstituted a chain gang and reestablished harsh vagrancy laws, blacks, with the assistance of some laboring whites, attempted to take control of the party's executive council. Although the insurgents failed, they nearly split the ticket by voicing their frustrations. Thereafter, moderates became a bit more accommodating. When voting precincts were redrawn in 1871, blacks were virtually given their own ward, thus assuring radical representation on city council. Also in 1871, party officials tried to distribute some of the spoils to blacks by appointing Sam Kelso postmaster general and naming twenty-seven other blacks as grand jurors on the corporation court for the coming year.[42]

Although these concessions may have encouraged local blacks, they remained vigilant in the protection of their rights and eager to expand their freedoms, especially after Conservatives regained a foothold in both state and municipal politics during the early 1870s. In 1872, after the

Conservative-dominated state legislature amended the city charter, blacks condemned several of the new charter's features, including its call to postpone elections for a year, the lack of adequate police reforms, and the legislature's refusal to let the people of Lynchburg ratify the charter. In addition, blacks criticized the city council's failure to protest the legislature's action. Blacks feared that the new charter was part of a larger conspiracy to deny them political power. In response, black community leaders organized several indignation meetings to protest the action. In the end, they were not able to stop the new charter, but they did gain one small victory: they forced the city council to hold municipal elections the following month, as originally planned. In that election, the radicals retained control of the Third Ward and reelected George Burch as mayor, an outspoken critic of the new charter.[43]

In Lynchburg, as in other Southern cities, a corollary of blacks' effort to assert their political and economic independence was the establishment of an autonomous black community. Almost immediately, blacks began to organize voluntary associations to assist one another. Some of these organizations grew from the workplace and operated as trade guilds. Others emerged from shared moral and social interests. By 1870, Lynchburg blacks had founded a debating club, a temperance society, a women's social circle, and several fraternal organizations, some of which replicated the names and rituals of white organizations. Most of these associations offered their members the same thing—emotional support, financial assistance, a common identity, and opportunities for advancement within the community.[44]

These organizations became the most visible indication of blacks' growing independence from Lynchburg's white community. Through the group solidarity that these clubs provided, blacks annually celebrated the Fourth of July, Lee's surrender, and the enactment of the Emancipation Proclamation through parades, picnics, and fairs. The ability to celebrate their freedom publicly was itself a revelation for many. Jacob Yoder noted the enthusiasm with which blacks embraced their first procession, a June 1866 parade commemorating the first anniversary of the first black-run Sunday schools. According to Yoder, many had spent extra money for clothes, with most of the girls "tastefully attired" in white dresses. To the accompaniment of local singers and musicians, some fifteen hundred blacks marched down Lynchburg's main streets, most carrying banners with political, religious, and moral messages. One banner included Lincoln's photograph mounted alongside two Union flags and the statement "With Malice toward None and Charity to All." Other messages included "Do Right," "Love the Truth," "Do Not Despise These Little Ones," "Faith, Hope, Charity," and "Lynchburg Sabbath Schools Founded June 5, 1865." As the procession made its way through town, the crowd gave hurrahs for various purposes, offering up loud cheers to all but Andrew Johnson. When it was over, an older freedman told Yoder, "This looks like the better day coming of which I had heard when I was a boy but was not permitted to see till now."[45]

As black institutions solidified, black entrepreneurs began to lay the economic basis for a separate black community. After the war, a small number of blacks made slight but significant inroads into certain professional occupations, working as teachers and ministers. Although evidence is fragmentary, extant sources show that there were at least two black groceries, several saloons and restaurants, one funeral hall, and four black barbershops. Except for the barbershops, these catered almost exclusively to the town's black population.[46]

In addition, a small number of artisans also entered the ranks of proprietorship. Although most of these worked in crafts that whites denigrated as "nigger work"—for instance, as barbers and blacksmiths—or in crafts that were endangered because of technological advances and Northern competition—as shoemakers and cabinetmakers—the overall increase in the number of black shopkeepers from four in 1860 to twenty-one in 1870 suggests that a separate black business community had begun to solidify. The success of a few artisans may have helped other black laborers. Although it is risky to make comparisons with preemancipation black occupational patterns, it appears that the total number of black artisans in Lynchburg after the war increased from 71 in 1860 to 118 in 1870.[47]

In many Southern communities, the development of a separate black business community was part of a larger trend toward the spatial separation of the races.[48] It is tempting to make a similar claim for Lynchburg. The available sources suggest that black entrepreneurs and shopkeepers probably clustered in two parts of the town. According to the city's 1873 business directory, some settled southwest of town, near the Fair Grounds, while many more settled on the town's eastern edge in the city's Third Ward.[49]

Blacks settled in the outskirts of town for a variety of reasons. The town's chronic lack of affordable housing probably forced many to move toward the periphery, where rents were lower and the poorest could build squatters' huts. In addition, many places of employment were located on the outskirts of town, including tobacco factories, warehouses, railroad terminals, and foundries. Finally, living on the periphery of town provided blacks greater freedom from Southern whites. Although the city police regularly patrolled the central business district, they lacked the resources to oversee the river basin and the outlying hills. Thus, in the postwar years, blacks moved many of their community institutions from the inner-city alleys to the outlying neighborhoods. The black community's newest church, Jackson Street Methodist, was located on Lynchburg's periphery, as were several of the Freedmen's Bureau schools.[50]

Blacks were not completely successful in their quest for autonomy. For one thing, the spatial separation between the races was never complete. Because the steep hills made much of the town uninhabitable, Lynchburg remained a cramped city, forcing the two races to live in close proximity to each other. Moreover, the economic and social forces that compelled blacks to move to the outskirts of town also acted upon lower-class whites. Thus, the eastern edge of town included as many white shoemaking shops as black shoemaking shops. Then, too, many blacks remained tied to the inner city for a variety of reasons. At night and on weekends, poorer blacks and whites continued to frequent the Buzzard's many grogshops, gambling halls, and houses of ill fame. During the day, blacks also continued to play a crucial role in the city's central business district. Throughout the period, many blacks continued to work in downtown businesses and homes as servants, laborers, draymen, vendors, and porters. As such, blacks remained a conspicuous part of the downtown milieu. For these reasons, racial separation was never complete, despite the predilections of blacks and whites. Voting records suggest this as well as anything. In the 1871 state election, Conservatives outpolled Republicans by slim majorities in the First and Second Wards. In the Third Ward, a radical stronghold, one-third of all voters voted Conservative.[51]

Nor did most Lynchburg blacks experience economic progress in the years after emancipation. Instead, the majority remained dependent and poor, working in the same jobs that they held in slavery—as servants, factory and railroad hands, and menial laborers for small shop owners. As in slavery, most of these jobs offered little pecuniary reward and few opportunities for advancement. By the end of the decade, 98 percent of Lynchburg's unskilled black laborers possessed neither real nor personal property.[52] Indeed, many unskilled black laborers found that their economic circumstances deteriorated in the five years after the war because of the decline of the tobacco trade. The industry's early postwar prosperity was not a portent of things to come. Although tobacco manufacturing remained a lucrative business, Lynchburg's flush times had ended—at least for the time being. During the late 1860s and early 1870s, the industry fluctuated wildly. As it did several tobacconists closed their factories, while others formed partnerships to pool their resources and lower their costs.[53]

As the tobacco industry declined, many in the black community suffered. Throughout the late 1860s and early 1870s, tobacco strikes became a near-annual occurrence. In contrast to 1867, however, black workers found it exceedingly difficult to win concessions from the manufacturers. As factories closed due to the decline of the industry, surviving manufacturers hired unemployed workers as strikebreakers and slowly broke the collective will of the workers. As this happened, labor conflicts of the late 1860s and early 1870s became increasingly volatile. During a long and bitter strike in the winter of 1869–1870, Perry of the *News* twice accused strikers of violence. According to Perry, strikers tried to intimidate both manufacturers and strikebreakers. In one instance, Perry claimed, strikers tried to murder James Carter, a tobacco worker who refused to participate in the strike.[54] Although Perry never proved that the unidentified assailants were strikers, it is true that black workers were becoming increasingly desperate, though not always in the way Perry portrayed. As the strike wore on, hundreds left town in search of work, often with the prodding of labor agents who shipped them off to work on the railroads or on black-belt cotton plantations. As a result, and despite the large influx of black refugees into the city during the early years of Reconstruction, Lynchburg's black population actually declined slightly during the 1860s, from 3,353 in 1860 to 3,051 in 1870.[55]

Those blacks who remained suffered considerably as Lynchburg's economic base eroded. According to observers, many in Lynchburg's black community subsisted on the barest of necessities. Jacob Yoder, a Freedmen's Bureau schoolteacher, spent many of his off-hours visiting black families. He described one home as a "small room nearly in the ground ... made of the roughest kind of wall." The shack was located "out of town, almost unapproachable, on a piece of ground valueless for anything" except the desperate poor, who "prefer it to living out of doors." The landlord charged three dollars per month for the shack—a price Yoder described as excessive. Yet this house may have been better than most; the renter was a woman of some stature within the black community, Sam Kelso's mother. Those who were even worse off continued to live in the shanties infamously known as Fort Snacks. Writing in the *Lynchburg News* in August 1871, "Fickacken" satirically described the shantytown as a "hotel kept on the European plan," with a staff of "some six or eight hundred colored residents." He observed that "the inside walls are neatly papered with *Harpers' Weekly* and *Police Gazette*," while the "roofing is a composition of tin, iron, slate, shingles, planks, and canvass . . . very durable" and "certainly very costly." For warmth and cooking, the residents constructed fireplaces of brick and mud that "curve in the shape of a crescent" as they gradually deteriorated. According to Bureau agents, many of the habitants did without most common household furnishings, such as beds, tables, and chairs.[56]

Some white Lynchburgers responded to black poverty with the same paternalist care they had shown before the war. Many prosperous whites claimed that they were only too willing to help individuals who had proved themselves loyal and faithful in the past. Maurice Langhorne's granddaughter recalled that her grandfather provided for most of his former slaves during their first years of freedom because they were unable to support themselves. Charles Blackford claimed that he was equally generous to his former free black servant John Scott. Although Scott found work elsewhere after the war, Blackford continued to provide for him as long as he lived.[57] Wealthy whites also extended assistance to blacks through more formal means. Through direct donations and participation in fund-raising events, civic leaders dutifully and conspicuously helped blacks build two churches in the years immediately after the war. In addition, the Lynchburg Tobacco Association also donated money to build a home for poor and infirm blacks.[58]

For the most part, however, white benevolence to blacks was neither as consistent nor as extensive as it had been before the war. Some gave only to confirm to themselves and to white Northerners that blacks would not be able to survive without their supervision and guidance. Others believed that emancipation effectively ended their responsibilities to black Lynchburg residents. During presidential Reconstruction, Freedmen's Bureau agents complained that civic leaders demonstrated little interest in extending public relief to blacks. Local agent Louis Stevenson reported to his superiors that while city council regularly set aside funds to feed and clothe poor whites, "it has been nearly a month since I was informed that the City Council had made an appropriation to aid the colored poor."

Nevertheless, council continued to collect taxes from blacks. As a result, Stevenson lamented, "the freedmen are supporting the entire white pauper population in my subdistrict." When Stevenson asked to meet with council to discuss this matter, council ignored his request.[59]

Reluctantly, the Bureau often assumed the role of charitable institution, even though it lacked the resources to do an effective job. The Bureau was especially active during the winter months, when need was greatest. In January 1868, Lacey agreed to donate the Bureau's hospital bedding to destitute blacks, to be fashioned into clothing. A few weeks later, another Bureau agent informed Lacey that more aid was needed. Because "civil authorities will not aid them," the agent told Lacey, "there are a number of sick freedmen . . . destitute of food and unable to get any." Unsure of what he could do, Lacey vaguely promised that he would look into the matter. In desperation, he tried to solicit help from his superiors in Richmond, asking them to send him one hundred pairs of shoes. The plan failed when his superiors meekly responded that they did not have enough shoes on hand to fill the order. Evidently, they, too, were either unwilling or unequipped to provide prolonged assistance to impoverished blacks. Thus, poor blacks had little choice but to stay in their homes during the cold months. That winter, Stevenson observed that many students were reluctant to attend Bureau schools because "they have not the clothing to make them comfortable in doing so."[60]

According to many native whites, Lynchburg blacks simply did not deserve their benevolence. As they saw it, most blacks had betrayed their kindnesses, had belied the organic relationship that bound them together, and were now, thanks to unscrupulous and "mean" whites, out to destroy them. In August 1867, Perry warned blacks that they should not expect to keep their jobs if they planned to use their newly gained right to vote against their employers. Claiming that he was "and always has been the friend of the colored man," Perry "kindly and sincerely" urged blacks to "repudiate those political societies" that would try to convince them "that their interests are antagonistic to their employers." If they remained politically active, Perry cautioned, their employers might feel compelled to fire them. Five months later, when blacks elected two radical Republicans to the constitutional convention, Button informed blacks that whites were now prepared to move beyond threats. According to Button, many whites were now "in favor of cutting loose at once and unconditionally from the negroes since they have leagued themselves together against the whites." Already, Button observed, employers were planning a meeting to

"inaugurate prompt measures for the introduction of labor from Europe."
Although the meeting never came off, a growing number of whites became attracted to the idea of replacing blacks with foreign labor. For the
next several years, conservative whites devised schemes to bring immigrants, either Europeans or Chinese, to Lynchburg. Although all their
efforts failed, this did not stop angry white civic leaders from threatening
blacks with social and economic ostracism. Toward the end of Reconstruction, Perry warned blacks that unless they began to "identify themselves
with the communities in which they live and refuse to be made the
slaves and tools of demagogues," they would face the united wrath of all
whites.[61]

To most blacks, conservatives' understanding of events must have
seemed horribly skewed. Although some prominent blacks were willing
to allow that some former masters had been well intentioned during
slavery, most former slaves knew otherwise. And since emancipation,
blacks had experienced greater competition for jobs that were once theirs
alone, wage reductions in several large industries, and a general unwillingness by the white community to assist them in their poverty. Throughout
the period, whites, no less than blacks, retreated from the old organic
model of race relations. With black emancipation, most stopped providing sustained benevolent assistance to their former slaves. For many
residents of property and standing, unadulterated power, not power disguised by personalism, became the new prescription for race relations.
Symptomatic of the new racial ethic, Perry suggested that employers
detach themselves from even their most trusted of house servants. "Familiarity with servants is a mistake," Perry counseled. Better to "keep them
at a respectful distance," so that they will know "your superiority . . . by
your high bearing." Although Perry allowed that employers should be
courteous, patient, and considerate with the hired help, he cautioned
that too much conviviality "breaks down all barriers" and "encourages
impudence." "Uniform civility and politeness," Perry suggested, "is power
over them."[62]

Alienated from Southern whites and unable to secure adequate aid
from the federal government, many blacks had little choice but to fend
for themselves. As was true during the Civil War, many turned to thievery
as a way to survive. Indeed, black theft continued unabated from the Civil
War. A few months after Lee's surrender, Button reported that "burglaries, robberies, &c." were becoming "so common around here, that it
will not be thought worth while to chronicle them after a time." He

predicted that within a short while, every property owner would "have to elect himself a sentinel, and stand guard over his family supplies." In response, council replaced the night watch with a professional police force of twenty-four in January 1866, then later expanded it to thirty-two. Indicative of how civic leaders perceived the problem, the new force made a special point of searching out and catching black thieves. During sample periods in 1866 and 1868, the police apprehended 104 thieves—more than three times the number arrested during a similar prewar period. Of these, 87 percent were black.[63]

Prosecution of these criminals taxed the local judicial system to its limits. Grand juries of the circuit court periodically complained that hearing the large number of cases against blacks made it impossible for them to perform their other duties. In reaction, council established a special grand jury for the hustings court, to hear only cases of petit larceny. When this failed to clear the docket, Button suggested that the mayor be given greater discretionary power to pass summary judgments in cases of petty thievery. Meanwhile, because the vast majority of suspects were convicted, the city jail was chronically full, if not overcrowded. To alleviate the congestion, the hustings court on two separate occasions petitioned local and state officials to allow it to impose whipping as a punishment for petty crimes.[64]

Postwar black crime differed from its prewar antecedents in one crucial respect. In contrast to antebellum and even wartime crime patterns, when blacks often stole as a way to participate in the gray market, postwar blacks were more likely to commit crimes against property to procure the basic necessities of life. For this reason, blacks generally stole items that they could consume themselves—namely, small amounts of food, clothing, and fuel—rather than items that they could barter through local grocers and grogshop keepers, such as boxes of plug tobacco and railroad iron. In 1866, less than one-fifth of all thefts by blacks were for items that blacks commonly sold on the gray market, while nearly two-thirds were for food, fuel, and clothing.[65]

For their part, propertied whites generally recognized that blacks stole out of necessity yet remained unmoved by their plight, believing that poverty, especially black poverty, was simply a result of laziness. In the winter of 1866, Perry observed that there "seems to be a perfect *fence rail mania* among the negroes of the town," who "must steal the wood they burn" because they "won't work." To stop the nightly thefts, he suggested that "*cold lead* be tried . . . a sovereign remedy when all others have failed."

Later, Perry suggested the same remedy for the ubiquitous garden thieves that appeared every summer.[66]

As white civic leaders tried to solve the problem of race control in a free society, many laboring whites became convinced that black emancipation adversely affected their lives. Despite blacks' precarious economic status, many laboring whites believed that blacks' modest postwar advances posed a serious threat to their own social and economic security. Writing in the *Lynchburg News* in 1867, "Brutus" gave full expression to laboring whites' fears. Brutus suggested that blacks often advanced at the expense of white laborers and craftsmen. He observed that white employers routinely employed black carpenters, bricklayers, blacksmiths, and painters "to the *exclusion of white men* seeking the *same* work." Although the writer assured his readers that these employers had operated under the most charitable of motives—"to aid your former slaves in getting a start in the world and to convince them that you really had no ill-will towards them"—he contended that the results had been disastrous. Because of their actions, "it has been the general subject of remark that the negroes got all the jobs . . . while the white mechanics had either to live in want, or go to some new business or move away." According to Brutus, the outcome of the recent tobacco strike only aggravated the problem. Because the factory workers won, all blacks now acted like "arrogant and imperious dictators" in their dealings with whites. Still, Brutus contended that employers were as much to blame as anyone. Because the tobacconists had foolishly shown that they "can not do without them," blacks "feel that they can now dictate terms to you, and that you are obliged to yield to them."[67]

White laborers' fear that ex-slaves and their white employers threatened the livelihoods of laboring whites was not without justification—though not for the reasons described by Brutus. From 1860 to 1870, the number of white artisans declined 45 percent (412 to 227), while the number of black artisans may have increased by as much as 70 percent (70 to 118). As a result, the percentage of white skilled workers in the overall skilled workforce declined from 85 percent to 66 percent during the period.[68] Black competition was not the only reason that many skilled white laborers found it difficult to remain in Lynchburg. From the fall of the Confederacy in 1865 through the panic of 1871, Lynchburg's economic decline hurt the town's white artisans and laborers nearly as much as it hurt black workers. Just as Lynchburg's former prominence as a tobacco town had once benefited most of the town's residents, so, too, did the industry's postwar decline cause many to suffer. Without the huge profits from the tobacco trade to fuel the economy, many artisans found themselves without patrons to employ them and thus more vulnerable to the volatile national economy.

As the economic base of the town eroded, many white artisans simply decided to leave town rather than face an uncertain future. Civic leaders did little to try to stop them. Indeed, in their more candid moments, boosters admitted that Lynchburg was no longer an attractive location for skilled craftsmen. In 1868, Perry instructed out-of-town mechanics not to come to Lynchburg because there were no jobs and too many *"do noth-ings"* in town already. Four years later, city council was equally forthright, admitting in its promotional literature for the town that "the disastrous consequences of the war have so crippled this whole community" that its mills, shops, and factories were still "worked only to a limited extent." Council predicted that "it will be some years before the town reaches its former prosperity."[69]

As the number of white skilled workers declined in Lynchburg, the number of white, male unskilled laborers increased slightly from 155 to 169. These individuals concentrated in jobs that most considered the least desirable occupations in town. Although stigmas against "nigger work" remained after the war, a small but growing number of whites began to accept jobs once reserved for blacks. From 1860 to 1870—at a time when the number of tobacco factory workers was less than half of what it had been ten years before—the number of white tobacco factory laborers nearly doubled, from forty-five to eighty-four. By 1870, nearly 40 percent of all white unskilled laborers worked in these factories. In addition, the number of whites in personal service positions nearly tripled. In 1870, roughly one out of seven (14 percent) unskilled white laborers worked as servants of some sort.[70]

More than likely, most poorer whites had no choice but to take these jobs. In the fall of 1867, times were so bad that "Brutus" speculated many unskilled whites would be glad to take jobs traditionally reserved for blacks, for instance, as porters, gardeners, cooks, and house servants. Perhaps it was not blacks who crowded whites out of jobs but whites who crowded out blacks. Either way, black and white laborers found that economic circumstances compelled them to compete with one another at the marketplace. Thus, in contrast to the prewar period, each group would find it increasingly difficult to avoid the other.[71]

White laborers' declining job status directly affected their economic well-being. The percentage of laborers with neither personal nor real property dramatically increased during the period. In 1860, 27 percent of white, nonproprietor skilled workers and 58 percent of white unskilled workers reported that they owned neither real nor personal property; by 1870, the percentage had risen to 73 percent for skilled workers and 93 percent for unskilled workers.[72] In addition, unemployment became a constant, as opposed to a seasonal, problem. In 1868, Button reported that small-time hucksters, most of them unemployed clerks, artisans, and laborers, populated every street in town, selling apples or small wares. To help them, Button occasionally recommended their services to his readers. In doing so, he was forced to admit that many white laborers in the town were impoverished.[73]

All white laborers seemed to suffer. Native white workers experienced the most extreme decline in job status. By 1870, native white Virginians accounted for 65 percent (twenty of thirty-one) of the white population that worked in personal service occupations and 96 percent (eighty-one of eighty-four) of the white population that took jobs in the tobacco factories. Ironically, the Irish, the town's largest and most despised immigrant group, were far more successful in avoiding occupations that carried the stigma of "nigger work." Of Lynchburg's twenty-one unskilled Irish laborers, only two (one male, one female) held personal service occupations and only one worked in a tobacco factory. Even so, theirs was hardly a success story. Although four skilled laborers owned their own shops (two tailors, one plumber, and one cigarmaker), most continued to toil in the same jobs that they and their kin had held before the war, working as outdoor laborers, railroad hands, and wagoners. Among the poorest of the ethnic groups in Lynchburg before the war, they remained poor after the war. The percentage of skilled Irish laborers with neither real nor personal property rose from 46 percent to 58 percent, while the percentage of propertyless unskilled Irish laborers rose from 64 percent to 75 percent. Like native whites and blacks, many Irish laborers may have been forced to leave town as the job market tightened. From 1860 to 1870, the number of skilled Irish laborers in Lynchburg declined from seventeen to twelve, and the number of unskilled Irish laborers declined from forty-six to twenty-five. In short, most Irish laborers remained poor and economically vulnerable.[74]

White female laborers, regardless of ethnicity, also suffered from the town's economic decline. Northern ready-made clothing, introduced before the war, became more available after the war, making it difficult for most of the town's seamstresses to find work. As early as June 1865, Button claimed that he was "shamed and mortified" to see so many well-dressed people promenading the streets, dressed in "foreign" ready-mades. To stimulate home industries, he urged residents to patronize local seamstresses, hatters, and tailors rather than "fatten those who have evinced anything but a brotherly love for us." Few took Button's advice. By 1870, the number of seamstresses in town declined from 187 to 41. Because this work was one of the few respectable jobs open to white women, the decline of the trade made it difficult for many to find employment. Because many of these women were single heads of households, there was an exponential rise in the number of impoverished children. To care for this growing group, a few well-intentioned private citizens began to make plans to build an orphanage.[75]

Many laboring whites' material circumstances slowly deteriorated as their economic prospects declined. An examination of laboring whites' housing provides a case in point. Although laborers had long considered Lynchburg an expensive place to live, Button reported that they were ill prepared for the rents that greeted them when they returned from the war. Unable to afford anything else, white laborers joined blacks in converting "kitchens, cabins, and smokehouses" into homes. Here they lived with "pigs, dogs, cows, and horses almost under the same shelter." So many opted for these arrangements that a correspondent for the *New York Herald* described postwar Lynchburg as a collection of "tumble down and half shingled shanties." The poor paid dearly for these "crowded holes." Perry believed that "many landlords, and sub-landlords especially, are realizing handsomely by letting every nook of their premises that will hold a carcass, without regard to anything else than the *main chance*." When rents rose during the winter of 1866–1867, Button made several pleas to property holders to hold the line. When most refused to do so, some renters set up tents and moved out of their rooms in protest. This "antirent movement" gained considerable attention but little reform. The next year, "Sufferer," writing in the *Lynchburg Virginian*, again asked property holders to lower their rents.[76]

With no other recourse, some whites joined blacks in squatting in various abandoned buildings on the outskirts of town. Immediately after the war, several white families took up quarters in the abandoned buildings of the defunct Lynchburg College. A year later, the place remained crowded with impoverished families. Out of sympathy, Jannett Cleland asked the elders of her church, First Presbyterian, if she could start a mission for the white residents. They rebuffed her, informing her that the church was broke and could not afford the added expense. The grand jury was even less charitable. In June 1866, they cited the college as a public nuisance and ordered the trustees to evict "those who made it disreputable." Federal officials nullified the directive, however, realizing that the indigent had nowhere else to go.[77]

Like some blacks, whites turned to crime to help make ends meet. Although local newspaper reports suggest that white thievery never matched black thievery either before or after the war, there is evidence that some poorer whites remained immersed in criminal networks. As blacks slowly abandoned the gray market to concentrate on more immediate needs, many whites—including children—entered it, stealing railroad iron and gasoline caps to barter to grocers and grogshop keepers. In 1866, five of the fourteen mayor's court prosecutions against iron thieves were against whites. Implicitly, council admitted that the number of white thieves was increasing: when council members decided to expand the poorhouse in 1871, they included a workhouse designed as a place of refuge for white women and children convicted of petty thievery, so that these could escape the corrupting influences of jail yet "be made to contribute towards their support."[78]

White civic leaders were uncertain how to respond to the increase in the number of impoverished whites. At first, many treated poor whites with considerable compassion. Button, in particular, expounded on the need to help returning Confederate veterans find a place in society. According to Button, most were eager to find work and were not too proud to take jobs that once only slaves had performed. And yet most were "without work, without means, and on very short allowances." By his view, it was the community's responsibility to find work for these people.[79]

Yet in the years immediately after the war, financial constraints made it difficult for civic leaders to assist poorer whites as they had once done. Public support simply could not keep up with need, even when Conservatives held power and systematically excluded blacks from public assistance. Thus, when Conservative councilman Henry Latham proposed that the city establish a soup kitchen to feed poor whites during the winter of 1866–1867, other council members rejected the measure because the city was already too much in debt. For the rest of the decade, council was unable to increase the city's commitment to the poor. Finally, in the early 1870s, council allocated additional funds. In January 1870, the city established a dispensary to "regulate the medical service to the poor" of the town. A year later, council allocated funds to enlarge the poorhouse. By these acts, municipal authorities tacitly admitted that poverty in the town had increased.[80]

As before the war, Southerners hoped that private assistance would augment public support. Yet here, too, aid did not match prewar levels. Before the war, winter fund-raising drives to assist the poor were an annual event. After the war, charitable events occurred less frequently and were more modest in scale. Although the winter of 1866–1867 was a severe one, the only organized charitable event was a Calico Ball, in which wealthy women wore plain dresses to a lavish party and then donated their attire to destitute white women at the end of the evening.

The next winter was nearly as harsh, but once again, most citizens of property were reluctant to give. In response, Button, who before the war had often praised his readers for their benevolence, now chastised them for their indifference. Button lamented that "the active personal exercise of charity" was now "left entirely to a few men and women" who, because of public apathy, had to work unceasingly "to obtain the means from the wealthy" to "relieve the suffering of the poor."[81]

Even when calamity struck, assistance was not always forthcoming. In late September 1870, a severe flood destroyed hundreds of homes and businesses along the James River basin, leaving many poorer residents homeless. Although several leading citizens organized a flood relief drive, most residents were slow to contribute. Several weeks after the flood, Button reported that the organization had raised only a "small amount . . . for distribution" to the poor. As a result, the relief committee reluctantly determined to "confine the charity to the most destitute—to infirm persons and widows with little children." No others would be eligible.[82]

Recognizing that their mastery over the community had always depended on their economic ascendancy, civic leaders proposed a number of schemes to revitalize the economy. Some hoped that the postwar slump would provide an opportunity to bring much-needed reform to Lynchburg's economic structure. Those who wanted greater industrial diversification could now point to black emancipation and the stagnant tobacco trade as reasons to refashion Lynchburg's economic base. Not surprising, this group received considerable support from Northern in-dustrialists who hoped to reconstruct the South's economic base so that it

Lynchburg topography: Church Street between Twelfth and Thirteenth Streets (JML). During the 1860s, wealthy residents used Lynchburg's dramatic topography to isolate themselves from the rest of the community. The footbridge provided the only direct access from this wealthy neighborhood to downtown Lynchburg until 1870, when the ravine was filled in. By then, the neighborhood had become the exclusive domain of the town's wealthiest residents. The mansion of Maurice Moore, Lynchburg's wealthiest postwar tobacconist, stands at the far left of the photograph.

would resemble the industrial North. These two groups quickly seized the initiative. Almost immediately after the war, Button encouraged the town's business leaders to show the same "Yankee" energy and activity that they demonstrated before the war. At the same time, he cautioned that the new way to prosperity would not be through tobacco but through iron manufacturing, coal mining, and textiles. To underscore the point, Button even suggested that some of the outlying farms switch from tobacco to foodstuffs, in anticipation of the large workforce that Lynchburg manufacturing would attract. Button predicted that Lynchburg would become "a second Lowell [Massachusetts] in point of manufacturing interest." Perry seconded Button's proposal and suggested that the town's artisans and mechanics would be the prime beneficiaries of the movement away from an agriculture-based economy. Writing in June 1866, Perry urged the town's business community to take full advantage of the region's soil, climate, mineral deposits, and water power, so that the laboring classes could enjoy flush times again.[83]

During the next several years, city boosters worked to expand Lynchburg's economic base. Initially, Button and Perry seemed to believe that it was enough to encourage consumers to support home manufacturing and to encourage craftsmen to import Northern machines and manufacturing methods. As they and other boosters became more aware of the immensity of the task, they only became more ambitious. Some residents joined the Virginia Immigration Society, to attract more skilled workers from Europe and the North. To stimulate investments, Button told wealthy residents to stop investing in land, to sell what land they had to entrepreneurs, and to use the profits to invest in manufacturing. At the same time, other boosters offered a variety of railroad construction schemes to expand Lynchburg's markets south to the Carolinas and Georgia. City council also endorsed efforts to improve Lynchburg's economic base. Almost immediately after the war, when the city was in debt, council promoted a subscription scheme to build a railroad to Danville. When the city began to settle its debts, council became more active. In 1871, council established a Bureau of Immigration to attract entrepreneurs and investors to the region. Later in the year, Council published a promotional booklet to send to manufacturers and investors throughout the United States, Europe, and Canada. The following year, council established tax incentives to encourage natives to invest in new industries and to attract "experienced manufacturers from abroad" to settle in Lynchburg.[84]

Not every plan worked. In June 1868, Max Guggenheimer, one of Lynchburg's wealthiest and most ambitious merchants, announced that he intended to enter the textile industry so that he would not have to buy Northern ready-mades. By 1880, three-fourths of his inventory was manufactured in the South but none of it in Lynchburg. For a short while, Lynchburg was in the running for a large nail factory that would have employed more than fifty families, but the town lost out when no local investors came forward. Because of the town's poor finances, the railroad schemes proposed in the mid-1860s did not come to fruition until the early 1870s. Lack of investment capital wasn't the only problem. Trying to retain control of the town's place in the evolving national economy also proved difficult. In the late 1860s, coastal cities, with the support of Northern investors, encouraged railroad consolidation, a scheme that most Lynchburg boosters feared would make the town a way station under outside control, making it impossible for Lynchburg to develop as a railroad and manufacturing hub.[85]

Nevertheless, Lynchburg's economic structure changed markedly during the period. The number of banks and investment houses doubled from four in 1859 to eight in 1873. The town became home for a wide variety of new and expanding industries. As more individuals began to take the initiative to transform the town's economy, Button's outlook brightened. In 1872, after surveying the town's efforts to reclaim its former prosperity, he boasted that Lynchburg had done more than any city in the state to stimulate immigration and commercial development.[86]

The transformation—limited as it was—had a mixed impact on Lynchburg residents. Some manufacturers and craftsmen realized substantial profits by pooling their resources to take advantage of the town's links to national markets. During the late 1860s, E. J. Folkes and J. L. Winston, furniture- and cabinetmakers, purchased a variety of new machines that transformed their business into one of the largest and most technologically advanced in the state. After Button toured their factory in 1868, he proudly predicted that Folkes and Winston would soon be able to "furnish the whole region of the country with furniture."[87] The leather tanning industry underwent an even more radical transformation. Sometime after the war, two German immigrants, Frederick Myers and A. B. Goodman, began to replicate Northern methods of production for their small factory. By employing skilled craftsmen from the North to oversee the operation and by installing state-of-the-art machines and production methods, they produced harness, bridle, and shoe leather for manufacturers in Philadelphia and Baltimore. A writer for a trade journal reported that their plant rivaled those of the Northeast. In 1870, they manufactured over $36,000 in leather goods.[88]

Other entrepreneurs did not do quite as well. By 1870, many industries that consolidated and modernized production had not yet realized substantial profits for their efforts. For instance, from 1860 to 1870, the number of iron foundries in Lynchburg and vicinity decreased from six to five while capital investment increased from $48,600 to $63,585. Yet despite the greater capital outlay for better machines, profits decreased from $104,000 to $86,000. During the same period, coach manufacturing went through a similar process of consolidation and expansion. From 1860 to 1870, the number of coachmakers decreased from four to three while capital investments tripled, from $6,650 to $20,600. Yet here, too, demand did not yet meet expectations. John Bailey, Lynchburg's largest antebellum coachmaker, must have been especially frustrated. By buying steam-powered machinery, his capital investment increased from $4,000 to $20,000. Yet his product value decreased from $30,000 to $11,676.[89]

Whatever success capitalists enjoyed at this time did not necessarily translate into success for workers. In the long run, mechanization hurt many craftsmen. According to Button, Folkes and Winston's machinery was so good that they produced a better product than "mere hands." Partially as a result of their productivity, the number of cabinetmakers in town declined by half during the decade, from fourteen to seven. Goodman and Myers had an even more profound impact on artisans in trades related to their industry. Manufacturing census data suggest that their production methods were so efficient that the enterprise created few new jobs for skilled workers. In 1870, they employed just twenty workers, most of whom were black and unskilled.[90]

Meanwhile, Myers and Goodman's establishment helped change Lynchburg's shoe manufacturing industry. Although they did not manufacture shoes, they probably provided leather to small shoemakers in Lynchburg and the surrounding country. For this reason, the number of Lynchburg shoemakers who owned their own shops expanded at this time, from six in 1860 to twenty-six in 1870. But most of these were not the skilled craftsmen of the prewar era. As many as sixteen were jobbers who bought their leather precut by Myers and Goodman and constructed their shoes to the company's specifications. As a result, they probably possessed few of the traditional skills of the craft and lacked the independence of their predecessors.[91]

Other artisans and laborers were also adversely affected by the economic transformation. Despite boosters' efforts to encourage residents to purchase locally made products, many craftsmen and laborers simply could not compete with Northern-made products and were thus ill served by Lynchburg's closer ties to regional and national markets. During the 1860s, Lynchburg's four hatters closed their shops, and the number of seamstresses and dressmakers declined from 187 to 41. Both crafts were victims of Northern ready-mades.[92]

The town's new iron-rolling mill provided an even more glaring example of the lamentable consequences of industrialization. Situated along the river basin a few miles outside town, the mill was constructed shortly after Secession to cater to the Confederacy's expanding need for railroad iron. By the end of the decade, the mill employed hundreds of workers. Although some of these were skilled artisans, a large number were unskilled and semiskilled, most of whom were dispossessed farmers, newly arrived from the countryside. Single men with financial obligations to family members back home, they lived in crowded tenements built by the company. Resentful of their poverty and their growing indebtedness to the mill owners, these workers rejected community leaders' sporadic efforts to integrate them into the white community.[93]

Lynchburg's boosters expected the postwar economic transformation to improve the quality of life for most white laborers. Its failure to do so made some civic leaders fearful of class conflict and, in their worst nightmares, labor agitation that crossed racial boundaries. At first glance, these concerns seem unwarranted. For the most part, white and black laborers viewed each other as competitors, not as allies in a contest against capital. Yet cautious conservatives were wary of the possibility. As they well knew, skilled and unskilled laborers from both races were poor and getting poorer. In their poverty, they were beginning to share common work experiences and similar living circumstances. Such were the unintended consequences of black emancipation and the transformation of the town's economic structure.

White men of property worried that some white laborers were forsaking the Conservative Party to align with blacks in the Republican Party. Unfortunately, it is extremely difficult to determine the composition of Lynchburg's Republican Party during Reconstruction. The local party organ, the *Lynchburg Press*, has survived only in fragmentary form. Occasionally, rival newspapers published the names of party leaders and officeholders. Most of these were men of some means, including merchants, tobacconists, and grocers. These men often resembled their political adversaries in nativity, wealth, and prewar stature. Yet a few others were prosperous craftsmen, mostly longtime Lynchburg residents, who may have been attracted to the Republican Party's progressive economic policies. This group included Samuel Dawson, a saddlemaker; Alex Sutphin, a wealthy jeweler; James Edwards, a tailor; and John P. Wright, a printer. Wright began his career in Lynchburg with the *Lynchburg Virginian*, sometime before the war. A few years after the war, he and other family members established two Republican newspapers in the area, the *Lynchburg Press* and the *Marion Record*. Through these newspapers, Wright endorsed a number of policies designed to help poorer whites in the South, including land confiscation and redistribution, expansion of the suffrage, public schools, and disfranchisement of former rebels to break the power of the Southern "aristocracy." By the late 1870s, the paper attained its reputation as the "working-man's journal" of the region.[94]

It is much more difficult to determine what sorts of whites helped comprise the rank and file of the Republican Party. Although their numbers were small, anecdotal evidence suggests that at least some were artisans who embraced ideas that were repugnant to the majority of prosperous whites. John Wright's son James was a member of the party and president of the local typographers' union. Charles Flynn, dubbed the "radical wheelwright" by the Conservative press, was considered even more sinister. Flynn, a native Virginian and longtime Lynchburg resident, had been something of a rough character before the war. Although he was a member of Centenary Methodist for a time, he was also something of a street brawler. Court records show that he was arrested several times—mostly for fighting with others of his class at local doggeries. Apparently, he sat out the war, although there is no evidence that he actively opposed it. After the war, he emerged as a leader of the local Republican Party. In his public statements, Flynn laced his critique of the South with appeals to both racial and class equality. In an 1869 letter to the House Select Committee on Reconstruction, Flynn vowed that he would "always be a Republican" because he believed that "all men were born with equal and inalienable rights" and because he wanted to "secure equal justice to the poor whites and blacks of the South." That year, he made an impassioned speech on the steps of the Court House, in which he denounced the "aristocracy" that ruled the country and predicted its overthrow by a coalition of blacks and poor whites. Within the Republican Party, Flynn presented himself as the voice of the laboring white man and consistently suggested that many more like him were in Lynchburg. While noting that fear of reprisal kept most from voting Republican, Flynn asserted that many poorer whites were sympathetic to the Republican cause. After the 1869 state election, he told Congress that he knew of "hundreds of white citizens in Lynchburg and the county of Campbell that would have voted the Republican ticket but for fear of persecution."[95]

Although Flynn offered no evidence to support his assertion, Conservatives found his assessment unsettling nonetheless. By their view, he was at least half right. The truth was that while most laboring whites did not vote the Republican ticket, they were also reluctant to support Conservative candidates. Time and again, Conservatives blamed defeat on their failure to attract larger numbers of poorer whites to their cause. Although Button and Perry usually tried to pass off poorer whites' lack of political involvement as simple apathy and inherent laziness, they occasionally admitted that they suspected laboring whites did not vote because they had become alienated from Conservative elites and were sympathetic to the Republican Party. Others came to a similar conclusion. Writing in the *Lynchburg Virginian* in 1868, "Seneca" suggested that because laboring whites did not vote Conservative, they should be considered part of the opposition. By his view, the present political struggle was a battle between propertied whites and "indigent and designing" blacks and whites.[96]

To counter the persistent indications of white laborers' alienation, Conservatives hoped to regain their loyalty by persuading them that race mattered more than class. In harrowing terms, Conservative leaders described what would happen to white Southerners if blacks realized their political ambitions. According to Perry, "ignorant negroes" would "control and govern white men," substituting "anarchism . . . for constitutional law" and "mob violence . . . for civil justice." Once this had occurred, Perry predicted, "the poorest citizen will suffer equally with the highest." To stop this from happening, Perry cautioned, poorer whites would do well to remember that political contests "were no longer between parties, but between races."[97]

Because they believed the stakes in the contest were so high, Conservatives censured those whites who supported the Republican Party as traitors to the South and to their race. In a particularly passionate rebuke, Button denounced any white man "who elected to join the black cohorts of Radicalism" as "unworthy of his lineage, a reproach to his Creator . . . a standing witness to the doctrine of innate depravity." According to Button, such a man aided the "mission of Radicalism" by "elevating one race by the deterioration of another." These traitors, Button warned, would pay for their disloyalty: "They not only separate themselves from their own people, but they earn and will receive the contempt of their race everywhere." Perry agreed. The editor warned white Republicans that "intelligent and honorable gentlemen" would judge them by the associations they made. If their associates were "ignorant, vicious, and depraved" blacks, respectable whites would judge them accordingly and deny them a place in white society.[98] To underscore the need for white racial solidarity, Button suggested that the names of the two political parties be changed to the "White Man's Party" and the "Negro Party," believing that once this was done, "very few white men will be found willing to separate from their race and alienate themselves from its respect and sympathy, to unite with a party whereof more than 95 in every 100, in this community, are negroes."[99]

Conservatives' efforts to attract lower-class whites must have been difficult for many wealthy whites. For some, class prejudice was almost as strong as racial prejudice. Eager to create a reliable workforce in the wake of black emancipation, many employers encouraged poorer whites to assume jobs once designated as "nigger work," then criticized them for refusing to do so. Addressing himself to the "young men of Lynchburg," "Merchant" encouraged unemployed white men to show less pride and more industry, telling them that if they demonstrated an eagerness to sweep floors, make a fire, or bring water, they would be "preferred to negroes who are so certain and insolent when spoken to about their business."[100] In the years immediately after the war, Perry also criticized poorer whites for their refusal to take jobs that required manual labor. He confessed that he could not understand why most poorer whites did not work harder to succeed. By his view, opportunities for social and economic mobility created a "perfect equalization of all white men." Whatever inequalities existed, Perry argued, were the result of "differences in . . . natural powers and . . . virtue." Thus, poorer whites had only themselves to blame for their poverty and low status. At times, Perry likened poorer whites to blacks, ridiculing both for their lack of steady habits and capitalist acumen. When the circus came through town in April 1867, Perry noted that the town was "completely demoralized" because it was a "moral impossibility" to get "darkies" and "a great many whites" to do "a lick of work." Disgusted, Perry asserted that neither group seemed to "care a continental for anything . . . but the spotted horses, Baby Annie, and 'sich.' "[101]

As Conservatives realized they had no hope of defeating the radicals without near-complete racial solidarity, the class-oriented criticisms against lower-class whites slowly abated. The turning point came in 1867, when local radicals swept the constitutional convention election of 1867. Conservatives believed that radicals won the close contest largely because they did a better job of getting their party members to the polls. Soon after the results of the election were known, Button lamented that they had lost the election because whites had been too apathetic and disorganized. To make sure the same did not happen again, Button urged Conservative leaders to "press it upon the attention of our people" that unless they "put forth all their strength," Lynchburg would have "a negro Council, a negro mayor, and negro police." Although Button did not specifically mention laboring whites as a target group at this time, subsequent events suggest that party leaders were eager to gain their allegiance. Almost immediately, public criticism of Lynchburg's laboring whites ended. Slowly, Conservatives began to demonstrate far more sympathy for the interests of white laborers and mechanics.[102]

For the next several years, the Conservative press regularly published essays on the dignity of labor and supported a variety of issues that were attractive to white laborers, including the establishment of local mechanics' organizations, lower housing rents, shorter workdays, and regular payment to employees. In addition, Conservative leaders tried to suggest that they, not the radicals, were the true friends of labor. During the state election of 1869, for instance, Conservative newspapers proudly noted that a meeting of "Lynchburg mechanics"—an assembly that also included grocers, clerks, and petty public officials, as well as several well-to-do artisan-proprietors—had unanimously endorsed the Conservative ticket. Two years later, when Conservative civic boosters tried to pass a railroad subscription plan, they emphasized that the proposed railroad would be especially advantageous for laborers. On the eve of the election, the *Lynchburg News* endorsed the proposal with the simple headline "KEEP OUR MECHANICS."[103]

At times, Lynchburg Conservatives' efforts to win the laboring white vote went against the national party's campaign strategies. Thus, in 1872, Perry condemned his party for deriding the Republican candidate for vice president because he came from a working-class background. In an obvious effort to win the support of Lynchburg mechanics, Perry suggested to party leaders that it was "time that the aristocratic sentiments of a former age and country . . . died out." After all, Perry noted, "it is one of the greatest glories of our country that so many of our most distinguished public men have risen from some obscure position to the highest official trusts."[104]

As Lynchburg's Conservative leaders tried to attract laboring whites to their party, they gradually stopped the tiresome Irish-baiting of the prewar years. Although Button and Perry occasionally made light of the Fenians—a mostly Northern organization intent on making Canada an Irish republic—they no longer portrayed the local Irish population as morally repugnant and a threat to social order. Indeed, Button now referred to the Irish as "friends" to the community and characterized the local chapter of the Fenians as "dignified" and "respectable," implying that their ethnicity no longer separated them from other whites. The editors were not alone in this new spirit of rapprochement. Before the war, native whites had often observed Saint Patrick's Day by ridiculing and abusing the local Irish population. This changed after the war. In 1866, for the first time in memory, Saint Patrick's Day passed without incident.[105]

However earnest their efforts, Conservatives were not completely successful in attracting lower-class whites to their side. White laborers had long come to expect benevolence and patronage in return for their acceptance of elite rule. After the war, financial constraints and the emergence of a more competitive and impersonal economic structure precluded elites from providing as they once had. Now all they could offer poorer whites was the recognition of their whiteness if they voted the Conservative ticket. For many laboring whites, this may not have been enough; for at the same time that elites emphasized the importance of the color line, their infatuation with industrial development, their criticism of poorer whites who refused to take menial jobs, and their failure to provide greater patronage and support to struggling white artisans undercut poorer whites' ability to avoid the taint of blackness. In February 1871, Perry reported that many magistrates had begun to urge the courts to put white "loafers" on the chain gang alongside blacks. For many laboring whites, the heightened attention to race may have exposed their own precarious status and their greater affinity with blacks.[106]

Lynchburg's civic leaders realized the crisis they were in. Political suasion and economic paternalism were clearly not having the desired effect. As the depth of the crisis became clearer, a growing number began to suggest that there was but one option left—religion. With growing evangelical fervency, Lynchburg's residents looked to God to do what they had failed to do—save the community from collapse.

CHAPTER FIVE

"To Crown Our Hearty Endeavors": Religion, Race, and Class, 1865–1872

B efore and during the war, devout Lynchburg residents had looked
to evangelical Christianity as a source of stability, security, and
reassurance. Now, in the aftermath of war and facing the uncertainties of black emancipation and Yankee rule, it was only natural that
many Lynchburg residents continued to look to their religious leaders for
spiritual and emotional support. Just a few weeks after Lee's surrender,
Jannett Cleland listened intently to a sermon by her minister, James
Ramsey of First Presbyterian Church. Ramsey, though visibly shaken
by defeat and fearful of the impending Yankee occupation, assured his
congregation that they were still "kings and priests of God." He reminded
his congregation to "put their trust in God and lay up their treasures in
heaven." Though Ramsey's message was simple, he spoke with such
power and conviction that Cleland recorded in her diary that she was now
"willing to trust God for everything in the future."[1]

For his part, Ramsey believed that the only way white Southerners
could remedy their present difficulties was through their faith in God.
While civic leaders tried to solve the town's social and political fragmentation through economic expansion and the politics of race, Ramsey and
other religious leaders suggested a solution of their own—a regeneration
of community through a collective recommitment to the South's evangelical heritage. In December 1865, Ramsey penned letters to every member

of the congregation, encouraging each to remain "faithful to your high and holy calling." In these letters, he warned his congregation that the "remarkable history of the present year gives special emphasis to the teachings of its closing hours." To help his congregation face the uncertainty of this tumultuous time, Ramsey advised members to put their spiritual affairs in order. Specifically, Ramsey admonished believers to confess their sins and to recommit themselves to Christ. Yet Ramsey was not interested only in the spiritual state of the congregation. He was also concerned for the fate of the community. To help Lynchburg survive the chaos of defeat, Ramsey advised members to consider their collective responsibilities. Specifically, he advised wealthier members to "forsake all self-indulgences" and to "govern all . . . expenditures." If they did so, Ramsey suggested, they would be better able to provide for "God's servants" who were "in actual want."[2]

John Warwick Craig, a local Episcopal minister, shared many of Ramsey's concerns. In a sermon preached three times in the two years after the war, Craig asserted that defeat and Yankee rule were not necessarily signs that God had abandoned the South or its cause. True, God had punished the South. But in doing so, Craig suggested, God acted not as a wrathful judge but as a "tender father striving to correct his children by the discipline of suffering." Indeed, the "terrible ordeals" of defeat and "military despotism" were really signs of God's abiding "care and love." By chastening the South, God provided Southerners an opportunity to examine their hearts, confess their sins, and repent. Craig predicted that when Southerners humbled themselves and rededicated their lives to God, God would not only pardon the South but "crown our hearty endeavors with abundant success." Although Craig did not elaborate the point, Lynchburgers undoubtedly understood his point: collective repentance offered the South a way to turn military defeat into a transcending victory.[3]

Ramsey's letter and Craig's sermon anticipated much of what historian Charles Reagan Wilson has termed "the religion of the Lost Cause." Like other Southern ministers in the years after the war, Ramsey and Craig maintained that Southerners possessed a unique and intimate relationship with God because of their history of spiritual devoutness. Although they interpreted defeat as a sign of God's wrath, they convinced themselves that God would not have punished them so severely if He did not love them so much. As long as Southerners repented and rededicated themselves to God, God would again exalt the South.[4]

The caveat was that white Southerners would have to set aside their differences to make common cause in Christ. For this reason, Ramsey, Craig, and other Southern ministers encouraged their congregations to make theirs a religion of spiritual unity. Rather than chastising individuals for their sins, ministers encouraged members to work out their faith by helping to fortify the evangelical community. Thus, Craig urged his followers to "refrain from all censoriousness—to exercise a liberal and charitable judgment on the conduct and character of our neighbors." He further warned that a critical temperament "is a great impediment to the spread of our Redeemer's kingdom, for it engenders strife . . . and alienates those whom we would willingly bring into the fold of Christ." As Craig, Ramsey, and others saw it, Southerners had sinned collectively as well as individually; therefore, repentance must be collective as well as individual.[5] Thus, the religion of the Lost Cause intertwined with and ultimately supported the political and social agenda of Southern conservatives. By placing harmony at the center of religion, white religious leaders hoped to unite Southerners through a process of moral regeneration that would transcend the social divisions that had become so visible during the war and after.

Unfortunately, Lynchburg's churches were in no condition to lead the sort of revival of community that postwar ministers envisioned. Instead, Lynchburg's postwar Protestant churches confronted a variety of crises that—at least, temporarily—led to a period of spiritual stagnation that distracted them from a complete embrace of their spiritual mission.

The withdrawal of blacks from the predominantly white churches was one such crisis. Although white church leaders originally expressed relief that they would no longer be burdened by the ignorant and barbaric religious customs of their former slaves, this initial reaction soon gave way to more complex feelings. While most Southern whites worried about the political implications of separate black religious institutions, many reacted as though they had been personally betrayed when blacks left to form separate churches. Whites showed their wounded pride in a variety of ways, none of which fully expressed the depth of their feelings toward blacks. Some predicted that the racial separation of the churches would be short-lived. Black worship services would become so barbaric and unruly, they contended, that whites would soon be forced to supervise their proceedings. Still others asserted that black congregations would flounder because members would not have the wherewithal to manage their institutions. Thus, when the African Baptist Church burned to the ground in 1866, Charles Button of the *Lynchburg Virginian* smugly observed that blacks "could not be induced ... to save their own house of worship," while "whites did everything they could to prevent its destruction."[6]

As it became obvious that blacks were not about to return, white religious leaders began to search for new ways to reestablish the bonds of paternalism. For many, the religion of the Lost Cause provided the proper justification for continued interference in black life. Idealizing the historical relationship between masters and slaves, whites argued that blacks still needed their spiritual supervision and guidance.[7] Most often, whites tried to be somewhat indirect in their efforts to reestablish control. Some tried to use patronage to compel blacks into a new type of dependency. When members of the newly formed Colored Methodist Church announced plans to buy an abandoned tobacco factory and turn it into a church, Perry of the *Lynchburg News* encouraged white residents to play a conspicuous role in the congregation's fund-raising efforts. At the groundbreaking some months later, a number of prominent whites participated in the ceremony, including the editors of all three Conservative newspapers, the mayor, the president of city council, ministers from several white churches, and the officers of the local order of the Knights Templar. Button remarked that the ceremony proved that "none know better than the negroes themselves ... that the Southern people are their best friends, despite the pretensions ... of mischievous and hypocritical Yankees." At about the same time, wealthy whites also patronized special fund-raising programs to rebuild the African Baptist Church.[8]

At other times, whites tried more overt ways to reassert ecclesiastical control over blacks and their religious institutions. Just months after the Freedmen's Bureau set up schools in the town, representatives from the town's white Protestant churches formulated a plan by which they would assume control. Although the scheme failed, white evangelicals remained convinced that they knew what was best for Lynchburg blacks. In October 1866, ministers petitioned the Bureau again—this time with a plan for the churches to assume full control of public assistance for all black residents. Meanwhile, some denominations tried to reestablish ecclesiastical control over their black members. In the pages of the *Religious Herald*, the Baptist state journal, church leaders debated how best to supervise black churches affiliated with their denomination. In August 1868, the Lynchburg District Conference for the Methodist Church requested that the presiding elder of the local conference "secure pastoral supervision" over all the black Methodist congregations in the area. First Presbyterian was even more direct. A few months after the war, church elders reopened their black Sunday school program, even though they did not have cash on hand to fund the venture.[9]

Try as they might, however, there was little that white church leaders could do to reestablish their former influence over the town's African American churches. Instead, the consequences of their efforts were mostly deleterious. Although few white religious leaders were willing to admit it, the only things that they received for their efforts were a nagging sense that they had failed in their divine mission and the ever-festering conviction that blacks had betrayed them.[10]

Internal problems also hurt many of Lynchburg's white churches. For almost a year, members of First Baptist quarreled with their minister. Although extant records do not reveal the cause of the dispute, the conflict forced the minister's resignation and left the church without a pastor for several months. Members of Protestant Methodist also quarreled at this time. Here the issue was not the minister but unification with the Court Street Methodist congregation. After nearly two years of heated debate, the congregation decided by a small majority not to unify. After the vote, several members of the losing faction quit the church. Meanwhile, the deteriorating health of ministers and lay leaders at several churches also contributed to Lynchburg's postwar spiritual malaise. At First Presbyterian, James Ramsey's health began to deteriorate during the late 1860s. As he grew more feeble, the church began to experience a slow decline. Although the congregation hired a second minister to assist Ramsey in 1868, the church continued to weaken. The session's 1869 annual report candidly observed that, in numbers and wealth, the church was "feebler . . . than it has been for ten years." In addition, the session noted, many of the church's wealthiest members had died or moved away, leaving the church weak "from the poverty of those who remain." The session was equally cryptic in its assessment of the church's spiritual state. Although the session acknowledged that many members displayed "manifest evidence" of spiritual growth, it confessed that "in some among us there is such want of . . . spirituality as to bring their whole state into doubt." The clerk of session candidly reported that he could not recall the last time anyone in the congregation had restored a backslider or converted a sinner from the world.[11]

Second Presbyterian experienced a similar decline, as several key members of the congregation advanced in years. In 1868, a special report of the session of Second Presbyterian stated that despite Jacob Mitchell's sincere effort to "make a good and lasting impression" on his congregation through sermons and door-to-door visitations, the church was "not spiritually growing ... and gives little evidence of growth in grace." Freedmen's Bureau teacher Jacob Yoder agreed with the session's observation. After a May 1866 visit to the church, he noted that Mitchell's "powerful preaching does not seem to take hold on the hearts of his people." During the years after the war, regular attendance at the church steadily declined. From 1865 to 1868, an average of just over 100 attended the church each Sunday; in the two years before the war, more than 170 had attended the church regularly. By late 1869, the two Presbyterian churches were in such spiritual and numerical decline that they briefly considered whether it might be more cost-effective to unite than to carry on as separate entities.[12]

As difficult as these problems were, the most debilitating obstacle that Lynchburg's churches faced in their effort to reunite the community spiritually was financial. Because of the town's postwar economic collapse, most Lynchburg churches were broke. Conditions at First Baptist, probably the town's least wealthy church, were especially bad. In September 1866, the church treasurer reported that the church's savings had dwindled to only $14.53. Even Court Street Methodist, the town's wealthiest church, did not completely escape the financial crisis. A year after the war, the treasurer reported that the church, "though not entirely free from debt, is entirely free from embarrassment" and would remain so as long as members continued to give as they had done.[13]

Poverty hurt the churches in two ways. First, economic concerns distracted ministers and elders from religious matters and may even have weakened their spiritual zeal. Centenary Methodist, in contrast to the evangelistic fervor that it had shown in the prewar years, seemed singularly preoccupied with its bleak postwar finances. During the two years after the war, church stewards discussed little besides ways to encourage members to make and meet their tithes. Meanwhile, the trustees of First Baptist, Protestant Methodist, the two Presbyterian churches, and St. Paul's Episcopal Church searched for new ways to raise funds so that they could pay their debts and become financially solvent.[14]

Second, the impoverished condition of the churches made them ill prepared to respond to the growing poverty of the town's white residents.

This was calamitous not only for the poor but also for the evangelical community. Before the war, public benevolence—usually in the form of cash and supplies to needy residents—had been one way in which churches helped poorer residents become at least marginally integrated into the life of the religious community. Now the churches found that they were unable to provide as they once had. As a result, they curtailed charitable giving to a fraction of what it had once been. A year after the end of the war, First Baptist had less than two dollars in its poor fund. When Jannett Cleland asked the elders of her church, First Presbyterian, to assist the poor residents squatting at the abandoned college, the elders told her that they could not afford to do so.[15]

Unable to provide as generously as they once had, churches began to experiment with new ways to assist the poor. Rather than give money outright, churches began to place more emphasis on home missions. The primary function of these new institutions was not to provide charity outright but to give poor whites, especially children, some semblance of an education. Although church leaders still expressed a desire to integrate poorer whites into the evangelical community through benevolence, they recognized that the scale of the problem outstripped their ability to provide assistance. Inspired by public institutions created during the war—namely the hospitals—organizers strove to develop efficient modes of benevolence. Leaders became especially intrigued with the role education could play in reform. By their view, schools provided financially strapped churches a more cost-effective and rational way to distribute their limited financial resources to a larger population of poorer residents. Using only rudimentary supplies and relying on female volunteers as teachers, the missions and schools required a minimal cash outlay to operate.[16]

In a short time, what had begun as a matter of financial expediency became a preferred form of charity. Even after Lynchburg's economy recovered slightly in the late 1860s, local churches continued to put more and more energy into their home mission programs. Church leaders quickly realized that the home missions had more advantages than just cost-effectiveness. For one, civic leaders believed that the missions might help solve the growing problem of social disorder and immorality in the city. With large numbers of impoverished blacks and whites roaming the streets, civic leaders recognized that they could no longer be as tolerant of lower-class impropriety as they once had been. For civic leaders, the missions and schools provided an opportunity to teach poorer whites the more disciplined values of self-control and self-regulation. At the same time, the objectives of the missions and schools corresponded with business leaders' desire to create a new economic order. Through these new institutions, civic leaders hoped that poorer whites would learn the values and social skills necessary to compete in a more complex and competitive world.[17]

Church leaders converted so completely to this new system of charity that they slowly retreated from one of the primary attributes of the old system of benevolence—personalism. Beginning in the late 1860s, several churches began to control charity by keeping ledgers and by changing their bylaws so that lay committees, not ministers, would decide the merits of each case. Under this new system, it became more difficult for poorer residents to receive straight monetary assistance. Quite often, when individuals or families became too dependent, church leaders denied further support. Consider the fate of the Gregory family of Court Street Methodist. Throughout the late 1860s and into the 1870s, Mrs. Nannie Gregory, a single mother with a large family, regularly applied to Court Street Methodist for assistance. At first, the Board of Stewards proved rather generous, giving her money or provisions on a near-monthly basis. After a time, however, the stewards grew tired of her constant appeals and began to lecture her, informing her in April 1872 that they "expect Mrs. Gregory and her family to exert themselves for their support." Thereafter, Mrs. Gregory stopped receiving regular assistance from Court Street Methodist.[18]

Domestic missions became so popular that by the end of 1871, five of Lynchburg's Protestant churches—First Presbyterian, Court Street Methodist, Centenary Methodist, First Baptist, and St. Paul's Episcopal— had started missions to assist indigent whites of the town. These missions ranged in size according to the church's financial resources. First Baptist's effort was probably the most modest. In early 1868, the School Committee resolved to hire a teacher and open a small school "on behalf of the poor for those whose moral and mental improvement we are bound as Christians to have a care." During the next few years, the church raised money for the program, while continuing to rely on volunteers to staff the endeavor. By 1871, they settled on a permanent location at the old college, still home to many indigent whites and blacks.[19]

Affluent Court Street Methodist was far more ambitious in its efforts to reach laboring poor whites. In 1866, church stewards established a Board of Domestic Missions and hired a minister, F. M. Edwards, to oversee its operation. With some assistance from Centenary Methodist, Edwards started Sabbath schools for destitute whites in three of the poorest neighborhoods in town—the Rolling Mill, Franklin's Hill, and the Fair Grounds. Because Court Street's stewards made support of the mission program a litmus test for church members' commitment to their faith, the missions received considerable financial and volunteer assistance. With an administrative supervisor, three paid teachers, and as many as eighty volunteers, the board operated missions at as many as three locations at once. At these they conducted Sabbath schools and, later, daily schools. At their peak, the Sunday schools attracted as many as three hundred children and adolescents, while the combined enrollment at the daily schools was probably close to one hundred. Meanwhile, the church's Dorcas Society, a female Methodist benevolent society, also expanded its efforts. During the period, the organization maintained its regular Sabbath school program for poorer whites and added a day school.[20]

The Lynchburg Bible Society was an even more ambitious effort than the various mission school programs. In December 1867, ministers and laymen from six of the seven white evangelical churches organized to distribute Bibles to the poor of the city.[21] As with the mission schools, church leaders envisioned a program that would expose the poor of the town to Lynchburg's religious community in a more thorough and systematic manner than had previous outreach programs. According to the bylaws, the Society hoped to visit every family in the district, determine their spiritual needs, and "take note of the name and residence of the destitute who are not able to pay for a bible." Toward this end, the chairman of the Society, the Reverend Thomas Early of Court Street Methodist, divided the city into twelve sections and assigned a minister or laymen to visit each section.[22]

Despite organizers' aspirations, most domestic missions did not match expectations. The Bible Society, for one, never developed beyond the planning stage. Perhaps because volunteers realized the immensity of the task, they eventually lost their enthusiasm for door-to-door fact-finding and proselytizing. After only a few meetings, the Society disbanded. Some other domestic missionary endeavors lasted longer but also failed to become permanent entities. St. Paul's Episcopal and First Presbyterian both suspended operations of their domestic missions after only a few years.[23]

Even Court Street Methodist Church's well-funded mission program experienced problems. At first, Edwards and his assistants received considerable praise for their efforts. Less than a year after making the appointment, the stewards commended Edwards for his "fidelity, zeal, and marked efficiency" in ministering to those who "have been almost entirely destitute of ministerial care and instruction." A few years later, the stewards again complimented Edwards and the Mission Board, stating that in their "judgment, no work within the bounds of the Conference is more truly of a missionary character and no part of our Missionary fund more profitably expended." Civic leaders were equally impressed by the church's commitment to the poor. After Court Street Methodist announced plans to open a mission in the suburbs, Button praised the church on behalf of the town, noting that it "deserves great credit for its praiseworthy exertions" for the indigent children of the city.[24]

Despite these laudatory remarks, there are several reasons to suspect that Court Street's mission program was not as successful as church and civic leaders portrayed it. First, extant attendance figures suggest that the schools did not experience the slow, steady growth that one might expect from a successful missionary program. During one two-year span, average attendance at the Sabbath schools rose from about 124 to 300, only to decline again to about 150. Second, the Mission Board failed to find permanent homes for two of its missions. Although the church built a permanent structure at the Rolling Mill, its other missions experienced a more transitory existence—opening, moving, and closing as student and, perhaps, teacher interest waxed and waned. As a result, the church was unable to keep the two other schools in operation over an extended period. Finally, Court Street Methodist largely failed to attract any of the families of their "young scholars" into the permanent church body. From 1865 to 1872, only two unskilled laborers joined Court Street Methodist Church.[25]

Perhaps it is not surprising that the poor were not attracted to Court Street Methodist. The church was not only the wealthiest in town, it also had the reputation of being the most ostentatious. Freedmen's Bureau teacher Jacob Yoder, a deeply religious man, claimed to love Methodism "above all other" denominations but despised Court Street Methodist. In 1866, after his second visit to Court Street, he condemned it as "the most aristocratic church in this place," more adapted "to draw out the fashionable folks than the spirit of God." Yet Lynchburg's other churches—including those that had sizable numbers of white laborers—fared only slightly better than Court Street Methodist in attracting poorer residents into the full life of the church after the war. In all, only fifteen unskilled whites, 10 percent of all new members, joined Lynchburg's eight Protestant churches in the five years after the war. Of these, ten joined Centenary Methodist.[26]

It is difficult to determine what poorer residents thought of Lynchburg's evangelical churches. Certainly, longtime residents must have been struck by the different intent of postwar benevolent outreach. Before the war, most church programs operated under the premise that the unregenerate changed only after they voluntarily accepted God into their lives and joined a Christian community. Thus, prewar ministers tended to preach conversion first, moral reform second. After the war, however, religious leaders were no longer willing to wait for poorer whites to reform. Eager to solve the problem of public disorder even as they tried to enhance the bonds of racial solidarity, religious leaders tried to place poorer whites in institutions that would ready them for conversion through discipline and instruction.[27]

From the perspective of many poorer whites, it was probably difficult to discern which was more important to the domestic missionaries— conversion or discipline. At times, the missionaries seemed to act as if these were one and the same. In an 1869 Methodist Conference quarterly report, the stewards of Court Street Church noted that the improvement of the children at one of their mission schools had been "very decided and in some instances quite remarkable." Gathered "from the most destitute parts of the city and its suburbs, they were ignorant, rude, and in many instances filthy almost beyond belief." Since attending the mission school, however, "they are now decent, respectful, easily controlled, studious, and give promise of a degree of usefulness in life that will amply vindicate the wisdom of the enterprise."[28]

Lower-class whites responded to the proselytizing efforts of the mission schools in a variety of ways. Some, no doubt, found the values of the missionaries attractive and converted to them. In addition, some students, especially children, probably developed strong attachments to their teachers, many of whom still tried to abide by the ethic of personalism. Female teachers seem to have been especially caring. At the Dorcas Society mission school, for example, regular attendees spent day after day with the same teachers, young women who earnestly tried to help their students. Jannett Cleland, who became a teacher at First Presbyterian Church's mission school, was equally devoted to her young charges. Cleland took a special interest in each of her students and used what she considered to be her feminine instincts—namely, maternal love, patience, and compassion—to educate them.[29]

Yet one wonders how well personalism operated in this new institutional environment. Most families found it difficult to attend the missions regularly because of their uncertain economic circumstances and unstable family situations. Not only were children of these families unable to develop close relationships with their teachers, they probably remained largely unmoved by the missions' efforts to convert them to the new moral code of self-control. Privately, teachers complained that many of their students misbehaved and were reluctant learners. Cleland, for one, candidly lamented in her diary that her students tried to "provoke" her daily, despite her obvious devotion to them. The wild fluctuations in classroom attendance from week to week and even day to day, no matter what the cause, also indicate that the "young scholars" did not internalize the self-discipline their teachers tried to instill in them. In December 1870, the Dorcas Society conceded that attendance at its Sabbath school "has been so irregular" that the Society could no longer estimate what attendance might be from week to week.[30]

Evidently, students of the Dorcas Society's Sabbath school developed a decidedly pragmatic view of the Society's home mission program. A large number evidently took what they could from the schools but otherwise remained detached from the evangelical community. Extant records suggest that attendance at the schools increased during times of extreme want but receded during flush times. Thus, the school experienced a sharp rise in attendance during the eighteen months after the war but a gradual decline during the next year, as the health of the economy improved. Thereafter, many laboring families continued to try to manipulate their benefactors. The treasurer of the Dorcas Society observed that when she tried to determine the organization's benevolence budget, she had to assume that virtually all those who attended the school, no matter how irregularly, would apply for the annual distribution of clothes and shoes. Economic constraints may have compromised poorer whites' ability to be independent, but they did not compromise their desire to manipulate elites when they could.[31]

The spiritual malaise of Lynchburg's white congregations lasted into the 1870s. Then, it abruptly ended with a spiritual reawakening that contemporaries called the Great Revival of 1871—an event that lasted nearly four months, spread through nearly all the town's white Protestant churches, and led to the conversion of more than five hundred area residents. This was not the first revival Lynchburg had experienced. As was the case throughout the South, many of Lynchburg's churches planned annual protracted meetings to satisfy their congregations' desire for an experiential relationship with God. These were usually very organized affairs, each staged by a single church. Congregations prepared for revivals months in advance by holding weekly and sometimes nightly prayer meetings. Long before the revival began, ministers contracted with important itinerants who specialized in revivalist preaching to share the pulpit. To reach the largest possible audience, most churches planned their revivals for the fall, to accommodate the agricultural business cycle.[32]

Despite Lynchburg's long history of revivalism, the town had never experienced anything that compared to the awakening in 1871. Although extant sources do not provide a full explanation of the revival's causes, it appears that it began in much the same way as its predecessors. In December 1870, First Baptist invited A. B. Earle, an itinerant revivalist, to preach at the church. Earle had been touring in the South for several months, sparking religious enthusiasm at virtually every stop. He arrived in Lynchburg in early January. Although he stayed for less than a week, the response was extraordinary. Each night, he preached to larger and more enthusiastic audiences, converting at least ten a night. By the end of his stay, the church was holding meetings twice a day and had received eighty new members into its fellowship.[33]

Although Earle ignited the religious enthusiasm, it soon took on a life of its own. After Earle left, First Baptist hastily called on two more itinerants to help the regular minister, C. C. Bitting, carry the preaching load. After nearly a month of nightly sermons and daily prayer vigils, the religious enthusiasm spread to Centenary Methodist. From there, the revival moved to the two Presbyterian churches and Court Street Methodist. Finally, after nearly four months of sermons, prayer vigils, altar calls, baptisms, and love feasts, the revival ended.[34]

Civic and religious leaders, eager to find evidence of white racial solidarity wherever they could, emphasized the community-wide enthusiasm that the revival generated. Early on, a correspondent for the *Religious Herald*, a Baptist journal, noted that "all classes flocked to hear" the famous Earle. A bit later, when the revival had spread throughout the white evangelical community, Perry of the *Lynchburg News* made a similar observation, noting that the religious enthusiasm "seems to reach every class of the community, and seems to be increasing every day." After the revival, W. E. Judkins, Court Street Methodist's minister, noted that the revival had been singularly "remarkable" because of its popular appeal. In his quarterly statement to the denomination, Judkins suggested that the awakening had established a new religious community that transcended lines of class and social status. At his own church, "one hundred and sixty souls were converted," including men and women "of every age and every position in life. . . . The most cultural and intellectual . . . the veteran of three score and ten, the little child of ten or twelve Summers, the poor, the unlettered, all bowed together before the cross and rejoiced together in a Savior's love." Button, ever eager to enhance the stature of the town's elite citizens, emphasized the conspicuous role that civic leaders had played in the revival as it unfolded. In a mid-February account of the revival's progress, he noted that the converts at Court Street Methodist included "many prominent business men," whose "accessions to the church and whose examples will exert a most salutary influence" on the community.[35]

These observations had at least some basis in fact. For one thing, the revival spread to a large cross section of the town's white community. Nearly half of the converts were men. In terms of occupation, roughly half of the 514 converts can be identified through either the manuscript census or the 1873 business directory. Of these, 25 percent came from laborers' families, 44 percent came from professionals' families, and 20 percent came from the families of minor professionals. Moreover, the revival may have complemented elites' efforts to unify local whites. Indeed, conforming to the expectations of the burgeoning religion of the Lost Cause, the revival either coincided with or anticipated several other events that white civic leaders hailed as indications of the community's growing racial solidarity.

The first of these was a vote for municipal subscription for the Danville-Lynchburg railroad. On February 15, the town voted overwhelmingly for subscription by a vote of 1,610 to 169. Conservatives had campaigned hard for public funding of the road. Both Button of the *Virginian* and Perry of the *News* endorsed the scheme, arguing that the new Southern railroad would give the town an opportunity to regain its industrial base by providing local entrepreneurs a direct link to the natural resources and markets of southern Virginia and North Carolina. Although the near-unanimous victory suggested that the plan received considerable support from the black community, Conservatives generally ignored blacks' electoral contribution and instead interpreted the victory as an indication of the growing solidarity among whites. Button, for one, argued that the lopsided victory made the black vote irrelevant, since the referendum would have passed without blacks' support.[36]

Second, after years of Republican domination, Lynchburg's Conservative Party began to reclaim its hold on the local government. During the late 1860s, loyalty oaths and other voting restrictions had kept many of Lynchburg's Conservatives from running for state or municipal office. In the state election of 1869, however, Conservatives attracted moderate Republicans by raising the specter of black political rule. The result was a stunning victory for the Conservative Party. In that election, Conservatives elected their candidate for governor, gained a majority in both state houses, and defeated a referendum that would have disfranchised many of the town's most prominent citizens.[37] In the ensuing months, Lynchburg's Conservatives, thanks largely to the politics of race, ascended to power. In November 1870, they elected their candidate for Congress in a narrow victory. Then, in the May 1871 municipal elections, whites outregistered blacks for the first time in five years to take ten of fifteen city council seats, losing only those seats in the largely black Third Ward.[38]

Finally, within weeks of the revival, several ex-soldiers, white men of all classes, reorganized the Home Guard—the town's first and most prestigious Civil War regiment. In the ensuing months, the organization participated in a variety of public holidays and ceremonies. Although these new duties paled in comparison to their wartime activities, the Guard retained an important symbolic role. If nothing else, it embodied white Lynchburg residents' belief that neither the war nor Reconstruction had defeated them.[39]

The revival, of course, did not cause any of these events, but it did complement these activities by affirming a developing community consensus through the very public demonstration of repentance and conversion. Yet even as the revival strengthened the bonds of the white community on one level, it did not unite rich and poor as civic and religious leaders had intended. In part, this was because most of the town's poorest whites remained obstinately outside the town's religious community. Never a large portion of the town's churchgoing population, unskilled white laborers became an even smaller segment after the revival. In 1870, one in ten church members came from the families of unskilled laborers; during the four months of the revival, only one in twenty new church members came from these families.[40]

Moreover, those laborers who did participate in the revival, mostly skilled artisans, did not necessarily act in ways that helped civic and religious leaders achieve the unity of purpose that they desired. For one thing, laborers did not play their prescribed role as followers during the revival. Instead, the course of the revival suggests that they, not the town's traditional leaders, led the procession to the altar. The revival started at the church with the largest number of laborers and their families, First Baptist, and then spread to the church with the second largest number, Centenary Methodist. Moreover, laborers who joined a church during the revival demonstrated a decided preference to worship in churches other than those attended by the town's most prominent citizens and civic leaders. Over 90 percent of all laborers who joined a church during the revival joined First Baptist, Centenary Methodist, and First Presbyterian. Conversely, only 3 percent joined either Court Street Methodist or St. Paul's Episcopal, the churches with the wealthiest and most prestigious members.[41]

Given the reputations of First Baptist and Centenary Methodist, it is not surprising that laborers preferred to join these two churches above all others. As before the war, these churches remained committed to the evangelical traditions of spiritual equality and conservative morality. Although the postwar economic crisis and spiritual malaise hindered their ability to attract new members, both churches held fast to those customs that had made them popular among laborers before the war. Each church continued to provide less wealthy members greater opportunity for church leadership, and each demonstrated an unwavering commitment to upholding the bonds of community through church discipline.

Laborers' developing attraction to First Presbyterian requires a bit more explanation but further supports the contention that the town's pious artisans, shopkeepers, and laborers wanted a very distinctive brand of evangelical Protestantism. Before the war, the church attracted a few artisans and their families but was mostly dominated by merchants, tobacconists, and professionals. As death and membership transfers deprived the church of many of the latter members, skilled artisans and petty clerks began to assume more responsibilities in the life of the church. By the late 1860s, the church's lay leaders included a wide cross section of the town's social structure, including artisans, petty merchants, and office clerks, as well as merchants and professionals.[42]

As this group assumed responsibility for the spiritual life of the church, they gradually transformed its evangelical style, adopting many of the same policies that governed First Baptist and Centenary Methodist. Thus, during the late 1860s and early 1870s, church members committed themselves to purifying their congregation through church discipline. In the five years before the war, First Presbyterian's elders disciplined only three members; in the seven years after the war, elders disciplined ten members—second only to First Baptist, which disciplined twenty-six members during the period. Six of these disciplinary actions occurred during the eighteen months after the revival. Like First Baptist and Centenary Methodist, the elders of First Presbyterian disciplined members for a wide variety of offenses, including public drunkenness, dancing, and infrequent church attendance. By comparison, congregations that did not have sizable numbers of laborers became less reluctant to discipline members. In 1867, the stewards of Protestant Methodist decided that they would no longer discipline members for "nonattendance," because they did not believe that "such conduct" would "necessarily exclude believers from the kingdom of grace and glory." After the war, the church disciplined only three members—all for selling alcohol. Court Street Methodist, with roughly three times the membership of First Presbyterian, held only eight disciplinary hearings in the seven years immediately after the war—all for either profanity or public drunkenness. In each case, the elders lectured the transgressor but took no other action. Conversely, First Baptist and First Presbyterian suspended or expelled about half of all transgressors brought before each congregation.[43]

Although church discipline was not a daily part of church life, its relative frequency at First Baptist, Centenary Methodist, and First Presbyterian suggests that members of these churches remained wedded to a strict code of morality and a traditional conception of Christian fellowship. Evidently, the objects of church discipline shared these values as well. Although some recent studies have demonstrated that church members became unwilling to submit to church discipline during the late nineteenth century, the example of Lynchburg suggests class variations in this trend. At the town's least wealthy churches, disciplined members tended to submit to the collective will of their congregations. Only about one-third ignored their church's efforts to discipline them. But most of these may have long since left the church: in nearly every one of these cases, the church initiated disciplinary hearings because of the member's prolonged absence.[44]

Not that all came quietly. A few others bristled a bit before finally submitting to the church's authority. In August 1870, the elders of First Presbyterian summoned Alex McCorkle, the son of a prosperous merchant and grocer, to censure him for his frequent bouts with alcohol. For several months, McCorkle refused the summons. Finally, in March 1871, McCorkle wrote to the session, informing the elders that he did not want to submit to their "inquest." At the same time, however, he asked them not to expel him, because he did not want to be "humiliated" and because he wanted to remain a part of the church's fellowship. At their next meeting, session rejected McCorkle's plea and decided to take disciplinary action. Evidently, session's resolute response scared McCorkle. He now realized that he was at risk of being excommunicated—a fate he did not want to bring upon himself. Two weeks after asserting that he would not submit to session, McCorkle appeared before the church elders to confess his sins. Session promptly suspended him for one year. At the end of the year, McCorkle asked for, and was granted, reinstatement.[45]

As McCorkle's case suggests, church members at Lynchburg's less wealthy churches remained determined to protect the traditional bonds of Christian fellowship—even as some tried to test the strength of those bonds. Indeed, church discipline may have gained a new poignancy for many less wealthy residents in the years immediately after the war. Anxious about their status in the new social order, and feeling estranged from elites, Lynchburg's less wealthy residents may have used church discipline to strengthen the one institution that still gave them a place in society. Moreover, church discipline offered less wealthy residents a way to show meddlesome and self-righteous wealthy residents that they could determine for themselves what constituted proper behavior.

Of course, the separation of wealthy and less wealthy evangelicals was never complete. Although the two groups continued to approach religion differently, both were still part of a common evangelical culture. Thus, a small percentage of wealthier residents continued to join First Baptist, Centenary Methodist, and First Presbyterian. During the revival, for instance, roughly one-sixth of Centenary Methodist's and First Baptist's and one-third of First Presbyterian's new members were professionals or wealthy proprietors. Yet when wealthy residents joined these churches, they understood that the rituals and traditions of the congregations encouraged a distinctive style of social interaction—one that emphasized collective responsibility, strict morality, and spiritual equality.[46]

Although the Great Revival of 1871 may have temporarily soothed intraracial class tensions in Lynchburg, it could not make them go away. Instead of abandoning their class interests within the broad drive for racial solidarity, laboring whites stubbornly adhered to distinctive value systems. While many simply refused to participate in the revival, others used what civic leaders wistfully interpreted as a consensus-building event to articulate a distinctively egalitarian and morally conservative worldview that contained in its historical origins a critique of the less morally rigorous upper classes.

Yet class lines were made even more complex by the activities of Lynchburg's poorest whites, the unskilled laborers, whose response to the revival was almost negligible. Thus, the very values that separated all laborers from the propertied classes divided them internally as well. Perhaps this helps to explain why Lynchburg laborers did not use their evangelical theology to articulate a broad-based political attack against the upper classes. Nevertheless, municipal leaders feared the potential for conflict. Just a few months after the revival and the sweeping political victories of the early 1870s, Button repeated his doubts concerning the loyalty of the town's white laborers. Admitting that there was considerable enmity between the propertied classes and poor whites, he again urged employers to hire those of their own race, not blacks. Perhaps Button had grasped the central truth of class relations in Lynchburg. Civic leaders might gain lower-class whites' support during moments of extreme political crisis, but in the daily activities of life, poorer whites—as demonstrated by their religious preferences—proved far more elusive to elites' plea for intraracial class harmony.[47]

CHAPTER SIX

"The Mauling Science": Black and White Violence and Vigilance, 1865–1872

On Tuesday, August 7, 1866, J. G. Perry, local editor for the *Lynchburg News*, reported two weekend incidents of interracial violence, the likes of which were virtually unknown before black emancipation. The first had occurred the previous Saturday evening. On that night, a black gang accosted a white man, whom Perry identified only as an ex-Confederate soldier, as he walked along Twelfth Street on his way home. According to Perry, the incident began when one of the assailants shoved the man against a wall, cursing him as a "d—d rebel son of a ——." For a brief moment, the ex-soldier fought back by brandishing a small knife; but when it broke in the arm of one of the assailants, he was defenseless. In a matter of seconds, the gang knocked the man to the ground and began pummeling him with heavy sticks and rocks. Although the man pleaded with white onlookers to help him, they refused, apparently intimidated by the growing number of blacks who had gathered around to watch the assault. Somehow, the white man freed himself from his assailants. As he fled, the black gang continued the assault by pelting him with rocks.

The next day, Sunday, blacks and whites again clashed—but this time with radically different results. On a busy street, two white youths, J. W. Padget and J. M. Rodgers—both children of Lynchburg artisans— accosted three unidentified blacks. According to the youths, the dispute began when they confronted the black men on the sidewalk and ordered them to step aside. When the men not only refused but responded with insults, the youths decided that this was provocation enough: they assaulted the three men, stopping only after the police arrived.[1]

Although white males were clearly the aggressors in one of the weekend incidents, Perry interpreted both as confirmation that the "lower class of negroes in this city" were becoming increasingly ruthless in their behavior toward whites. To stop such "outrages," Perry encouraged his readers to act with more resolve—or face the possibility of a full-scale race riot, as had occurred in Memphis just a few months earlier. "They have got to be stopped," Perry warned, "or there will be no such thing as living with them. If allowed to go on as they are going, insulting and trampling upon white men at their pleasure ... the result will be a repetition of the deplorable scenes that have been enacted in some of the other Southern cities."[2]

By encouraging whites to be more aggressive against blacks, Perry implicitly appealed to the complementary ethics of honor and vigilance. Most lower-class whites probably did not need the encouragement. As products of a distinctly Southern community, they accepted violence as an effective and legitimate way to impose order on society. Indeed, Lynchburg's poorest white residents probably adhered to the ethic of honor more ardently than ever, because black emancipation and the economic transformation of the town made status a more contested commodity than it had been before the war. For this reason, postwar interracial interaction is perhaps best understood within the broader context of the ethic of honor.

As before the war, most incidents of postwar violence occurred in defense of individual or family honor. Civic leaders' growing intolerance of public disorder did little to curb lower-class Southerners' penchant for violence when they felt their honor threatened. Indeed, Perry's advice suggests that some civic leaders believed violence—unencumbered by rule of law—often worked best, at least insofar as the governance of blacks was concerned.

Even the imposition of a modern police force in 1866, created to stop the epidemic of petty thievery that gripped the town immediately after the war, proved ineffectual in stopping violent acts of vengeance. Indeed, many policemen—themselves products of Southern culture—occasionally resorted to violence to defend their honor. In one incident, Edward

Akers, an auctioneer, stood by a Republican rally, badgering the black speakers. Police sergeant Edwin Diuguid, a former carpenter, approached Akers, instructing him to keep the peace. At first, Akers complied. But when Diuguid allowed a group of blacks to boisterously applaud a speaker, Akers accused Diuguid of creating a double standard. "Why don't you stop your cousins?" he sarcastically asked the policeman. Diuguid, a Conservative himself, took violent exception to Akers's insult and attacked him with his billy club. Only after some effort were other policemen able to separate Diuguid from his detractor.[3] In another instance, the town's longtime city jailer Hughey Hughes got into a scuffle with Charles Green at a neighborhood bar. After trading insults, Green attacked Hughes with a cane, hitting him in the face several times. In retaliation, Hughes drew his pistol and fired two shots at Green, missing him both times but hitting an innocent bystander. Finally, other bar patrons stopped the fight by holding the two men down.[4]

The courts also made only half-hearted efforts to curb white honor-based violence in Lynchburg. Although the city magistrates and state court judges occasionally tried to bring belligerents to justice, juries often allowed older standards of behavior to prevail when personal honor was at stake. On a July night in 1871, William H. Miller met Morris O. Thomas at a bar. The two began to discuss an old grudge that dated back to the war. Tempers flared. When Thomas called Miller a "damned lying, thieving son of a bitch," Miller drew his pistol. Thomas, seeing it, dared him to fire. Miller did so, fatally wounding Thomas in the abdomen. Although witnesses testified that Thomas was unarmed when he dared Miller, the jury—containing an equal representation of artisans, merchants, and clerks—deliberated for only one hour before deciding that Miller had acted in self-defense and was thus not guilty. In his report of the case, Perry praised the jury for its judicious and humane ruling.[5]

John McAlister got off nearly as light. McAlister, the steward of the Washington House, shot Fred Douglas, the baker of the hotel, in the leg, during a dispute about the baker's abilities. McAlister was tried by the state court for malicious assault. After a short deliberation, the jury returned a verdict of guilty but asked the judge for a minimum sentence—a one-cent fine and one hour in jail. The judge waived the fine when McAlister claimed that he did not have the proper change.[6]

Thus unimpeded by either the law or community disapprobation, whites went about defending their honor much as they had before the war. In most cases, individuals retaliated quickly and decisively when insulted. When James Bobbitt, a white clothing-store clerk, criticized John Pitts, a white cabinetmaker, for his shoddy workmanship, Pitts responded by insulting Bobbitt. Predictably, Bobbitt replied with a few "rough words" of his own. Pitts, now enraged, decided that trading insults would no longer suffice. Instead, he drew a small "saloon pistol" and shot Bobbitt, wounding him in the arm.[7]

While most aspects of lower-class honor-based violence resembled prewar behavior, there was one significant change: after the war, incidence of interracial violence increased precipitously. Before emancipation, interracial affairs of honor were relatively rare, largely because the South's social structure was stable enough to assure whites that they need not feel threatened by blacks and rigid enough to dissuade blacks from challenging the status of lower-class whites.[8] After the war, however, black emancipation and ongoing civil rights legislation made social and legal distinctions between blacks and whites less clear. Because the defense of honor was one of the principal ways in which individuals achieved or retained status in the nineteenth-century South, some whites became increasingly sensitive to what they perceived as personal affronts by blacks.[9] And when whites chose to assault blacks to avenge their honor, they often did so with an unusual degree of ferocity. For instance, although white men rarely attacked white women in public, white men did not always extend black women the same courtesy. John Bowles, a white laborer, engaged in a heated argument with a black female neighbor over the conduct of her child. According to Bowles, the woman became verbally abusive. In reaction, Bowles fetched his gun, filled it full of buckshot, and fired at the woman. The spray of the shot hit mother and child, killing both instantly.[10]

Contemporary observers recognized that lower-class white violence against blacks in the name of honor had become a common occurrence after the war. When federal officials learned that a local entertainment hall had invited a lecturer to speak on the virtues of dueling, they immediately closed the hall, fearing it would provoke Southern whites to further violence against both blacks and Yankees. According to a Freedmen's Bureau agent, the speaker intended to urge white men to avenge Confederate defeat through violent acts of honor and vengeance. The agent contended that most white Lynchburgers did not need the encouragement. As it was, the agent reported, many residents believed it a "private right ... to shoot, assault, and harass Yankees and blacks," insouciantly "calling it Southern chivalry." Indeed, he believed that "most of the

outrages occurring in this District have been prompted by this spirit."
According to the agent, lower-class whites were the worst offenders.
While the most "respectable portion of the people" usually minded their
own business, poorer whites made it a point to harass blacks verbally and
physically.[11]

The agent probably overstated lower-class whites' thirst for vengeance.
Although whites were often belligerent when they encountered blacks,
most did not roam the streets looking for a fight. Instead, most lower-
class whites and blacks tried their best to avoid one another—just as they
had done before the war. During the voter registration drive of 1867,
Perry complained that many lower-class whites refused to register because
they did not want to have to stand in line next to blacks. In addition,
several public places became enclaves for one or the other race. According
to newspaper accounts, whites loathed going to the train station, the
marketplace, and the streets along the river because too many blacks
congregated in those locales. Thus, when journalist Edward King stopped
in Lynchburg during his tour of the South at the end of Reconstruction,
he noted that he did not see a white person until he scaled the hill to the
streets that straddled the top of the business district. Once there, the only
blacks he saw were servants, drivers, and the like.[12]

In day-to-day leisure activities as well, lower-class whites and blacks
generally tried not to mix. Although most black and white bars and
amusement halls were in the same neighborhoods, both groups usually
sought the company of their own when they had time to socialize. Separate bars were especially important to many black laborers. To establish
some autonomy for themselves, Lynchburg blacks quickly set up their
own amusement halls and grogshops. In the days before blacks had
sufficient capital to establish more legitimate businesses, these doggeries,
saloons, and gambling halls became a center of black business activity. For
their part, whites already had their own bars and had no need to frequent
black doggeries. When an ex-Confederate soldier was arrested for gambling with eight blacks at a black bar in the Buzzard, Button made special
notice of the case only because it was so exceptional to find a white man
in a black tavern. Predictably, he condemned the ex-soldier as a disgrace
to his former regiment.[13]

Try as they might, however, lower-class blacks and whites found it
difficult to go their own way in postwar Lynchburg. Accidental encounters sometimes had fatal consequences. In one instance, Reuben Jackson,
a black day laborer, promised to meet one of his employers at a white

working-class bar. Unfortunately, he arrived before his boss. As he entered, two white artisans, Andrew Sprague and C. Castiglioni, confronted him, asking him if he thought of himself as "a damned nigger or a white man." When Jackson tried to ignore the two men, they became even more enraged. Both men began to beat Jackson, first with their fists and later with a whip. Finally, the bar owner intervened, momentarily freeing Jackson so that he could make his escape. But, as Jackson stumbled toward the door, Castiglioni stabbed him in the back, fatally wounding him.[14]

Most typical were the many street-corner confrontations, so numerous that both newspaper editors and federal officials mentioned them only in passing. Along the small, cramped streets of Lynchburg, laboring whites and blacks often passed one another. When they did, violence often erupted, no matter how circumspectly some blacks tried to behave. Spotswood Ryder, an unskilled white laborer, was especially sensitive to perceived affronts by blacks. On a winter's day in 1870, Ryder walked past a black man who remarked to a friend, "Here comes that d——d white rascal." This was hardly the first time "Spot" had been insulted. With a long history of criminal behavior, including drunkenness, petty thievery, and assault, Spot had acquired a reputation as the white community's most infamous ne'er-do-well. Thus, he endured constant ridicule from the public press—but never from the mouth of a black man. Believing that abuse from an inferior was intolerable, Spot, in the words of Perry, "practiced his mauling science" on the man, leaving him sprawled on the sidewalk. Later that day, the man made complaint to the mayor. Reluctantly, the mayor arrested Spot. When Spot came before the court, the mayor gave him a stern lecture but refused to send him on for further trial.[15] Perry, for one, believed Spot's behavior was necessary and desirable. Perry often encouraged lower-class whites to be assertive when they confronted black "loafers" who obstructed the city's sidewalks. "The 'white trash' have submitted to being forced into the gutters about as often as they intend to be," Perry warned; "unless the police abate the nuisance those who are thus outraged by it will take the matter in their own hands."[16]

Blacks and whites also began to clash on the shop floor. Before emancipation, white workers had little reason to feel threatened by black workers because most were slaves and thus their obvious inferiors. Moreover, the designation of some labor as "nigger work" helped separate whites from blacks. After the war, however, as blacks and whites began to compete for the same jobs and perform similar tasks, the artificial barriers of segregation broke down. Although the foundries and most of the tobacco factories tried to separate black and white workers, other businesses, including the railroads and the building trades, did not.[17] In these places, workplace violence seems to have increased after the war. Because most confrontation occurred away from the public eye, however, newspapers generally reported only the most sensational cases. Yet even these intermittent reports give some indication of the animosities that existed between white and black workers. From 1866 to 1872, newspapers reported four incidents of fatal or near-fatal racial violence in the town's iron factories alone. In each case, a white supervisor, usually a master craftsman, claimed that he had been provoked by the black worker's "impudence," an explanation that suggested that the black worker had challenged the status of the white boss by defying his order.[18]

As in street fights, white laborers on the job often counted on powerful and influential whites—in this case, the shop proprietors—to support their actions. In most instances, employers complied. S. B. Ferguson, the owner of a tobacco factory, personally arrested one of his black workers after the worker engaged in a fight with a white employee. Although Ferguson did not know who had started the fight, he determined that it was better to protect the white laborer than to protect the black. Only in rare instances did employers break the color line. In 1870, W. H. Ward, a supervisor at the ironworks, fired Pleasant Hubbard, a black worker, for impudence. When Hubbard appealed to Colonel Heath, one of the owners of the mill, Heath immediately reinstated Hubbard. Apparently, Ward resented Heath's interference and determined to even the score by abusing Hubbard. Eventually, Ward's taunts got the best of Hubbard. After a particularly nasty exchange, Hubbard retaliated by knocking Ward to the ground. A fellow white worker named Mayo rushed to Ward's aid by grabbing and pinning Hubbard. As he did, Ward drew his pistol and shot Hubbard in the abdomen, fatally wounding him. The incident did not end there, however. Colonel Heath personally saw to it that the police arrested Ward and Mayo. Ward, viewing Heath's prosecution as a breach of racial solidarity and a violation of his right to defend himself, sued Heath for malicious prosecution, claiming damages of five thousand dollars. Although this case was probably exceptional, the Hubbard-Ward affair suggests that business leaders sometimes allowed class considerations to override racial solidarity. When they did so, laboring whites often found themselves in an extremely precarious position.[19]

No doubt, the very precariousness of their status helps to explain why some lower-class whites retaliated against blacks with such ferocity. Although excessive brutality might lay them open to arrest and criminal prosecution, most believed they had no choice but to act, given the dictates of the code of honor. Because they believed blacks were their inferiors, lower-class whites could not risk defeat. Small wonder that whites often resorted to firearms and bowie knives to gain the final victory. Rather than assail a black man in a bare-knuckles brawl, many whites elected to end the dispute with a bullet or a knife, so that they would not have to face the dishonor of being punched and beaten by a social inferior. In this regard, one of the more tragic developments of the postwar South was that laboring whites' deepest anxieties about status coincided with the introduction of the handgun as an affordable item for many working men. White Southerners may not have been well armed for the Civil War, but they certainly were for the postwar battle for control.[20]

For their part, blacks did not always offer whites an easy out from violent confrontations. Despite the risks of white retribution, many freedmen refused to tolerate the daily insults and threats that they once had to endure. Blacks were especially determined to defend their honor against the abuses of lower-class whites. Although blacks sometimes engaged wealthier whites in violent confrontations, such incidents occurred less and less frequently—in large part because freedmen eventually realized that the "new" dependency of freedom was much like the "old" dependency of slavery. As a result, most became more circumspect when challenging a civic or business leader.[21] Conversely, blacks felt fewer constraints in their behavior toward laboring whites, whose economic wealth and political power was closer to their own. Thus if laboring whites were sensitive about their status, in part it was because many blacks forced them to be by challenging their honor.

Whatever the cause, many freedmen took the offensive against abusive laboring whites. As the many street-corner fights suggest, blacks were now just as apt to trade insults with white belligerents as they were to step out of their way. Yet, given white racial attitudes, this meant that even the smallest incident could escalate into a violent brawl—often with tragic results. In one such case, Robert Waddell, a white man, insulted his black neighbor, Henry Clay. That night, Clay vowed to his family that he would get revenge. The next day, Clay found Waddell digging in his potato patch. Evidently, Clay began to ridicule Waddell, just as Waddell had done to him the day before. Unwilling to tolerate such behavior from a black man, Waddell brandished a pocketknife. When this threat failed to silence Clay, Waddell determined that he had run out of options, save one: Waddell stabbed Clay twice in the breast, killing him instantly. Waddell immediately surrendered to the authorities. At his trial, he claimed that Clay had provoked him to violence. The jury believed him and ruled the act justifiable homicide.[22]

Personal honor was not the only source of interracial violence in postwar Lynchburg. Because of the weaknesses of the state, white Southerners also continued a long tradition of vigilante justice, especially against blacks.[23] The establishment of a modern police force—at least, in its early years—did not impede Southern vigilance, nor did civic leaders intend it to do so. In 1867, Button encouraged suburban residents to form a citizens' patrol, to protect themselves against thieves. In the city, too, civic leaders encouraged citizens to learn to protect their property. When thieves attempted to break into Patrick McDivitt's house on Fifth Street late one evening, Perry used the incident to lecture his readers on the necessity of personal vigilance. Although Mrs. McDivitt had been spared by the timely return of her husband, Perry noted that she might have been killed, because she had no means to protect herself. Rather than being defenseless, Perry advised, "housekeepers" should "be on the alert, and . . . at all times keep loaded firearms convenient," without "hesitating a moment to use them."[24] Perry meant what he said. When James Chenault, a white man, shot Fendall Patterson, a black man, in the legs for stealing wood, Perry's only regret was that Chenault "should have aimed a little higher, and thus have caused more fatal results than are likely to ensue."[25]

In most instances, the courts supported individual acts of white vigilantism. After repeated raids of his potato patch, James McKinney hired C. H. Turner, the son of a laborer, to stand guard at night. At about two o'clock one morning, Turner spied a black man raiding McKinney's garden. As the man ran to make his escape, Turner fired his rifle, hitting the man in the side. The black man died the next day, from what the coroner's inquest quizzically described as "nervous shock caused by a gunshot wound." A jury composed of twelve white men ruled the shooting justifiable homicide.[26]

Usually, white vigilantes and the civil authorities who endorsed their methods simply relied on the dictum that since all blacks were, by nature, petty thieves, the only way to stop them was to shoot them. Thus, blacks rarely gained the sympathy of the court, no matter how badly they had been wounded or how circumstantial the evidence. Early one morning, an unidentified black man appeared in the mayor's court to make complaint against a white assailant for an unprovoked assault the night before. According to the black man, the incident had occurred as he was walking home late at night, after traveling several miles in the country to search for work. As he passed through town, he inadvertently trespassed through someone's yard. The owner of the property noticed him and without warning, sprayed him with buckshot, inflicting serious wounds on his legs, back, and arms. Unmoved by the man's story and his condition, Mayor Branch refused to take action. According to Button, the mayor believed "the more probable story" that the black man was "interfering with some one's chicken roost or pig pen."[27]

It is difficult to determine how often white property owners took the law into their own hands to punish black thieves. Usually, authorities found out about such an occurrence only when the sentry either killed or maimed the thief. Otherwise, neither the thief nor the vigilant property owner was likely to report the incident. Even when wounded, black victims were hesitant to talk. Early one morning, Claiborne Calloway was found on the street with a severe bullet wound in his leg and several "ugly and possibly dangerous wounds" on his head. The night before, a night watchman at a woodyard on Jefferson Street had assaulted a would-be thief. Perry of the *News* believed Claiborne was probably the thief, but Claiborne "obstinately refused to give any information," for fear he would be arrested for the crime.[28]

It is also difficult to determine if laboring whites were more apt than upper-class whites to use force against black thieves, although it is tempting to draw this conclusion. Of the four cases reported in Lynchburg newspapers in which whites either maimed or murdered thieves, three of the vigilantes were skilled or unskilled white workers. Certainly, laboring whites must have felt especially victimized by black thievery—no matter how petty such occurrences were. Although white laborers did not have the ornate possessions that graced the homes of wealthier whites, black thieves stole from them just the same. According to court records, white laborers were victims in nearly 40 percent of all thefts attributed to blacks.[29]

Black thieves found white laborers attractive marks for a variety of reasons. For one, white laborers had what they wanted. Extant evidence suggests that most black thieves stole what was most useful to them, primarily food, clothing, firewood, and tools—items that most white working-class households possessed. Second, racism effectively kept blacks out of those economic circles where they might have practiced the most lucrative forms of crime, such as forgery, swindling, and grand larceny. Finally, black thieves tended to steal from those who were most accessible to them. In Lynchburg, this meant that black thieves practiced their art on two groups. Some, primarily servants, stole from their employers—usually a bit at a time, in hopes that their appropriations would not be noticed. Others stole from those in their own neighborhoods. This meant that many blacks often stole from those of their own race. But it also meant that many stole from the shops and homes of white laborers and artisans, individuals who, like most blacks, settled in the deep ravines along Diamond Hill, on the eastern side of town. Away from the center of town, these individuals were hidden from the watchful eye of the police but not from the equally observant eye of would-be perpetrators.[30]

Evidently, proximity to black thieves exasperated many laboring whites, leading some to protect their property to the point of murder. The few fragments of surviving court testimony reveal that laboring whites who violently assaulted presumed thieves justified their behavior by claiming that black recidivism and police indifference had simply worn them down, leaving them with no other option but to take matters into their own hands. In this, the case of William Walker may be typical. Walker, a white carpenter, lived on the corner of Twelfth and Polk, streets that bordered the primarily black Third Ward. After his chicken coop had been raided of fifteen chickens, Walker made complaint to both the civil and military police; each told Walker that they could not help him because he lived beyond their immediate jurisdiction, the central business district. Frustrated, Walker resolved to stop the thief himself. After lying in wait for several nights, he finally spied a suspicious black man lurking around his chicken coop. According to Walker, he warned the man, later identified as Charles Dixon, to stop; when he did not, Walker shot him. Dixon lingered until sunrise before dying. After the incident, Walker expressed considerable regret at his action. In a pretrial inquest, he repeated several times that he had wanted Dixon arrested, not killed. He further claimed that he had given Dixon ample warning before shooting him. Although much of Walker's testimony may be the pleas of a desperate man trying to avoid a possible murder charge, his words also reflect a man who believed that he had no recourse other than to act forcefully and decisively in the face of lawlessness.[31]

Evidently, Walker was not alone in this regard. Living on the outskirts of town, near a race of people whom they wanted to avoid, poorer whites learned and practiced an assertiveness and truculence that often ended in violence. Although historians sometimes argue that the proximity of black and white lower classes created real bonds of interracial intimacy and fleeting moments of interracial class unity, more often the opposite was true. Lynchburg's close quarters exacerbated racial animosities.[32]

After the war, blacks successfully established control over many public places, including the Old Lynchburg Market, once a hub of the town's economic life. (Edward King, *The Great South: A Record of Journeys in Louisiana, Texas, the Indian Territory, Missouri, Arkansas, Mississippi, Alabama, Georgia, Florida, South Carolina, North Carolina, Kentucky, Tennessee, Virginia, West Virginia, and Maryland* [Hartford, Conn.: American Publishing Company, 1875])

If much of white violence against blacks was intended to complement or maintain existing laws and social relations through individual and collective acts of vigilance, much of black violence against whites was meant to challenge these laws and social relations through extralegal methods of their own. In Lynchburg, it did not take blacks long to realize that the town's postwar system for law and order rarely dispensed justice fairly across the color line. At nearly every turn, blacks believed, the law worked against their interests. In 1869, John Averitt, a black Republican leader, told the congressional House Select Committee on Reconstruction that any black man who "gets arrested . . . don't stand much chance of being cleared." In a letter to the same committee, Gaston Curtis, a white resident, argued that blacks were "practically denied the protection of the laws." According to Curtis, they were regularly "tried for small offenses, and sentenced to the Penitentiary for long terms, and in many instances, upon slight testimony." "No wonder," Curtis remarked, "they long for the advent of the good time coming when they shall be honestly dealt with." In contrast, whites often acted with impunity. John Boisseau, a white tobacconist and chairman of city council during congressional Reconstruction, reported that he did not "know of an instance, where the . . . colored man has been shot down or murdered, that these [ex-Rebels] have shown any disposition to bring the offending party to justice, but in every instance that I know of the offending party has escaped justice.[33]

These Republicans exaggerated the situation only slightly, if at all. As before the war, Lynchburg's municipal and state courts continued to be inefficient, allowing many suspected thieves and rowdies—both white and black—to escape punishment. Even so, the town's criminal justice system, including the police, local magistrates, and the state court, generally treated black suspects more harshly than whites.

For every type of crime, more blacks were arrested than whites. In all, blacks accounted for 87 percent of all arrests for property crimes and 76 percent of all arrests of violent crimes. Although these percentages may indicate that most criminals were black, they also suggest that the police judged blacks more harshly than whites and that they may have provided whites alternatives to the harsh formality of the judicial system. Only in the area of nuisance crimes were whites arrested in anything close to equal numbers as blacks. As civic leaders began to embrace the new ethic of self-control, they became less tolerant of certain aspects of lower-class white leisure behavior. After the war, nearly 40 percent of all arrests for drunkenness, disorderly behavior, vagrancy, and gambling were white.[34]

Blacks' criticisms of Lynchburg's legal system began with the behavior of the police themselves. As in other Southern cities, Lynchburg's police force was composed primarily of white, working-class men.[35] Although civic leaders portrayed the police as impartial emissaries of the law, professional in training and demeanor, blacks believed otherwise. By their view, the police retained the prejudices of their class and of their society. In their petitions to the Freedmen's Bureau, the lone agency in Lynchburg that heard their complaints, blacks claimed that the police commonly used undue force when making arrests, maliciously beat male and female black suspects for no cause, and failed to take blacks' testimony if they could find white witnesses.[36] In one instance, a white man named Williams accosted Lewis Saunders, a black man, in a Buzzard alley and attempted to club him with a stone. When Saunders fought back, Williams took out his gun. In response, Saunders drew his pistol. Finally, the police intervened and arrested Saunders. To make their case, police took the word of a white prostitute, ignoring several black witnesses.[37]

In addition, blacks accused the police of harassing them without cause. According to blacks, the police regularly ransacked their persons and their homes in search of stolen items; prohibited them from carrying weapons, such as guns and knives; and abused them when they were walking the streets at night.[38] Moreover, blacks claimed that the Lynchburg police rarely acted as peacekeepers. At political rallies and on the streets, the police occasionally joined other whites in insulting blacks. When white rowdies drove black speakers from the podium at a Republican political rally at the Campbell County Court House, one of the instigators was George Bruce, Jr., a Lynchburg constable.[39]

Throughout the period, members of the black community implored Republican members of city council to reform the police system. Unfortunately, council often proved less than sympathetic. Even during federal occupation, city council refused to hire blacks as policemen, fearful that such an act would only increase racial animosities and decrease the Republican Party's appeal among native white voters. In addition, most Republican council members shared Conservatives' belief that government had to take a hard line against recalcitrant blacks so that they would learn the rules of free society.[40]

If blacks could not rely on city council to act on their concerns, neither could they hope for much support from the federal government. Although freedmen originally took many of their complaints about the police and the courts to federal officials, these officials became increasingly reluctant to defend individual blacks. Freedmen's Bureau agents and military personnel stopped the worst and most flagrant abuses of justice, but after a time, they determined that they could not create wholesale reform without the cooperation of the town's civic leaders. A few days after police arrested Saunders for beating Williams, members of the black community complained to the Freedmen's Bureau that the police had ignored black witnesses and that the two white prostitutes had lied. Bureau agents looked into the matter, determined that Saunders's complaint had merit, and asked a local judge and the mayor to review the case. They refused. The Freedmen's Bureau then asked Williams to appear before the Bureau court. Williams ignored the summons, and Saunders remained in jail for disorderly conduct. Although the commanding officer of the Military Subdistrict of Lynchburg, Colonel F. M. Cooley, could have ordered Williams's arrest and Saunders's release, he decided not to do so.[41]

The tenure of John McClain as chief of police provides an even more poignant example of council's and federal agents' reluctance to intervene on behalf of the black community. Cooley nominated McClain as chief of police in June 1868. Although Cooley had known McClain only a few months, he selected him because local white Republicans assured Cooley that McClain was a loyal "Union man" who opposed the restoration of Conservative rule. Within a year, however, blacks discovered that McClain's anti-Conservative sentiments did not make him any less racist than most ex-rebels. In February 1869, black leaders within the Republican Party petitioned Cooley to remove McClain from office. In their complaint, they claimed that McClain failed to discipline abusive officers, encouraged white residents to taunt blacks and federal soldiers, and generally allowed "his prejudices to . . . oppress the colored people unnecessarily."[42] In response, the Republican council suspended McClain. But when Conservatives, once McClain's ardent enemies, raised a spirited defense on his behalf, several Republicans wavered. According to Button of the *Virginian*, several "prominent citizens" told council that wholesale change might damage the town's quest for law and order. "Despite the carpings of niggers and scalawags," Conservatives claimed, McClain had proven himself to be an efficient and effective officer. Eventually, they convinced city council. After debating the issue for a month, council decided to set aside blacks' complaints and voted to retain McClain.[43]

Because of incidents like this, Bureau agents concluded that if they wanted to accomplish anything, it was more expedient to work with Lynchburg's civic leaders than to investigate every charge of mistreatment. At base, many federal agents suspected that because blacks lacked a strong moral sense, they were to blame for most of their problems with civic authorities. By the agents' view, it was simply imprudent to impede the restoration of civil government for the sake of those blacks who habitually disobeyed the law.[44] After 1867, federal officials referred all cases of theft and assault to the mayor's court. If blacks did not like the mayor's brand of justice, they could appeal to the Bureau, but it was unlikely that they would get a much more sympathetic hearing there. The previous year, the Bureau had reviewed only seven of the mayor's judgments and overturned only one of his decisions.[45]

Once arrested, Lynchburg blacks and whites continued to have very different experiences with the legal system. By blacks' view, the courts suffered from many of the same problems as did the police. Most lawyers, judges, and jurors were Southern whites; indeed, no blacks were selected to the grand jury until 1871.[46] The results were predictable. For crimes of property, blacks were more likely than whites to be sent on to the state courts for trial, and far more likely to be found guilty by the state court. For crimes of violence, whites were more likely than blacks to be released without punishment, while blacks were far more likely than whites to receive a fine or prison term as summary judgment by the mayor's court. Only in the area of nuisance crimes were blacks and whites treated the same by the mayor. About 90 percent of all blacks and whites who came before the mayor for public drunkenness, prostitution, vagrancy, or gambling received a summary punishment.[47]

When sent on for trial to the state courts, blacks were again more likely than whites to be found guilty. In all, state courts convicted less than one-third of whites arrested for either violent or property crimes. In contrast, state tribunals convicted over two-thirds of blacks arrested for these crimes. This discrepancy suggests not only that many whites profited from better legal representation but that judge and jury were more likely to view white suspects sympathetically than they would black suspects.[48]

The range of punishments handed down by the courts also varied by race. Although the penal code made no formal racial distinctions, in practice, blacks tended to feel the full weight of the law more often than did whites. Punishments for crimes in which blacks were almost exclusively convicted tended to be extremely harsh. Immediately after the war, Conservative-controlled courts routinely sentenced blacks to public whippings and forced labor, in a conscious effort to retain some of the vestiges of slavery. Republican-led penal reform at the state level and the

Freedmen's Bureau review of local court decisions ended the worst of the abuses, but only for a short time and not uniformly. Freedmen's Bureau agents could be just as insensitive and cruel as local courts in determining punishments for black offenders. In September 1867, local agents endorsed city council's proposal to place black prisoners in chain gangs to clean the streets. In another instance, the Freedmen's Bureau court accepted the decision of the civil court to whip a black man thirty lashes for stealing a sheep.[49]

As Conservatives regained power in the late 1860s and early 1870s, they overturned whatever slight advances blacks had made during federal occupation. As before congressional Reconstruction, Southern whites increased punishments for crimes associated with blacks. The deterioration of blacks' status before the courts is most visible in sentencing for petty thievery. During the sample years of 1866 and 1868, 80 percent of blacks convicted of petit larceny in the state courts received prison sentences of three months or less; in the sample years of 1870 and 1872, only half received sentences of three months or less, while nearly one-third received prison terms of one year or more. Meanwhile, at the local level, virtually all blacks convicted of a municipal infraction at the mayor's court served their sentences on the newly created chain gang, where armed guards manacled them to iron balls, ranging in weight from ten to thirty pounds. In 1871, an all-white grand jury made an even more obvious attempt to turn back the clock when it recommended that the judge of the corporation court employ the whip for cases of black petit larceny.[50]

The courts were far more lenient in their response to white lawbreakers. Although civic leaders' effort to impose a new moral order on Lynchburg translated into slightly higher arrest rates for whites, juries were often reluctant to convict white suspects, especially when the victim was black. When Sprague and Castiglioni were tried for stabbing Reuben Jackson, they defended themselves by claiming that they were drunk and thus unaccountable for their actions. Much to the horror of the black community, the strategy worked. Although both admitted guilt, each was fined only fifty dollars and sentenced to two months in jail. Some whites did not receive even that much. As long as a white person could reasonably claim that he had been provoked to violence, he could hope to gain the court's and the community's sympathy. Shortly after the war, Gilbert Haythe, a planter who lived just outside Lynchburg, was convicted by a Union military commission for killing one of his former slaves. The commission sentenced Haythe to eighteen years in jail. Prominent citizens, including several magistrates, took up Haythe's cause and petitioned President Andrew Johnson for a full pardon. Johnson complied. After serving three months in the city jail, Haythe was released.[51] In June 1868, Robert Waddell, described by Button as "a worthy and estimable gentleman," shot Henry Clay, a black agricultural laborer, during an altercation. Waddell claimed he had acted in self-defense. Judge and jury agreed, so Waddell walked.[52]

For less serious crimes, local magistrates sometimes refused to make an arrest. In December 1866, a black man asked the mayor to arrest a "white gentleman" for beating him. According to the complainant, the beating occurred after he accused the "gentleman" of stealing a small sum of money from him. The mayor ignored the complaint. Perry, for one, was glad of it. In yet another effort to encourage whites to greater vigilance of the racial code, he suggested that the white gentleman be granted the right to hit the black man again, for insulting his character.[53]

This is not to say that whites always escaped punishment. In July 1871, James Daugherty, a white man, shot Waddy Buckner, a black man, during a drinking spree. Although Daugherty employed a similar defense to Castiglioni and Sprague's, the all-white jury didn't buy it this time. They convicted Daugherty of second-degree murder and sentenced him to five years in jail. Button praised the verdict, claiming that the trial provided "striking proof of the even-handed justice with which the courts of Virginia administer the laws without reference to class or color." It was not that simple. The trial was delayed several days because the judge could not find jurors who would even consider convicting a white man for killing a black man—even though Daugherty admitted his guilt. At one point, the judge became so frustrated with the mood of the town that he asked Button to stop reporting on the case, because he feared that Button's sympathetic portrayal of Daugherty had prejudiced the community. Meanwhile, the black community thronged the Court House during the trial, to pressure the legal community to avenge Buckner's death. In truth, the trial proved not that blacks could find justice in Lynchburg but that whatever justice blacks secured was incomplete, hard-won, and came largely by their own vigilance. Sadly, the Daugherty trial provided one of the few times that Button had occasion to claim that justice was color-blind.[54]

Unable to win redress through legal means, many blacks opted for extra-legal methods to protect themselves. Most common, black suspects simply resisted arrest. After Sullivan Schoolfield "kicked up a row" on Fifth Street, police attempted to arrest him, but—according to newspaper reports—Schoolfield swore he would "not be taken by no d——d white man." When police grabbed Sullivan, he jerked away and ran for his life. After a short chase, police captured him a second time and carried him off to the jail. Police had an even harder time subduing Lee Brown. Brown's employer called the police after Brown assaulted him. When three policemen attempted to arrest Brown, he declared he would not go peacefully and attempted to brandish a small weapon concealed in his clothing. In reaction, the police proceeded to bludgeon him with a dirk cane and then manacled him. Beaten, but not bowed, Brown continued to fight with his captors until they made it to the jail.[55]

Some blacks used other means besides force of arms to demonstrate their contempt of Lynchburg justice. After being sentenced to the state penitentiary for one year for petit larceny, Aron Wills lashed out at the court in an impassioned speech, calling the all-white jury and the presiding judge "scoundrels" for imposing such a harsh punishment. Kendall Banks tried a different tack to demonstrate his contempt for Lynchburg law. Perry recorded that while Banks was serving on the chain gang for larceny, he refused to cooperate with the prison guards. Instead, he "evinced a mutinous disposition and positively refused to work" for several days. Even after guards attempted to break him by ladening him down with "balls and chains as a punishment," Banks remained, in Perry's words, "obstinate as a mule," standing in the "broiling sun the whole day without ever showing the least sign of submission."[56]

Of course, blacks were not alone in opposing the police and the courts. Many whites also criticized the town's new peacekeeping efforts. Lower-class whites, in particular, viewed the police as an attempt by civic leaders to impose middle-class standards of public behavior in their neighborhoods. After a drunken brawl, Benjamin Reynolds attempted to evade police. When an officer finally caught up with him, Reynolds attacked him. After a long struggle, the police finally dragged Reynolds to jail. When Perry reported the incident in his newspaper, he remarked that resisting arrest was "becoming altogether too common here." In reaction, he encouraged the mayor and the grand jury to make an example of Reynolds. Unless such "rowdies and roughs" were punished severely, Perry observed, the force might "as well be disbanded at once, and the city given over to the tender mercies of the violators of the law."[57]

Yet if both lower-class whites and blacks opposed the imposition of the police, blacks' efforts to resist arrest eclipsed whites' efforts in several respects. When whites resisted, they usually acted alone and rarely carried their protest beyond the moment of the actual arrest. Few whites, if any, dared to challenge the legitimacy of the police per se. After all, white lawbreakers could rarely hope to garner much community support in their efforts to flout the law. Virtually all property holders, no matter how meager their estates, welcomed the police's efforts to stop the town's postwar crime wave. Then, too, Lynchburg's police usually came from the same economic class, neighborhoods, and even families as most white lawbreakers. In contrast, most members of the black community seemed willing to thwart the efforts of the police. Perhaps because they were more often singled out for abuse, blacks often displayed a collective opposition to any police activity they deemed inappropriate.

These incidents did not always end in violence. In March 1866, police attempted to search the home of Solomon Field, a popular Buzzard bar owner, to find a side of stolen bacon. When Field refused to let them in because they had no cause, the officers forced their way in. Although outnumbered, Field continued to resist. Eventually, the police subdued Field, but only after the altercation had attracted many of his black neighbors. Angry that the police would harass one of their community's most popular figures, the crowd—"numbering at least one hundred and . . . muttering curses loud and deep," according to Perry—followed Field to the cage, staying until Field won his release later that day. Not to be outdone, the police returned the next day—this time with federal soldiers, who arrested Field for resisting arrest the previous day. Again, Field's neighbors gathered in support and followed Field to prison. This time, however, Field did not get off so easy and was fined for his conduct.[58]

Occasionally, blacks used mass action to free one of their own after an arrest. In April 1868, blacks from the surrounding countryside entered the city for a political rally. As they often did when attending such events, some gathered in military formation, as a way of protecting themselves from threatening whites. R. Rudd, a policeman, stopped one of these groups, demanding all who owned weapons to turn them over to him. In response, one unidentified black man stepped forward, stating that although he owned a musket, he would not relinquish it. Rudd told the man that he would have to arrest him. According to black and white witnesses, the man agreed to go peacefully, but only on the assurance that Rudd would not take his gun. As the two walked toward the jail, the man's friends followed them. As they continued down the street, more irate blacks joined the group. Fearful of the growing crowd behind him, Rudd grabbed his prisoner's weapon. This only enraged the crowd. They encircled Rudd and demanded that he release his prisoner. At this point, testimonies conflict. According to Rudd, several blacks lowered their guns to the ready position. Black witnesses—including two of the town's most prominent Republican leaders—denied this, stating that no one pointed a gun at Rudd. Regardless, Rudd panicked, inadvertently releasing the prisoner as he blew his whistle for help. The mob, including the arrested gun owner, ran away. Evidently, they had obtained their objective: as he ran off, the arrested man assured Squire Taliaferro, one of the organizers of the rally, "It's all right. I have got my gun and I am agoing home."[59]

Black vigilantes sometimes acted with less restraint when accosted by the police. In one such instance, two constables arrested John Jeffries on suspicion of stealing a gun from John Pick's store. As they walked to town, they passed some of Jeffries's friends. Evidently, Jeffries signaled his friends to follow him. When they reached a deserted area on the outskirts of town, the black gang attacked the policemen, severely beating one of the two, and freed the prisoner. In another instance, Bannister Spruell, a black man and former Union soldier, happened upon Police-Master Diuguid chastising an unidentified black man. Spruell entered the dispute, instructing the man not to "mind what the d——d white man said," and "commenced swearing at an outrageous rate." Diuguid then arrested Spruell and started to take him to jail. On their way to the cage, a third black man, Thomas Orris, also a former federal soldier and a friend of Spruell's, attempted a rescue. Spruell and Orris struggled with Diuguid, until Diuguid shot Spruell in the leg. Other policemen then helped Diuguid take the two to the cage.[60]

Blacks also worked on the other side of the law, to harass or persecute white wrongdoers whom the police and courts refused to punish. After a drunken Christmas celebration, L. F. and F. G. Swatz beat up a black man, William Brookins, at the railroad depot. A black mob found the two men at the depot and proceeded to encircle them. Whatever the mob's intent, it was interrupted by the police who, under the pretense of arresting the Swatz brothers, allowed the two men to escape. Incensed, the black mob ran the brothers down, returned them to the police, and demanded that the police arrest them. To make sure that the police carried out their duty, they followed the two men to jail with, as Button described it, "a threatening attitude." Yet once the two men were caged, the crowd dispersed in an orderly fashion.[61]

A few months later, the depot was the scene for another incident of black vigilance. While escorting passengers to the train, two policemen ordered Wyatt Padgett, a black man, to get out of their way. When Padgett refused, the police attempted to arrest him. Padgett resisted, prompting a young white man named Wright to come to the policemen's aid. According to black witnesses, Wright punched and kicked Padgett until police came to march Padgett to jail. In reaction, blacks formed two groups—one to march to the jail to demand Padgett's release, the other to find Wright, to retaliate for his unwarranted treatment of Padgett. Luckily for Wright, the police found him first and escorted him back to the jail, to protect him from his pursuers.[62]

When the police and the courts did not act to the black community's satisfaction, blacks sometimes took matters into their own hands. In July 1866, two white men, James and Jerry Moore, attacked a black man named John Green. Green tried to fight back but was restrained by federal soldiers, who promptly marched the Moore brothers to jail to be charged. The mayor, however, refused to cooperate with the federal authorities; instead, he released the Moore brothers without so much as a hearing. Frustrated, members of the black community decided to take matters into their own hands. A "crowd of fourteen or fifteen" blacks followed the Moores to their home, verbally abusing them as they walked. They stopped only after federal troops ordered them to leave.[63]

Although these incidents suggest a wide range of black vigilance activity, they are linked by a few common patterns. First, and most obvious, mobs played a central role in black vigilance. While blacks often had to be servile when they stood alone against the police and vigilant whites, they could be far more assertive when they acted in concert. Second, few of these mob actions were random attacks on the police. In virtually every case, blacks attempted to correct or draw attention to a perceived injustice—the persecution of a favorite bar owner, police misconduct, unwarranted abuse by citizens or the police, and harassment for using public places. Finally, despite whites' accusations to the contrary, the mobs were generally composed in their behavior. In most cases, they acted with specific objectives and disbanded when these objectives were realized. Indeed, black vigilantes often seemed more intent on monitoring the judicial system than on taking justice into their own hands. In some instances, the mob's primary function was not to free an incarcerated black by force of arms but to protect him from abuse, by making sure that neither the police nor the jailer assaulted him.

When necessary, Lynchburg's black mobs could be extremely aggressive, using force and the threat of force to chasten their white adversaries. During federal occupation, blacks periodically demonstrated their martial resolve by marching in military formation with their old units or the local chapter of the Union League. According to newspaper accounts and testimonies of federal officials, blacks did their best to remain well armed after the war. During the early months of radical Reconstruction, Perry claimed that one of the first things rural blacks did when they removed to the city was to buy a gun. Although the guns were often cheaply made and thus unsafe, Perry observed that blacks took great pride in their ability to wield firearms nonetheless. According to Perry, many blacks displayed their weaponry conspicuously across their chests, as though they were still soldiers. During the October 1867 political campaign, the first election in which blacks had the right to vote, members of the Lynchburg Union League made a number of public appearances in military garb, to display both their collective might and their determination to vote. That year, a local Freedmen's Bureau agent reported that a black Republican club across the river in Amherst County acted as a quasi-military organization, complete with mandatory drills. In Lynchburg, blacks' interest in military organization continued for some time after this first election. In June 1869, Button reported that he now had it "upon good authority" that several local blacks had organized "a military organization" that met regularly for drills.[64]

By such acts as these, Lynchburg's black community may have anticipated a change of behavior that would affect much of American black society in the ensuing years of the late nineteenth century. Where slaves had once used disguise and deception to survive within an oppressive system, postwar urban blacks adopted a new collective persona of aggression and intimidation.[65] Although civic leaders may have exaggerated the extent of blacks' belligerence to the law, the panicked behavior of the town's police suggests that many whites were indeed terrified by blacks' more assertive tactics. After nearly every incident of perceived black aggression, Lynchburg's newspaper editors warned their readers to arm themselves, fearing that the town was on the verge of race war. Even federal agents were concerned. In August 1867, a local federal official complained that Lynchburg blacks made the racial climate worse because they were "clannish" and hostile to virtually all whites.[66]

Whites' fears of collective black violence were furthered by conflicts and turmoil within their own community. White civic leaders not only feared the behavior of blacks but were also anxious about their own race's lack of coordinated resolve in stopping such incidents. Whites could not help but notice how their efforts at racial vigilance differed from the efforts of the black community: while white vigilance against blacks was usually carried out by individuals, black vigilance against whites was often performed by mobs, sometimes as large as a hundred or more. No matter that whites had the law, most of the firearms, and virtually all the political and economic resources on their side; blacks had a collective will. And in a town that was nearly 45 percent black, with new migrants arriving seemingly every day, this was indeed a frightening phenomenon.

Of course, it had not always been this way. Before the war, white mob violence had played a crucial role in policing the often jagged lines of race relations in Lynchburg. Through militias and more spontaneous vigilante groups, whites of all classes not only disciplined defiant slaves and free blacks but demonstrated their own allegiance to the slave regime. After the war, whites attempted to use their tradition of collective vigilance to intimidate blacks once again. According to Bureau agents, gangs of whites regularly attended Republican rallies to hoot and jeer at the speakers. Some of these rallies became riotous affairs. At a Republican gathering at nearby Campbell County Court House in 1868, for example, a small group of drunken whites—including at least one Lynchburg artisan and a city constable—mounted the speaker's podium, ordered a black orator to sit down at the point of a gun, and ripped up the Union flag. According to Sam Kelso and John Averitt, two county magistrates refused to take action as they watched the incident from the crowd. Election days could be equally volatile. On several occasions, whites threatened to roam the streets, ready to do violence to any black man who dared to vote. Undeterred, many blacks simply armed themselves with bowie knives, pistols, and shotguns and walked to polling places in groups.[67]

Only on rare occasions, however, did whites make good on their threats of mass vigilance. For a brief period during the height of congressional Reconstruction, the Ku Klux Klan (KKK) organized in Lynchburg. In early 1868, advertisements with mysterious messages—complete with allusions to "signal fires," "Clansmen," "the White Palace," and the "Shrouded Night"—began to appear in the local Conservative papers. A few weeks later, Button reported that the Klan had organized in Lynchburg and was meeting on the edge of town at—ironically enough—the abandoned Quaker Meeting House. According to Button, the Klan made occasional midnight rides through town, looking for vagrant blacks to abuse. In one instance, they attempted to catch a black hotel waiter on his way home from work but failed when the waiter ducked back into the hotel. Button made the most of the incident, suggesting that "the narrow escape of this negro should be a warning to others . . . run no unnecessary risks." On the same night, posters appeared throughout the town bearing the message "K.K.K. GATHER AT MIDNIGHT IN SILENCE."[68]

Despite these activities, mob violence was never as pronounced in postwar Lynchburg as it had been in the prewar period. When blacks complained to Congress and the Freedmen's Bureau about the town's racial climate, they usually described individual acts of aggression relating to the brutal treatment accorded petty thieves or assertive blacks. Klan and other vigilante efforts were apparently too weak and ineffectual to be of much concern to Lynchburg blacks. Black leaders never made formal complaint against the KKK or any other vigilante organization, even though federal officials in Washington occasionally invited them to do so.

Similarly, Freedmen's Bureau agents and military officials recorded few incidents of white mob activity in their monthly reports to their supervisors. Indeed, they sometimes concluded that the lack of mob violence in Lynchburg indicated racial harmony. During a political campaign in the summer of 1867, Louis Stevenson, an officer for the Freedmen's Bureau, asserted that "the feelings between the races is good . . . proven by the number of political meetings which are being held, where the greatest latitude has been allowed in regard to the expression of sentiment," without "difficulty of any kind."[69] Stevenson probably overstated the case. The lack of mob violence did not mean that Lynchburg was a congenial place for blacks to live. Constant threats and the many acts of aggression suggest that Lynchburg whites were not only antagonistic to blacks but often violently so. For this reason, blacks regularly pleaded with federal government officials to declare martial law to protect them. By their view, Lynchburg was a grievously dangerous place to live. John Averitt cogently summarized blacks' situation by telling a congressional committee that blacks faced daily "outrages . . . from very slight cause or no cause at all."[70]

Yet if the lack of mob violence did not reflect interracial harmony, it did indicate the lack of racial and political solidarity within the white community. Throughout the period, nagging conflicts divided Lynchburg's lower classes, making them a difficult group to mobilize. As church membership patterns, crime patterns, and reactions to the police suggest, white laborers were hardly of one mind when it came to matters of public behavior. Perhaps the one thing that they could agree on was their opposition to black equality. Yet this was not enough to make lower-class whites sympathetic to civic leaders' political ambitions. Evidently, most lower-class whites neglected to vote out of indifference or as a silent protest against elite rule. Their apathy—and sometimes antipathy—to the so-called White Man's Party undoubtedly figured into the relative weakness of white mass extralegal tactics in Lynchburg. Before the war, laboring whites had played a crucial role in ritualistic mob actions, but after the war, no longer. Estranged from elites, Lynchburg's laboring whites proved reluctant to participate in activities that might further elites' political plans. Instead, they expressed their racial antipathies in matters that were of the most immediate concern to themselves—the retention of segregated bars and other leisure establishments, the defense of personal honor, and the protection of property.

White civic leaders had good reason to view these developments with some foreboding. By their view, laboring whites' political and social independence were grim reminders that the leaders had yet to resolve the social fragmentation and conflict that had scarred their community in the last years of the war. If this was not enough, civic leaders also had to contend with an army of occupation and a burgeoning black community that consistently demonstrated an enviable collective will. Even as the federal government retreated from Reconstruction, Lynchburg's white civic leaders could not confidently assume that they would again be masters of their community.

Lynchburg's Centennial and Beyond

From October 12 through October 15, 1886, present and former Lynchburg residents gathered at the Fair Grounds to celebrate the town's Centennial. According to one chronicler of the event, the occasion "proved a grand success." From fifty thousand to seventy-five thousand people gathered to hear speeches, observe dramatic presentations and tableaux, and visit the many exhibits that showed off the talents of Lynchburg housewives, artisans, entrepreneurs, and manufacturers. Opulent decorations transformed Lynchburg from an aging factory town to a miracle of colors and lights. "From one end [of town] to the other," the writer observed, "street vistas were worthy of the grandest of gala days." Organizers hoped the event would serve three purposes: commemorate the past, celebrate the present, and anticipate the future. To most, the three were inextricably entwined. Orator after orator came to virtually the same conclusions: Lynchburg's present was the fulfillment of its noble past and a guarantee of a bright and prosperous future.[1]

Lost in the celebration, however, was any sort of reckoning with the previous twenty years of the town's history. When John Warwick Daniel, the town's eminent statesman and public orator, surveyed the history of the town in his keynote address, he conveniently neglected to mention Confederate defeat, black emancipation, and political Reconstruction.[2] Perhaps these events were still too painful for Daniel, a disabled war veteran, to discuss. Perhaps he did not want to broach such dark subjects in a speech meant to glorify and celebrate. Just as likely, however, Daniel believed that the era did not deserve much consideration. By 1886, most white Southerners had persuaded themselves that defeat and federal occupation had been transitory setbacks for Southern civilization. Now that the ordeal had ended, they resolutely tried to re-create the tranquillity, harmony, and prosperity that they believed characterized the Old South. In their most optimistic moments—as during Lynchburg's Centennial celebration, for example—white Southerners could almost believe they had achieved their goal.[3]

In reality, the past could not be so easily denied. True, the town's economic fortunes brightened during the decade after Reconstruction. In the early 1870s, boosters feared that the town would no longer be able to count on the tobacco trade to give the town fame and prosperity. During the late 1870s, however, the trade revived and, as it did, Lynchburg's prospects brightened. By 1883, thirty factories manufactured over six million pounds of the weed for chewing and smoking. By 1886, celebrants at the Centennial claimed that their town again deserved the title "Tobacco City."[4]

Unfortunately for Lynchburg's citizens of property and standing, flush times in the tobacco trade no longer spelled peace and prosperity for the entire town. Instead, war, emancipation, and the turmoil of Reconstruction made race and class conflict unremitting attributes of town life. Thus, Lynchburg society was every bit as disunited in the 1880s as it had been in the previous two decades.

For their part, blacks continued to seek greater autonomy by developing distinctive social and economic institutions to serve their needs. By 1880, the town's black community supported 66 black-owned businesses, including ten groceries, two liveries, thirteen produce stalls at the city market, three saloons, two bathhouses, and a variety of small artisan shops. In addition, myriad professionals, including physicians, lawyers, and an undertaker, served the needs of the town's growing black population. Five years later, there were 101 black-operated business establishments, including twenty-eight grocers, three builders, six saloons, four blacksmith shops, two undertaking establishments, and three confectionery stores.[5]

More ominous than blacks' business successes, however, were the activities of the town's black tobacco factory workers, who remained contentious of white authority. In 1883, the all-black Lynchburg Labouring

Association organized a strike against the factories for higher wages. Some thirteen hundred black factory laborers participated, effectively shutting down the tobacco industry for several weeks. In 1886, black factory laborers, in a quest for greater power, joined in a rare coalition with whites to form the Knights of Labor.[6]

Occasionally, white laborers joined black laborers in a mutual fight for autonomy and equality. In these brief instances, laboring whites and blacks once again terrified civic leaders with the specter of a biracial working-class coalition. The first such movement occurred early in the decade. In 1881, hundreds of laboring whites bolted the local Democratic Party, complaining that conservatives within the party had assumed near dictatorial control of the city government. Almost immediately, they allied with Lynchburg's blacks—a group that shared lower-class whites' sense of alienation. Together, the two groups organized a new political party. Calling themselves the Regulators, blacks and whites sought to return civic government to a lost age of mutualism and democracy. During the campaign, party leaders vowed to improve public education and to end political favoritism, so that the "privileges of the city" would be "judiciously divided" for the "general benefit and not used for the support of a favored few." Although Democratic race-baiting destroyed the coalition within a few years, in 1881, the party of laboring whites and blacks was strong enough to elect six of the town's fifteen councilmen, including five in the mostly black Third Ward.[7]

Conservatives' hold on lower-class whites after the dissolution of the Regulators was short-lived. In 1886, lower-class whites bolted the Democratic Party again, to re-form the biracial coalition—this time under the banner of the Knights of Labor. Through the Knights, black and white laborers created what one local historian has described as "a powerful and highly democratic organization." During the 1887 municipal election campaign, the party went beyond the Regulators' demands to espouse a truly biracial message. The party demanded that the "patronage of the city" be "divided between white and colored men." Apparently, the demand was not just rhetorical. Black and white party members lived up to their commitment by nominating and voting for a biracial slate of candidates. Seven of the fifteen Knights candidates for city council were black. Four of the seven Knights candidates elected to council were black. This marked only the second time since 1867 that blacks were elected to city council.[8]

The immediate causes of the class conflicts of the 1880s are beyond the scope of this study, but the long-term causes take us back to the era of military defeat and Reconstruction. After the war, Lynchburg's gentlemen of property and standing slowly broke from prewar traditions of personalism, paternalism, and tolerance. As they tried to reestablish their fortunes and their mastery over the community, they became more interested in imposing order and seeking private gain than in looking out for the public good. Although the transformation was incomplete by the close of Reconstruction, it began in earnest in the years immediately after the war. Civic and business leaders might not have been ready to articulate a theory of community that allowed for the individual's right to seek personal success and independence, but their behavior suggests that they were moving in that direction.[9]

This transformation compounded lower-class whites' problems. As the postwar economic slump and black emancipation undermined their economic well-being and their social status, lower-class whites turned to the town's traditional leaders for assistance—just as they had always done in times of crisis. This time, however, elites rebuffed them. Instead of patronage, charity, and protection, wealthy residents offered moralisms and institutionalized benevolence but otherwise left laborers to their own devices. Only at election time did civic leaders seem to have much use for less-wealthy white people, whose deference they then needed. In flush times, laboring whites might have welcomed the opportunity for greater independence from elite control; but these were not flush times. Frustrated, lower-class whites remained devoted to an older ethic of community, one that emphasized mutual support and communal responsibility. They demonstrated their loyalty to this ethic mostly clearly in their religious practices, their allegiance to the twin ethics of honor and vigilance, and—for a brief period in the 1880s—their political behavior.

In this new environment, Lynchburg blacks had it at once easier and harder than lower-class whites: easier, in that they expected and wanted less from the town's civic leaders, so that elites' snubs did not wound them as deeply; harder, in that their social, political, and economic status was even more precarious than that of laboring whites. Amid their suffering, they retained a collective resolve that was the envy of the white community. Although the power of blacks' collectivism was circumscribed by their limited political and economic resources, whites were truly fearful of its existence; and none more so than laboring whites, who viewed themselves as alone and vulnerable near the bottom of Lynchburg's social hierarchy. These fears help explain why laboring whites made few sustained efforts to create a political coalition with their black counterparts. At base, they believed blacks were not simply a threat to their status but competition for their jobs, their homes, and their place in Lynchburg society.

Blacks were equally reluctant to forge alliances with laboring whites. At base, they wanted to experience freedom for themselves and to forge autonomous social, economic, and political institutions. Then, too, blacks had good reason to fear laboring whites. By their view, most laboring whites were a violent and malicious people, who seemed to resent blacks' every effort to survive in Lynchburg's hostile environment. Over time, Lynchburg's blacks learned that they could not even trust those whites who helped fill the ranks of the Republican Party. Most whites simply could not divorce themselves from their ancient prejudices and were thus reluctant to share power with blacks. Moreover, bitter experience taught blacks that many laboring whites preferred to ally themselves with white elites and would not be fully committed to a biracial working-class coalition. Thus, blacks often had to go beyond politics to preserve and extend their liberty. Through collective vigilance, and by establishing their own institutions, Lynchburg's black community found some semblance of security, autonomy, and freedom. Tragically, these tactics only furthered laboring whites' anxieties.

Whether Lynchburg elites recognized the fragility of the town's biracial coalition is not known. What probably concerned them as much as anything was not so much that laboring whites and blacks occasionally found common cause but that both groups—often acting independent of each other—consistently behaved in ways that undermined elite authority. In doing so, they created an unstable political environment. Race-baiting might have brought lower-class whites to heel for a time, but it did not make them any less resentful of elite control.

Perhaps this helps explain why many civic leaders eventually embraced disfranchisement of both blacks and lower-class whites as a solution to their problems. When Virginia revised its constitution in 1902, the chief architect of the state's disfranchisement clause was Carter Glass, former editor of the *Lynchburg News* and son of Robert Glass, the former editor of the *Lynchburg Republican*. The disfranchisement clause Glass created was among the harshest devised by the Southern states. In writing it, Glass contrived a plan by which all the disfranchising devices then used by Southern states, including the poll tax, the grandfather clause, the literacy test, and the understanding clause, would be employed against both blacks and poor whites. When asked if his plan was discriminatory, Glass explained that "discrimination is . . . precisely what we propose; that, exactly, is what this convention was elected for." Glass hoped that his constitutional revision would roll back the deleterious effects of Reconstruction, making it possible for the supporters of tradition and the old order to rule unchallenged again.[10]

Ironically, the creation of the new constitution was an indication of both elites' power and their weakness. On the one hand, they reestablished control and destroyed the opposition in doing so. On the other hand, they had to resort to political fiat, rather than popular support, to do it. This might have been good enough for Carter Glass's generation, but it is doubtful whether it would have been good enough for Robert Glass's.

Appendixes

Occupation Categories for Analysis of the 1860 and 1870 Manuscript Censuses

Assigning occupational categories is an arbitrary and often tortuous task. In this study, I have relied on Stephen Ash's categorization of occupations, making only minor changes to fit Lynchburg's urban setting.

Professional or proprietor: apothecary, banker, broker, clergyman, coal dealer, dentist, engineer, hotelkeeper, insurance agent, lawyer, manufacturer, merchant, newspaper editor, physician, professor, storekeeper, tobacco inspector.

Minor professional: baggage master, bank clerk, barkeep, boardinghouse keeper, bookkeeper, city employee, clerk, express agent, huckster, mail agent, peddler, policeman, railroad agent, salesman, schoolteacher.

Skilled: baker, barber, blacksmith, bookbinder, butcher, cigarmaker, confectioner, cooper, engineer on railroad, foreman, gunsmith, harnessmaker, leather finisher, machinist, marble cutter, mechanic, miller, molder, photographer, plumber, printer, saddler, shoemaker, silversmith, tailor, tanner, telegraph operator, tinner, wagonmaker.

Skilled building trades: bricklayer, cabinetmaker, carpenter, mason, painter, plasterer, stonecutter.

Unskilled: boatman, cook, factory laborer, foundry worker, gardener, hack driver, messenger, porter, sexton, wagon driver, waiter, whitewasher.

Unskilled clothing trades: mantuamaker, milliner, seamstress.

Unskilled day laborer: day laborer, laborer.

Unskilled tobacco factory worker: tobacco factory laborer.

Tables

TABLE I:I
Lynchburg by Race, Gender, and Status, 1860

Race	Male	Female	T
White	1,970	1,832	3,802
Free Black	154	203	357
Slave	1,524	1,170	2,694
TOTAL	3,648	3,205	6,853

SOURCE: Data from the U.S. Bureau of the Census, *Population of the United States in 1860* (Washington, D.C.: Government Printing Office, 1864).

NOTE: Published reports in 1860 census did not include either place of birth or ethnicity as variables for Lynchburg. For Campbell County, of which Lynchburg was then a part, the foreign population was 416 males and 241 females. Probably most of these lived in or near Lynchburg.

TABLE I:2
Occupation Groups by Race, 1860

Occupation Group	White	Black
Tobacconist	67	0
Professional or Proprietor	216	0
Minor Professional	263	1
Grocer	62	1
Proprietor, skilled	31	4
Proprietor, skilled—building trades	9	0
Proprietor, seamstress	6	0
Skilled	230	17
Skilled, building trades	139	8
Unskilled, clothing	155	7
Unskilled, tobacco factory	45	73
Unskilled, labor	100	27
Other Unskilled	71	51
Unclassified	47	16
Unknown	24	0
Other	36	2
TOTAL	1,501	207

SOURCE: Data from Manuscript of Population Schedule microfilm, Lynchburg, Virginia, 1860.

TABLE 1:3
Occupation Groups by Place of Birth

Occupation Group	Virginia	Other South	North	Ireland	Germany	Other Europe
Tobacconist	66	1	0	0	0	0
Professional or proprietor	167	8	18	7	13	3
Minor Professional	232	6	7	7	8	2
Grocer	34	2	0	2	32	2
Proprietor, skilled	23	2	1	1	2	5
Proprietor, skilled—building trades	9	0	0	0	0	0
Proprietor, seamstress	4	0	1	0	1	0
Skilled	159	10	25	18	14	10
Skilled, building trades	125	5	7	5	3	2
Unskilled, clothing	145	4	6	5	1	0
Unskilled, tobacco factory	117	1	0	0	0	0
Unskilled, labor	76	0	4	45	2	0
Other Unskilled	103	2	3	11	0	1
Unclassified	58	1	0	1	1	1
Unknown	19	0	0	2	1	0
Other	37	0	1	0	0	0
TOTAL	1,374	42	73	125	48	26

SOURCE: Data from Manuscript of Population Schedule microfilm, Lynchburg, Virginia, 1860.

TABLE 1:4
Slave Artisans, 1860

Occupation of owner	N
baker	1
barber	2
blacksmith	1
cabinetmaker	4
carpenter	4
confectioner	10
jeweler	1
master builder	2
master mason	6
plasterer	3
shoemaker	3
stonecutter	1
stone mason	1
tinker	1
wheelwright	1
TOTAL	41

SOURCE: Data from Manuscript of Population Schedule microfilm, Lynchburg, Virginia, 1860; Manuscript of Slave Schedule microfilm, Lynchburg, Virginia, 1860.

TABLE 1:5

Unskilled Laborers by Race, Place of Birth, and Gender, 1860

Place of birth	Clothing		Tobacco		Day Labor		Other	
	M	F	M	F	M	F	M	F
Ireland	1	4	0	0	44	1	6	5
Other Europe	0	1	0	0	2	0	0	1
Northern U.S.	0	7	0	0	4	0	1	2
South U.S. White	1	160	34	11	45	4	15	20
South U.S. Black	1	6	20	53	23	4	14	37
TOTAL	3	178	54	64	118	9	36	65

SOURCE: Data from Manuscript of Population Schedule microfilm, Lynchburg, Virginia, 1860.

TABLE 2:1
Church Membership, 1860 by Occupation of Head of Household

Church	Professional or proprietor	Minor professional	Proprietor, skilled	Skilled	Unskilled	Other
First Presbyterian	32	15	1	16	4	17
Second Presbyterian	35	3	1	7	1	4
Court Street Methodist	56	23	0	17	9	18
Centenary Methodist	33	16	8	47	28	19
First Baptist	34	12	3	23	20	16
St. Paul's Episcopal	77	18	6	16	2	10
TOTAL	267	87	19	126	64	84

Church Membership by Occupation of Head of Household
(in percentages)

Church	Professional or proprietor	Minor professional	Proprietor, skilled	Skilled	Unskilled	Other
First Presbyterian	38	18	1	19	5	20
Second Presbyterian	69	6	2	14	2	8
Court Street Methodist	46	19	0	14	7	15
Centenary Methodist	22	11	5	31	19	12
First Baptist	31	11	3	21	19	15
St. Paul's Episcopal	60	14	5	12	2	8

SOURCE: Compiled from the membership rolls of First Presbyterian Church, Second Presbyterian Church, Court Street Methodist Church, Centenary Methodist Church, First Baptist Church, St. Paul's Episcopal Church.

NOTE: Protestant Methodist Church membership rolls were not available. Category "other" includes the following manuscript census designations: farmer, gentleman, no occupation, and overseer.

TABLE 2:2
Church Membership by Gender, 1860

Church	Male	Female
First Presbyterian	55	106
Second Presbyterian	34	78
Centenary Methodist	74	204
Court Street Methodist	70	127
First Baptist	77	204
St Paul's Episcopal	59	192
TOTAL	369	911

SOURCE: Compiled from the membership rolls of First Presbyterian Church, Second Presbyterian Church, Centenary Methodist Church, Court Street Methodist Church, First Baptist Church, St. Paul's Episcopal Church.

TABLE 2:3
Late Antebellum Church Leaders by Occupation Group

Church	Year	Title	N	Professional or proprietor	Minor professional	Skilled laborer	Unskilled laborer
St. Paul's Episcopal	1860	vestry	12	12			
Court Street Methodist	1860	steward	4	4			
		trustee	4	4			
		class leader	3	3			
Centenary Methodist	1859	steward	7	6		1	
		trustee	8	8			
		lay preacher	2			2	
First Presbyterian*	1860	elder	5	4			
Second Presbyterian	1860	elder	6	5		1	

*The occupation of one elder from First Presbyterian could not be identified.
SOURCE: Compiled from the First Presbyterian Church Minutes, 1860, Second Presbyterian Church Minutes, 1860, Court Street Methodist Church Minutes, 1860, Centenary Methodist Church Minutes, 1859, St. Paul's Episcopal Church Minutes, 1860.
NOTE: Although the Baptist Church constitution provided for stewards and trustees, church records do not list these officers for antebellum period.

TABLE 2:4
*Mayor's Court Verdicts by Race, Status, Ethnicity, and Gender, for sample years
1858 and 1860*

Group	N	Released	Bond	Fine	Jail	Whipped	Grand Jury
ASSAULTS							
Native White Male	27	8	4	0	4	0	11
Native White Female	1	1	0	0	0	0	0
European White Male	5	2	1	0	0	0	2
Subtotal	33	11	5	0	4	0	13
Free Black Male	3	0	0	1	1	1	0
Free Black Female	1	0	0	0	0	1	0
Male Slave	11	1	0	0	7	0	3
Female Slave	0	0	0	0	0	0	0
Subtotal	15	1	0	1	8	2	3
TOTAL	48	12	5	1	12	2	16
FIGHTING							
Native White Male	6	3	2	0	1	0	0
Native White Female	1	1	0	0	0	0	0
European White Male	3	0	2	0	0	0	1
Subtotal	10	4	4	0	1	0	1
Free Black Male	4	0	0	0	0	4	0
Free Black Female	3	0	0	1	0	2	0
Male Slave	14	2	0	0	0	12	0
Female Slave	0	0	0	0	0	0	0
Subtotal	21	2	0	1	0	18	0
TOTAL	31	5	4	1	1	18	1
THEFTS							
Native White Male	5	1	0	0	1	0	3
Native White Female	0	0	0	0	0	0	0
European White Male	3	2	0	0	0	0	1
Subtotal	8	3	0	0	1	0	4
Free Black Male	2	1	0	0	0	1	0
Free Black Female	2	1	0	0	0	1	0
Male Slave	18	4	0	0	0	12	2
Female Slave	2	0	0	0	0	2	0
Subtotal	24	6	0	0	0	16	2
TOTAL	32	9	0	0	1	16	6

SOURCE: Compiled from the *Lynchburg Virginian*, September 1858 through June 1859 and January 1860 through September 1860.

TABLE 2:5

Mayor's Court Verdicts by Occupation Group

Occupation Group	N	Released	Bond	Fined	Whipped	Jail	Grand Jury
ASSAULTS							
Professional	1	0	0	0	0	0	1
Minor Professional	2	2	0	0	0	0	0
Skilled	7	3	0	0	0	1	3
Unskilled	7	1	1	0	0	0	5
TOTAL	17	6	1	0	0	1	9
FIGHTING							
Professional	0	0	0	0	0	0	0
Minor Professional	0	0	0	0	0	0	0
Skilled	2	0	2	0	0	0	0
Unskilled	4	0	2	0	2	0	0
TOTAL	6	0	4	0	2	0	0

SOURCE: Compiled from the *Lynchburg Virginian*, September 1858 through June 1859 and January 1860 through September 1860.

TABLE 2:6

Mayor's Court Verdicts for Public Drunkenness by Race, Status, Ethnicity, and Gender

Group	N	Released	"Caged"	Fined	Bond	Evicted	Whipped
Native White Male	36	7	19	2	2	6	0
Native White Female	2	2	0	0	0	0	0
Irish Male	20	4	7	3	0	6	0
Subtotal	58	13	26	5	2	12	0
Free Black Male	10	1	2	0	0	0	7
Free Black Female	11	2	2	0	0	0	7
Female Slave	2	0	0	0	0	0	2
Male Slave	15	10	0	0	0	14	0
Subtotal	38	4	4	0	0	0	30
TOTAL	96	17	30	5	2	12	30

SOURCE: Compiled from the *Lynchburg Virginian*, September 1858 through June 1859 and January 1860 through September 1860.

TABLE 2:7
Mayor's Court Verdicts for Public Drunkenness by Occupation Group

Occupation Group	N	Released	"Caged"	Fined	Bond	Evicted	Whipped
Professional or Proprietor	0	0	0	0	0	0	0
Minor Professional	0	0	0	0	0	0	0
Skilled	7	2	4	0	1	0	0
Unskilled	13	3	8	0	0	1	1
Slave	17	1	0	0	0	0	16
TOTAL	37	6	12	0	1	1	17

SOURCE: Compiled from the *Lynchburg Virginian*, September 1858 through June 1859 and January 1860 through September 1860.

TABLE 2:8
Race and Ethnicity of Assailants and Victims for Crime of Assault Brought before the Mayor's Court

Assailant	Black	Native white	Irish
		Victim	
Black	7	6	0
White	0	16	0
Irish	0	1	1

Race and Ethnicity of Assailants Brought before the Mayor's Court for Crime of Fighting

Alleged Instigator	Black	Native white	Irish
		Adversary	
Black	18	0	0
White	4	0	0
Irish	0	0	3

SOURCE: Compiled from the *Lynchburg Virginian*, September 1858 through June 1859 and January 1860 through September 1860.

TABLE 2:9
State Court Felony Trials 1858, 1860 by Gender, Race, and Ethnicity of Defendant

Group	N	Theft	Violence*	Gambling	Violation of liquor laws	Other
Native White Male	110	5	17	76	8	4
Native White Female	3	0	1	0	2	0
Irish Male	5	0	1	0	4	0
European Male	5	0	1	0	4	0
Free Black Male	2	0	1	0	0	1
Male Slave	4	0	1	0	0	3
Unknown Male	14	8	3	1	1	0
TOTAL	143	13	25	77	19	8

*Includes: assault, murder, attempted murder, rape, poisoning.
SOURCE: Compiled from the Hustings Court Minute Books, Criminal Cases, 1858, 1860; Circuit Court Minute Books, Criminal Cases, 1858, 1860. Both in Lynchburg City Clerk's Office (hereafter LCC).

TABLE 2:10
State Court Felony Trials by Occupation Group of Defendant

Group	N	Theft	Violence*	Gambling	Violation of liquor laws	Other
Professional or Proprietor	10	0	3	5	0	2
Minor Professional	3	2	0	1	0	0
Grocer	13	0	0	4	7	2
Skilled	35	1	8	21	5	0
Unskilled	11	2	5	3	1	0
Unclassified	6	0	0	4	2	0
Slave	4	0	1	0	0	3
TOTAL	82	5	17	38	15	7

* Includes: assault, murder, attempted murder, rape, poisoning.
SOURCE: Compiled from the Hustings Court Minute Books, Criminal Cases, 1858, 1860, LCC; Circuit Court Minute Books, Criminal Cases, 1858, 1860, LCC.
NOTE: Occupation was determined by cross-checking names through the 1860 manuscript census. 57% were identified through this method.

TABLE 2:11
State Court Verdicts by Race and Gender, Legal Status, and Ethnicity

Group	N	Guilty	Not guilty	Dropped	Fine	Prison	Other	Unknown
CRIMES OF THEFT								
White Male	4	1	1	2	0	1	1	0
White Female	1	0	1	0	0	0	0	0
Free Black Male	0	0	0	0	0	0	0	0
Free Black Female	0	0	0	0	0	0	0	0
Male Slave	0	0	0	0	0	0	0	0
Female Slave	0	0	0	0	0	0	0	0
Unknown Male	8	5	0	3	0	5	0	0
TOTAL	13	6	2	5	0	6	1	0
CRIMES OF VIOLENCE AGAINST PERSONS								
Native White Male	12	4	7	1	0	1	1*	0
European White Male	2	1	1	0	0	1	0	0
Black Male	2	2	0	0	0	1	2**	0
Unknown Male	3	1	2	0	1	0	0	0
TOTAL	19	8	10	1	1	3	3	0

*Hanged for murder
**Whipped
SOURCE: Compiled from the Hustings Court Minute Books, Criminal Cases, 1858, 1860, LCC; Circuit Court Minute Books, Criminal Cases, 1858, 1860, LCC.

TABLE 3:1

Year and Cause of Termination of Service for Lynchburg Soldiers Who Joined the Confederate Army in 1860
(N = 401)

Year	Unknown	Death	Illness	Wound	Transfer	Deserted	Court-martial	Hired a substitute	Detailed	Last year recorded on military rolls
1861	32	12	8	1	3	0	0	1	6	4
1862	38	28	15	11	2	3	0	7	11	16
1863	2	5	2	2	0	4	2	0	5	10
1864	4	9	2	1	0	9	0	0	3	29
1865	1	1	1	0	4	4	0	0	0	4
Date unknown	1	0	1	5	4	0	0	0	0	—
TOTAL	77	55	29	20	9	20	2	8	25	63

Assumed to have served through entire war: 93

SOURCE: Compiled from the military rosters collected by George Morris and Susan Foutz, *Lynchburg in the Civil War: The City, the People, the Battle* (Lynchburg, Va.: E. H. Howard, 1984).

TABLE 3:2
Desertions by Year for
Lynchburg Soldiers

Year	N
1861	0
1862	3
1863	4
1864	9
1865	4
TOTAL	20

SOURCE: Compiled from the military rosters collected by George Morris and Susan Foutz, *Lynchburg in the Civil War: The City, the People, the Battle* (Lynchburg, Va.: E. H. Howard, 1984).

TABLE 4:1
Occupation Groups, 1870
(by Race)

Occupation group	White N	White %	Black N	Black %	Total N
Professional	221	98	4	2	225
Minor professional	312	97	10	3	322
Grocer	84	87	13	13	97
No occupation	160	46	189	54	349
Proprietor, skilled	45	70	19	30	64
Proprietor, skilled — building trades	12	86	2	14	14
Proprietor, seamstress	1	100	0	0	1
Skilled craftsmen	105	68	49	32	154
Skilled builders	65	58	48	42	113
Unskilled, labor	79	14	497	86	576
Unskilled, clothing	28	70	12	30	40
Unskilled, railroad	18	22	65	78	83
Unskilled, servant	31	6	527	94	558
Unskilled, tobacco factory	84	17	409	83	493

SOURCE: Data from the Manuscript of Population Schedule microfilm, Lynchburg, Virginia, 1870.

TABLE 4:2
Changes in the White Workforce, 1860–1870

| | 1860 | | 1870 | | |
Occupation group	N	%	N	%	% Change
Professional	284	19	221	19	−22
Minor professional	263	18	312	26	19
Grocer	63	4	84	7	33
Proprietor, skilled	35	2	45	4	29
Proprietor, skilled—building trades	9	1	12	1	33
Skilled craftsmen	229	16	105	9	−54
Skilled builders	139	10	65	6	−53
Unskilled, labor	140	9	79	7	−44
Unskilled, servant	12	1	31	3	158
Unskilled, clothing	174	12	28	2	−84
Unskilled, tobacco factory	45	3	84	7	87
Other*	84	6	69	6	−18
TOTAL	1,477		1,135		

*Includes the following occupation groups: apprentice, farmer, overseer, and unclassified (prostitutes, gamblers).
SOURCE: Data from the Manuscript of Population Schedule microfilm, Lynchburg, Virginia, 1870.

TABLE 4:3
Mayor's Court Verdicts Thefts, Summary Judgments: 1866, 1868

| | | Verdict | | | | Summary judgment | | | |
Group	N	Not guilty	Guilty	Fine	Prison	Bond	Evicted	No punishment	Grand jury
Black (F)	20	0	20	1	1	1	0	1	16
Black (M)	41	7	34	0	3	0	1	5	25
White (F)	2	0	2	0	0	0	0	0	2
White (M)	9	0	9	1	1	1	1	0	5
TOTAL	72	7	65	2	5	2	2	6	48

SOURCE: Compiled from the *Lynchburg News*, 1866, 1868; *Lynchburg Virginian*, 1866, 1868.

TABLE 4:4
State Court Verdicts and Punishments Crimes against Property, 1866, 1868

| | | Verdict | | | Punishment | | |
Group	N	Not guilty	Guilty	Dropped	Prison	Whipped	Unknown*
White (M)	10	5	3	1	3	0	1
White (F)	1	0	0	0	0	0	1
Black (M)	48	3	37	0	37	8	11
Black (F)	12	2	7	1	7	0	0
TOTAL	71	10	47	2	47	8	13

*In most instances, the individual was probably at large.
SOURCE: Compiled from the Circuit Court Minute Books, Criminal Cases, 1866, 1868, LCC; Hustings Court Minute Books, Criminal Cases, 1866, 1868, LCC.

TABLE 5:1

Occupation and Membership of New Church Members, 1865–1871, by Occupation Group of Head of Household

Church	Proprietor or professional	Minor professional	Skilled	Unskilled	Other	Total
First Presbyterian	7	4	6	1	4	22
Second Presbyterian	8	4	0	1	1	14
Court Street Methodist	19	6	3	0	6	34
Centenary Methodist	10	10	16	10	1	47
First Baptist	11	1	8	1	2	23
St. Paul's Episcopal	7	2	0	2	0	11
TOTAL	62	27	33	15	14	151

SOURCE: Compiled from the membership roles of First Presbyterian Church, Second Presbyterian Church, Court Street Methodist Church, Centenary Methodist Church, First Baptist Church, St. Paul's Episcopal Church, all for 1865–1871.

NOTE: Protestant Methodist Church membership role was not available.

TABLE 5:2

Occupation and Membership of *1871* Revivalists *by Occupation Group of Head of Household*

Church	Proprietor or professional	Minor professional	Skilled	Unskilled	Other	Total
First Presbyterian	10	6	9	3	0	28
Second Presbyterian	4	3	1	0	3	11
Court Street Methodist	35	17	2	1	4	59
Centenary Methodist	10	10	30	12	4	66
First Baptist	14	21	34	6	13	88
TOTAL	73	57	76	22	24	252

SOURCE: Compiled from the membership rolls of First Presbyterian Church, Second Presbyterian Church, Court Street Methodist Church, Centenary Methodist Church, First Baptist Church, all for 1871.

TABLE 6:1

Mayor's Court Punishments: Crimes of Property by Race and Gender

Group	N	Fine	Prison	Postbond	Evicted	Released	Grand Jury
White (M)	14	1	3	1	1	0	8
White (F)	5	0	1	0	0	2	2
Black (M)	99	2	21	0	1	25	50
Black (F)	31	2	2	1	0	5	21
TOTAL	149	5	27	2	2	32	81

SOURCE: Compiled from the *Lynchburg News* and *Lynchburg Virginian* for 1866, 1868, 1870, 1872.

TABLE 6:2

Mayor's Court Punishments: Crimes of Violence by Race and Gender

Group	N	Fine	Prison	Postbond	Evicted	Released	Grand Jury
White (M)	52	5	3	17	0	15	15
White (F)	9	3	0	3	0	3	0
Black (M)	109	38	15	13	0	27	17
Black (F)	89	50	9	7	2	22	1
TOTAL	259	96	27	40	2	67	33

SOURCE: Compiled from the *Lynchburg News* and *Lynchburg Virginian* for 1866, 1868, 1870, 1872.

TABLE 6:3

State Court Verdicts: Violent Crimes by Race and Gender

Group	N	Guilty	Not guilty	Dropped	Unknown	Fine	Prison
White (M)	21	7	4	4	3	6	7
White (F)	2	0	1	0	1	0	0
Black (M)	9	7	1	1	0	6	3
Black (F)	3	1	1	0	1	1	1
TOTAL	35	15	7	5	5	13	11

SOURCE: Compiled from the Hustings Court Minute Books, Criminal Cases, 1866, 1868, 1870, 1872, LCC; Circuit Court Minute Books, Criminal Cases, 1866, 1868, 1870, 1872, LCC.

TABLE 6:4

State Court Verdicts: Crimes of Property by Race and Gender

Group	N	Guilty	Not guilty	Dropped	Unknown	Fine	Prison	Whipped
White (M)	13	4	6	1	2	0	4	0
White (F)	1	0	0	0	1	0	0	0
Black (M)	69	50	9	0	10	1	49	8
Black (F)	18	12	2	1	1	0	12	0
TOTAL	101	66	17	2	14	1	65	8

SOURCE: Compiled from the Hustings Court Minute Books, Criminal Cases, 1866, 1868, 1870, 1872, LCC; Circuit Court Minute Books, Criminal Cases, 1866, 1868, 1870, 1872, LCC.

TABLE 6:5
Mayor's Court Punishments: Moral Crimes by Race and Gender

Group	N	Fine	Jail	Security	Evicted	Released
White (M)	83	47	18	5	1	8
White (F)	11	8	0	0	2	1
Black (M)	70	44	13	7	3	6
Black (F)	83	52	14	3	4	10
TOTAL	247	151	45	15	10	25

SOURCE: Compiled from the *Lynchburg News* and *Lynchburg Virginian* for 1866, 1868, 1870, 1872.

Notes

1. Robert C Kenzer, *Kinship and Neighborhood in a Southern Community: Orange County, North Carolina, 1849–1881* (Knoxville: University of Tennessee Press, 1987); Paul D. Escott, *Many Excellent People: Power and Privilege in North Carolina, 1850–1900* (Chapel Hill: University of North Carolina Press, 1985); Jonathan M. Wiener, *Social Origins of the New South: Alabama, 1860–1885* (Baton Rouge: Louisiana State University Press, 1978).

2. Michael Wayne, *The Reshaping of Plantation Society: The Natchez District, 1860–1880* (Baton Rouge: Louisiana State University Press, 1983); Stephen V. Ash, *Middle Tennessee Society Transformed, 1860–1870: War and Peace in the Upper South* (Baton Rouge: Louisiana State University Press, 1988); Steven Hahn, *The Roots of Southern Populism: Yeoman Farmers and the Transformation of the Georgia Upcountry, 1850–1890* (New York: Oxford University Press, 1983); Wayne K. Durrill, *War of Another Kind: A Southern Community in the Great Rebellion* (New York: Oxford University Press, 1990); J. William Harris, *Plain Folk and Gentry in a Slave Society: White Liberty and Black Slavery in Augusta's Hinterlands* (Middletown, Conn.: Wesleyan University Press, 1985).

3. See, especially, C Vann Woodward, "*Strange Career* Critics: Long May They Persevere," *Journal of American History* 75 (1988): 864. Others that argue who race relations were largely determined by elites include Joel Williamson, *The Crucible of Race: Black-White Relations in the American South since Emancipation* (New York: Oxford University Press, 1984); J. Morgan Kousser, *The Shaping of Southern Politics: Suffrage Restriction and the Establishment of the One-Party South, 1880–1910* (New Haven, Conn.: Yale University Press, 1974); John W. Cell, *The*

Highest Stage of White Supremacy: The Origins of Segregation in South Africa and the American South (Cambridge: Cambridge University Press, 1982); Howard N. Rabinowitz, *Race Relations in the Urban South, 1865–1890* (Urbana: University of Illinois Press, 1980).

4. 1860 Census, Population Schedule manuscript microfilm, Lynchburg, Virginia. These statistical ratios are fairly similar to other cities and towns in the Upper South. See the following for demographic comparisons: Suzanne Gehring Schnittman, "Slavery in Virginia's Urban Tobacco Industry, 1840–1860" (Ph.D. diss., University of Rochester, 1986), 21–67; Richard C. Wade, *Slavery in the Cities: The South, 1820–1860* (New York: Oxford University Press, 1964), 3–27; Ira Berlin and Herbert Gutman, "Natives and Immigrants, Free Men and Slaves: Urban Workingmen in the Antebellum American South," *American Historical Review* 88 (1983): 75–1200.

5. Woodward, "*Strange Career* Critics," 857–61.

6. Wade, *Slavery in the Cities*; Claudia Dale Goldin, *Urban Slavery in the American South, 1820–1860: A Quantitative History* (Chicago: University of Chicago Press, 1976); David Goldfield, "The Urban South: A Regional Framework," *American Historical Review* 86 (1981): 1009–34.

7. Rabinowitz, *Race Relations*; Peter J. Rachleff, *Black Labor in the South: Richmond, Virginia, 1865–1890* (Philadelphia: Temple University Press, 1984); Edward L. Ayers, *Vengeance and Justice: Crime and Punishment in the Nineteenth Century American South* (New York: Oxford University Press, 1984), 76.

NOTES TO CHAPTER ONE

1. Joseph Clarke Robert, *The Tobacco Kingdom: Plantation, Market, and Factory in Virginia and North Carolina, 1800–1860* (Durham, N.C.: Duke University Press, 1938), 72–74, 80–82; Joseph Clarke Robert, *The Story of Tobacco in America* (New York: Alfred A. Knopf, 1949), 67–71, 187–88; W. Asbury Christian, *Lynchburg and Its People* (Lynchburg, Va.: J. P. Bell, 1900), 103; Anne Royall, *Mrs. Royall's Southern Tour or Second Series of the Black Book*, vol. 2 (Washington, D.C., 1839), 100; *Lynchburg Virginian*, 30 August 1858; 29 July 1865.

2. Robert, *Tobacco Kingdom*, 182; S. Allen Chambers, Jr., *Lynchburg: An Architectural History* (Charlottesville: University Press of Virginia, 1981), 30–32, 86, 87; Suzanne Gehring Schnittman, "Slavery in Virginia's Urban Tobacco Industry, 1840–1860" (Ph.D. diss., University of Rochester, 1986), 39–40.

3. Schnittman, "Slavery," 39–40; Robert, *Tobacco Kingdom*, 181–84.

4. Robert, *Tobacco Kingdom*, 164, 181–83; Schnittman, "Slavery," 39–40; 1860 Census, Manufacturing Schedule manuscript microfilm, Campbell County, Virginia; *Lynchburg Virginian*, 12 June 1856.

5. Eugene L. Schwaab, ed., *Travels in the Old South: Selected from Periodicals of the Times* (Lexington: University Press of Kentucky, 1973), 535; *Lynchburg Virginian*, 23 July 1856.

6. 1860 Census, Population Schedule manuscript microfilm, Lynchburg, Virginia; 1860 Census, Manufacturing Schedule manuscript microfilm, Campbell County, Virginia.

7. Schnittman, "Slavery," 40–41.

8. Robert, *Tobacco Kingdom*, 32–50.

9. Ibid., 222–26; David R. Goldfield, *Urban Growth in the Age of Sectionalism: Virginia, 1847–1861* (Baton Rouge: Louisiana State University Press, 1977), 5, 237–38; *Lynchburg Virginian*, January 1858.

10. *Lynchburg Virginian*, 11 January 1858; 23 July 1856; Robert, *Tobacco Kingdom*, 74; "Tobacco Trade in Virginia," *Hunt's Merchants' Magazine and Commercial Review* 40 (1859): 341–45; "Tobacco Trade in Virginia," *Hunt's Merchants' Magazine and Commercial Review* 42 (1860): 341–45.

11. Chambers, *Lynchburg*, 118, 119, 131, 148, 199, 203; George Morris and Susan Foutz, *Lynchburg in the Civil War: The City, the People, the Battle* (Lynchburg: E. H. Howard, 1984), 1; Virginia and Tennessee Railroad Company, *A Prospectus of the Virginia and Tennessee Railroad Co., concerning the sale of $1,000,000 of their bonds, under an act of the legislature of Virginia; together with the opinions of the leading journals of the country upon the means and prospects of the company* (Richmond: Dispatch Job Office, 1855).

12. *Lynchburg Virginian*, 4 March 1856; 7 March 1856; 29 July 1856; 30 March 1858; *Virginia and Tennessee Railroad Company, Prospectus*.

13. "Tobacco Trade in Virginia," *Hunt's Merchants' Magazine and Commercial Review* 40 (1860): 736–39.

14. 1860 Census, Manufacturing Schedule manuscript microfilm, Campbell County, Virginia.

15. *Lynchburg Virginian*, 28 March 1860; 2 May 1860.

16. David S. Forbes to his mother, 12 December 1859; cited in Chambers, *Lynchburg*, 197.

17. *Lynchburg Virginian*, 28 March 1860; 31 May 1858; 1860 Census, Manufacturing Schedule manuscript microfilm, Campbell County, Virginia.

18. 1860 Census, Population Schedule manuscript microfilm, Lynchburg, Virginia; 1860 Census, Slave Schedule manuscript microfilm, Lynchburg Virginia.

19. It is impossible to determine the exact number of free and slave laborers employed in the tobacco factories. The slave schedule for 1860 does not provide occupational information and the manufacturing schedule does not differentiate between slave and free laborers. As a result, rough estimates must suffice. The forty-five factories in Lynchburg owned or hired a total of 1,001 slaves—857 male and 144 female. If all of these worked in tobacco factories, and if this number accounts for all slaves who worked in Lynchburg tobacco factories, then 95 percent of all tobacco laborers in Lynchburg were slaves. However, some of the 1,001 were probably domestics or other nonfactory workers. Moreover, some probably did not work as full hands—ninety were under the age of ten. As a result, this estimate is probably high. A more conservative method to estimate the total number of slave workers in the tobacco factories is to omit all children below the age of ten and to identify three workers per firm as domestics. Using this method, the conservative estimate still suggests that 74 percent—776 workers— were slaves. See 1860 Census, Population Schedule manuscript microfilm, Lynchburg, Virginia; 1860 Census, Slave Schedule manuscript microfilm, Lynchburg, Virginia.

20. Recently, historian Barbara Fields has argued that slavery was largely antagonistic to Southern urban development. According to Fields, urban slave-holders' desire to control the person, not simply the person's labor, was "anachronistic" in a capitalistic economy. For this reason, Fields concludes, slavery retarded the growth of Southern cities and Southern economic development. The system of slavery that developed in Lynchburg's tobacco factories supports Fields's argument. See Barbara Jeanne Fields, *Slavery and Freedom on the Middle Ground: Maryland during the Nineteenth Century* (New Haven, Conn.: Yale University Press, 1985), 47–57. For general descriptions of the economics of tobacco factory labor see Richard C. Wade, *Slavery in the Cities: The South, 1820–1860* (New York: Oxford University Press, 1964), 34–35; Robert S. Starobin, *Industrial Slavery in the Old South* (New York: Oxford University Press, 1970), 135–37; Goldfield, *Urban Growth*, 138–39; Schnittman, "Slavery," 139–44.

21. Schnittman, "Slavery," 139–41.
Tobacconists in other Virginia cities were less reticent to use white labor. In 1859, *Hunt's Merchants' Magazine* reported that a few Richmond and Petersburg tobacconists set aside workrooms for young white women. The correspondent branded the experiment a success, noting that the " 'lumps' made by the skillful hands of a white girl . . . surpass in neatness and symmetry, those turned out by a negro of longer experience." Furthermore, the correspondent suggested that "consumers of 'the weed' would turn their quids with additional zest, if they were conscious of the fact that the plugs had passed through the hands of comely maidens, instead of through the paws of some 'imp of darkness.' " See "White Girls in Tobacco Factories," *Hunt's Merchants' Magazine* 40 (1859): 522–23.

22. For the influence of the South's rural culture on Southern cities, see Elizabeth Fox-Genovese, *Within the Plantation Household: Black and White Women in the Old South* (Chapel Hill: University of North Carolina Press, 1988), 70–77; David R. Goldfield, *Cotton Fields and Skyscrapers: Southern City and Region* (Baton Rouge: Louisiana State University Press, 1982), 29–79; David R. Goldfield, "Urban-Rural Relations in the Old South: The Example of Virginia," *Journal of Urban History* 2 (1976): 146–68.

23. Beginning in the 1850s, a number of inventions were introduced to replace the muscle power used to press the plug into shape. The most celebrated of these was the hydraulic press. Yet by 1860, only six factories in Lynchburg used this new machine. The rest continued to use hand-powered screws and levers. See 1860 Census, Manufacturing Schedule, manuscript microfilm, Campbell County, Virginia.

24. Frederick F. Siegel, *The Roots of Southern Distinctiveness: Tobacco and Society in Danville, Virginia, 1780–1865* (Chapel Hill: University of North Carolina Press, 1987), 132–35; Robert, *Tobacco Kingdom*, 209–18; Wade, *Slavery in the Cities*, 35; Charles Weld, *A Vacation Tour in the United States of America* (London, 1855), 313–14.

25. Philip Lightfoot Scruggs, *The History of Lynchburg, Virginia, 1786–1946* (Lynchburg, Va.: J. P. Bell, 1946), 57; Robert, *Tobacco Kingdom*, 197. Unknowing observers believed that these chants reflected the slaves' general contentment and their masters' general benevolence. See Schwaab, ed., *Travels in the Old South*, 535.

26. *Lynchburg Virginian*, 18 December 1858; Peter J. Rachleff, *Black Labor in the South: Richmond, Virginia, 1865–1890*, (Philadelphia: Temple University Press, 1984) 13–34, and John T. O'Brien, "Factory, Church, and Community: Blacks in Antebellum Richmond," *Journal of Southern History* 44 (1978): 509–36, note a similar trend among Richmond factory workers.

27. It is virtually impossible to estimate the number of house servants in Lynchburg because of the idiosyncrasies of nineteenth-century census takers. Some names listed in the slave schedules do not appear in either the 1860 census schedule or the 1859 city business directory; as a result, the masters of more than two hundred slaves could not be located. Unfortunately, this information is vital to infer the occupation of the slave. As a result, rough estimates based on the available information must suffice. To determine the number of house servants, I assumed that all slave women between the ages of fifteen and sixty were domes-tics—except those owned by the tobacconists and seamstresses. In addition, I assumed that all male slaves not held by either artisans or tobacconists were also house servants. Using this method, as many as one-third (551 women and 283 men) of Lynchburg's slaves whose masters could be identified in the census were house servants. This procedure probably overestimates the number of house servants, but it still intimates general trends. Ira Berlin and Herbert Gutman, "Natives and Immigrants, Free Men and Slaves: Urban Workingmen in the Antebellum American South," *American Historical Review* 88 (1983): 1182, employ a similar methodology to determine the number of slave artisans in the urban South.

28. Ira Berlin, *Slaves without Masters: The Free Negro in the Antebellum South* (New York: Oxford University Press, 1974), 177–81, 220–21; Wade, *Slavery in the Cities*, 23–24, 120–21; Leonard Curry, *The Free Black in Urban America, 1800–1850: The Shadow of the Dream* (Chicago: University of Chicago Press, 1981), 1–37.

29. Marcus R. Roediger, *The Wages of Whiteness: Race and the Making of the American Working Class* (New York: Verso Press, 1991), 47–50; Christine Stansell, *City of Women: Sex and Class in New York, 1789–1860* (Chicago: University of Illinois Press, 1987), 155–68; Hasia R. Diner, *Erin's Daughters in America: Irish Immigrant Women in the Nineteenth Century* (Baltimore: Johns Hopkins University Press, 1983), 70–94.

30. The best studies of household servant-master relations include: Eugene D. Genovese, *Roll, Jordan, Roll: The World the Slaves Made* (New York: Vintage Books, 1972), 70–75, 327–65; Fox-Genovese, *Within the Plantation Household*; Suzanne Lebsock, *The Free Women of Petersburg: Status and Culture in a Southern Town, 1784–1860* (New York: W. W. Norton & Co., 1985), 137–45; Jacqueline Jones, *Labor of Love, Labor of Sorrow: Black Women, Work, and the Family, from Slavery to the Present* (New York: Vintage Books, 1985), 25–29. Jacob Duche Mitchell, Diary, 28 January 1857, Lynchburg Museum System (hereafter LMS); Mrs. John Meem Payne, "A Brief Outline of My Life for the Benefit of My Children" n.d., LMS.

31. *Lynchburg Virginian*, 19 June 1860. For similar trends in other Southern cities, see Edward L. Ayers, *Vengeance and Justice: Crime and Punishment in the Nineteenth-Century American South* (New York: Oxford University Press, 1984),

101–5; Wade, *Slavery in the Cities*, 80–81, 98–102; William H. Pease and Jane H. Pease, *The Web of Progress: Private Values and Public Styles in Boston and Charleston, 1828–1843* (New York: Oxford University Press, 1985), 162–66; Fields, *Slavery and Freedom*, 52–54.

32. Anonymous, "Our Queen," n.d., LMS; R. H. Early, *Campbell Chronicles and Family Sketches Embracing the History of Campbell County, Virginia, 1782–1926* (Lynchburg, Va., J. P. Bell, 1927), 263–66.

33. Charles Blackford to Mary Blackford, 24 December 1858, Blackford Family Papers, Jones Memorial Library, Lynchburg, Virginia (hereafter JML).

34. Wade, *Slavery in the Cities*, 62–75; Starobin, *Industrial Slavery*, 57–62.

35. George Bagby, "Cornfield Peas," in *Selections from the Miscellaneous Writings of George W. Bagby* (Richmond: Whittet & Shepperson, 1884), 1:174; William W. Blackford, *War Years with Jeb Stuart* (Baton Rouge: Louisiana State University Press, 1993), 12–13.

36. "A Friend of Oral Sunday School for Africans," *Lynchburg Virginian*, 29 January 1859; *Lynchburg Virginian*, 12 February 1859.

37. Ayers, *Vengeance and Justice* 102–3; Wade, *Slavery in the Cities*, 94–97; Michael Stephen Hindus, *Prison and Plantation: Crime, Justice, and Authority in Massachusetts and South Carolina, 1767–1878* (Chapel Hill: University of North Carolina Press, 1980), 86–99, 150–61.

38. *Lynchburg Virginian*, 29 January 1858; 17 March 1858.

39. Orra Langhorne, *Southern Sketches from Virginia, 1881–1901*, ed. Charles E. Wynes (Charlottesville: University Press of Virginia, 1964), 116–18. Manumissions, though rare, continued through the war. In 1860, Anne Bryce amended her will so that her slaves would be "liberated" upon her death "and permitted to go to any free state they may choose." Will of Anne Bryce, 1860 Will Book E, 1130, Lynchburg City Clerk's Office (hereafter LCC).

40. Genovese, *Roll, Jordan, Roll*, 327–65; Fox-Genovese, *Within the Plantation Household*, 152–65, 178–86; Lebsock, *Free Women of Petersburg*, 137–45; Jones, *Labor of Love*, 25–29.

41. Letter of William Luck, 15 August 1864, Lynchburg Family Papers, Alderman Library, University of Virginia (hereafter AL). As occurred in most Southern communities, Lynchburg residents constantly circulated rumors of more sensational acts of retribution by black servants, including arson and poisoning. Only on rare occasions were the accusations substantiated, much less brought to court. See chapter 2, below.

42. Blackford seems to have recognized as much. He noted that his servants feared that without the ceremony, "they would lose all claim upon me" (Charles Blackford to Mary Blackford, 24 December 1858).

43. Wade, *Slavery in the Cities*, 34–35; *Lynchburg Virginian*, 24 March 1851; 17 June 1867; Robert, *Tobacco Kingdom*, 200–205; 1860 Census, Manufacturing Schedule manuscript microfilm, Campbell County, Virginia. Approximately 49 percent of all Lynchburg's tobacco factory slaves were hired in 1860. By all accounts, slave hiring became increasingly popular during the 1850s. According to Robert, the number of hired slaves working in Virginia factories from 1850 to 1860 increased by 164 percent, while the number of tobacconist-owned slaves

increased by only 80 percent. Small tobacconists preferred to hire slaves because it saved them the financial burden of buying slaves in order to expand; allowed them to make annual and seasonal adjustments in their workforce; and protected them from financial loss should a slave become injured or die.

44. Scruggs, *History of Lynchburg*, 57; Robert, *Tobacco Kingdom*, 205; Siegel, *Roots of Southern Distinctiveness*, 131.

45. Charles Ostrander, diary, 11 September 1864, Charles Ostrander Papers; Jacob Duche Mitchell, diary, 8 April 1860, Jacob Mitchell Papers, Perkins Library, Duke University (hereafter PL). Local whites also emphasized how exceptionally well they treated their slaves. Wyatt Hill, the son of a tobacconist, recalled that his father believed he had to treat his slaves well because it was in his economic interest to do so (interview with Wyatt Tucker Hill, Works Project Administration, Folklore Collection, Civil War Recollections, Virginia State Archives [hereafter VSA]), 13.

46. Robert, *Tobacco Kingdom*, 203.

47. *Lynchburg Virginian*, 16 November 1852.

48. Historians generally agree that the gray market was extensive. For analyses of its economic and social significance to the black community, see J. William Harris, *Plain Folk and Gentry in a Slave Society: White Liberty and Black Slavery in Augusta's Hinderlands* (Middletown, Conn.: Wesleyan University Press, 1985) 57–61; Wade, *Slavery in the Cities*, 155–56; Genovese, *Roll, Jordan, Roll*, 599–607; Ayers, *Vengeance and Justice*, 125–130.

49. Harris, *Plain Folk and Gentry*, 94–122; Stephen V. Ash, *Middle Tennessee Society Transformed 1865–1870: War and Peace in the Upper South*, (Baton Rouge: Louisiana State University Press, 1988) 44–49; Robert C. Kenzer, *Kinship and Neighborhood in a Southern Community: Orange County, North Carolina, 1849–1881* (Knoxville: University of Tennessee Press, 1987), 29–51; James Oakes, *The Ruling Race: A History of American Slaveholders* (New York: Vintage Books, 1982), 229–32.

50. Oakes, *Ruling Race*, 228–30; James Oakes, *Slavery and Freedom: An Interpretation of the Old South* (New York: Vintage Books, 1990), 80–136.

51. Barbara Bellows, *Benevolence among Slaveholders: Assisting the Poor in Charleston, 1670–1860* (Baton Rouge: Louisiana State University Press, 1993), 160–61; 183–92; Pease and Pease, *Web of Progress*, 121–23, 177–78.

52. John Meem Payne, "Recollections of Lynchburg," n.d., 5–7; JML; *Payne and Blackford's Lynchburg Business Directory* (Lynchburg, Va.: J. P. Bell, 1859); 1860 Census, Population Schedule manuscript microfilm, Lynchburg, Virginia. For descriptions of the decline of the preindustrial workshop in Northern cities, see Paul E. Johnson, *A Shopkeeper's Millennium: Society and Revivals in Rochester, New York, 1815–1837* (New York: Hill & Wang, 1978); Mary Ryan, *Cradle of the Middle Class: The Family in Oneida County, New York, 1790–1865* (New York: Cambridge University Press, 1981); Alan Dawley, *Class and Community: The Industrial Revolution in Lynn* (Cambridge, Mass.: Harvard University Press, 1976).

53. Daniel W. Crofts, *Old Southampton: Politics and Society in a Virginia County, 1834–1869* (Charlottesville: University Press of Virginia, 1992), 126–31, 155–62; Kenzer, *Kinship and Neighborhood*, 55–61; Rhys Isaac, *The Transformation of Virginia 1740–1790*, (Chapel Hill: University of North Carolina Press, 1982), 88–

114; Thomas Bender, *Community and Social Change in America* (Baltimore: Johns Hopkins University Press, 1978), 100–105.

54. *Lynchburg Virginian*, 19 September 1859. George W. Bagby also ridiculed the ignorance of the poor in his famous "Mozis Addums" stories. In these stories, a poor white named Moses Adams describes his life, revealing his ignorance and lack of civility in the process. See "Meekins's Twinses" and "Flize," in Bagby, *Miscellaneous Writings*, 273–84, 333–37.

55. Sabra Ramsey to James B. Ramsey, 2 November 1860, Ramsey Family Papers, PL; L. Minor Blackford, *Mine Eyes Have Seen the Glory: The Story of a Virginia Lady, Mary Berkeley Minor Blackford, 1802–1896, Who Taught Her Sons to Hate Slavery and to Love the Union* (Cambridge, Mass.: Harvard University Press, 1954), 80, 81, 84.

56. Harris, *Plain Folk and Gentry*, 96–100; Goldfield, *Urban Growth*, 178–79, 219–20.

57. Isaac, *Transformation of Virginia*, 29.

58. Samuel Garland, Jr., and Charles Slaughter, attorneys at law, account book, 1857–1861, Garland and Slaughter Papers, JML.

59. Samuel Garland, Jr., and Charles Slaughter, day book, 1861–1863, Garland and Slaughter Papers, JML.

60. eorge Washington Clement, account book, JML.

61. Bruce Laurie, *Artisans into Workers: Labor in Nineteenth-Century America* (New York: Noonday Press, 1989), 55–56, 108–12.

62. *Lynchburg Republican*, 18 August 1856; 9 April 1860.

63. 1860 Census, Population Schedule manuscript microfilm, Lynchburg, Virginia.

64. *Lynchburg Virginian*, 28 December 1858.

65. Ibid., 23 April 1859; 28 April 1860. Historians who have noted the personal nature of Southern urban benevolence include: Fox-Genovese, *Within the Plantation Household*, 77–83; Pease and Pease, *The Web of Progress*, 144–46; Bellows, *Benevolence among Slaveholders*; Lebsock, *Free Women of Petersburg*, 195–236.

66. Mitchell diary, 1857, 1861, 1862, LMS; Mitchell diary, 1860, PL.

67. *Lynchburg Virginian*, 15 January 1856; 21 January 1861; Lebsock, *Free Women of Petersburg*, 225–30; Bellows, *Benevolence among Slaveholders*, 166–67.

68. *Lynchburg Virginian*, 31 January 1856; 26 November 1860; 13 December 1860; 28 January 1861; "Query," *Lynchburg Virginian*, 13 January 1858; "Old Kriss," *Lynchburg Virginian*, 22 December 1860.

69. Ibid., 21 January 1861.

70. Ibid., 28 December 1858; 28 January 1861.

71. Ibid., 24 July 1851; 4 June 1859.

72. Crofts, *Old Southampton*, 139–69; Bender, *Community and Social Change*, 101–5; Harry L. Watson, *Liberty and Power: The Politics of Jacksonian America* (New York: Noonday Press, 1990), 3–15; J. Mills Thornton III, *Politics and Power in a Slave Society: Alabama, 1800–1860* (Baton Rouge: Louisiana State University Press, 1978), 3–58.

73. Letters by "Virginius," *Lynchburg Virginian*, 3 January 1861; 8 January 1861; see also *Lynchburg Virginian*, 5 September 1859; 8 November 1852.

74. *Lynchburg Virginian*, 28 December 1860.

75. For a useful summary of the political ideologies of Whigs and Democrats, see Watson, *Liberty and Power*, 237–48. Watson also concludes that the differences between Whigs and Democrats were not as distinct as historians have previously believed.

76. *Lynchburg Republican*, 23 February 1859; 21 May 1859; 19 May 1857.

77. *Lynchburg Virginian*, 1 April 1856; 3 April 1856; 6 April 1859; 4 April 1860. Crofts, *Old Southampton*, 165–68, sees a similar development in Southampton County.

78. *Lynchburg Virginian*, 18 March 1859.

79. Isaac, *Transformation of Virginia*, 111–13; Crofts, *Old Southampton*, 139–40; Charles S. Sydnor, *The Development of Southern Sectionalism, 1819–1848* (Baton Rouge: Louisiana State University Press, 1948), 288–93.

80. Elijah Fletcher to Calvin Fletcher, 28 December 1850; 30 May 1851; in Martha von Briesen, ed, *The Letters of Elijah Fletcher* (Charlottesville: University Press of Virginia, 1965), 226, 229; Blackford, *Mine Eyes Have Seen the Glory*, 114–15.

81. Johnson, *Shopkeeper's Millennium*; Ryan, *Cradle of the Middle Class*; Dawley, *Class and Community*.

82. Chambers, *Lynchburg*, 190–93.

83. *Lynchburg Virginian*, 5 February 1858; 16 March 1858.

84. Will of N Kabler, 1860 Will Book E, 137–39, LCC.

85. *Payne and Blackford's*.

86. *Lynchburg Virginian*, 24 July 1851; 28 December 1858; 2 May 1859; 4 June 1859. Although the workhouse was not built until after the war, others repeated the call for its construction. Button, for one, was an ardent supporter of the idea that the idle and intemperate poor should be forced to work. At one point, he endorsed a plan that would have the "old soakers" who crowded the jail and sidewalks fix the city streets. He believed it an offense that drunkards were regularly sent to jail with no other punishment than "to be fed, and warmed at the expense of the city." See also *Lynchburg Virginian*, 18 February 1859; 2 May 1859; 22 August 1859.

87. Anne Royall, *Mrs Royall's Southern Tour or Second Series of the Black Book* (Washington, D.C., 1830), 1: 109; Robert, *Tobacco Kingdom*, 183, 215.

88. Chambers, *Lynchburg*, 114, 200; Susan Leigh Blackford, *Letters From Lee's Army: Or Memoirs of Life in and out of the Army of Virginia during the War between the States* (New York: Charles Scribner's Sons, 1947) 2–3.

89. Douglas Summers Brown, *A History of Lynchburg's Pioneer Quakers and Their Meeting House, 1754–1936* (Lynchburg, Va.: J. P. Bell, 1936), 87–88; Crofts, *Old Southampton*, 117–19.

90. John B. Douglas, "Recollections of a Refugee," n.d., JML.

91. Berlin and Gutman, "Natives and Immigrants," 1182, use a similar methodology. See Table 1:4 in the Appendix for a list of slave artisans.

92. 1860 Census, Population Schedule manuscript microfilm, Lynchburg, Virginia.

93. 1860 Census, Population Schedule manuscript microfilm, Lynchburg, Virginia.

94. Berlin and Gutman, "Natives and Immigrants," 1175–1200. According to the Berlin-Gutman study, Northern and foreign-born immigrants comprised as much as 70 percent of the free laboring population in some Southern cities.

95. 1860 Census, Population Schedule manuscript microfilm, Lynchburg, Virginia.

96. Berlin and Gutman, "Natives and Immigrants," 1194–96; Bruce Levine, *Half Slave and Half Free: The Roots of Civil War* (New York: Hill & Wang, 1992), 43–44; Button occasionally accused the North's European immigrants of encouraging abolitionist fanaticism in the North; see *Lynchburg Virginian*, 6 October 1855.

97. Of the nine foreign and native-born shopkeepers, six held slaves; thirteen of fifty-nine (22 percent) nonproprietors held slaves.

98. Thornton, *Politics and Power*, xviii; Roediger, *Wages of Whiteness*, 59–60.

99. 1860 Census, Population Schedule manuscript microfilm, Lynchburg, Virginia.

100. *Payne and Blackford's*; Garland and Slaughter day book 1859–1864, JML.

101. *Lynchburg Virginian*, 6 April 1859.

102. Henry Didlake to William Massie, n.d., William Massie Papers, PL.

103. J. M. Cobb to William Massie, 6 February 1862, William Massie Papers, PL.

104. Blackford, *Mine Eyes Have Seen the Glory*, 114–15, 272; "Annual Report of the Lynchburg Dorcas Society," *Lynchburg Virginian*, 24 July 1851.

105. *Lynchburg Virginian*, 9 June 1859.

106. For discussions of urban police in the Old South, see Ayers, *Vengeance and Justice*, 82–30; Hindus, *Prison and Plantation*, 39–40; Pease and Pease, *Web of Progress*, 100–101; Goldfield, *Urban Growth*, 144–46. For lower-class whites' desire for autonomy, see Steven Hahn, *The Roots of Southern Populism: Yeoman Farmers and the Transformation of the Georgia Upcountry, 1850–1890* (New York: Oxford University Press, 1983), 52–77, 86–116; Kenzer, *Kinship and Neighborhood*; Paul D. Escott, *Many Excellent People: Power and Privilege in North Carolina, 1850–1900* (Chapel Hill: University of North Carolina Press, 1985), 3–31; Ash, *Middle Tennessee Society Transformed*, 44–48; Harris, *Plain Folk and Gentry*, 25–34.

107. Drew Gilpin Faust, *The Creation of Confederate Nationalism: Ideology and Identity in the Civil War South* (Baton Rouge: Louisiana State University Press, 1988), 32, 82–84; Thornton, *Politics and Power*; Crofts, *Old Southampton*, 141–69; Levine, *Half Slave and Half Free*, 135–44; Escott, *Many Excellent People*, 15–24; Wayne K. Durrill, *War of Another Kind: A Southern Community in the Great Rebellion* (New York: Oxford University Press, 1990) 11–16.

NOTES TO CHAPTER TWO

1. Jannett Cleland, diary, 6 January 1861, Jones Memorial Library, Lynchburg, Virginia (hereafter JML).

2. Ibid.

3. Session Minutes of First Presbyterian Church of Lynchburg, Virginia, 5 May 1860; 9 May 1860.

4. Cleland diary, 11 November 1864; 17 February 1864.

5. Donald G. Mathews, *Religion in the Old South* (Chicago: University of Chicago Press, 1977), xvi-xviii, 57–58. Also see Dickson D. Bruce, Jr., *And They All Sang Hallelujah: Plain-Folk Camp-Meeting Religion, 1800–1845* (Knoxville: University of Tennessee Press, 1974), 62–69; Rhys Isaac, *The Transformation of Virginia, 1740–1790* (Chapel Hill: University of North Carolina Press, 1982), 163–72; Anne C. Loveland, *Southern Evangelicals and the Social Order, 1800–1860* (Baton Rouge: Louisiana State University Press, 1980), 1–18.

6. Mathews, *Religion in the Old South*, 38. Also see Isaac, *Transformation of Virginia*, 260–65, 285–89, 314–17; Paul D. Escott, *Many Excellent People: Power and Privilege in North Carolina, 1850–1900* (Chapel Hill: University of North Carolina Press, 1985), 23–27.

7. A number of local studies have examined the makeup of the South's rural churches. Virtually without exception, these emphasize the egalitarian nature of the evangelical denominations. For examples, see J. William Harris, *Plain Folk and Gentry in a Slave Society: White Liberty and Black Slavery in Augusta's Hinterlands* (Middletown, Conn.: Wesleyan University Press, 1985), 102; Robert C. Kenzer, *Kinship and Neighborhood in a Southern Community: Orange county, North Carolina, 1849–1881* (Chapel Hill: University of North Carolina Press, 1987), 11–12; Daniel W. Crofts, *Old Southampton: Politics and Society in a Virginia County, 1834–1869* (Charlottesville: University Press of Virginia, 1992), 94–95; Stephen V. Ash, *Middle Tennessee Society Transformed, 1865–1870: War and Peace in the Upper South* (Baton Rouge: Louisiana State University Press, 1988), 32–38, 57–58; Orville Vernon Burton, *In My Father's House Are Many Mansions: Family and Community in Edgefield, South Carolina* (Chapel Hill: University of North Carolina Press, 1985), 21–28, 57–61; John B. Boles, ed., *Masters and Slaves in the House of the Lord: Race and Religion in the American South, 1740–1870* (Lexington: University Press of Kentucky, 1988).

8. John Warwick Daniel to his sister, 5 November 1861, John Warwick Daniel Papers, Alderman Library, University of Virginia (hereafter AL).

9. Jacob Duche Mitchell, diary, 18 February 1860, Perkins Library, Duke University (hereafter PL); Jacob Duche Mitchell, diary, 15 January 1861, Lynchburg Museum System (hereafter LMS).

10. Mathews, *Religion in the Old South*, 26.

11. Cleland diary, 6 January 1861; Mitchell diary, 15 January 1857, LMS.

12. According to church minutes, the number of disciplinary cases for Lynchburg's evangelical churches from January 1, 1858, to April 1, 1861, were as follows:

Church	Discipline Hearings
Centenary Methodist	0
Court Street Methodist	1
Protestant Methodist	2
First Presbyterian	2
Second Presbyterian	0
First Baptist Church	7

13. Minutes of the First Baptist Church of Lynchburg, Virginia, 10 January 1859; 14 February 1859.

14. Historians generally agree that churches exercised considerable care in their disciplinary proceedings. See Mathews, *Religion in the Old South*, 44–46; Kenzer, *Kinship and Neighborhood*, 13; Burton, *In My Father's House*, 57–58; Ash, *Middle Tennessee Society Transformed*, 37.

15. Minutes of the First Baptist Church, 3 October 1859.

16. In contrast, professionals, proprietors, and their families accounted for about 40 percent of Lynchburg's church membership. See Table 2:1 in the Appendix.

17. According to Mathews, women outnumbered men in evangelical churches by a ratio of sixty-five to thirty-five (*Religion in the Old South*, 47). In Lynchburg, the ratio was seventy-one to twenty-nine. See Table 2:2 in the Appendix. Throughout the South, women, not men, were the mainstays of evangelical churches. Lynchburg's laboring women were probably attracted to religion for many of the same reasons as most Southern women. Although churches rarely allowed women to assume leadership roles, they did offer women prestige and status in less tangible ways. By emphasizing the importance of family and family religion, evangelicals helped establish women's role as moral caretakers. And through various church activities, from religious worship to church organizations, women gained community and a larger purpose in life than the South's patriarchal order usually allowed—even though churches themselves often worked to bolster patriarchy. See Mathews, *Religion in the Old South*, 101–3; Burton, *In My Father's House*, 131–33; Suzanne Lebsock, *The Free Women of Petersburg: Status and Culture in a Southern Town, 1784–1860* (New York: W. W. Norton & Co., 1985), 215–18; Jean E. Friedman, *The Enclosed Garden: Women and Community in the Evangelical South, 1830–1900* (Chapel Hill: University of North Carolina Press, 1985), 128–30; Elizabeth Fox-Genovese, *Within the Plantation Household: Black and White Women in the Old South* (Chapel Hill: University of North Carolina Press, 1988), 43–46.

18. See Table 2:1 in the Appendix.

19. See Table 2:3 in the Appendix.

20. Mitchell diary, 18 September 1857; 18 November 1857; 3 December 1857, LMS. Little is known about Crawford. He is not listed in either the 1859 business directory or the 1860 manuscript census. Mitchell's brief entries suggest that he was a man of few financial resources.

21. Mitchell diary, 1–18 August 1857, 1–31 January 1861, PL. I do not use gender as a variable here because nineteenth-century propriety often discouraged ministers from meeting alone with their female members. For the record, Mitchell met with eleven women and sixteen men during the August 1857 period and seventeen women and twenty-seven men during the January 1861 period.

22. Loveland, *Southern Evangelicals*, 95–96; Minutes of the Church Board of Trustees, Court Street Methodist Church, Lynchburg, Virginia, 19 April 1858.

23. These included eight skilled proprietors, forty-seven skilled laborers, and twenty-eight unskilled laborers (Membership Roll of First Baptist Church of Lynchburg, Virginia, 1858–1860; Membership Roll of Centenary Methodist Church, Lynchburg, Virginia, 1858–1860).

24. Minutes of the First Baptist Church, 29 May 1859; 5 June 1859.

25. Membership Roll of Centenary Methodist Church, 1858–1860.

26. Alfred A. Kern, *Court Street Methodist Church, 1851–1951* (Richmond: Dietz Press, 1951), 7–8; 1860 Census, Population Schedule manuscript microfilm, Lynchburg, Virginia.

27. Kern, *Court Street Methodist Church*, 8. For discussions of the ethical differences between rich and poor evangelicals, see Burton, *In My Father's House*, 60; Mathews, *Religion in the Old South*, chap. 1; Isaac, *Transformation of Virginia*, 161–208.

28. Patricia C. Click, *The Spirit of the Times: Amusements in Nineteenth-Century Baltimore, Norfolk, and Richmond* (Charlottesville: University Press of Virginia, 1989), sees a similar trend in her study of nineteenth-century amusement culture.

29. A number of historians have explored workers' efforts to demonstrate respectability by joining churches and moral improvement organizations. See Bruce Laurie, *Artisans into Workers: Labor in Nineteenth-Century America* (New York: Noonday Press, 1989), 183–85; Ronald G. Walters, *American Reformers, 1815–1860* (New York: Hill & Wang, 1978), 141–42; Paul E. Johnson, *Shopkeepers' Millennium: Society and Revivals in Rochester, New York, 1815–1837* (New York: Hill & Wang, 1978), 95–115.

30. Kern, *Court Street Methodist Church*, 9–10.

31. Interview with Mrs. Mary Barbara Grant Moorman, Works Project Administration Virginia Folklore Collection, AL, 3.

32. Mathews, *Religion in the Old South*, 26–28, 41–45; Ted Ownby, *Subduing Satan: Religion, Recreation, and Manhood in the Rural South, 1865–1920* (Chapel Hill: University of North Carolina Press, 1990), 144–57; Loveland, *Southern Evangelicals*, 71–90; James B. Ramsey, *"The Elders That Rule Well": A Sermon Preached at Lexington, Virginia, April 4th, 1855, at the Opening of Lexington Presbytery* (Lexington, Va.: Smith & Fuller, 1855), 7–8; Wilbur F. Davis to "Dear Wife," 27 October 1853, Beale-Davis Family Papers, Southern Historical Collection, University of North Carolina at Chapel Hill (hereafter SHC).

33. Peter Kolchin, *American Slavery, 1619–1877* (New York: Hill & Wang, 1993), 115–7; Larry M. James, "Biracial Fellowship in Antebellum Baptist Churches," in Boles, ed., *Masters and Slaves*, 37–57.

34. Minutes of the First Baptist Church, 12 January 1852.

35. Ibid.

36. Ibid., 8 November 1852.

37. Ibid., July 1853; 15 July 1853. First Baptist Church records do not provide names or any other identifying features of the leadership of African Baptist.

38. Ibid., 8 December 1856; 7 March 1859.

39. *Lynchburg Virginian*, 27 October 1860; Minutes of the First Baptist Church, 21 December 1860.

40. *Lynchburg Virginian*, 4 June 1859; 14 January 1860; 18 December 1860.

41. At First Baptist, this practice led to some rather cumbersome name entries in the church minutes. For instance, when Charles Ryan's wife was brought before the church for repeated drunkenness, church records referred to her as Sister Charles Ryan (Minutes of the First Baptist Church, 12 March 1860).

42. "Minutes of the Dorcas Society," *Lynchburg Virginian*, 20 December 1855; 4 June 1859, 14 January 1860.

43. Fox-Genovese, *Within the Plantation Household*, 109; Bertram Wyatt-Brown, *Southern Honor: Ethics and Behavior in the Old South* (New York: Oxford University Press, 1982), 294–96; Friedman, *Enclosed Garden*.

44. Diary of an anonymous woman, 17 June 1854; 18 June 1854; 10 August 1854, David B. Harris Collection, PL.

45. *Lynchburg Virginian*, 7 December 1859.

46. Ibid., 19 January 1860; 20 September 1859; 27 April 1860.

47. Ibid., October 1859.

48. Information of this incident comes from a letter by Dacre's son John, written some forty years after the affair. John, by then clerk of session of the same church that expelled his father, asked that the letter be included in the church minutes as a way to explain his father's behavior and to defend his reputation. John Kinnier to First Presbyterian Church, 24 September 1899, First Presbyterian Church Records.

49. Edward L. Ayers, *Vengeance and Justice: Crime and Punishment in the Nineteenth-Century American South* (New York: Oxford University Press, 1984), 27–31; Dickson D. Bruce, Jr., *Violence and Culture in the Antebellum South* (Austin: University of Texas Press, 1979), 103–13; Elliott J. Gorn, " 'Gouge and Bite, Pull Hair and Scratch': The Social Significance of Fighting in the Southern Backcountry," *American Historical Review* 90 (1985): 18–43; Elliott J. Gorn, " 'Good-bye Boys, I Die a True American': Homicide, Nativism, and Working-Class Culture in Antebellum New York City," *Journal of American History* 74 (1987): 388–410.

50. The most thorough analyses of Southern honor tend to emphasize upper-class behavior and minimize the class differences in the use of honor. See Ayers, *Vengeance and Justice*, 9–33; Wyatt-Brown, *Southern Honor*, 3–61; Steven M. Stowe, *Intimacy and Power in the Old South: Ritual in the Lives of the Planters* (Baltimore: Johns Hopkins University Press, 1987), 1–24.

51. See Table 2:10 in the Appendixes.

52. *Lynchburg Virginian*, 31 December 1859; 26 January 1859; *Lynchburg Republican*, 3 September 1860. For discussions of the public nature of vengeance, see Wyatt-Brown, *Southern Honor*, 43–47. Wyatt-Brown argues that acts of vengeance and affairs of honor required a public, because Southerners believed that the opinions of others were an "inseparable part of personal identity and a gauge of self-worth."

53. *Lynchburg Virginian*, 21 April 1859; 2 September 1859; October 1859; 9 September 1859.

54. Ibid., 10 May 1859; 12 January 1859.

55. According to most interpretations of honor, Southern men expected women to be passive and fragile. Placed on a pedestal, women could serve as arbiters of honor but could not actively participate in the defense of family honor because, as Ayers argues, honor was a male, not a female, attribute. Among the lower classes, however, women may have been more openly contentious. See Wyatt-Brown, *Southern Honor*, 231–35; Ayers, *Vengeance and Justice*, 13.

56. *Lynchburg Virginian*, 16 August 1859; *Mary Snyder v. William Stone*, Ended

Law Papers for the Circuit Court of Lynchburg, Virginia, Criminal Proceedings, Virginia State Archives (hereafter VSL).

57. Darrett Rutman and Anita Rutman, in their study of colonial Middlesex County, Virginia, found that citizens often used slander suits to protect their reputations and seek revenge. See Darrett B. Rutman and Anita H. Rutman, *A Place in Time: Middlesex County, Virginia, 1650–1750* (New York: W. W. Norton & Co., 1984), 82, 111, 136.

58. *Snyder v. Stone.*

59. For discussions of the South's view of the state, see Ayers, *Vengeance and Justice*, 31–33; Michael Stephen Hindus, *Prison and Plantation: Crime, Justice, and Authority in Massachusetts and South Carolina, 1767–1878* (Chapel Hill: University of North Carolina Press, 1980), 3–25; Wyatt-Brown, *Southern Honor*, 362–65. *Lynchburg Virginian*, 10 November 1859.

60. *Lynchburg Virginian*, 3 September 1859. For the best discussion of how Southerners exploited the courts to satisfy personal grievances, see Hindus, *Prison and Plantation*, 95–98.

61. *Lynchburg Virginian*, 26 January 1859.

62. Newspaper accounts are used because the actual records for the mayor's court no longer exist. There are some problems with this approach. Button did not keep a regular journal of the mayor's court proceedings but reported only those cases that space allowed. Undoubtedly, he was selective in the process. Given his hierarchy of prejudices, he probably underreported cases involving native whites and overreported cases involving Irish and blacks. In addition, he seems to have withheld most cases in which the accused was an upper-class white. Professionals appear in only 3 of the 279 cases in which the plaintiff's occupation can be determined. Yet if mayor's court proceedings, as they appear in the newspapers, do not provide a complete picture of crime in Lynchburg, they are a helpful source in gauging how criminals—especially lower-class criminals—were treated by the town's criminal justice system.

63. *Lynchburg Virginian*, 8 November 1858. See Table 2:4 in the Appendixes.

64. Occupations for the other alleged assailants included a gentleman and a merchant.

65. Circuit Court Minute Book, 1860, Lynchburg City Clerk's Office (hereafter LCC); *Lynchburg Republican*, 3 September 1860.

66. See Table 2:7 in the Appendixes. Of the 115 cases of drunkenness reported in the *Virginian*, I could find the occupation group for only 37. Of these 7 were skilled workers, 13 were unskilled workers, and 17 were slaves. Most of the rest probably belonged to the large shifting population of laborers who came in and out of town.

67. See Table 2:6 in the Appendixes. Half of all those asked to leave town for drunkenness were Irish. Moreover, more than one-third of all Irish convicted of drunkenness (six of sixteen) were asked to leave town.

Although Button did not usually provide information on jail terms for drunks, he often inferred that the individual would be released after sobering up. Surprisingly, some laborers viewed jail as a relatively quick, though humiliating, cure for drunkenness. On a few occasions, individuals asked the jailer for lodging until they dried out. Of course, most of those arrested for drunkenness made the opposite plea—to be released from jail. On occasion, the mayor responded with humanity. In one instance, Mayor Branch released an "ancient and dilapidated" John O'Connor after O'Connor wrote Branch several notes from jail. Perhaps to rid the town of one more nuisance, Branch even paid O'Connor's railroad fare to his hometown, Richmond. See *Lynchburg Virginian*, 18 March 1859; 8 October 1859.

68. *Lynchburg Virginian*, 18 March 1858; 23 August 1859.

69. Mayor's court records for the sample years 1858 and 1860 show only two arrests of prostitutes. Both were charged with vagrancy after being arrested on a city street late at night. State courts indicted another two women for running houses of prostitution. One woman was released without trial; the other was fined twenty dollars. On the South's view of the passionate man, see Ayers, *Vengeance and Justice*, 9–25; Wyatt-Brown, *Southern Honor*, 50–55, 292–94; Hindus, *Prison and Plantation*, xxvii, 49–53; Stowe, *Intimacy and Power*, 77–78, 229–30; Bruce, *Violence and Culture*, 8–12, 39–43; Kenneth Greenberg, "The Nose, the Lie, and the Duel in the Antebellum South," *American Historical Review* 95 (1990): 57–74.

70. Savannah's ratio was about one prostitute for every thirty-nine men and Norfolk's was one to twenty-six. See Wyatt-Brown, *Southern Honor*, 293.

71. *Law Order Book of the Hustings Court of Lynchburg, Virginia*, 8 May 1860, LCC; *Law Order Book of the Circuit Court of Lynchburg, Virginia*, 6 June 1860, LCC.

72. The origin of the name Buzzard's Roost is unclear. During the 1930s, Wyatt Tucker Hill recalled that the Buzzard was simply one "long frame building." Other sources also refer to the Buzzard as a bar. Nevertheless, residents also used the appellation to describe the entire neighborhood. See the interview with Wyatt Tucker Hill, Works Project Administration Folklore Collection, Civil War Recollections, VSA, 10; John Meem Payne, "Recollections of Lynchburg," n.d., JML, 2.

73. *Lynchburg Virginian*, 18 November 1859; Hill interview, 10. This description of laboring-class leisure life is consistent with other studies of Northern and Southern nineteenth-century cities. See Ayers, *Vengeance and Justice*, 73–105; Sean Wilentz, *Chants Democratic: New York City and the Rise of the American Working Class, 1788–1850* (New York: Oxford University Press, 1984), 257–70; Click, *Spirit of the Times*, 17–19; Johnson, *Shopkeeper's Millennium*, 55–61. Also useful is Roy Rosenzweig, *Eight Hours for What We Will: Workers and Leisure in an Industrial City, 1870–1920* (New York: Cambridge University Press, 1983), 36–46.

74. Karen Halttunen, *Confidence Men and Painted Women: A Study of Middle-Class Culture in America, 1840–1870* (New Haven, Conn.: Yale University Press, 1982), 61–62; John F. Kasson, *Rudeness and Civility: Manners in Nineteenth-Century Urban America* (New York: Noonday Press, 1990), 36–44.

75. For discussions of Southern fatalism as it related to social reform movements, see Loveland, *Southern Evangelicals*, 161–171; Wyatt-Brown, *Southern Honor*, 28–29; Bruce, *And They All Sang Hallelujah*, 99–100; Ayers, *Vengeance and Justice*, 56–57; William H. Pease and Jane H. Pease, *The Web of Progress: Private Values and Public Styles in Boston and Charleston, 1828–1843* (New York: Oxford University Press, 1985), 153–70.

76. *Lynchburg Virginian,* 29 December 1858; 18 March 1859.

77. Ibid., 31 August 1859. In another instance, Button defended his lengthy description of a black domestic dispute by teasing his patrons that he knew they preferred to "read nonsense in this column rather than sense in another part of the paper. We have them in this instance as much as we think their delicate stomachs can well digest at one time" (4 November 1858).

78. Ibid., January 1859; 13 January 1859; 5 April 1859.

79. Alexander Patten, cited in Eugene L. Schwaab, ed., *Travels in the Old South: Selected from Periodicals of the Times* (Lexington: University Press of Kentucky, 1973), 535–42; Roger Lane, *Roots of Violence in Black Philadelphia, 1860–1900* (Cambridge, Mass.: Harvard University Press, 1986), 146–47. See also James Borchert, *Alley Life in Washington: Family, Community, Religion, and Folklife in the City, 1850–1970* (Urbana: University of Illinois Press, 1980); Lawrence W. Levine, *Black Culture and Black Consciousness: Afro-American Folk Thought from Slavery to Freedom* (New York: Oxford University Press, 1977); Ayers, *Vengeance and Justice,* 234–36.

80. See Table 2:6 in the Appendixes.

81. *Lynchburg Virginian,* 19 October 1858; 26 January 1860.

82. Wyatt-Brown, *Southern Honor,* 46.

83. *Lynchburg Virginian,* 12 November 1859; 30 November 1859; 16 December 1859; 16 December 1859; 17 December 1859; 24 December 1859.

84. Ibid., 27 January 1860.

85. Wyatt-Brown, *Southern Honor,* 402–34. See also Steven A. Channing, *Crisis of Fear: Secession in South Carolina* (New York: W. W. Norton & Co., 1970); Dan T. Carter, "The Anatomy of Fear: The Christmas Day Insurrection Scare of 1865," *Journal of Southern History* 42 (1976): 345–64; Charles B. Dew, "Black Ironworkers and the Slave Insurrection Panic of 1856," *Journal of Southern History* 41 (1975): 321–38.

86. John Rawlings to Alexander Brown, 12 November 1860, Alexander Brown Papers, PL; Sabra Ramsey to James B. Ramsey, November 1860, Ramsey Family Papers, PL; Robert Dudley to "Dearest Sister," 5 November 1859, John Dudley Papers, PL; John B. Douglas, "Recollections of a Refugee," n.d., JML, 3.

87. John Rawlings to Alexander Brown, 12 November 1860.

88. Sabra Ramsey to James B. Ramsey, November 1860. Some were more sanguine about such incidents of hysteria. From Cincinnati in 1859, Robert Dudley heard the rumors of insurrection in Lynchburg and teased his sister, then a resident of the town, that he "hoped niggers and insurrectionists have not taken over the Old Burgh" (Robert Dudley to "Dearest Sister," 5 November 1859).

89. Douglas, "Recollections," 3.

90. Ibid.

91. Escott, *Many Excellent People,* 57–60; Harris, *Plain Folk and Gentry,* 144–56; Wayne K. Durrill, *War of Another Kind: A Southern Community in the Great Rebellion* (New York: Oxford University Press, 1990), 11–18, 30–37.

Lynchburg Goes to War

1. Steven A. Channing, *Crisis of Fear: Secession in South Carolina* (New York: W. W. Norton & Co., 1970), 145–47; Paul D. Escott, *Many Excellent People: Power and Privilege in North Carolina, 1850–1900* (Chapel Hill: University of North Carolina Press, 1985), 29–31; J. William Harris, *Plain Folk and Gentry in a Slave Society: White Liberty and Black Slavery in Augusta's Hinterlands* (Middletown, Conn.: Wesleyan University Press, 1985), 135–38.

2. *Lynchburg Virginian*, 6 November 1860; 16 January 1861; 25 January 1861; 2 February 1861; 9 April 1861.

3. Ibid., 15 January 1861; 16 January 1861; 3 April 1861; L. Minor Blackford, *Mine Eyes Have Seen the Glory: The Story of a Virginia Lady, Mary Berkeley Minor Blackford, 1802–1896, Who Taught Her Sons to Hate Slavery and to Love the Union* (Cambridge, Mass.: Harvard University Press, 1954), 128, 131, 137; Susan Leigh Blackford, ed., *Letters From Lee's Army: Or the Memoirs of Life in and out of the Army of Virginia during the War between the States* (1894; reprint, New York: Charles Scribner's Sons, 1947), 1–3; W. H. Morgan, *Personal Reminiscences of the War of 1861–5* (Lynchburg, Va.: J. P. Bell, 1911), 17–24; Robert T. Bell, *The Eleventh Virginia Infantry* (Lynchburg, Va.: H. E. Howard, 1985), 2–4.

4. Daniel W. Crofts, *Reluctant Confederates: Upper South Unionists in the Secession Crisis* (Chapel Hill: University of North Carolina Press, 1989), ably chronicles the growing disunity among Unionists. See George Reese, ed., *Proceedings of the Virginia State Convention of 1861* (Richmond: Virginia State Library, 1965), 3:377–81; Blackford, *Mine Eyes Have Seen the Glory*, 149–57; *Lynchburg Virginian*, 9 April 1861.

5. *Lynchburg Virginian*, 9 April 1861

6. Morgan, *Personal Reminiscences*, 28; Robert Enoch Withers, *Autobiography of an Octogenarian* (Roanoke, Va., Stone Printing, 1907), 155; Peter Houck, *A Prototype of a Confederate Hospital Center in Lynchburg, Virginia* (Lynchburg, Va.: Warwick House, 1986), 52–58; John J. Terrell, "Reminiscences of Dr. John J. Terrell," n.d., John J. Terrell Papers, Lynchburg Museum System (hereafter LMS), 1.

7. Blackford, *Mine Eyes Have Seen the Glory*, 187.

8. *Lynchburg Republican*, 17 April 1861; *Lynchburg Virginian*, 16 April 1861. Rosters were compiled by George Morris and Susan Foutz, *Lynchburg in the Civil War: The City, the People, the Battle* (Lynchburg, Va.: E. H. Howard, 1984).

9. Morris and Foutz, *Lynchburg in the Civil War,* 8–10.

10. William D. Branch to Governor John Letcher, 31 July 1861, in *The War of the Rebellion: A Compilation of the Official Records of the Union and Confederate Armies* (Washington, D.C., 1882), series 2, 2:1363–65 (hereafter OR).

11. John B. Douglas, "Recollections of a Refugee," n.d., Jones Memorial Library, Lynchburg, Virginia (Hereafter JML), 6–12; Blackford, *Mine Eyes Have Seen the Glory*, 172, 183, 188, 249–50.

Lynchburg At War

1. Susan Blackford to Charles Blackford, 21 April 1861, Blackford Family Papers, JML; John L Henry and Peter B. Akers, "A History of a Campaign, Compiled from Copious Notes Taken on the Field, as the Incidents Occurred," n.d., JML, 1–2, 9–10; *Lynchburg Virginian*, 24 April 1861.

2. Reid Mitchell, *Civil War Soldiers: Their Expectations and Their Experiences* (New York: Simon & Schuster, 1988), 18–23; see also Robert C. Kenzer, *Kinship and Neighborhood in a Southern Community: Orange County, North Carolina, 1849–1881* (Knoxville: University of Tennessee Press, 1987), 71–74.

3. Mitchell, *Civil War Soldiers*; Reid Mitchell, "The Northern Soldier and His Community," in Maris Vinovskis, ed., *Toward a Social History of the American Civil War: Exploratory Essays* (New York: Cambridge University Press, 1990), 78–92; Reid Mitchell, *The Vacant Chair: The Northern Soldier Leaves Home* (New York: Oxford University Press, 1993); Gerald Linderman, *Embattled Courage: The Experience of Combat in the American Civil War* (New York: Free Press, 1987), pp. 80–110.

4. Henry and Akers, "History of a Campaign," 3, 5–6.

5. Edmond Moorman, "Records and Events of the Beauregard Rifles," (edited by Hunter Marshall, 1907), JML, 9.

6. Charles Blackford to Susan Blackford, 26 June 1861, Blackford Family Papers, JML.

7. Ibid., 7 December 1861, JML; Robert Garlick Hill Kean to Jane Kean, 15 October 1861, Robert Garlick Hill Kean, Papers, Alderman Library, University of Virginia (hereafter AL).

8. *Lynchburg Virginian*, 24 June 1861; Charles Blackford to Susan Blackford, 29 October 1862, JML; Morris and Foutz, *Lynchburg in the Civil War*, 59.

9. *Lynchburg Virginian*, 9 July 1861; Charles Blackford to Susan Blackford, 26 June 1861; 26 August 1861, 10 October 1861, JML. According to Linderman, Blackford was probably right in blaming boredom—rather than cowardice, as a previous generation of historians argued—as a cause of military alcoholism. See Linderman, *Embattled Courage*, 119–21. Through constant vigilance of his own spiritual health, Blackford resisted most of the temptations of camp life. Nevertheless, he did opt for a slightly more acceptable alternative, opium, which he used as a cure for aches and pains and as a sedative for a nervous condition that he believed was brought on by the burden of command and the hours of boredom.

10. Moorman, "Records and Events," 11; Henry and Akers, "History of a Campaign," 24–25; Charles Blackford to Susan Blackford, 10 December 1861, JML.

11. See chapter 2, above.

12. Withers, *Autobiography*, 151; Henry and Akers, "History of a Campaign," 40–41; Charles Blackford to Susan Blackford, 26 August 1861.

13. *Lynchburg Virginian*, 9 January 1863; 23 December 1864; Samuel Oakey to "Cousin," 30 January 1863, Oakey Family Papers, Perkins Library, Duke University (hereafter PL).

14. Henry and Akers, "History of a Campaign," 12–14, 24–25; Morgan, *Personal Reminiscences*, 199–200.

15. Bell, *Eleventh Virginia Infantry*, 3–5; *Lynchburg Virginian*, 2 October 1861.

16. William King to Annie King, 6 November 1861, King Family Papers, AL; Charles Blackford to Susan Blackford, 10 October 1861; *Lynchburg Virginian*, 27 September 1861; 2 January 1862; 14 January 1862; 7 February 1862.

17. *Lynchburg Virginian*, 19 November 1863.

18. Ibid., 27 September 1861; 21 October 1861.

19. Linderman, *Embattled Courage*, 43–60.

20. Charles Blackford to Susan Blackford, 13 June 1861; 23 June 1861, JML.

21. 6Ibid., 13 June 1861; 23 June 1861; 3 July 1861; 26 August 1861; 27 July 1861, JML; Susan Blackford to Charles Blackford, 9 June 1861, JML. See the following for fuller discussions of wartime religion in the South: Mitchell, *Civil War Soldiers*, 173–74; Linderman, *Embattled Courage*, 102–10; Drew Gilpin Faust, "Christian Soldiers: The Meaning of Revivalism in the Confederate Army," *Journal of Southern History* 53 (1987): 63–89.

22. Charles Blackford to Susan Blackford, 26 June 1861.

23. Susan Blackford to Charles Blackford, 4 June 1861; 9 June 1861; 10 July 1861; 12 July 1861; JML.

24. Charles Blackford to Susan Blackford, 9 July 1861, JML.

25. Ibid., 6 June 1861; 28 August 1861; 10 November 1861; 12 November 1861; 16 November 1861; 27 November 1861; 28 December 1861, JML; Blackford, ed., *Letters from Lee's Army*, 21, 154.

26. Susan Blackford to Charles Blackford, 19 September 1861; 26 September 1861, JML; Charles Blackford to Susan Blackford, 20 December 1861; 4 May 1862; 6 February 1862; 3 December 1862, JML.

Charles Blackford was not unique. Other officers also made grand gestures to gain the loyalty of their soldiers, only to feel abused afterward. Colonel Robert T. Preston of the Twenty-eighth Virginia Infantry, a unit that included many Lynchburg soldiers, relied on many of the same strategies that Charles Blackford employed. Preston cared little about discipline and preferred to gain the support of his men through personal indulgences. He referred to his soldiers as "My People" and bragged that he knew all of his soldiers by name. Colonel Samuel Garland, original commander of the Home Guard, also tried to gain his men's fidelity. Even after he accepted a higher office, one that placed him out of personal contact with his old regiment, he cultivated their devotion. When they petitioned to be transferred to a more glamorous and less taxing artillery division, he complained to friends that he felt personally betrayed. See Withers, *Autobiography*, 151; Morgan, *Personal Reminiscences*, 25–26; Robert Garlick Hill Kean, diary, 24 September 1861, Robert Garlick Hill Kean Papers, AL.

27. Charles Blackford to Susan Blackford, 4 November 1861; 27 November 1861; 6 November 1861, JML; Susan Blackford to Charles Blackford, 9 October 1861, JML; William King to Annie King, 6 November 1861; Henry and Akers, "History of a Campaign," 38.

Evidently, John Langhorne was so ashamed of his failure to retain the loyalty of his men that it remained a sensitive topic for him and his family well after the war. In a tribute to Langhorne given in the early 1890s, Thomas Munford, a friend of Langhorne and a Confederate officer from Lynchburg, denied that Langhorne ever had trouble with command and asserted that his retirement from the field stemmed solely from his relationship with Radford. See Thomas T. Munford, "Address to the Garland-Rodes Camp: Presenting a Portrait of Major John S. Langhorne," n.d., Munford-Ellis Papers, George Munford Division, PL.

28. Withers, *Autobiography*, 159.

29. William W. Blackford, *War Years with Jeb Stuart*, n.d., (Baton Rouge: Louisiana State University Press, 1993) 51–53. Linderman, *Embattled Courage*, 169–79 has aptly called the military reforms "the new severity." See also Bell Irvin Wiley, *The Life of Johnny Reb: The Common Soldier of the Confederacy* (Baton Rouge: Louisiana State University Press, 1971), 217–43.

30. Kean diary, 28 January 1862; Charles Phelps to Mary Lee, 12 March 1862, Charles Phelps Papers, AL; Murray L Brown, ed., "The Civil War Letters of James W. Old," *Manuscripts* 42 (1990): 132.

31. Blackford, *War Years with Jeb Stuart*, 255, 280. According to Blackford, the soldier was released on appeal.

32. Escott, *Many Excellent People*, 59–84; Wayne K. Durrill, *War of Another Kind: A Southern Community in the Great Rebellion* (New York: Oxford University Press, 1990), 166–85; Stephen V. Ash, *Middle Tennessee Society Transformed 1865–1870: War and Peace in the Upper South* (Baton Rouge: Louisiana University Press, 1988), 84–105; Harris, *Plain Folk and Gentry*, 140–66; Steven Hahn, *Roots of Southern Populism: Yeoman Farmers and the Transformation of the Georgia Upcountry, 1850–1890* (New York: Oxford University Press, 1983), 124–33.

33. OR, series 4, 3:802–16; Morgan, *Personal Reminiscences*, 24; *Lynchburg Virginian*, 16 July 1864.

34. Morris and Foutz, *Lynchburg in the Civil War*, 57–110. This is not a criticism of Morris and Foutz's efforts. Their roster contains much valuable information and has saved me considerable time and energy. By my estimate, of the 401 Lynchburg residents who enlisted in 1861, only 23 percent served until the end of the war, while an equal number left the service through resignations, desertion, or substitution. See Table 3:1 in the Appendixes.

35. William King to Annie King, 7 February 1862, AL; Robert Garlick Hill Kean to Jane Hill, 23 December 1861, AL; Charles Blackford to Susan Blackford, 15 October 1862, JML.

36. Morris and Foutz, *Lynchburg in the Civil War*, 57–58; Linderman, *Embattled Courage*, 176–77; H. C. Sommerville, diary, 10 April 1865, Virginia State Archives (hereafter VSA). Historians have yet to explore the regional variations of Confederate desertion rates; North Carolina has received the most attention, perhaps because desertion rates were higher among North Carolina troops than any another. See Kenzer, *Kinship and Neighborhood*, 81–83; Phillip Shaw Paludan, *Victims: A True Story of the Civil War* (Knoxville: University of Tennessee Press, 1981), 70–76; Escott, *Many Excellent People*, 32–58; James M. McPherson, *Battle Cry of Freedom: The Civil War* (New York: Oxford University Press, 1988), 694–95. Other regional studies that suggest high desertion rates include: Harris, *Plain Folk and Gentry*, 178–81; Hahn, *Roots of Southern Populism*, 124–29; James Marten,

Texas Divided: Loyalty and Dissent in the Lone Star State 1856–1874 (Lexington: University Press of Kentucky, 1990), 94–103.

37. Escott, *Many Excellent People*, 32–58; Paul D. Escott and J. J. Crow, "The Social Order and Violent Disorder: An Analysis of North Carolina in the Revolution and the Civil War," *Journal of Southern History*, 52 (1986): 372–402; Paul D. Escott, "The Failure of Confederate Nationalism: The Old South's Class System in the Crucible of War," in Harry P. Owens and James J. Cooke, eds., *The Old South in the Crucible of War* (Jackson: University Press of Mississippi, 1983), 15–28.

38. Morgan, *Personal Reminiscences*, 24.

39. Mitchell, *Civil War Soldiers*, 170–71; Wiley, *Life of Johnny Reb*, 135–36; Fred Arthur Bailey, *Class and Tennessee's Confederate Generation* (Chapel Hill: University of North Carolina Press, 1987), 99–104.

40. William Allen to his mother, 17 March 1865; Willam Allen to Henry Allen, 24 March 1865; Thomas Allen to "Sister Sallie," 30 March 1866, all in Allen Family Papers, JML.

41. *Lynchburg Virginian*, 21 September 1863; Escott, "Failure of Confederate Nationalism," 15–28.

42. Blackford, *War Years with Jeb Stuart*, 280.

43. Brown, ed., "Civil War Letters of James W. Old," 132, 138–39.

44. Ibid., 137–38.

45. Thomas Kelley to Martha Sublett, 6 June 1864; Samuel Sublett to a friend, 18 January 1862; Samuel Sublett to a friend, 4 March 1862, Papers, Thomas Kelley, PL.

46. John R. Dennett, *The South as It Is, 1865–6*, ed. Henry M. Christman (New York: Viking Press, 1965), 63–64.

47. Thomas Kelley to Martha Sublett, 6 June 1864.

48. Ibid.

49. Lewis Blackford to William Blackford, Sr., 30 September 1861, Blackford Family Papers, Southern Historical Collection, University of North Carolina at Chapel Hill (hereafter SHC); Henry and Akers, "History of a Campaign," 28, 30–31.

50. *Lynchburg Virginian*, 22 June 1864; Morris and Foutz, *Lynchburg in the Civil War*, 38–49.

51. Henry and Akers, "History of a Campaign," 31; Thomas Kelley to Martha Sublett, 6 June 1864.

52. Thomas Kelley to Martha Sublett, 11 October 1864, PL; Thomas Kelley to Martha Sublett, 6 June 1864; Walter Henderson to "Puss," 24 October 1864, Walter Henderson Papers, JML.

53. Mitchell, *Civil War Soldiers*, 172; Henry and Akers, "History of a Campaign," 15, 26–27.

54. Thomas Kelley to Martha Sublett, 11 October 1864; Blackford, ed., *Letters From Lee's Army*, 260–61.

55. Bell, *Eleventh Virginia Infantry*, 39–42; Morgan, *Personal Reminiscences*, 199–200; Sommerville diary, 9 April 1865.

56. Morgan, *Personal Reminiscences*, 271–79; Charles Blackford to Nannie Blackford, 2 August 1864, Blackford Family Papers, JML; Blackford, *War Years*

with Jeb Stuart, 166; Thomas H. Munford, "Circular to Soldiers," 21 April 1865, Munford-Ellis Papers, PL.

57. Charles Blackford to Susan Blackford, 21 September 1861; 22 January 1863, JML; Morris and Foutz, *Lynchburg in the Civil War*, 78.

58. Charles Blackford to Susan Blackford, 19 December 1861; 30 December 1861; 18 June 1864, JML.

59. Samuel Sublett to a friend, 18 January 1862, Thomas Kelley, Papers, PL.

60. *Lynchburg Virginian*, 7 March 1863; 22 October 1863.

61. George Munford to his father, 30 July 1863, Munford-Ellios Papers, PL.

62. Susan Blackford to Charles Blackford, 27 April 1863; 18 November 1861; letter 101A (n.d.), JML.

63. N. E. Lucas to John James Dillard, n.d., John James Dillard Papers, PL; Blackford, *Mine Eyes Have Seen the Glory*, 239–40; *Lynchburg Virginian*, 21 February 1865.

64. Charles Blackford to Susan Blackford, 28 July 1864, JML; Withers, *Autobiography*, 211–12.

The War in Lynchburg

1. *Lynchburg Virginian*, 1 May 1861; 20 July 1861; 30 April 1862.

2. Ibid., 28 January 1862; 18 April 1862; Houck, *Prototype of a Confederate Hospital*, 70–93; Mary Forsberg, "Hospital Reminiscences," 1901, JML; Narcissa Owen, *Memoirs of Narcissa Owen, 1831–1907* (Washington, D.C., 1907), 74–77.

3. Blackford, *Mine Eyes Have Seen the Glory*, 213–14; Henry and Akers, *History of a Campaign*, 21; Moorman "Beauregard Rifles," 33; Charles Blackford to Susan Blackford, 16 July 1863, JML.

4. Houck, *Prototype of a Confederate Hospital*, 58–61; Susan Blackford to Charles Blackford, 8 July 1861; 7 May 1864, JML; Forsberg, "Hospital Reminiscences."

5. *Lynchburg Virginian*, 29 March 1862; 18 April 1862.

6. Susan Blackford to Charles Blackford, 12 November 1861; 22 November 1861; 12 December 1861; 15 May 1863; 1 August 1863, JML.

7. Jacob Duche Mitchell, diary, 6 June 1862, LMS; Cornelius M. Buckley, ed., *a Frenchman, a Chaplain, a Rebel: The War Letters of Pere Louis-Hippolyte Gache, S.J.* (Chicago: Loyola University Press, 1981), 190–91, 210, 216.

8. William Blackford, Sr., to Launcelot Blackford, 20 April 1861, Blackford Family Papers, SHC.

9. *Lynchburg Virginian*, 20 March 1862.

10. Ibid., 13 May 1861; 13 December 1861.

11. Ibid., 30 December 1861; 25 February 1862; 29 March 1862; 1 April 1862; 5 May 1862; 26 July 1862.

12. Ibid., 26 March 1862; 29 March 1862.

13. Ibid., 29 March 1862; 31 March 1862; 1 April 1862.

14. Ibid., 5 May 1862; Morris and Foutz, *Lynchburg in the Civil War*, 27.

15. Morris and Foutz, *Lynchburg in the Civil War*, 27; *Lynchburg Republican*, 5 May 1863.

16. Lucy Rodes to Alexander Brown, 5 June 1862, Alexander Brown Papers, PL; Blackford, *Mine Eyes Have Seen the Glory*, 180.

17. *Lynchburg Virginian*, 11 February 1864; 25 June 1864; 9 August 1864.
18. Susan Blackford to Charles Blackford, 16 November 1861; 30 October 1862, JML; Charles Blackford to Susan Blackford, 30 April 1863, JML.
19. Terrell, "Reminiscences," 29; *Lynchburg Virginian*, 9 August 1864.
20. Henry and Akers, "History of a Campaign," p 9; Susan Blackford to Charles Blackford, 15 May 1863.
21. William Andrew Fletcher, *Rebel Private: Front and Rear* (reprint, 1908; Austin: University of Texas Press, 1954), 36; *Lynchburg Republican*, 15 August 1863.
22. Faust, "Christian Soldiers," 63–89; Mitchell, *Civil War Soldiers*, 173.
23. *Lynchburg Republican*, 14 January 1863; Robert Brown to Alex "Sandy" Brown, 25 March 1862, Alexander Brown Papers, PL.
24. Mitchell diary, 1861, 1862, LMS; John Lipscomb Johnson, *Autobiographical Notes* (privately printed, 1958), 161–63; Buckley, ed., *A Frenchman, a Chaplain, a Rebel*, 192–93; Houck, *Prototype of a Confederate Hospital*, 94–105.
25. Linderman, *Embattled Courage*, 252–57; Samuel Oakey to "Cousin," 6 October 1863, Oakey Family Papers, PL.
26. Lucy Rodes to Alex "Sandy" Brown, 6 May 1862; 20 July 1862; 29 October 1862, Alexander Brown Papers, PL.
27. Buckley, ed, *A Frenchman, a Chaplain, a Rebel*, 199–201, 209–11, 216.
28. *Lynchburg Virginian*, 24 January 1862; 20 February 1863. For analyses of Southern entrepreneurs' expectations, see David R. Goldfield, *Urban Growth in the Age of Sectionalism: Virginia, 1847–1861* (Baton Rouge: Louisiana State University Press, 1977), 226–70; Laurence Shore, *Southern Capitalists: Ideological Leadership of an Elite, 1832–1885* (Chapel Hill: University of North Carolina Press, 1986), 79–98; James Russell, *Atlanta: City Building in the Old South and the New* (Baton Rouge: Louisiana State University Press, 1988), 91–115; Mary DeCredico, *Patriotism for Profit: Georgia's Urban Entrepreneurs and the Confederate War Effort* (Chapel Hill: University of North Carolina Press, 1990), 21–46. For summaries of the Confederacy's economic advances but continued woes, see DeCredico, *Patriotism for Profit*, 72–80; Emory Thomas, *The Confederacy as a Revolutionary Experience* (Englewood Cliffs, N.J.: Prentice-Hall, 1971), 79–99; Emory Thomas, *The Confederate Nation, 1861–1865* (New York: Harper & Row, 1979), 206–14; Don H. Doyle, *New Men, New Cities, New South: Atlanta, Nashville, Charleston, Mobile, 1860–1910* (Chapel Hill: University of North Carolina Press, 1990), 22–50.
29. Drew Gilpin Faust, *The Creation of Confederate Nationalism: Ideology and Identity in the Civil War South* (Baton Rouge: Louisiana State University Press, 1988), 41–57; Anne C. Rose, *Victorian America and the Civil War* (New York: Cambridge University Press, 1992), 68–71.
30. *Lynchburg Virginian*, 11 November 1861; 12 November 1861; 13 November 1861; 14 October 1862.
31. Ibid., 10 March 1863; 14 October 1862; Mitchell diary, 26 November 1862, LMS; Kean diary, 7 March 1863.
32. *Lynchburg Virginian*, 10 March 1863; Charles Blackford to Susan Blackford, 30 July 1863, JML.
33. Susan Blackford to Charles Blackford, 18 November 1861; 1 August 1863; Johnson, *Autobiographical Notes*, 155–67.

34. *Lynchburg Virginian,* 21 January 1865; Dennett, *The South as It Is,* 47–50; Whitelaw Reid, *After the War: A Tour of the Southern States,* C. Vann Woodward (reprint, 1866; New York: Harper & Row, 1965), 331–32.

35. Samuel Sublett to "dear friend," 4 March 1862, Thomas Kelley Papers, PL; *Lynchburg Republican,* 17 October 1862; 1 March 1864.

36. Jannett Cleland, diary, 11 August 1863, JML; Susan Blackford to Charles Blackford, 22 November 1861; 6 August 1864, JML.

37. Douglas, "Recollections of a Refugee," 3–5; *Lynchburg Virginian,* 23 December 1864.

38. *Lynchburg Virginian,* 16 December 1861.

39. Ibid., 4 April 1862.

40. Buckley, ed., *A Frenchman, a Chaplain, a Rebel,* 159–61; *Lynchburg Virginian,* 10 March 1863. For analyses of Confederate food riots, see Escott, *Many Excellent People,* 65–67; Thomas, *Confederate Nation,* 203–5; Emory Thomas, *The Confederate State of Richmond: A Biography of the Capital* (Austin: University of Texas Press, 1971), 119–22.

41. *Lynchburg Republican,* 27 June 1862.

42. *Lynchburg Virginian,* 20 February 1863; 30 March 1863.

43. Ibid., 15 August 1864.

44. Ibid., 23 July 1862; 3 March 1864; 10 March 1864, 28 March 1864; 26 December 1864; *Lynchburg Republican,* 20 January 1863; 21 January 1863; 29 May 1863.

45. *Lynchburg Virginian,* 20 January 1863; *Lynchburg Republican,* 21 January 1863.

46. Session Minutes of the First Presbyterian Church of Lynchburg, Virginia, 30 January 1864.

47. Of the twenty-nine individuals sent to state court for crimes of theft in 1862 and 1864, five were arrested for stealing food, six for clothes, two for weaponry, five for money, one each for books and a watch, and nine for items not listed in the court records; *Lynchburg Virginian,* 3 February 1865.

48. Others have concluded that crimes against property reflected a far more profound alienation from the war See Escott, *Many Excellent People,* 36–44; Hahn, *Roots of Southern Populism,* 124–33; Michael Shirley, *From Congregation Town to Industrial City: Culture and Social Change in a Southern Community* (New York: New York University Press, 1994), 136–43.

49. This argument runs counter to the conclusions of a number of historians, including Thomas, *Confederacy as a Revolutionary Experience,* 117; Orville Vernon Burton, "On the Confederate Homefront: The Transformation of Values From Community to Nation in Edgefield, South Carolina" (paper presented at the Woodrow Wilson International Center for Scholars, Washington, D.C., 19 July 1989), 18.

50. "Annual Report of the First Presbyterian Church of Lynchburg, Virginia," 1861; 1862; 1863.

51. Houck, *Prototype of a Confederate Hospital,* 76–89; Owen, *Memoirs,* 74–78; Blackford, *Mine Eyes Have Seen the Glory,* 188, 234.

52. *Lynchburg Virginian,* 31 July 1863; 1 August 1863; Owen, *Memoirs,* 74.

53. *Lynchburg Virginian,* 15 August 1864.

54. Susan Blackford to Charles Blackford, 14 August 1864; 30 September 1864, JML; Charles Blackford to Susan Blackford, 5 October 1864, JML; George Ramsey to Sabra Ramsey, 24 August 1864, Ramsey Family Papers, PL.

55. *Lynchburg Virginian*, 6 October 1864; 22 August 1864; 21 January 1865.

56. Ibid., 29 July 1863; 3 September 1864.

57. Ibid., 23 June 1862; 24 July 1862.

58. Ibid., 23 June 1864.

59. Jacob Yoder, diary, 2 May 1866, VSA.

60. *Lynchburg Virginian*, 25 June 1864; 16 July 1864; 3 June 1864; *Lynchburg Republican*, 3 June 1863.

61. *Lynchburg Virginian*, 4 April 1862; 30 November 1863; Blackford, *Mine Eyes Have Seen the Glory*, 206.

62. Susan Blackford to Charles Blackford, 4 November 1862, JML; *Lynchburg Virginian*, 21 January 1863; 24 January 1863; 30 October 1863.

63. Ibid., 16 November 1861; 30 October 1862; Charles Blackford to Susan Blackford, 30 April 1863; 21 August 1863, JML; Blackford, ed., *Letters from Lee's Army*, 162.

64. Susan Blackford to Charles Blackford, 22 November 1861; 25 November 1861; 5 December 1861; Charles Blackford to Susan Blackford, 3 December 1861; 17 December 1861, JML.

65. Charles Blackford to Susan Blackford, 25 October 1863, JML.

66. Susan Blackford to Charles Blackford, 22 December 1862; 9 January 1863, JML.

67. Ibid., 22 January 1863; 9 January 1863; 21 August 1863, JML.

68. Ibid., 29 November 1861; 30 October 1861; letter 168, (n.d.), JML.

69. *Lynchburg Virginian*, 3 February 1865.

70. Ibid., 2 November 1863.

71. Lieutenant-Colonel J C. Shields to Captain C. B. Duffeld, in OR, series 4, 3:1194; James H. Brewer, *The Confederate Negro: Virginia's Craftsmen and Military Laborers, 1861–1865* (Durham, N.C.: Duke University Press, 1969), 23–26, 122; Houck, *Prototype of a Confederate Hospital*, 106–11.

72. *Lynchburg Virginian*, 13 February 1864; Quarterly Meeting Reports of the Stewards of Court Street Methodist Church, Lynchburg, Virginia, 1861–1865.

73. *Lynchburg Republican*, 7 April 1863.

74. Ibid., 8 June 1863.

75. *Lynchburg Virginian*, 30 January 1864.

76. Ibid., 30 January 1864; 5 February 1864; 9 February 1864.

77. Ibid., 15 June 1861; 21 June 1862.

78. Joel Williamson, *The Crucible of Race: Black-White Relations in the American South since Emancipation* (New York: Oxford University Press, 1984), 50–57.

79. *Lynchburg Virginian*, 9 August 1864.

80. *Lynchburg Republican*, 29 May 1863.

81. *Lynchburg Virginian*, 30 July 1863.

82. Ibid., 3 March 1864; A W. Owen to Medical Director's Office, 29 April 1864, Records of the Confederacy, RG 109, Records of the Medical Department: Letters Sent and Received, Medical Director's Office, Richmond, Virginia, chap.

6, vol. 364, National Archives (hereafter NA); Complaints of Joshua Burns, 11 January 1868, Records of the Bureau of Refugees, Freedmen, and Abandoned Lands (hereafter Freedmen's Bureau), RG 105, Records of the Subassistant Commissioner, Seventh District of Virginia, Register of Complaints, series 4086, vol. 304, NA.

83. *Lynchburg Virginian*, 20 October 1864; 11 November 1864; 18 February 1865; *Lynchburg Republican*, 2 April 1865. Glass was not enthusiastic about using black troops, believing it would be a travesty to force impoverished whites to provide sustenance to black soldiers. Noting that he had only two slaves fit for military service, he told his readers that he "would put one of them in, and sell the other to any man who will put him in. Don't all call at once!"

84. *Lynchburg Virginian*, 25 March 1864; 27 March 1864; 2 April 1864; 3 April 1864.

85. Ibid., 2 April 1864; 3 April 1864; 4 April 1864.

86. Ibid., 3 April 1864; Susan Blackford To Charles Blackford, 15 May 1863.

87. "Memorial of the Citizens of Lynchburg to the State Legislature of Virginia," 9 February 1865, Petitions to the State Legislature, VSA.

88. R. E. Colston to James Seeddon, 16 December 1864, in OR, series 1 vol. 43:2, 940; Francis Nicholls to General S. Cooper, 16 December 1863, in OR series 1, vol. 29:1, 876–79; Francis Nicholls to General S. Cooper, 4 April 1864, in OR series 4, vol. 3:268–9; James Longstreet, *From Manassas to Appomattox: Memoirs of the Civil War in America* (reprint, 1896; Bloomington: Indiana University Press, 1976), 645.

89. *Lynchburg Virginian*, 29 June 1863; 30 June 1863.

90. Harris, *Plain Folk and Gentry*, 147–53; Escott, *Many Excellent People*, 45; Mitchell, *Civil War Soldiers*, 161–67; Charles P. Roland, *The Confederacy* (Chicago: University of Chicago Press, 1960), 59–60.

91. Cleland diary, 11 October 1864; 14 October 1864; William Waller to his wife, 5 December 1864, Chamberlayne Family Papers, section 62, Virginia Historical Society (hereafter VHS); Withers, *Autobiography*, 211–13.

92. *Lynchburg Virginian*, 6 January 1865; 7 January 1865.

93. Ibid., 6 January 1865; 8 January 1865.

94. Ibid., 2 March 1865.

95. Morris and Foutz, *Lynchburg in the Civil War*, 51–53.

96. J. C. Breckinridge to General J. E. Johnson, 8 April 1865, in OR, series 1, vol. 47:3, 767.

97. Jedediah Hotchkiss, *Make Me a Map of the Valley: The Civil War Journal of Stonewall Jackson's Topographer*, ed. Archie McDonald (Dallas: Southern Methodist University Press, 1973), 263–65.

98. Mary Washington Cabell Early, diary, 9–15 April 1865, Early Family Papers, VHS; Sommerville diary, n.d. but after 10 April 1865.

99. William Lyne Wilson, *A Borderland Confederate*, ed. Festus P. Summers (Pittsburgh: University of Pittsburgh Press, 1962), 102–5; Sommerville Diary, n.d. but after 10 April 1865.

100. Report of Major General Edward, in OR, series 1, vol. 46:1, 1160–63; Report of Brevet Major General John W. Turner, 26 April 1865, in OR, series 1,

vol. 46:1, 1214–19; Report of Brigadier General Ranald S. Mackenzie, 8 May 1865, in OR, series 1, vol. 46:1, 1244–53; Walter Martin to "Dear Hart," 9 April 1865, in OR, series 1, vol. 51:2, 1068–69; Sommerville diary, n.d. but after 10 April 1865; General George Munford to Elizabeth Munford, 30 April 1865, Munford-Ellis Papers, PL.

    101. Cleland, diary, 20 April 1865.

    102. Sommerville, diary, n.d. but after 10 April 1865.

    103. Blackford, ed., *Letters From Lee's Army*, 292.

NOTES TO CHAPTER FOUR

    1. Susan Leigh Blackford, ed., *Letters from Lee's Army: Or the Memoirs of Life in and out of the Army in Virginia during the War between the States* (1894 reprint, New York: Charles Scribner's Sons, 1947), 291–95.

    2. Ibid.; Charles Blackford, "Personal Narrative of the Events following the Civil War," n.d., Blackford Family Papers, Jones Memorial Library, Lynchburg, Virginia (hereafter JML), 5–6.

    3. Charles Blackford to Susan Blackford, 18 June 1865, Blackford Family Papers, JML.

    4. Robert Garlick Hill Kean, diary, 27 June 1865, Robert Garlick Hill Kean Papers, Alderman Library, University of Virginia (hereafter AL).

    5. Charles Blackford to Mary Blackford, 11 June 1865, Blackford Family Papers, JML; L. Minor Blackford, *Mine Eyes Have Seen the Glory: The Story of a Virginia Lady, Mary Berkeley Minor Blackford, 1802–1896, Who Taught Her Sons to Hate Slavery and to Love the Union* (Cambridge, Mass.: Harvard University Press, 1954), 240–41. J. Irvin Gregg to General N. M. Curtis, 1 June 1865, Records of the U. S. Army Continental Commands (hereafter Continental Commands), RG 393, Letters and Circulars Sent from Headquarters at the Military Subdistrict of Lynchburg, Virginia (hereafter Letters Sent), series 299, National Archives (hereafter NA).

    6. Weekly Report of the Military District of Lynchburg, 13 August 1865, 25 September 1865, Continental Commands, RG 393, Letters Sent, series 7000, NA; J. Irvin Gregg to General N. M. Curtis, 20 May 1865; 17 June 1865; 20 June 1865, Continental Commands, RG 393, Letters Sent (Inventory III), series 299, NA.

    7. John R Dennett, *The South as It Is, 1865–6* ed. Henry M. Christman (New York: Viking Press, 1965), 45, 46–47, 49.

    8. *Lynchburg Virginian*, 29 June 1865; 9 August 1865; Dennett, *The South as It Is*, 35, 67, 85–86; Whitelaw Reid, *After the War: A Tour of the Southern States*, ed. C. Vann Woodward (reprint, 1866; New York: Harper & Row, 1965) 331.

    9. Louis Stevenson to General O. Brown, 31 January 1867, Records of the Bureau of Refugees, Freedmen, and Abandoned Lands (hereafter Freedmen's Bureau), RG 105, Records of the Assistant Subassistant Commissioner, Seventh District of Virginia (hereafter Records of the Subassistant), series 4082, NA; Captain R. S. Lacey to Superintendent of Culpeper County, 13 November 1865, Freedmen's Bureau, RG 105, Records of the Subassistant Commissioner, series

4072, NA; Weekly Reports, 25 September 1865; 7 October 1865, Continental Commands, RG 393, series 7000, NA; *Lynchburg Republican*, 13 June 1865; *Lynchburg News*, 16 April 1866; 27 July 1866.

10. Kean diary, 6 July 1865; Continental Commands, RG 393, General Orders and Special Orders of Military Subdistrict of Lynchburg, Virginia, series 301, NA; Launcelot Blackford to Lewis Blackford, 21 May 1865, Blackford Family Papers, Southern Historical Collection, University of North Carolina at Chapel Hill (hereafter SHC).

11. J. Irvin Gregg to General N. M. Curtis, 24 May 1865, Continental Commands, RG 393, Letters Sent, series 299, NA; *Lynchburg Virginian*, 4 April 1866.

12. Captain R. S. Lacey to Assistant Commissioner Orlando Brown, 16 November 1865, Freedmen's Bureau, RG 105, Records of the Subassistant Commissioner, Unentered Letters Received to the Assistant Subassistant, series 4075, NA; *Lynchburg Virginian*, 24 December 1865.

13. T. P. Wodell to Captain R. S. Lacey, 16 February 1866, Freedmen's Bureau, RG 105, Records of the Subassistant Commissioner, Letter Received, series 4073, NA; Reid, *After the War*, 329–34.

14. J. Irvin Gregg to General N. M. Curtis, 20 May 1865; *Lynchburg Virginian*, 11 August 1865; 17 February 1866; *Lynchburg News*, 18 January 1866.

15. J. Irvin Gregg to General N. M. Curtis, 20 May 1865; *Lynchburg Virginian*, 11 August 1865; 17 February 1866.

16. Jacob Yoder, diary, 28 April 1866; 2 May 1866; 6 May 1866; 16 May 1866, Virginia State Archives (hereafter VSA).

17. Ibid., 7 May 1866; 22 June 1866; 26 January 1870; Richard Lowe, *Republicans and Reconstruction in Virginia, 1856–1870* (Charlottesville: University Press of Virginia, 1991), 106–7.

18. *Lynchburg Virginian*, 19 June 1865; 17 January 1866; 26 May 1866; Kean diary, 8 October 1865.

19. *Lynchburg Virginian*, 8–10 August 1865; Philip Lightfoot Scruggs, *The History of Lynchburg, Virginia, 1786–1946*, (Lynchburg, Va.: J P. Bell, 1946), 121.

20. Captain R. S. Lacey to Assistant Commissioner Orlando Brown, 6 February 1866, Freedmen's Bureau, RG 105, Records of the Subassistant Commissioner, Letter Sent, series 4072, NA.

21. *Lynchburg Virginian*, 17 January 1866; 26 May 1866; 10 September 1866; 31 October, 1866; 6 December 1866.

22. Lowe, *Republicans and Reconstruction*, 31–35; Eric Foner, *Reconstruction: America's Unfinished Revolution, 1863–1877* (New York: Harper & Row, 1988), 190–91; *Lynchburg Virginian*, 2 April 1866; 5 April 1866.

23. Lowe, *Republicans and Reconstruction*, 72–96; Foner, *Reconstruction*, 271–80.

24. *Lynchburg Virginian*, 16 April 1868; 27 January 1869; 12 May 1869; 18 June 1869; *Lynchburg Republican*, 29 October 1867; W. H. Morgan, *Personal Reminiscences of the War of 1861–5* (Lynchburg, Va.: J. P. Bell, 1911), 273–280; Robert Enoch Withers, *Autobiography of an Octogenarian*, (Roanoke, Va.: Stone Printing, 1907), 246–50 and passim. For conservatives' antidemocratic message, see Eric Foner, "Reconstruction and the Problem of Free Labor," in *Politics and*

Ideology in the Age of the Civil War (New York: Oxford University Press, 1980), 121.

25. Thomas Kelley to "Cousin," 12 April 1866, Thomas Kelley Papers, Perkins Library, Duke University (hereafter PL); Kean diary, 7 July 1865.

26. Blackford, *Mine Eyes Have Seen the Glory*, 245.

27. Mrs John Meem Payne, "A Brief Outline of My Life for the Benefit of My Children," n.d., Lynchburg Museum System (hereafter LMS), 10; J. Irvin Gregg to General N. M. Curtis, 1 June 1865; Testimony of John Averitt before the House of Representatives Select Committee on Reconstruction, 28 January 1869, Records of the U. S. House of Representatives, Fortieth and Forty-first Congress (hereafter House Select Committee on Reconstruction), RG 233, Box 7, NA.

28. Charles Blackford to Mary Blackford, 7 September 1865, SHC. Evidently, Blackford never completely got over his slaves' betrayal. Years later, he came across his 1858 inventory of slave property. At the bottom of the list of servants—some of whom he had known for years—he wrote, "All became free and were reduced to beggary by Gen. Lee's surrender." See Charles Blackford, "Registry of Negroes," 12 December 1858, Blackford Family Papers, JML.

29. Payne, "Brief Outline of My Life," 10; Kean diary, 7 July 1865; John J. Terrell, "Reminiscences of Dr. John J. Terrell," John J. Terrell Papers, LMS, 38. For more extended studies of the postwar master-servant relationship, see Leon F. Litwack, *Been in the Storm So Long: The Aftermath of Slavery* (New York: Vintage Books, 1979), 293–96, 346–51, 354–58; James L. Roark, *Masters without Slaves: Southern Planters in the Civil War and Reconstruction* (New York: W. W. Norton & Co., 1977), 144–49.

30. Blackford, *Mine Eyes Have Seen the Glory*, 253–58.

31. Ibid., 247; Payne, "Brief Outline of My Life," 12.

32. *Lynchburg Virginian*, 4 January 1867.

33. Register of Complaints, Freedmen's Bureau, RG 105, Records of the Assistant Subassistant Commissioner of the Seventh District of Virginia (hereafter Records of the Assistant Subassistant), series 4086, vol 304, NA. Bureau agents were less than systematic in recording freedmen's job-related complaints; as a result, there are large gaps in the record, making analysis of the subject difficult.

34. *Lynchburg News*, 31 March 1870; City Council of Lynchburg, *Resources and Advantages of Lynchburg, Virginia and Tributary Country*, (Lynchburg, Va.: Virginian Job Office 1872).

35. For brief mentions of the tobacco factories' importance for the black community, see *Lynchburg Virginian*, 20 July 1865; 27 July 1866; 28 December 1865; 30 March 1866; 10 July 1866.

36. Armstead L Robinson, "Plans Dat Comed from God: Institution Building and the Emergence of Black Leadership in Reconstruction Memphis," in Orville Vernon Burton and Robert C. McMath, Jr., eds., *Toward a New South? Studies in Post-Civil War Southern Communities* (Westport, Conn.: Greenwood Press, 1982), 71–102.

37. *Lynchburg Virginian*, 13 May 1867; *Lynchburg News*, 13 May 1867.

38. *Lynchburg Virginian*, 17 May 1867; *Lynchburg News*, 8 August 1867.

39. Richard Lowe, "Virginia's Reconstruction Convention: General Schofield

Rates the Delegates," *Virginia Magazine of History and Biography* 80 (1972): 341–60; Lowe, *Republicans and Reconstruction*, 122–29.

40. In April 1868, city council included five merchants, three tobacconists, a former Union military officer assigned to Lynchburg (R. S. Lacey), and three individuals who could not be identified by either the 1860 or the 1870 manuscript census. Register of Civil Officers in the Subdistrict of Lynchburg, n.d., Continental Commands, RG 393, series 5335, vol. 343, NA; Cooley to Colonel S. F. Chalfin, 16 April 1868, Continental Commands, RG 393, letters, telegraphs, and orders sent by the Military Commissioner, Twenty-third Division of Virginia, series 302; Lowe, *Republicans and Reconstruction*, 158–59.

41. Alrutheus Ambush Taylor, *The Negro in the Reconstruction of Virginia* (New York: Russell & Russell, 1926), 231, 235, 277.

42. *Lynchburg Republican*, 6 August 1868; *Lynchburg Virginian*, 1 April 1869; 28 August 1869; 21 March 1871; 4 March 1872; *Lynchburg News*, 4 February 1870; 12 February 1870; 22 December 1870; 8 April 1871.

43. *Lynchburg News*, 9 April 1872; 10 April 1872; 12 April 1872; *Lynchburg Virginian*, 10 April 1872.

44. *Lynchburg News*, 21 November 1866; 14 March 1867; 16 July 1870; 1 February 1871; 11 August 1871; *Lynchburg Virginian*, 24 September 1870; 18 March 1871; 16 June 1871.

45. *Lynchburg News*, 22 May 1866; *Lynchburg Virginian*, 5 November 1868; 10 April 1869; 25 June 1869; 24 September 1870; Yoder diary, 5 June 1866.

46. Luther Porter Jackson, *Negro Office-Holders in Virginia, 1865–1895* (Norfolk, Va.: Guide Quality Press, 1945), 59.

47. 1870 Census, Population Schedule manuscript microfilm, Lynchburg, Virginia; 1870 Census, Manufacturing Schedule manuscript microfilm, Campbell County, Virginia.

48. Howard N. Rabinowitz, *Race Relations in the Urban South, 1865–1890* (Urbana: University of Illinois Press, 1980), 97–124; Janette Thomas Greenwood, *Bittersweet Legacy: The Black and White "Better Classes" in Charlotte, 1850–1910* (Chapel Hill: University of North Carolina Press, 1994); Michael Shirley, *From Congregation Town to Industrial City: Culture and Social Change in a Southern Community* (New York: New York University Press, 1994), 164–65; Don H. Doyle, *Nashville in the New South, 1880–1930* (Knoxville: University of Tennessee Press, 1985), 107–116.

49. *Lynchburg Business Directory* (Lynchburg, Va., 1873).

50. Ibid.

51. *Lynchburg News*, 10 November 1871; Edward King, *The Great South: A Record of Journeys in Louisiana, Texas, The Indian Territory, Missouri, Arkansas, Mississippi, Alabama, Georgia, Florida, South Carolina, North Carolina, Kentucky, Tennessee, Virginia, West Virginia, and Maryland* (Hartford, Conn.: American Publishing Company, 1875), 554. Harold Woodman, "Economic Reconstruction and the Rise of the New South," in James B. Boles and Evelyn Thomas Nolen eds. *Interpreting Southern History: Historiographical Essays in Honor of Sanford W. Higginbotham* (Baton Rouge: Louisiana State University Press, 1987), 298–99, provides a succinct summary of similar patterns in other Southern cities.

Lynchburg may have resembled Charleston, South Carolina in its pattern of racially mixed neighborhoods. See Don H. Doyle, *New Men, New Cities, New South: Atlanta, Nashville, Charleston, Mobile, 1860–1910* (Chapel Hill: University of North Carolina Press, 1990), 301–6; John P. Radford, "Race, Residence, and Ideology: Charleston, South Carolina in the Mid-Nineteenth Century," *Journal of Historical Geography* 24 (1976): 329–46.

52. 1870 Census, Population Schedule manuscript microfilm, Lynchburg, Virginia.

53. *Lynchburg Business Directory*. In 1873, the city directory listed twenty-five tobacco factories in Lynchburg; of these, fifteen (60 percent) were partnerships. In 1859, the business directory had listed forty-eight factories; twenty-two (46 percent) were partnerships. For descriptions of the transformation of the tobacco industry, see Joseph Clarke Robert, *The Story of Tobacco in America* (New York: Alfred A. Knopf, 1949), 184–86; Frederick F. Siegel, *The Roots of Southern Distinctiveness: Tobacco and Society in Danville, Virginia, 1780–1865* (Chapel Hill: University of North Carolina Press, 1987), 156.

54. *Lynchburg News*, 7 January 1870; 10 January 1870.

55. Yoder diary, 17 January 1870; 10 February 1870; US. Bureau of the Census, Ninth Census, *The Statistics of the Population of the United States: Compiled from the Original Returns of the Ninth Census (June 1, 1870)* (Washington, D.C.: Government Printing Office, 1872).

56. Yoder diary, 14 June 1866; *Lynchburg News*, 15 August 1871.

57. Payne, "Brief Outline of My Life," 10; Blackford, ed., *Letters from Lee's Army*, 292; For more extended studies of the postwar master-servant relationship, see Litwack, *Been in the Storm So Long*, 293–96, 346–51, 354–58; Roark, *Masters without Slaves*, 144–49.

58. *Lynchburg News*, 7 June 1866; 23 December 1866; *Lynchburg Virginian*, 3 October 1866; 28 January 1867; 4 September 1867.

59. Yoder diary, 5 May 1866; Louis Stevenson to Orlando Brown, 31 December 1867, Freedmen's Bureau, RG 105, Records of the Assistant Subassistant Commissioner, series 4082, vol. 299, NA.

60. Louis Stevenson to General O. Brown, 31 January 1867. R. S. Lacey to Louis Stevenson, 3 January 1868; A. B. Kinney to R. S. Lacey, 27 January 1868; J. M. Studling to R. S. Lacey 15 February 1868, all in Freedmen's Bureau, RG 105, Records of the Subassistant Commissioner, Register of Letters Received and Endorsement, series 4073, vol. 291, NA.

61. *Lynchburg Virginian*, 1 November 1867; 11 December 1867; *Lynchburg News*, 22 February 1867; 6 August 1867; 19 November 1870.

62. *Lynchburg News*, 31 March 1870; 13 October 1871.

63. *Lynchburg Virginian*, 17 July 1865; 9 April 1866; 13 January 1871; 9 February 1871; *Lynchburg News*, 7 April 1866; 23 January 1867, 8 February 1871.

64. Whipping was permitted for a brief period in 1866—until the federal government responded to complaints from blacks and stopped the practice *Lynchburg Virginian*, 25 June 1866; 17 August 1868; 13 January 1871; 9 February 1871; *Lynchburg News*, 19 March 1866; 23 March 1866; 9 August 1866; 22 October 1866; 8 February 1871. See Tables 4:3 and 4:4 in the Appendixes for municipal and state verdicts against property crimes.

65.

Item Stolen	N
Unidentified Clothing	13
Coat	6
Shoes	8
Cloth	5
Vegetables	7
Meat	12
Iron	14
Fuel (wood, coal)	4
Money	8
Watches	3
Tools	4
Tobacco	1
Other	3
TOTAL	88

SOURCE: Compiled from the *Lynchburg News*, 1866; *Lynchburg Virginian*, 1866.

66. *Lynchburg News*, 12 February 1866; 6 August 1870; 15 June 1872.

67. "To the Young Men of Lynchburg," *Lynchburg News*, 29 October 1867.

68. See Tables 4:1 and 4:2 in the Appendixes.

69. *Lynchburg Virginian*, 10 November 1868; 23 August 1872; *Lynchburg News*, 8 January 1870; 24 May 1872; City Council, *Resources and Advantages of Lynchburg*, 5.

70. These included five cooks, one carriage driver, two gardeners, thirteen unspecified servants (five males, eight females), eight nurses, and two porters (1870 Census, Population Schedule manuscript microfilm, Lynchburg, Virginia). In 1860, only twelve whites, 8 percent of all unskilled white laborers, held these types of jobs.

71. "To the Young Men of Lynchburg," *Lynchburg Virginian*, 29 October 1867.

72. 1870 Census, Population Schedule manuscript microfilm, Lynchburg, Virginia.

73. *Lynchburg Virginian*, 9 December 1868; 24 April 1867.

74. 1860 Census, Population Schedule manuscript microfilm, Lynchburg, Virginia; 1870 Census, Population Schedule manuscript microfilm Lynchburg, Virginia.

75. *Lynchburg Virginian*, 29 June 1865.

76. *Lynchburg News*, 21 March 1866; *Lynchburg Virginian*, 14 December 1865; 2 April 1866; 22 January 1867; 3 June 1867; "The Landlord and the Tenant," *Lynchburg Virginian*, 26 March 1868.

77. Jannett Cleland, diary, 15 June 1866, JML; *Lynchburg Virginian*, 9 June 1866; 24 November 1866.

78. *Lynchburg Virginian*, 30 March 1871.

79. Ibid., 10 August 1865; 21 August 1865; 9 December 1865.

80. Ibid., 3 January 1867; 28 March 1867; 30 March 1868; 21 November 1870; 4 March 1871; 30 March 1871.

81. Ibid., 16 January 1867; 25 October 1867; 31 December 1867.

82. Ibid., 7 December 1870; *Lynchburg News,* 19 January 1867; 30 September 1870; 3 October 1870; 4 October 1870.

83. Laurence Shore, *Southern Capitalists: Ideological Leadership of an Elite, 1832–1885* (Chapel Hill: University of North Carolina Press, 1986), 114–19; Shirley, *Congregation Town,* 144–71; *Lynchburg Virginian,* 29 July 1865; 10 November 1868; see also *Lynchburg Virginian,* 7 December 1868; 31 December 1868; 3 April 1869; *Lynchburg News,* 6 June 1866.

84. The new law remitted "all taxes on capital invested, machinery, new buildings and improvements necessary to conduct the same and the profits arising therefrom . . . for the space of ten years." In addition, council would publish the law and appoint a committee of "public-spirited citizens" to distribute it "to all the manufacturing districts of this country and Europe"; *Lynchburg Virginian,* 22 November 1872; City Council, *Resources and Advantages of Lynchburg.*

85. *Lynchburg Virginian,* 26 March 1867; 28 May 1867; 13 June 1868; John Warwick Daniel, "Lynchburg Past and Present," in Hinton Helper, ed, *Centennial Souvenir of Lynchburg Virginia* (New York: South Publishing Company, 1887), 25; W. Asbury Christian, *Lynchburg and Its People* (Lynchburg, Va.: J. P. Bell, 1900), 254–56; Scruggs, *History of Lynchburg,* 131–32; Lowe, *Republicans and Reconstruction,* 150–52; Withers, *Autobiography,* 242–44.

86. Lynchburg Business Directory; *Lewis's Southern Directory, 1871–2* (n.p., n.d.), 169–75; *Lynchburg Virginian,* 23 August 1872.

87. *Lynchburg Virginian,* 5 September 1867; 8 April 1868 Unfortunately, the census taker for the 1870 manufacturing census failed to record several businesses in his report, including Folkes and Winston's cabinet shop. As a result, it is not known how many workers they employed.

88. For a description of the Myers and Goodman tannery, see *Lynchburg Virginian,* 28 April 1869 Button cited a recent article in *Shoe and Leather Reporter,* a trade journal, as his source.

89. 1870 Census, Manufacturing Schedule manuscript microfilm, Campbell County, Virginia.

90. *Lynchburg Virginian,* 5 September 1867; 8 April 1868.

91. The number of jobbers was determined by checking the manufacturing census against contemporary business directories. Ten of the twenty-six leather shop owners were listed as shoemakers who also sold their product; the rest probably produced for local merchants See *Lewis's Southern Directory* and *Lynchburg Business Directory.* The argument here is speculative but based on similar developments in other areas. For descriptions of the evolution of the shoe industry, see Ross Thomson, *The Path to Mechanized Shoe Production in the United States* (Chapel Hill: University of North Carolina Press, 1989); and Alan Dawley, *Class and Community: The Industrial Revolution in Lynn* (Cambridge Mass.: Harvard University Press, 1976).

92. 1870 Census, Population Schedule manuscript microfilm, Lynchburg, Virginia; 1870 Manufacturing Schedule manuscript microfilm. Campbell County, Virginia.

93. Contemporary sources provide only scant information on the rolling mill; hence, I relied on secondary works to guide my discussion See Daniel J. Walko-

witz, *Worker City, Company Town: Iron and Cotton-Worker Protest in Troy and Cohoes, New York, 1855–84* (Urbana: University of Illinois Press, 1978), on the transformation of the iron industry during the mid-nineteenth century; Shirley, *Congregation Town*, 207–13; 232–33 and Jacquelyn Dowd Hall, James LeLoudis, Robert Korstad, Mary Murphy, LuAnn Jones, and Christopher B. Daly, *Like a Family: The Making of a Southern Cotton Mill World* (Chapel Hill: University of North Carolina Press, 1987), on the uneasy transition that Southern rural immigrants made to Southern industrial towns.

94. In June 1867, twenty Lynchburg residents attended a Republican state convention; fourteen of these were identified from the 1870 manuscript census This group included nine merchants or grocers, two city officials, one insurance agent, one hotel clerk, and one brick mason. In May 1871, the *Lynchburg News* printed a list of fifteen Lynchburg Republican Party officers. This group included five merchants and grocers, four tobacconists, five skilled artisans (including a machinist, a silversmith, a tanner, a tailor, and a saddler), and one city employee. See *Lynchburg Virginian*, 15 June 1867; *Lynchburg News*, 19 May 1871; *Marion Record*, 18 June 1867; Lestor Cappon, *Virginia Newspapers, 1821–1935: A Bibliography with Historical Introduction and Notes* (New York: D. Appleton-Century, 1936), 121, 127.

95. Charles Flynn to General Baker, 11 December 1869, House Select Committee on Reconstruction, RG 233, Box 10, NA; Lynchburg Virginian, 1 June 1869; 3 January 1871; *Lynchburg News*, 22 December 1870; 3 January 1871.

96. "Seneca," *Lynchburg Virginian*, 16 April 1868 For similar assessments of the Republican rank and file, see *Lynchburg Virginian*, 6 September 1866; 2 March 1869; 10 February 1871; 30 May 1871; and *Lynchburg News*, 22 October 1867; 27 September 1870; 16 October 1871.

97. *Lynchburg News*, 21 October 1867; 2 November 1867.

98. *Lynchburg Virginian*, 26 September 1867; *Lynchburg News*, 22 October 1867.

99. *Lynchburg Virginian*, 30 May 1871.

100. Ibid., 29 October 1867.

101. *Lynchburg News*, 11 February 1867; 26 March 1867; 18 April 1867.

102. *Lynchburg Virginian*, 3 November 1867.

103. Ibid., 12 June 1869; 24 November 1870; *Lynchburg News*, 20 January 1870; 23 August 1870; 15 February 1871.

104. *Lynchburg News*, 30 September 1872.

105. *Lynchburg Virginian*, 16 March 1866; 19 March 1866; 9 June 1866; *Lynchburg News*, 10 April 1866.

106. *Lynchburg News*, 4 February 1870; 12 February 1870; *Lynchburg News*, 8 January 1870.

NOTES TO CHAPTER FIVE

1. Jannett Cleland, diary, 16 April 1865, Jones Memorial Library, Lynchburg, Virginia (hereafter JML).

2. Cited in Mary Elizabeth Kinnier Bratton, *Our Goodly Heritage: A History of*

the First Presbyterian Church of Lynchburg, Virginia 1815–1940 (Lynchburg, Va.: J. P. Bell, n.d.), 48.

3. John Warwick Craig, "Sermon Preached at Castle Craig, Campbell County, 23 July 1865," John Warwick Craig Sermons, Virginia Historical Society (hereafter VHS).

4. Charles Reagan Wilson, *Baptized in Blood: The Religion of the Lost Cause, 1865–1920* (Athens: University of Georgia Press, 1980), 58–78; Gaines M. Foster, *Ghosts of the Confederacy: Defeat, the Lost Cause, and the Emergence of the New South* (New York: Oxford University Press, 1987), 13–14, 22–24. See also Gerald Linderman, *Embattled Courage: The Experience of Combat in the American Civil War* (New York: Vintage Books, 1987), 255–56; Drew Gilpin Faust, "Christian Soldiers: The Meaning of Revivalism in the Confederate Army," *Journal of Southern History* 53 (1987): 87–90.

5. Craig, "Sermon Preached at Castle Craig."

6. Leon F. Litwack, *Been in the Storm So Long: The Aftermath of Slavery* (New York: Vintage Books, 1979), 468–70; *Lynchburg Virginian*, 8 August 1865; 12 June 1866; 4 July 1866.

7. Wilson, *Baptized in Blood*, 100–104; Joel Williamson, *The Crucible of Race: Black-White Relations in the American South since Emancipation* (New York: Oxford University Press, 1984), 85–93.

8. *Lynchburg News*, 10 March 1866; *Lynchburg Virginian*, 3 October 1866.

9. *Lynchburg Virginian*, 28 September 1865; R. S. Lacey to General Orlando Brown, 29 December 1865, Records of the Bureau of Refugees, Freemen, and Abandoned Lands (hereafter Freedmen's Bureau) Letters Registered, Freedmen's Bureau, RG 105, Press copies of letters sent, series 4072; E. J. Early to R. S. Lacey, 31 October 1866, Freemen's Bureau, RG 105, Letters Received, series 4073, NA; "Proceedings of the Lynchburg District Conference," *Lynchburg Virginian*, 25 August 1868; *Lynchburg News*, 1 June 1872; Bratton, *Our Goodly Heritage, 1865–1890*, 49. Howard N. Rabinowitz, *Race Relations in the Urban South* (Urbana: University of Illinois Press, 1980), 97–98, 205, provides a thorough discussion of how increased segregation contributed to the postwar problem of race control.

10. For discussions of white-black church relations during emancipation and beyond, see Rabinowitz, *Race Relations in the Urban South*, 200–202; Litwack, *Been in the Storm So Long*, 464–71; John W. Blassingame, *Black New Orleans, 1860–1880* (Chicago: University of Chicago Press, 1973), 148–49; Clarence L. Mohr, *On the Threshold of Freedom: Masters and Slaves in Civil War Georgia* (Athens: University of Georgia Press, 1986), 247–65.

11. Minutes of the Protestant methodist Church at Lynchburg, Virginia, December 1869; Minutes of the First Baptist Church of Lynchburg, Virginia, 7 July 1867; 21 July 1867; "Report on the State of Religion of the First Presbyterian Church of Lynchburg, April 1869," in Minute Book of the Session of First Presbyterian Church of Lynchburg, Virginia, 1869; Session Minutes of First Presbyterian Church of Lynchburg, Virginia, 10 October 1869; 12 October 1869.

12. "Report on Reciprocal Duties," 8 April 1868, in Minute Book of the Session of Second Presbyterian Church of Lynchburg, Virginia, 1868; Jacob

Yoder, diary, 20 May 1866, Virginia State Archives (hereafter VSA). Extant records do not explain why the two churches abandoned the unification plan. Since First Presbyterian approved of the plan, it is possible that it was vetoed by either Second Presbyterian or the regional presbytery.

13. Minutes of the First Baptist Church, 10 September 1866; Minutes of the Stewards of Centenary Methodist Church, Lynchburg, Virginia, 1866–1867, passim; Minutes of the Fourth Quarterly Meeting of the Stewards of Court Street Methodist Church, Lynchburg, Virginia, November 1866.

14. Minutes of the Stewards of Centenary Methodist Church, 1866–1867, passim; Minutes of the First Baptist Church, 12 March 1866; 9 April 1866; 13 August 1866; 12 August 1867; Quarterly Meeting Report of the Stewards of the Protestant Methodist Church of Lynchburg, Virginia, December 1869; December 1871; "Report on the State of Religion of the First Presbyterian Church of Lynchburg, April 1869"; Vestry Minutes of St. Paul's Episcopal Church of Lynchburg, Virginia, 22 February 1870; 15 March 1870; 28 December, 1870.

15. Barbara Bellows, *Benevolence among Slaveholders: Assisting the Poor in Charleston, 1670–1860* (Baton Rouge: Louisiana State University, 1993), 121–27; Barbara Bellows, "'My Children, Gentlemen, Are My Own': Poor Women, the Urban Elite, and the Bonds of Obligation in Antebellum Charleston," in Walter J. Fraser, R. Frank Saunders, Jr., and Jon L. Wakelyn, eds., *The Web of Southern Social Relations: Women, Family, and Education* (Athens: University of Georgia Press, 1985), 52–53; Cleland diary, 15 July 1866.

16. Minutes of the First Baptist Church, 10 September 1866; Minutes of the Stewards of Centenary Methodist Church, 1866–1867, passim; Session Minutes of Second Presbyterian Church of Lynchburg, Virginia, 31 May 1869.

17. A similar transformation occurred in other Southern cities at about the same time. See Bellows, *Benevolence among Slaveholders*, 160–66; Michael Shirley, *From Congregation Town to Industrial City: Culture and Social Change in a Southern Community* (New York: New York University Press, 1994), 144–71; James Michael Russell, *Atlanta: City Building in the Old South and the New* (Baton Rouge: Louisiana State University Press, 1988), 171–76; Ted Ownby, *Subduing Satan: Religion, Recreation, and Manhood in the Rural South, 1865–1920* (Chapel Hill: University of North Carolina Press, 1990), 167–77.

18. Minutes of the First Baptist Church, 12 September 1870; Vestry Minutes of St. Paul's Episcopal Church, 15 March 1870; Minutes of the Stewards of Centenary Methodist Church, 8 January 1866; Minutes of the Stewards of Court Street Methodist Church, Lynchburg, Virginia, 29 April 1872.

19. Report of the School Committee, First Baptist Church of Lynchburg, Virginia, 13 January 1868; Minutes of the First Baptist Church, 28 May 1871.

20. Minutes of the Stewards of Court Street Methodist Church, 2 March 1869; Minutes of the Dorcas Society of Lynchburg, 21 December 1871, VSA.

21. Only First Baptist absented itself from the effort, because it was without a minister at the time.

22. *Lynchburg Virginian*, 8 January 1868; 11 January 1868.

23. Bratton, *Our Goodly Heritage*, 50, 57; Vestry Minutes of St. Paul's Episcopal Church, 20 November 1871.

24. Cited in Alfred A. Kern, *Court Street Methodist Church, 1851–1951* (Richmond: Dietz Press, 1951), 37–38; *Lynchburg Virginian*, 13 January 1869; 11 February 1869.

25. See Tables 5:1 and 5:2 in the Appendixes.

26. See Table 5:1 in the Appendixes; Yoder diary, 29 April 1866; 10 June 1866. Yoder later joined First Baptist.

27. For studies that explore the complex and sometimes less than benevolent motives of nineteenth-century urban reformers, see Bellows, *Benevolence among Slaveholders*; Paul E. Johnson, *A Shopkeeper's Millennium: Society and Revivals in Rochester, New York, 1815–1837* (New York: Hill & Wang, 1978), 116–35; Bruce Laurie, *Working People of Philadelphia, 1800–1850* (Philadelphia: Temple University Press, 1980), 33–52; Anthony F. C. Wallace, *Rockdale: The Growth of an American Village in the Early Industrial Revolution* (New York: W. W. Norton & Co., 1972), 296–349; Michael B. Katz, "Origins of the Institutional State," *Marxist Perspectives* 1 (1978): 6–22; David J. Rothman, *The Discovery of the Asylum: Social Order and Disorder in the New Republic* (Boston: Little, Brown, & Co., 1971).

28. "Report to the Third Quarterly Conference of the Methodist Church," 1 November 1869, cited in Kern, *Court Street Methodist Church*, 38.

29. Minutes of the Dorcas Society, 27 December 1871; Cleland diary, 10 March 1867.

30. Minutes of the Dorcas Society, 21 December 1870; Cleland diary, 10 March 1867.

31. Minutes of the Dorcas Society, 21 December 1870.

32. Ownby, *Subduing Satan*, 144–64; Edward L. Ayers, *The Promise of the New South: Life after Reconstruction* (New York: Oxford University Press, 1992), 166–68.

33. The Baptist journal *Religious Herald* covered Earle's complete tour. For a summary of Earle's work in Lynchburg, see "Revival in Lynchburg &c," *Religious Herald*, 19 January 1871.

34. *Lynchburg Virginian*, 6 January 1871; 17 January 1871; 17 February 1871; 22 April 1871; *Lynchburg News*, 10 January 1871; 12 January 1871; 21 February 1871.

35. *Religious Herald*, 19 January 1871; *Lynchburg News*, 19 January 1871; W. E. Judkins, "Conference Report of 31 July 1871," in the Minutes of the Stewards of Court Street Methodist Church; *Lynchburg Virginian*, 17 February 1871.

36. *Lynchburg News*, 6 February 1871; 16 February 1871; *Lynchburg Virginian*, 15 February 1871; 16 February 1871.

37. Richard Lowe, *Republicans and Reconstruction in Virginia, 1856–1870* (Charlottesville: University Press of Virginia, 1991), 164–82; Richard Lowe, "Another Look at Reconstruction in Virginia," *Civil War History* 32 (1986): 56–76; Virginius Dabney, *Virginia: The New Dominion* (New York: Doubleday, 1971), 353–73; Crandall Shifflett, "Gilbert Carlton Walker: Carpetbag Conservative," in Edward Younger, ed., *The Governors of Virginia, 1860–1978* (Charlottesville: University Press of Virginia, 1982), 57–67.

38. *Lynchburg Virginian*, 9 November 1870; 26 May 1871; *Lynchburg News*, 12 May 1871.

39. *Lynchburg News,* 27 April 1871; *Lynchburg Virginian,* 28 April 1871.

40. See Table 5:2 in the Appendixes.

41. See Tables 5:1 and 5:2 in the Appendixes.

42. Session Minutes of First Presbyterian Church, 10 October 1869; 12 October 1869.

43. Quarterly Meeting of the Stewards of the Protestant Methodist Church, January 1867. Centenary Methodist's discipline records—kept as part of its Sunday school records—are incomplete for the period.

44. Recent studies that examine the ritual and function of church discipline in Southern evangelical churches include: Nick Malavis, "Equality under the Lord's Law: The Disciplinary Process in Texas Baptist Churches, 1833–1870," *East Texas Historical Association* 31 (1993): 3–23; Ted Ownby, "Mass Culture, Upper-Class Culture, and the Decline of Church Discipline in the Evangelical South: The 1910 Case of the Godbold Mineral Well Hotel," *Religion and American Culture* 4 (1994): 107–32; Stephen M. Haines, "Southern Baptist Church Discipline, 1880–1939," *Baptist History and Heritage* 20 (1985): 14–27.

45. Session Minutes of First Presbyterian Church, 3 July 1870; 7 March 1871; 18 March 1871; 27 March 1872.

46. See Table 5:2 in the Appendixes.

47. *Lynchburg Virginian,* 30 May 1871.

NOTES TO CHAPTER SIX

1. *Lynchburg News,* 7 August 1866.

2. Ibid.

3. *Lynchburg News,* 18 October 1867; *Lynchburg Virginian,* 18 October 1867.

4. *Lynchburg Virginian,* 17 August 1871; *Lynchburg News,* 17 August 1871; 18 August 1871.

5. *Lynchburg Virginian,* 15 July 1871; 16 July 1871; 7 August 1871; *Lynchburg News,* 15 July 1871.

6. *Lynchburg Virginian,* 22 January 1868; *Law Order Book of the Hustings Court of Lynchburg Virginia,* 3 February 1868, Lynchburg City Clerk's office (hereafter LCC).

7. *Lynchburg Virginian,* 22 March 1867.

8. Edward L. Ayers, *Vengeance and Justice: Crime and Punishment in the Nineteenth-Century American South* (New York: Oxford University Press, 1984), 235–36; Eugene Genovese, "Yeoman Farmers in a Slaveholders' Democracy," in Eugene Genovese and Elizabeth Fox-Genovese, eds., *The Fruits of Merchant Capital: Slavery and Bourgeois Property in the Rise and Expansion of Capitalism* (New York: Oxford University Press, 1983), 249–62; George Fredrickson, *The Black Image in the White Mind: The Debate on Afro-American Character and Destiny, 1817–1914* (New York: Harper & Row, 1971), 64–69.

9. Bertram Wyatt-Brown, *Southern Honor: Ethics and Behavior in the Old South* (New York: Oxford University Press, 1982), 60–66.

10. *Lynchburg Virginian,* 26 September 1865.

11. O. B. Wilcox to Colonel S. F. Chaltin, 2 May 1867, Continental Com-

mands RG 393, Letters Sent From the Military Subdistrict of Lynchburg, Entry 302, v. 99, NA.

12. *Lynchburg Virginian,* 25 June 1867; Edward King, *The Great South: A Record of Journeys* (Hartford, Conn.: American Publishing Company, 1875), 552–60.

13. Roger Lane, *Roots of Violence in Black Philadelphia, 1860–1900* (Cambridge, Mass.: Harvard University Press, 1986), 30–31; R. S. Lacy to General O. Brown, 17 May 1867, Records of the Bureau of Refugees, Freedmen, and Abandoned Lands (hereafter Freedmen's Bureau), RG 105, Records of the Assistant Subassistant Commissioner, Letters Sent, series 4082, vol. 299, National Archives (hereafter NA); *Lynchburg News,* 9 March 1866.

14. *Lynchburg Virginian,* 2 April 1867; 5 April 1867.

15. *Lynchburg News,* 7 February 1870.

16. Ibid., 23 July 1866.

17. Because of the paucity of sources on postwar workshop organization in Lynchburg, evidence is derived from general works on Southern labor history, as well as scattered evidence from Lynchburg sources, especially Jonathan Woolard McLeod, "Black and White Workers: Atlanta during Reconstruction" (PhD. diss., University of California at Los Angeles, 1987), chap 3; Howard N. Rabinowitz, *Race Relations in the Urban South, 1865–1890* (Urbana: University of Illinois Press, 1978), 69–70; Peter J. Rachleff, *Black Labor in the South: Richmond, Virginia, 1865–1890* (Philadelphia: Temple University Press, 1984), 3–12; Eric Arnesen, *Waterfront Workers of New Orleans: Race, Class, and Politics, 1863–1923* (New York: Oxford University Press, 1991), 20–21, 32–34; John William Graves, *Town and Country: Race Relations in an Urban-Rural Context, Arkansas, 1865–1905* (Fayetteville: University of Arkansas Press, 1990), 102–33; Armstead L. Robinson, "Plans Dat Comed from God: Institution Building and the Emergence of Black Leadership in Reconstruction Memphis," in Orville Vernon Burton and Robert C. McMath, Jr., eds., *Toward a New South? Studies in Post-Civil War Southern Communities* (Westport, Conn.: Greenwood Press, 1982), 71–102; *Lynchburg Virginian,* 13 October 1868; 28 April 1869; *Lynchburg News,* 7 June 1872.

18. *Lynchburg Virginian,* 25 January 1866; 26 January 1866; *Lynchburg News,* 9 September 1866; 13 December 1870; 18 February 1872.

19. *Lynchburg News,* 13 December 1870; 18 February 1871; *Lynchburg Virginian,* 10 September 1866. Unfortunately, local newspapers did not publish the outcome of the two trials.

20. Lane, *Roots of Violence,* 137–43. Although Lane notes that handguns did not enter Northern cities until the late nineteenth century, impressionistic evidence suggests that many Southern laborers carried handguns as a matter of course immediately after the war. In addition, ex-soldiers may have had guns and muskets left over from the war. Blacks also possessed firearms at this time, but impressionistic evidence suggests that blacks were not as well armed as whites, in either the quality or the quantity of their weaponry.

21. For former masters' treatment of their ex-slaves see Leon F. Litwack, *Been in the Storm So Long: The Aftermath of Slavery* (New York: Vintage Books, 1979), 372–73; James L. Roark, *Masters without Slaves: Southern Planters in the Civil War and Reconstruction* (New York: W. W. Norton & Co., 1977).

22. *Lynchburg Virginian,* 6 June 1866; 9 June 1866; 6 August 1866.

23. Michael Stephen Hindus, *Prison and Plantation: Crime, Justice, and Authority in Massachusetts and South Carolina, 1767–1878* (Chapel Hill: University of North Carolina Press, xix.

24. *Lynchburg Virginian,* 18 September 1867; *Lynchburg News,* 8 December 1866.

25. *Lynchburg News,* 21 December 1870.

26. *Lynchburg Virginian,* 2 October 1866.

27. Ibid., 19 February 1869.

28. *Lynchburg News,* 15 February 1870.

29. Where the occupation of the victim could be determined, for the even-numbered years between 1866 and 1872, eighteen of forty-nine robberies were against white laborers Since poorer residents were more likely than the wealthy to be left out of both the manuscript census and the business directory, the percentage of laboring white victims was probably higher.

30. Lane, *Roots of Violence,* 95–133; Litwack, *Been in the Storm So Long,* 142–43; Ayers, *Vengeance and Justice,* 165–73; James Borchert, *Alley Life in Washington: Family, Community, Religion, and Folklife in the City, 1850–1970* (Urbana: University of Illinois Press, 1980), 185–95; John W. Blassingame, *Black New Orleans 1860–1880* (Chicago: University of Chicago Press, 1973), 162–63; Rabinowitz, *Race Relations,* 43–48.

31. *Lynchburg Virginian,* 28 May 1867; *Commonwealth v. Walker,"* Circuit Court of Lynchburg, Ended Law Papers for the Virginia, Virginia State Archives (hereafter VSA).

32. Richard C. Wade, *Slavery in the Cities: The South, 1820–1860* (New York: Oxford University Press, 1964), 156–57; Rachleff, *Black Labor in the South,* 63–65.

33. Testimony of John Averitt before the house of Representatives Select Committee on Reconstruction (hereafter House Select Committee on Reconstruction), item 136; 28 January 1869, Gaston Curtis to the House Select Committee on Reconstruction, n.d. (item 148); John Boisseau to the House Select Committee on Reconstruction, n.d. (item 142), all in Records of the U.S. House of Representatives, Fortieth and forty-first Congress: Select Committee on Reconstruction, RG 233, Box 10, NA.

34. Figures are based on a survey of the mayor's court proceedings that were published in the *Lynchburg News* and the *Lynchburg Virginian* during the years 1866, 1868, 1870, and 1872 There are obvious limitations to this source. Newspaper editors used discretion in printing the mayor's court proceedings. As a result, crimes by whites were probably underreported. State court records also have limitations. Because the mayor gave summary judgments against blacks more often than against whites, state court records do not provide a good indication of the actual number of arrested blacks. See Tables 6:1 through 6:5 in the Appendixes.

35. Ayers, *Vengeance and Justice,* 83–87.

36. Louis Stevenson to R. S. Lacey, n.d., Freedmen's Bureau, RG 105, Register of Letters Sent, Records of the Assistant Subassistant Commissioner, series 4083, vol. 91, NA; James Woodall to R. S. Lacey, 21 July 1866, Records of the Assistant Subassistant Commissioner, Freedmen's Bureau, RG 105, Register of

Letters Received, series 4082, vol. 299, NA; Colonel O. B. Wilcox to Colonel S. F. Chalfin, 14 February 1867, Records of the U. S. Army Continental Commands (hereafter Continental Commands), Letters, Telegrams, and Orders Received at the Military Subdistrict of Lynchburg, Virginia (hereafter Letters Received), RG 393, series 302, vol. 99, NA.

37. Register of Complaints to the Freedmen's Court, n.d. (but probably March 1867), Freedmen's Bureau, RG 105, series 4086, vol. 304, NA.

38. O. B. Wilcox to Lieutenant O. B. Read, 30 April 1868, Continental Commands, RG 393, Letters Received, series 304, NA; *Lynchburg News*, 6 January 1870.

39. Republicans of the City of Lynchburg to Colonel F. M. Cooley, 17 February 1869, Continental Commands, RG 393, Letters Received, series 304, NA; "Testimonies of Samuel Kelso, Squire Taliaferro, Robert A. Camm, and Houston Rucker concerning the Incident at Campbell County Court House," 11 May 1868, Continental Commands, RG 393, Reports Received, series 5328, box 3, NA.

40. On the generally conservative racial attitudes of Southern-born Republicans, see Eric Foner, *Reconstruction: America's Unfinished Revolution, 1863–1877* (New York: Harper & Row, 1988), 297–301; Daniel W. Crofts, *Old Southampton: Politics and Society in a Virginia County, 1834–1869* (Charlottesville: University Press of Virginia, 1992), 245–47; 252–54; Richard Lowe, *Republicans and Reconstruction in Virginia, 1856–1870* (Charlottesville: University Press of Virginia, 1991), 81–90.

41. *Commonwealth v. Lewis Williams*, Freedmen's Bureau, RG 105, Register of Complaints to the Freedmen's Court, n.d., series 4086, vol. 304, NA.

42. Colonel F. M. Cooley to Colonel S. F. Chalfin, 17 June 1868, Continental Commands, RG 393, Letters and Circulars Sent from Headquarters at the Military Subdistrict of Lynchburg, Virginia (hereafter, Sent), series 5325, vol. 323, NA; Republicans of the City of Lynchburg to Colonel F. M. Cooley, 17 February 1869, Continental Commands, RG 393, Letters Received, series 304, NA.

43. *Lynchburg Virginian*, 30 March 1869; 26 April 1869.

44. For discussions of the character and sensibilities of Freedmen's Bureau agents, see Litwack, *Been in the Storm So Long*, 282–89; Crofts, *Old Southampton*, 220–25, 229–34; Foner, *Reconstruction*, 148–52.

45. Register of Complaints to the Freedmen's Court, n.d., Freedmen's Bureau, RG 105, series 4086, vol. 304, NA.

46. *Lynchburg News*, 8 April 1871.

47. See Table 6:5 in the Appendixes.

48. See Tables 6:1 through 6:5 in the Appendixes.

49. Register of Complaints to the Freedmen's Court, n.d., but probably February 1867; Freedmen's Bureau, RG 105, series 4086, vol. 304; Wilcox to Colonel S. F. Chalfin, 9 September 1867, Continental Commands, RG 393, Letters Sent, series 302, vol. 99.

50. Ayers, *Vengeance and Justice*, 173–74; Lowe, *Republicans and Reconstruction*, 47–49; Rabinowitz, *Race Relations*, 51–52; Foner, *Reconstruction*, 150, 199–201, 204, 423; "To the Honorable Judge of the Corporation Court for the City of

Lynchburg from the Grand Jury," *Law Order Book of the Corporation Court of Lynchburg, Virginia,* 7 February 1871, LCC.

51. *Lynchburg Virginian,* 3 November 1865; 17 November 1865; 27 January 1866.

52. *Lynchburg News,* 8 June 1868; *Lynchburg Virginian,* 8 June 1868; *Law Order Book of the Hustings Court,* 6 August 1868.

53. *Lynchburg News,* 5 December 1866.

54. *Lynchburg Virginian,* 29 July 1871; 16 August 1871; 17 August 1871; 6 January 1872; 8 January 1872.

55. *Lynchburg News,* 8 October 1866; 9 October 1866; 25 September 1872.

56. *Lynchburg Virginian,* 6 August 1868; *Lynchburg News,* 6 August 1868; *Lynchburg News,* 27 February 1872; 20 August 1872.

57. *Lynchburg News,* 3 July 1872 See also Lane, *Roots of Violence,* 9–12; Eric Monkkonen, *Police in Urban America, 1860–1920* (Cambridge: Cambridge University Press, 1981).

58. *Lynchburg News,* 9 March 1866; 10 March 1866.

59. "Testimonies of Mr Rudd, D. C. Wright, John Averitt, and Squire Taliaferro before the Military Commissioner," 30 April 1868, Continental Commands, RG 393, Letters Received, series 304, NA; *Lynchburg Virginian,* 27 April 1868.

60. *Lynchburg News,* 18 January 1867; 9 October 1866.

61. *Lynchburg Virginian,* 28 December 1868.

62. Ibid., 13 February 1869.

63. *Lynchburg News,* 6 July 1866.

64. Ibid., 26 May 1866; 18 March 1867; 20 July 1867; 16 September 1867; O. B. Wilcox to Colonel S. F. Chalfin, 26 September 1867; 27 September 1867, Continental Commands, RG 393, Letters Sent, series 302, vol. 99, NA; Louis Stevenson to Charles F. Robe, 20 October 1867, Continental Commands, RG 393, Letters Received, series 304, NA; *Lynchburg Virginian,* 30 August 1867; 1 June 1869; 24 July 1870.

65. For studies of the postwar changes in urban black behavior, see Rabinowitz, *Race Relations,* 334–35; Lane, *Roots of Violence,* 146–47; Jannette Thomas Greenwood, *Bittersweet Legacy: The Black and White "Better Classes" in Charlotte, 1850–1910* (Chapel Hill: University of North Carolina Press, 1994), 215–16; Robinson, "Plans Dat Comed from God."

66. R. S. Lacey to General O. Brown, 31 August 1867, Freedmen's Bureau, RG 105, Records of the Subassistant Commissioner, Letter Sent, series 4082, NA.

67. "Testimonies of Samuel Kelso, Squire Taliaferro, Robert A Camm, and Houston Rucker concerning the Incident at Campbell County Court House," 11 May 1868, Continental Commands, RG 393, Reports Received, series 5328, box 3, NA; Louis Stevenson to O. Brown, 30 November 1867, Freedmen's Bureau, RG 105, Records of the Assistant Subassistant Commissioner, Letters Sent, series 4082, NA; *Lynchburg News,* 18 October 1867; Lieutenant Colonel Carlton Boyd to Lieutenant Colonel E. W. Stone, 23 August 1869, Continental Commands, RG 393, Letters Sent, series 5325, NA; O. B. Wilcox to Colonel S. F. Chalfin, 26 September 1867; 27 September 1867, Continental Commands; *Lynchburg Virginian,* 1 June 1869.

68. *Lynchburg Virginian*, 27 March 1868; 9 April 1868; 13 April 1868.

69. Louis Stevenson to O Brown, 31 July 1867, Freedmen's Bureau, RG 105, Records of the Assistant Subassistant Commissioner, Letter Sent, series 4082, NA.

70. *Lynchburg News*, 1 November 1871; Testimony of John Averitt before the House Select Committee on Reconstruction, 28 January 1869.

NOTES TO THE EPILOGUE

1. Hinton Helper, "Introduction," in Hinton Helper, ed., *Centennial Souvenir of Lynchburg, Virginia* (New York: South Publishing Company, 1887), 5, 6.

2. John Warwick Daniel, "Lynchburg Past and Present," in Helper, ed., *Centennial Souvenir*, 8–26.

3. Charles Reagan Wilson, *Baptized in Blood: The Religion of the Lost Cause, 1865–1920* (Athens: University of Georgia Press, 1980), 22–23, 73–77; Gaines M. Foster, *Ghosts of the Confederacy: Defeat, the Lost Cause, and the Emergence of the New South* (New York: Oxford University Press, 1987), 88–103.

4. Daniel, "Lynchburg Past and Present," 23–24; Michael J. Schewel, "Local Politics in Lynchburg, Virginia, in the 1880s," *Virginia Magazine of History and Biography* 89 (1981): 170–72.

5. John Langston Mitchell, "Negro Businesses in Lynchburg, 1880–1910" (M.A. thesis, Virginia State College, 1952), 59–62.

6. Schewel, "Local Politics in Lynchburg," 174–75; Leslie Sheldon Hough, "Discontent in a Southern Tobacco Town: Lynchburg, Virginia Workers in the 1880s," (M.A. thesis, University of Virginia, 1973), 29–44.

7. Schewel, "Local Politics," 170–3.

8. Ibid., 175–77; Harry S. Ferguson, "The Participation of the Lynchburg, Virginia, Negro in Politics, 1865–1900," (M.A. thesis, Virginia State College, 1950), 16–27; Hough, "Discontent in a Southern Tobacco Town," 45–50, 57–61.

9. Thomas Bender, *Community and Social Change in America* (Baltimore: Johns Hopkins University Press, 1978), 110–17.

10. Raymond H. Pulley, *Old Virginia Restored: An Interpretation of the Progressive Impulse, 1870–1930* (Charlottesville: University Press of Virginia, 1968), 83–84, 101–4; Allen Moger, *Virginia: Bourbonism to Byrd* (Charlottesville: University Press of Virginia, 1968), 188–97; Virginius Dabney, *Virginia: The New Dominion* (New York: Doubleday, 1971), 430–31, 435–36.

Selected Bibliography

MANUSCRIPT COLLECTIONS

Perkins Library, Duke University

Bagby, George. Papers.
Blackford, Charles, and Thomas Jellis, Kirpatrick. Papers.
Brodnox, J. G. Papers.
Brown, Alexander. Papers.
Burton, Robert Oswald. Papers.
DeSotie, J. Howard. Papers.
Dillard, John James. Papers.
Dimitry, John B. S. Papers.
Dudley, John. Papers
Garland, James. Papers.
Harris, David B. Diary of an anonymous woman.
Hewitt, Richard Newton. Papers.
Humphries, E. J. Papers.
Kelley, Thomas. Papers.
Massie, William. Papers.
Mitchell, Jacob Duche. Diary. 1860.
Moncure, St. Leger Landon. Papers.
Munford-Ellis Family. Papers. George Munford Division.
Murrell, John C. Papers.
Oakey Family. Papers.
Pace, William. Papers.

Ramsey Family. Papers.
Warwick and Read. Papers.
Weston, George Harry. Diary.
Winfree Family. Papers.

Jones Memorial Library, Lynchburg, Virginia

Allen Family. Papers
Blackford Family. Papers.
Cleland, Jannett. Diary.
Clement, George Washington. Account book.
Douglas, John B. "Recollections of a Refugee." N.d. Unpublished manuscript.
Evans, D. R. Papers.
Forsberg, Mary. "Hospital Reminiscences." 1901. Unpublished Manuscript.
Garland, Samuel Jr., and Charles Slaughter. Papers.
Graham, Tazewell T. Papers.
Henderson, Walter. Papers.
Henry, John L., and Peter B. Akers. "A History of a Campaign, Compiled from Copious Notes Taken on the Field, as the Incidents Occurred." N.d. Unpublished manuscript.
Kersey, James. Papers.
Langhorne Family. Papers.
Lynchburg City Ordinances. 1858–1866.
Moorman, Edmond. "Records and Events of the Beauregard Rifles" (edited by Hunter Marshall), 1907. Unpublished manuscript.
Ostrander, Charles. Diary
Payne, John Meem. "Recollections of Lynchburg." N.d. Unpublished manuscript.
Robertston, John. Papers.

Lynchburg Museum System

Anonymous. "Our Queen." N.d. Unpublished manuscript.
Mitchell, Jacob Duche. Diary. 1857, 1861, 1862.
Payne, Mrs. John Meem. "A Brief Outline of My Life for the Benefit of My Children." N.d. Unpublished manuscript.
Terrell, John J. Papers.

National Archives

United States Census Office. Manuscripts of Manufacturing Schedule microfilm, Campbell County Virginia, 1860 and 1870.
———. Manuscript of Population Schedule microfilm, Lynchburg, Virginia, 1860 and 1870.
———. Manuscript of Slave Schedule microfilm, Lynchburg, Virginia, 1860.
Records of the Bureau of Refugees, Freedmen, and Abandoned Lands. RG 105. Education Reports for the Superintendent of Education for the State of Vir-

ginia (microfilm copy). Records of the Subassistant Commissioner, Seventh District of Virginia. Letters Sent, Letters and Endorsements Received, Special Orders Issued, Orders and Circulars Received; Contracts and Indentures. Records of the Assistant Subassistant Commissioner, Seventh District of Virginia. Letters Sent; Letters Received and Endorsements; Letters and Orders Received; Proceedings of the Freedmen's Court and Arrest Register; Register of Complaints.

Records of the Confederacy. RG 109. Records of the Medical Department. Records of the Medical Directors. Records of Hospitals in Virginia.

Records of the U.S. Army Continental Commands, 1821–1920. RG 393. Letters and Circulars Sent from Headquarters at the Military Subdistrict of Lynchburg, Virginia. Letters, Telegrams, and Orders Received at the Headquarters of the Military Subdistrict of Lynchburg, Virginia. General Orders and Special Orders of the Military Subdistrict of Lynchburg, Virginia. Letters Sent by the Military Commissioner, Twenty-third Division of Virginia. Register of Letters Received by the Twenty-third Division of Virginia. Endorsements Sent by Twenty-third Division of Virginia. Register of Letters Received relating to civil cases in the Twenty-third Division of Virginia. Record of Appointed Civil Officers in the Twenty-third Division. Record of Civil Cases Pending and Disposed in Twenty-third Division of Virginia.

Records of the U.S. House of Representatives, Fortieth and Forty-first Congress, Select Committee on Reconstruction: Committee Papers.

Southern Historical Collection, University of North Carolina at Chapel Hill

Beale-Davis Family. Papers.
Blackford Family. Papers.
Blackford, Launcelot. Diary.
Confederate Papers.
Goodwin-Morris Family. Papers.
Kirby-Smith, Edward. Papers.
Meredith, Gustavus. Papers.
Perkins, Constantine Marrast. Papers.
Proffit Family. Papers.

Alderman Library, University of Virginia

Blackford Family. Papers.
Cabell, William D. Papers.
Daniel, John Warwick. Papers.
Garland, Slaughter, and Diggs Family. Papers.
Kean, Robert Garlick Hill. Papers.
King Family. Papers.
Lynchburg Families. Papers.
Phelps, Charles Richard. Papers.
Works Project Administration. Virginia Folklore Collection.

Virginia Historical Society

Bagby Family. Papers.
Chamberlayne Family. Papers.
Confederate Army. Papers.
Craig, John Warwick. Sermons.
Early Family. Papers.
Garland Family. Papers.
Martin, George Alexander. Diary.
Rives, William Cabell. Papers.
Roberts Family. Papers.
Williams, Septimus Ligon. Papers.

Virginia State Archives

Brookes, St. George Tucker. "Autobiography." N.d. Unpublished manuscript.
Dorcas Society of Lynchburg. Minutes. 1870–1872.
Ended Law Papers for the Circuit Court of Lynchburg. Criminal and Civil Cases,
    1858–1872.
Lynchburg Free Negro Register. 1860–1865.
Petitions to the State Legislature.
Sommerville, H. C. Diary.
Works Projects Administration. Folklore Collection: Civil War Recollections.
Yoder, Jacob. Diary.

CHURCH RECORDS

Centenary Methodist Church. Lynchburg, Virginia.
Court Street Methodist Church. Lynchburg, Virginia.
First Baptist Church. Lynchburg, Virginia.
First Presbyterian Church. Lynchburg, Virginia.
Grace Memorial Church. Lynchburg, Virginia.
Holy Cross Catholic Church. Lynchburg, Virginia.
Protestant Methodist Church. Lynchburg, Virginia.
Presbyterian Church. Lynchburg, Virginia.
St. Paul's Episcopal Church. Lynchburg, Virginia.

LYNCHBURG CITY CLERK'S OFFICE

Circuit Court Minute Books. Vols. 1858–1872.
Corporation Court Minute Books. Criminal Cases. Vols. 1858–1872.
Ended Law Papers. Miscellaneous.
Hustings Court Minute Books. Criminal Cases. Vols. 1858–1872.
Law Order Books of the Circuit Court of Lynchburg, Virginia, Vols. 1858–1872.

Law Order Book of the Corporation Court, Vols. 1858–1872.
Law Order Books of the Hustings Court of Lynchburg, Virginia, Vols. 1858–1872.
Register of Marriages. Vols. 1858–1872.
Will Books. Vols. 1858–1872.

PERIODICALS

Hunt's Merchants' Magazine and Commercial Review. 1858–1872.
Lynchburg News. 1866–1872.
Lynchburg Republican. 1863, 1865–1872.
Lynchburg Virginian. 1856–1872.
Marion Record. 1868.
Religious Herald. 1865–1872.

GOVERNMENT DOCUMENTS

U.S. Bureau of the Census. Eighth Census. *Agriculture of the United States in 1860; Compiled from the Original Returns of the Eighth Census.* Washington, D.C.: Government Printing Office, 1864.
———. Eighth Census. *Manufactures of the United States in 1860; Compiled from the Original Returns of the Eighth Census.* Washington, D.C.: Government Printing Office, 1864.
———. Eighth Census. *Population of the United States in 1860; Compiled from the Original Returns of the Eighth Census.* Washington, D.C.: Government Printing Office: 1864.
———. Ninth Census. *The Statistics of the Population of the United States; Compiled from the Original Returns of the Ninth Census (1870).* Washington, D.C.: Government Printing Office, 1872.
———. Ninth Census. *The Statistics of the Wealth and Industry of the United States; Compiled from the Original Returns of the Ninth Census (1870).* Washington, D.C.: Government Printing Office, 1872.
———. Tenth Census. *Statistics of the Population of the United States at the Tenth Census (1880).* Washington, D.C.: Government Printing Office, 1883.
The War of the Rebellion: A Compilation of the Official Records of the Union and Confederate Armies. Washington, D.C.: Government Printing Office: 1882.

PUBLISHED PRIMARY SOURCES

Bagby, George. *Canal Reminiscences: Recollections of Travel in the Old Days on the James River & Kanawha Canal.* Richmond: West, Johnson & Co., 1879.
———. *Selections from the Miscellaneous Writings of George W. Bagby.* Richmond: Whittet & Shepperson, 1884.

Blackford, L. Minor. *Mine Eyes Have Seen the Glory: The Story of a Virginia Lady, Mary Berkeley Minor Blackford, 1802–1896, Who Taught Her Sons to Hate Slavery and to Love the Union.* Cambridge, Mass.: Harvard University Press, 1954.

Blackford, Susan Leigh, ed. *Letters from Lee's Army: Or the Memoirs of Life in and out of the Army of Virginia during the War between the States.* 1894 Reprint. New York: Charles Scribner's Sons, 1947.

Blackford, William W. *War Years with Jeb Stuart.* 1945. Rev. ed. Baton Rouge: Louisiana State University Press, 1993.

Brown, Murray L., ed. "The Civil War Letters of James W. Old." *Manuscripts* 42 (1990), 129–142.

Buckley, Cornelius M., ed. *A Frenchman, a Chaplain, a Rebel: The War Letters of Pere Louis-Hippolyte Gache, S.J.* Chicago: Loyola University Press, 1981.

Caldwell, Roy Von. *The Genealogy of James Caldwell and His Descendants, 1750–68.* Newton, N.C.: n.p., 1968.

City Council of Lynchburg. *Resources and Advantages of Lynchburg, Virginia and Tributary Country.* Lynchburg, Va.: Virginian Job Office, 1872.

"The Confederate Column." *Lynchburg News.* 1959–1960.

Dennett, John R. *The South as It Is, 1865–6.* Edited by Henry M. Christman. New York: Viking Press, 1965.

Early, Jubal. *Autobiographical Sketch and Narrative of the War between the States.* Philadelphia, 1912.

Early, R. H. *Campbell Chronicles and Family Sketches Embracing the History of Campbell County, Virginia, 1782–1926.* Lynchburg: J. P. Bell, 1927.

Edwards, John, E. *The Confederate Soldier: Being a Memorial Sketch of George N. and Bushrod W. Harris, Privates in the Confederate Army.* New York: Blelock, 1868.

Fletcher, William Andrew. *Rebel Private: Front and Rear.* 1908 reprint. Austin: University of Texas Press, 1954.

Helper, Hinton, ed. *Centennial Souvenir of Lynchburg, Virginia.* New York: South Publishing Company, 1887.

Hotchkiss, Jedediah. *Make Me a Map of the Valley: The Civil War Journal of Stonewall Jackson's Topographer.* Edited. by Archie McDonald. Dallas: Southern Methodist University Press, 1973.

Johnson, John Lipscomb. *Autobiographical Notes.* Privately printed, 1958.

King, Edward. *The Great South: A Record of Journeys in Louisiana, Texas, the Indian Territory, Missouri, Arkansas, Mississippi, Alabama, Georgia, Florida, South Carolina, North Carolina, Kentucky, Tennessee, Virginia, West Virginia, and Maryland.* Hartford, Conn.: American Publishing Company, 1875.

Langhorne, Orra. *Southern Sketches from Virginia, 1881–1901.* Edited by Charles E. Wynes. Charlottesville: University Press of Virginia, 1964.

Lewis's Southern Directory, 1871–2. N.p., n.d.

Longstreet, James. *From Manassas to Appomattox: Memoirs of the Civil War in America.* 1896. Reprint. Bloomington: Indiana University Press, 1976.

Lynchburg Business Directory. Lynchburg, Va., 1873.

Morgan, W. H. *Personal Reminiscences of the War of 1861–5.* Lynchburg, Va.: J. P. Bell, 1911.

Owen, Narcissa. *Memoirs of Narcissa Owen, 1831–1907.* Washington, D.C., 1907.
Payne and Blackford's Lynchburg Business Directory. Lynchburg, Va.: J. P. Bell, 1859.
Pollack, Edward, and S. C. Jordan. *Sketchbook of Lynchburg and Its People and Trade.* Lynchburg, Va.: Virginian Job Office, 1887.
Ramsey, James B. *"The Elders That Rule Well": A Sermon Preached at Lexington, Virginia, April 4th, 1855, at the Opening of Lexington Presbytery.* Lexington, Va.: Smith & Fuller, 1855.
Reese, George, ed. *Proceedings of the Virginia State Convention of 1861.* Richmond: Virginia State Library, 1965.
Reid, Whitelaw. *After the War: A Tour of the Southern States.* ed. C. Vann Woodward. 1866. Reprint. New York: Harper & Row, 1965.
Royall, Anne. *Mrs. Royall's Southern Tour or Second Series of the Black Book.* 3 volumes. Washington, D.C., 1830.
Schwaab, Eugene L., ed. *Travels in the Old South: Selected from Periodicals of the Times.* Lexington: University Press of Kentucky, 1973.
Sketches and Recollections of Lynchburg by the Oldest Inhabitant. Richmond, 1858.
Virginia and Tennessee Railroad Company. *A Prospectus of the Virginia and Tennessee Railroad Co., concerning the sale of $1,000,000 of their bonds, under an act of the legislature of Virginia; together with the opinions of the leading journals of the country upon the means and prospects of the company.* Richmond: Dispatch Job Office, 1855.
von Briesen, Martha, ed. *The Letters of Elijah Fletcher.* Charlottesville: University Press of Virginia, 1965.
Weld, Charles. *A Vacation Tour in the United States of America.* London, 1855.
Wilson, William Lyne. *A Borderland Confederate.* Edited by Festus P. Summers. Pittsburgh: University of Pittsburgh Press, 1962.
Withers, Robert Enoch. *Autobiography of an Octogenarian.* Roanoke, Va: Stone Printing, 1907.

PUBLISHED SECONDARY SOURCES

Arnesen, Eric. *Waterfront Workers of New Orleans: Race, Class, and Politics, 1863–1923.* New York: Oxford University Press, 1991.
Ash, Stephen V. *Middle Tennessee Society Transformed, 1860–1870: War and Peace in the Upper South.* Baton Rouge: Louisiana State University Press, 1988.
Ayers, Edward L. *The Promise of the New South: Life after Reconstruction.* New York: Oxford University Press, 1992.
———. *Vengeance and Justice: Crime and Punishment in the Nineteenth-Century American South.* New York: Oxford University Press, 1984.
Bailey, Fred Arthur. *Class and Tennessee's Confederate Generation.* Chapel Hill: University of North Carolina Press, 1987.
Bell, Robert T. *The Eleventh Virginia Infantry.* Lynchburg, Va.: H. E. Howard, 1985.

Bellows, Barbara. *Benevolence among Slaveholders: Assisting the Poor in Charleston, 1670–1860.* Baton Rouge: Louisiana State University Press, 1993.

Bender, Thomas. *Community and Social Change in America.* Baltimore: Johns Hopkins University Press, 1978.

Beringer, Richard, Herman Hattaway, Archer Jones, and William Still, Jr. *Why the South Lost the Civil War.* Athens: University of Georgia Press, 1986.

Berlin, Ira. *Slaves without Masters: The Free Negro in the Antebellum South.* New York: Oxford University Press, 1974.

Berlin, Ira, and Herbert Gutman. "Natives and Immigrants, Free Men and Slaves: Urban Workingmen in the Antebellum South." *American Historical Review* 88 (1983): 1175–1200.

Billings, Dwight B., Jr. *Planters and the Making of a "New South": Class, Politics, and Development in North Carolina, 1865–1900.* Chapel Hill: University of North Carolina Press, 1979.

Blassingame, John W. *Black New Orleans, 1860–1880.* Chicago: University of Chicago Press. 1973.

———. *The Slave Community: Plantation Life in the Antebellum South.* New York: Oxford University Press, 1972.

Boles, John B., ed. *Masters and Slaves in the House of the Lord: Race and Religion in the American South, 1740–1870.* Lexington: University Press of Kentucky, 1988.

Boles, John B., and Evelyn Thomas Nolan, eds. *Interpreting Southern History: Historiographical Essays in Honor of Sanford W. Higginbotham.* Baton Rouge: Louisiana State University Press, 1987.

Borchert, James. *Alley Life in Washington: Family, Community, Religion, and Folklife in the City, 1850–1970.* Urbana: University of Illinois Press, 1980.

Bratton, Mary Elizabeth Kinnier. *Our Goodly Heritage: A History of the First Presbyterian Church of Lynchburg, Virginia, 1815–1940.* Lynchburg, Va.: J. P. Bell, n.d.

Brewer, James H. *The Confederate Negro: Virginia's Craftsmen and Military Laborers, 1861–1865.* Durham, N.C.: Duke University Press, 1969.

Brown, Douglas Summers. *A History of Lynchburg's Pioneer Quakers and Their Meeting House, 1754–1936.* Lynchburg, Va.: J. P. Bell, 1936.

Bruce, Dickson D., Jr. *And They All Sang Hallelujah: Plain-Folk Camp-Meeting Religion, 1800–1845.* Knoxville: University of Tennessee Press, 1974.

———. *Violence and Culture in the Antebellum South.* Austin: University of Texas Press, 1979.

Bruce, Kathleen. *Virginia Iron Manufacture in the Slave Era.* New York: Augustus M. Kelley, 1968.

Burton, Orville Vernon. *In My Father's House Are Many Mansions: Family and Community in Edgefield, South Carolina.* Chapel Hill: University of North Carolina Press, 1985.

Burton, Orville Vernon, and Robert C. McMath, eds. *Class, Conflict, and Consensus: Antebellum Community Studies.* Westport, Conn.: Greenwood Press, 1982.

———, eds. *Toward a New South? Studies in Post-Civil War Southern Communities.* Westport, Conn.: Greenwood Press, 1982.

Cain, Marvin R. "A 'Face of Battle' Needed: An Assessment of Motives and Men in Civil War Historiography." *Civil War History* 28 (1982): 5–27.

Campbell, Randolph B. *A Southern Community in Crisis: Harrison County, Texas, 1850–1880.* Austin: University of Texas Press, 1983.

Cappon, Lester. *Virginia Newspapers, 1821–1935: A Bibliography with Historical Introduction and Notes.* New York: D. Appleton-Century, 1936.

Carter, Dan T. "The Anatomy of Fear: The Christmas Day Insurrection Scare of 1865." *Journal of Southern History* 42 (1976): 345–364.

Cell, John W. *The Highest Stage of White Supremacy: The Origins of Segregation in South Africa and the American South.* Cambridge: Cambridge University Press, 1982.

Chambers, S. Allen, Jr., *Lynchburg: An Architectural History.* Charlottesville: University Press of Virginia, 1981.

Channing, Steven A. *Crisis of Fear: Secession in South Carolina.* New York: W. W. Norton & Co., 1970.

Christian, W. Asbury. *Lynchburg and Its People.* Lynchburg, Va.: J. P. Bell, 1900.

Click, Patricia C. *The Spirit of the Times: Amusements in Nineteenth-Century Baltimore, Norfolk, and Richmond.* Charlottesville: University Press of Virginia, 1989.

Clinton, Catherine. *The Other Civil War: American Women in the Nineteenth Century.* New York: Hill & Wang, 1984.

Clinton, Catherine, and Nina Silber, eds. *Divided Houses: Gender and the Civil War.* New York: Oxford University Press, 1992.

Cobb, James C. "Beyond Planters and Industrialists: A New Perspective on the New South." *Journal of Southern History* 54 (1988): 45–68.

Cooper, William J. *The South and the Politics of Slavery, 1828–1856.* Baton Rouge: Louisiana State University Press, 1978.

Crofts. Daniel W. *Old Southampton: Politics and Society in a Virginia County, 1834–1869.* Charlottesville: University Press of Virginia, 1992.

———. *Reluctant Confederates: Upper South Unionists in the Secession Crisis.* Chapel Hill: University of North Carolina Press, 1989.

Curry, Leonard. *The Free Black in Urban America, 1800–1850: The Shadow of the Dream.* Chicago: University of Chicago Press, 1981.

Dabney, Virginius. *Virginia: The New Dominion.* New York: Doubleday, 1971.

Daniel, W. Harrison. "Old Lynchburg College, 1859–1869." *Virginia Magazine of History and Biography* 88 (1980): 446–77.

———. *Virginia Baptists, 1860–1920.* Bedford, VA: The Print Shop, 1987.

Dawley, Alan. *Class and Community: The Industrial Revolution in Lynn.* Cambridge, Mass.: Harvard University Press, 1976.

DeCredico, Mary. *Patriotism for Profit: Georgia's Urban Entrepreneurs and the Confederate War Effort.* Chapel Hill: University of North Carolina Press, 1990.

Dew, Charles B. "Black Ironworkers and the Slave Insurrection Panic of 1856." *Journal of Southern History* 41 (1975): 321–38.

———. "Disciplining Slave Ironworkers in the Antebellum South: Coercion, Conciliation, and Accommodation." *American Historical Review* 79 (1974): 393–418.

Diner, Hasia R. *Erin's Daughters in America: Irish Immigrant Women in the Nineteenth Century.* Baltimore: Johns Hopkins University Press, 1983.

Doyle, Don H. *Nashville in the New South, 1880–1930.* Knoxville: University of Tennessee Press, 1985.

———. *New Men, New Cities, New South: Atlanta, Nashville, Charleston, Mobile, 1860–1910.* Chapel Hill: University of North Carolina Press, 1990.

Dublin, Thomas. *Women at Work: The Transformation of Work and Community in Lowell, Massachusetts, 1826–1860.* New York: Columbia University Press, 1979.

DuBois, W.E.B. *Black Reconstruction in America, 1860–1880.* New York: Meridian, 1935.

Dunaway, Wayland Fuller. *History of the James River and Kanawha Company.* New York: Columbia University Press, 1922.

Durrill, Wayne K. *War of Another Kind: A Southern Community in the Great Rebellion.* New York: Oxford University Press, 1990.

Escott, Paul D. *Many Excellent People: Power and Privilege in North Carolina, 1850–1900.* Chapel Hill: University of North Carolina Press, 1985.

Escott, Paul D., and J. J. Crow. "The Social Order and Violent Disorder: An Analysis of North Carolina in the Revolution and the Civil War." *Journal of Southern History* 52 (1986): 372–402.

Evans, Willie McKee. *Ballots and Fence Rails: Reconstruction on the Lower Cape Fear.* Chapel Hill: University of North Carolina Press, 1967.

Faust, Drew Gilpin. "Christian Soldiers: The Meaning of Revivalism in the Confederate Army." *Journal of Southern History* 53 (1987): 63–89.

———. *The Creation of Confederate Nationalism: Ideology and Identity in the Civil War South.* Baton Rouge: Louisiana State University Press, 1988.

Fellman, Michael. *Inside War: The Guerrilla Conflict in Missouri during the American Civil War.* New York: Oxford University Press, 1989.

Fields, Barbara Jeanne. *Slavery and Freedom on the Middle Ground: Maryland during the Nineteenth Century.* New Haven, Conn.: Yale University Press, 1985.

Foner, Eric. *Nothing but Freedom: Emancipation and Its Legacy.* Baton Rouge: Louisiana State University Press, 1983.

———. *Politics and Ideology in the Age of the Civil War.* New York: Oxford University Press, 1980.

———. *Reconstruction: America's Unfinished Revolution, 1863–1877.* New York: Harper & Row, 1988.

Foster, Gaines. *Ghosts of the Confederacy: Defeat, the Lost Cause, and the Emergence of the New South.* New York: Oxford University Press, 1987.

Fox-Genovese, Elizabeth. *Within the Plantation Household: Black and White Women in the Old South.* Chapel Hill: University of North Carolina Press, 1988.

Fraser, Walter J., Jr., R. Frank Saunders, Jr., and Jon L. Wakelyn, eds. *The Web of Southern Social Relations: Women, Family, and Education.* Athens: University of Georgia Press, 1985.

Fredrickson, George. *The Black Image in the White Mind: The Debate on Afro-American Character and Destiny, 1817–1914.* New York: Harper & Row, 1971.

Friedman, Jean E. *The Enclosed Garden: Women and Community in the Evangelical South, 1830–1900.* Chapel Hill: University of North Carolina Press, 1985.

Gallman, J. Matthew. *Mastering Wartime: A Social History of Philadelphia during the Civil War.* New York: Cambridge University Press, 1990.

Genovese, Eugene D. *Roll, Jordan, Roll: The World the Slaves Made.* New York: Vintage Books, 1972.

Genovese, Eugene, and Elizabeth Fox-Genovese, eds. *The Fruits of Merchant Capital: Slavery and Bourgeois Property in the Rise and Expansion of Capitalism.* New York: Oxford University Press, 1983.

Goldfield, David R. "Communities and Regions: The Diverse Cultures of Virginia." *The Virginia Magazine of History and Biography* 95(1987):429–452.

———. *Cotton Fields and Skyscrapers: Southern City and Region.* Baton Rouge: Louisiana State University Press, 1982.

———. *Urban Growth in the Age of Sectionalism: Virginia, 1847–1861.* Baton Rouge: Louisiana State University Press, 1977.

———. "Urban-Rural Relations in the Old South: The Example of Virginia." *Journal of Urban History* 2 (1976): 146–68.

———. "The Urban South: A Regional Framework." *American Historical Review* 86 (1981): 1009–34.

Goldin, Claudia Dale. *Urban Slavery in the American South, 1820–1860: A Quantitative History.* Chicago: University of Chicago Press, 1976.

Gorn, Elliott J. "Good-bye Boys, I Die a True American: Homicide, Nativism, and Working-Class Culture in Antebellum New York City." *Journal of American History* 74 (1987): 388–410.

———. "Gouge and Bite, Pull Hair and Scratch: The Social Significance of Fighting in the Southern Backcountry." *American Historical Review* 90 (1985): 18–43.

Graves, John William. *Town and Country: Race Relations in an Urban-Rural Context, Arkansas, 1865–1905.* Fayetteville: University of Arkansas Press, 1990.

Greenberg, Kenneth. "The Nose, the Lie and the Duel in the Antebellum South." *American Historical Review* 95 (1990): 57–74.

Greenwood, Janette Thomas. *Bittersweet Legacy: The Black and White "Better Classes" in Charlotte, 1850–1910.* Chapel Hill: University of North Carolina Press, 1994.

Gutman, Herbert G. *The Black Family in Slavery and Freedom, 1750–1925.* New York: Vintage Books, 1976.

———. *Work, Culture, and Society in Industrializing America: Essays in American Working-Class and Social History.* New York: Vintage Books, 1977.

Hackney, Sheldon, *"Origins of the New South* in Retrospect." *Journal of Southern History* 38 (1972): 193–216.

Hahn, Steven. *The Roots of Southern Populism: Yeoman Farmers and the Transformation of the Georgia Upcountry, 1850–1890.* New York: Oxford University Press, 1983.

Hahn, Steven, and Jonathan Prude, eds. *The Countryside in the Age of Capitalist Transformation: Essays in the Social History of Rural America.* Chapel Hill: University of North Carolina Press, 1985.

Haines, Stephen M. "Southern Baptist Church Discipline, 1880–1939." *Baptist History and Heritage* 20 (1985): 14–27.

Hall, Jacquelyn Dowd, James LeLoudis, Robert Korstad, Mary Murphy, LuAnn Jones, and Christopher B. Daly. *Like a Family: The Making of a Southern Cotton Mill World*. Chapel Hill: University of North Carolina Press, 1987.

Halhunen, Karen. *Confidence Men and Painted Women: A Study of Middle-Class Culture in America, 1840–1870*. New Haven, Conn.: Yale University Press, 1982.

Harris, J. William. *Plain Folk and Gentry in a Slave Society: White Liberty and Black Slavery in Augusta's Hinterlands*. Middletown, Conn.: Wesleyan University Press, 1985.

Hill, Samuel S., ed. *The Varieties of Southern Religious Experience*. Baton Rouge: Louisiana State University Press, 1988.

Hindus, Michael Stephen. *Prison and Plantation: Crime, Justice, and Authority in Massachusetts and South Carolina, 1767–1878*. Chapel Hill: University of North Carolina Press, 1980.

Hine, Darlene Clark. *The State of Afro-American History*. Baton Rouge: Louisiana State University Press, 1985.

Houck, Peter. *A Prototype of a Confederate Hospital Center in Lynchburg, Virginia*. Lynchburg, Va.: Warwick House, 1986.

Isaac, Rhys. *The Transformation of Virginia, 1740–1790*. Chapel Hill: University of North Carolina Press, 1982.

Jackson, Luther Porter. *Negro Office-Holders in Virginia, 1865–1895*. Norfolk, Va.: Guide Quality Press, 1945.

Johnson, Charles A. *The Frontier Camp Meeting: Religion's Harvest Time*. Dallas: Southern Methodist University Press, 1955.

Johnson, Michael P. *Toward a Patriarchal Republic: The Secession of Georgia*. Baton Rouge: Louisiana State University Press, 1977.

Johnson, Paul E. *A Shopkeeper's Millennium: Society and Revivals in Rochester, New York, 1815–1837*. New York: Hill & Wang, 1978.

Jones, Jacqueline. *Labor of Love, Labor of Sorrow: Black Women, Work, and the Family, from Slavery to the Present*. New York: Vintage Books, 1985.

Joyner, Charles. *Down by the Riverside: A South Carolina Slave Community*. Urbana: University of Illinois Press, 1984.

Karamanski, Theodore. *Rally 'round the Flag: Chicago and the Civil War*. Chicago: Nelson-Hall, 1993.

Kasson, John F. *Rudeness and Crudity: Manners in Nineteenth-Century Urban America*. New York: Noonday Press, 1990.

Katz, Michael B. "Origins of the Institutional State." *Marxist Perspectives* 1 (1978): 6–22.

Kenzer, Robert C. *Kinship and Neighborhood in a Southern Community: Orange County, North Carolina, 1849–1881*. Knoxville: University of Tennessee Press, 1987.

Kern, Alfred A. *Court Street Methodist Church, 1851–1951*. Richmond: Dietz Press, 1951.

Kimball, Gregg D. "Life and Labor in an Industrial City, 1865–1920" *Labor's Heritage: Quarterly of the George Meany Memorial Archives* 3 (1991): 42–65.

Knight, Charles Louis. *Negro Housing in Certain Virginia Cities*. Richmond: William Byrd Press, 1927.

Kolchin, Peter. *American Slavery, 1619–1877.* New York: Hill & Wang, 1993.

Kousser, J. Morgan. *The Shaping of Southern Politics: Suffrage Restriction and the Establishment of the One-Party South, 1880–1910.* New Haven, Conn.: Yale University Press, 1974.

Kusmer, Kenneth L. *A Ghetto Takes Shape: Black Cleveland, 1870–1930.* Urbana: University of Illinois Press, 1976.

Lane, Roger. *Roots of Violence in Black Philadelphia, 1860–1900.* Cambridge, Mass.: Harvard University Press, 1986.

Laurie, Bruce. *Artisans into Workers: Labor in Nineteenth-Century America.* New York: Noonday Press, 1989.

———. *Working People of Philadelphia, 1800–1850.* Philadelphia: Temple University Press, 1980.

Lebsock, Suzanne. *The Free Women of Petersburg: Status and Culture in a Southern Town, 1784–1860.* New York: W. W. Norton & Co., 1985.

Levine, Bruce. *Half Slave and Half Free: The Roots of Civil War.* New York: Hill & Wang, 1992.

Levine, Lawrence W. *Black Culture and Black Consciousness: Afro-American Folk Thought from Slavery to Freedom.* New York: Oxford University Press, 1977.

Linderman, Gerald. *Embattled Courage: The Experience of Combat in the American Civil War.* New York: Free Press, 1987.

Litwack, Leon F. *Been in the Storm So Long: The Aftermath of Slavery.* New York: Vintage Books, 1979.

———. *North of Slavery: The Negro in the Free States, 1790–1860.* Chicago: University of Chicago Press, 1961.

Loveland, Anne C. *Southern Evangelicals and the Social Order, 1800–1860.* Baton Rouge: Louisiana State University Press, 1980.

Lowe, Richard. "Another Look at Reconstruction in Virginia." *Civil War History* 32 (1986): 56–76.

———. *Republicans and Reconstruction in Virginia, 1856–1870.* Charlottesville: University Press of Virginia, 1991.

———. "Virginia's Reconstruction Convention: General Schofield Rates the Delegates." *Virginia Magazine of History and Biography* 80 (1972): 341–60.

Maddex, Jack P., Jr. *The Virginia Conservatives, 1867–1879: A Study in Reconstruction Politics.* Chapel Hill: University of North Carolina Press, 1970.

Malavis, Nick. "Equality under the Lord's Law: The Disciplinary Process in Texas Baptist Churches, 1833–1870." *East Texas Historical Association* 31 (1993): 3–23.

Marten, James. *Texas Divided: Loyalty and Dissent in the Lone Star State, 1856–1874.* Lexington: University Press of Kentucky, 1990.

Mathews, Donald G. *Religion in the Old South.* Chicago: University of Chicago Press, 1977.

McPherson, James M. *Battle Cry of Freedom: The Civil War.* New York: Oxford University Press, 1988.

McWhiney, Grady, and Jamieson, Perry D. *Attack and Die: Civil War Military Tactics and the Southern Heritage.* University AL: University of Alabama, 1982.

Miller, Randall. "The Enemy Within: Some Effects of Foreign Immigrants on Antebellum Southern Cities." *Southern Studies* 24 (1985): 30–53.

Mitchell, Reid. *Civil War Soldiers: Their Expectations and Their Experiences.* New York: Simon & Schuster, 1988.

———. *The Vacant Chair: The Northern Soldier Leave Home.* New York: Oxford University Press, 1993.

Moger, Allen. *Virginia: Bourbonism to Byrd.* Charlottesville: University Press of Virginia, 1968.

Mohr, Clarence L. *On the Threshold of Freedom: Masters and Slaves in Civil War Georgia.* Athens: University of Georgia Press, 1986.

Monkkonen, Eric. *America Becomes Urban: The Development of U.S. Cities and Towns, 1780–1980.* Berkeley: University of California Press, 1985.

———. *The Dangerous Class: Crime and Poverty in Columbus, Ohio, 1860–1885.* Cambridge, Mass.: Harvard University Press, 1975.

———. "A Disorderly People? Urban Order in the Nineteenth and Twentieth Centuries." *Journal of American History* 68(1981): 539–59.

———. "From Cop History to Social History: The Significance of the Police in American History." *Journal of Social History* 15 (1981): 575–88.

———. *Police in Urban America, 1860–1920.* Cambridge: Cambridge University Press, 1981.

Morgan, Edmund S. *American Slavery, American Freedom: The Ordeal of Colonial Virginia.* New York: W. W. Norton & Co., 1975.

Morris, George and Susan Foutz. *Lynchburg in the Civil War: The City, The People, The Battle.* Lynchburg, Va.: E. H. Howard, 1984.

Niehaus, Earl F. *The Irish in New Orleans, 1800–1860.* Baton Rouge: Louisiana State University Press, 1965.

Oakes, James. *The Ruling Race: A History of American Slaveholders.* New York: Vintage Books, 1982.

———. *Slavery and Freedom: An Interpretation of the Old South.* New York: Vintage Books, 1990.

O'Brien, John T. "Factory, Church, and Community: Blacks in Antebellum Richmond." *Journal of Southern History* 44 (1978): 509–36.

Owens, Harry P., and James J. Cooke, eds. *The Old South in the Crucible of War.* Jackson: University Press of Mississippi, 1983.

Ownby, Ted. *Subduing Satan: Religion, Recreation, and Manhood in the Rural South, 1865–1920.* Chapel Hill: University of North Carolina Press, 1990.

Owsley, Frank L. *Plain Folk of the Old South.* Baton Rouge: Louisiana State University Press, 1949.

Palladino, Grace. *Another Civil War: Labor, Capital, and the State in the Anthracite Regions of Pennsylvania, 1840–1868.* Urbana: University of Illinois Press, 1990.

Paludan, Phillip Shaw. *"A People's Contest": The Union and the Civil War, 1861–1865.* New York: Harper & Row, 1988.

———. *Victims: A True Story of the Civil War.* Knoxville: University of Tennessee Press, 1981.

Pease, William H., and Jane H. Pease. *The Web of Progress: Private Values and Public Styles in Boston and Charleston, 1828–1843.* New York: Oxford University Press, 1985.

Pocock, J. G. A. "The Classical Theory of Deference." *American Historical Review* 81 (1976): 516–47.

Prude, Jonathan. *The Coming of Industrial Order: Town and Factory Life in Rural Massachusetts, 1810–1860.* New York: Cambridge University Press, 1983.

Pulley, Raymond H. *Old Virginia Restored: An Interpretation of the Progressive Impulse, 1870–1930.* Charlottesville: University Press of Virginia, 1968.

Rabinowitz, Howard N. "More than a Thesis: Assessing *The Strange Career of Jim Crow.*" *Journal of American History* 75 (1988): 842–57.

———. *Race Relations in the Urban South, 1865–1890.* Urbana: University of Illinois Press, 1980.

Raboteau, Albert J. *Slave Religion: The "Invisible Institution" in the Antebellum South.* New York: Oxford University Press, 1978.

Rachleff, Peter J. *Black Labor in the South: Richmond, Virginia, 1865–1890.* Philadelphia: Temple University Press, 1984.

Radford, John P. "Race, Residence, and Ideology: Charleston, South Carolina in the Mid-Nineteenth Century." *Journal of Historical Geography* 2, 4 (1976): 329–46.

———. "Testing the Model of the Pre-Industrial City: The Case of Ante-Bellum Charleston, South Carolina." *Transactions of the Institute of British Geographers* 4 (1979): 392–410.

Ransom, Roger L., and Richard Sutch. *One Kind of Freedom: The Economic Consequences of Emancipation.* New York: Cambridge University Press, 1977.

Roark, James L. *Masters without Slaves: Southern Planters in the Civil War and Reconstruction.* New York: W. W. Norton & Co., 1977.

Robert, Joseph Clarke. *The Story of Tobacco in America.* New York: Alfred A. Knopf, 1949.

———. *The Tobacco Kingdom: Plantation, Market, and Factory in Virginia and North Carolina, 1800–1860.* Durham, N.C.: Duke University Press, 1938.

Roediger, Marcus R. *The Wages of Whiteness: Race and the Making of the American Working Class.* New York: Verso Press, 1991.

Roland, Charles P. *The Confederacy.* Chicago: University of Chicago Press, 1960.

Rose, Anne C. *Victorian America and the Civil War.* New York: Cambridge University Press, 1992.

Rosenzweig, Roy. *Eight Hours For What We Will: Workers and Leisure in an Industrial City, 1870–1920.* New York: Cambridge University Press, 1983.

Rothman, David J. *The Discovery of the Asylum: Social Order and Disorder in the New Republic.* Boston: Little, Brown & Co., 1971.

Russell, James Michael. *Atlanta: City Building in the Old South and the New.* Baton Rouge: Louisiana State University Press, 1988.

Rutman, Darrett B. and Anita H. Rutman. *A Place in Time: Middlesex County, Virginia, 1650–1750.* New York: W. W. Norton & Co., 1984.

Ryan, Mary. *Cradle of the Middle Class: The Family in Oneida County, New York, 1790–1865.* New York: Cambridge University Press, 1981.

Schewel, Michael J. "Local Politics in Lynchburg, Virginia, in the 1880's." *Virginia Magazine of History and Biography* 89 (1981): 170–80.

Scruggs, Philip Lightfoot. *The History of Lynchburg, Virginia, 1786–1946.* Lynchburg, Va.: J. P. Bell, 1946.

Shaffer, Janet. "Narcissa and Robert Owen: The Point of Honor Years." *Virginia Magazine of History and Biography* 89 (1981): 153–69.

Shifflett, Crandall A. *Patronage and Poverty in the Tobacco South: Louisa County, Virginia, 1860–1900.* Knoxville: University of Tennessee Press, 1982.

Shirley, Michael. *From Congregation Town to Industrial City: Culture and Social Change in a Southern Community.* New York: New York University Press, 1994.

Shore, Laurence. *Southern Capitalists: Ideological Leadership of an Elite, 1832–1885.* Chapel Hill: University of North Carolina Press, 1986.

Siegel, Frederick F. "Artisans and Immigrants in the Politics of Late Antebellum Georgia." *Civil War History* 27 (1981): 221–30.

———. *The Roots of Southern Distinctiveness: Tobacco and Society in Danville, Virginia, 1780–1865.* Chapel Hill: University of North Carolina Press, 1987.

Stampp, Kenneth M. *The Era of Reconstruction, 1865–1877.* New York: Vintage Books, 1865.

Stansell, Christine. *City of Women: Sex and Class in New York, 1789–1860.* Chicago: University of Illinois Press, 1987.

Starobin, Robert S. *Industrial Slavery in the Old South.* New York: Oxford University Press, 1970.

Stowe, Steven M. *Intimacy and Power in the Old South: Ritual in the Lives of the Planters.* Baltimore: Johns Hopkins University Press, 1987.

Sydnor, Charles S. *The Development of Southern Sectionalism, 1819–1848.* Baton Rouge: Louisiana State University Press, 1948.

Taylor, Alrutheus Ambush. *The Negro in the Reconstruction of Virginia.* New York: Russell & Russell, 1926.

Thernstrom, Stephan. *Poverty and Progress: Social Mobility in a Nineteenth-Century City.* New York: Atheneum, 1974.

Thomas, Emory. *The Confederacy as a Revolutionary Experience.* Englewood Cliffs, N.J.: Prentice-Hall, 1971.

———. *The Confederate Nation, 1861–1865.* New York: Harper & Row, 1979.

———. *The Confederate State of Richmond: A Biography of the Capital.* Austin: University of Texas Press, 1971.

Thomson, Ross, *The Path of Mechanized Shoe Production in the United States.* Chapel Hill: University of North Carolina Press, 1989.

Thornton, J. Mills, III. *Politics and Power in a Slave Society: Alabama, 1800–1860.* Baton Rouge: Louisiana State University Press, 1978.

Trotter, Joe William, Jr. *Black Milwaukee: The Making of an Industrial Proletariat, 1915–45.* Urbana: University of Illinois Press, 1985.

Tyler-McGraw, Marie, and Greg D Kimball. *In Bondage and Freedom: Antebellum Black Life in Richmond, Virginia.* Richmond: Valentine Museum, 1988.

Tyrrell, Ian R. "Drink and Temperance in the Antebellum South: An Overview and Interpretation." *Journal of Southern History* 48 (1982): 485–509.

Vinovskis, Maris, ed. *Toward a Social History of the American Civil War: Exploratory Essays.* New York: Cambridge University Press, 1990.

Wade, Richard C. *Slavery in the Cities: The South, 1820–1860.* New York: Oxford University Press, 1964.

Waldrep, Christopher. " 'So Much Sin': The Decline of Religious Discipline and the 'Tidal Wave of Crime.' " *Journal of Social History* 23 (1990): 535–52.

Walkowitz, Daniel. *Worker City, Company Town: Iron and Cotton-Worker Protest in Troy and Cohoes, New York, 1855–84.* Urbana: University of Illinois Press, 1978.

Wallace, Anthony F. C. *Rockdale: The Growth of an American Village in the Early Industrial Revolution.* New York: W. W. Norton & Co., 1972.

Walters, Ronald G. *American Reformers, 1815–1860.* New York: Hill & Wang, 1978.

Watson, Harry L. *Jacksonian Politics and Community: The Emergence of the Second American Party System in Cumberland County, North Carolina.* Chapel Hill: University of North Carolina Press, 1981.

———. *Liberty and Power: The Politics of Jacksonian America.* New York: Noonday Press, 1990.

Wayne, Michael. *The Reshaping of Plantation Society: The Natchez District, 1860–1880.* Baton Rouge: Louisiana State University Press, 1983.

Wiener, Jonathan M. *Social Origins of the New South: Alabama, 1860–1885.* Baton Rouge: Louisiana State University Press, 1978.

Wilentz, Sean. *Chants Democratic: New York City and the Rise of the American Working Class, 1788–1850.* New York: Oxford University Press, 1984.

Wiley, Bell Irvin. *The Life of Johnny Reb: The Common Soldier of the Confederacy.* 1943 Reprint. Baton Rouge: Louisiana State University Press, 1971.

Williamson, Joel. *After Slavery: The Negro in South Carolina during Reconstruction, 1861–1877.* Chapel Hill: University Press of North Carolina, 1965.

———. *The Crucible of Race: Black-White Relations in the American South since Emancipation.* New York: Oxford University Press, 1984.

Wilson, Charles Reagan. *Baptized in Blood: The Religion of the Lost Cause, 1865–1920.* Athens: University of Georgia Press, 1980.

Woodward, C. Vann. *Origins of the New South, 1877–1913.* Baton Rouge: Louisiana State University Press, 1951.

———. *The Strange Career of Jim Crow.* 3d ed. New York: Oxford University Press, 1974.

———. *"Strange Career* Critics: Long May They Persevere." *Journal of American History* 75 (1988): 857–58.

———. *Tom Watson: Agrarian Rebel.* New York: Macmillan, 1938.

Wyatt-Brown, Bertram. *Southern Honor: Ethics and Behavior in the Old South.* New York: Oxford University Press, 1982.

Yancey, Rosa Faulkner. *Lynchburg and Its Neighbors.* Richmond: Ferguson & Sons, 1935.

Younger, Edward, ed. *The Governors of Virginia, 1860–1978.* Charlottesville: University Press of Virginia, 1982.

SECONDARY LITERATURE: UNPUBLISHED SOURCES

Doss, Richard B. "John Warwick Daniel: A Study of Virginia Democracy." Ph.D. diss. University of Virginia, 1955.

Ferguson, Harry S. "The Participation of the Lynchburg, Virginia, Negro in Politics, 1865–1900." M.A. thesis, Virginia State College, 1950.

Hough, Leslie Sheldon. "Discontent in a Southern Tobacco Town: Lynchburg, Virginia Workers in the 1880's." M.A. thesis, University of Virginia, 1973.

McLeod, Jonathan Woolard. "Black and White Workers: Atlanta during Reconstruction." Ph.D. diss. University of California at Los Angeles, 1987.

Mitchell, John Langston. "Negro Businesses in Lynchburg, 1880–1910." M.A. thesis, Virginia State College, 1952.

Schnittman, Suzanne Gehring. "Slavery in Virginia's Urban Tobacco Industry, 1840–1860." Ph.D. diss. University of Rochester, 1986.

Index